OXFORD MONOGRAPHS ON MUSIC

Benedetto Vinaccesi

A Musician in Brescia and Venice in the Age of Corelli

MICHAEL TALBOT

CLARENDON PRESS · OXFORD
1994

Oxford University Press, Walton Street, Oxford OX2 6DP

Oxford New York Toronto
Delhi Bombay Calcutta Madras Karachi
Kuala Lumpur Singapore Hong Kong Tokyo
Nairobi Dar es Salaam Cape Town
Melbourne Auckland Madrid
and associated companies in
Berlin Ibadan

Oxford is a trade mark of Oxford University Press

Published in the United States
by Oxford University Press Inc., New York

British Library Cataloguing in Publication Data
Data available
ISBN 0-19-816378-9

Library of Congress Cataloging in Publication Data
Data available
ISBN 0-19-816378-9

Set by Hope Services (Abingdon) Ltd.
Printed in Great Britain
on acid-free paper by
Biddles Ltd
Guildford & King's Lynn

For Colin Timms

Preface

BENEDETTO Vinaccesi is not, and probably never will be, a name that springs immediately to the mind of the average music-lover when the subject of Italian baroque music is mentioned. True, he was a good and sometimes strikingly original composer whose motets, cantatas, sonatas, and dramatic works deserve at least a foothold in the repertory. But he founded no school and attracted comparatively little attention in his day. Had he not existed, the course of musical history would not have been deflected.

So how does one justify devoting an entire book to this worthy but minor figure? The answer has to be a composite one, the sum of many small justifications.

One may begin with Vinaccesi's own compositions. Although their style displays great homogeneity and integrity, it fits only with difficulty into familiar categories. Born thirteen years later than Corelli, Vinaccesi belongs to a generation of Italian—indeed, European—composers who almost to a man fell under the sway of the 'Divine Arcangelo'. Yet his indebtedness to the older man is surprisingly small. On one hand, Vinaccesi looks back to an earlier generation of Italian composers—that of Legrenzi, Stradella, and Colonna—which reached maturity in the third quarter of the seventeenth century. On the other, he looks forward to (and may in his turn have been influenced by) the dynamic current introduced by Albinoni and Vivaldi in Venice during the first two decades of the eighteenth century. So his music constitutes an unusual amalgam of elements that we identify, following our modern penchant for tidy classification, as 'middle' and 'late' baroque. The study of it can bring into focus many neglected aspects of stylistic evolution in the years around 1700.

During the second part of his career Vinaccesi served, as *maestro di coro* and organist respectively, two important Venetian institutions: the charitable foundation known as the Ospedale dei Poveri Derelitti ai Santi Giovanni e Paolo (more familiarly, the Ospedaletto) and the *cappella* of the ducal church of San Marco. On both institutions and their musical life much has already been written; yet when one examines closely the activity of a single individual within a large and complex organization, one inevitably encounters new facts of general relevance. This book therefore contains a small, but I hope not trivial, contribution to the history of both the Ospedaletto and the ducal church.

Vinaccesi spent his youth and the first part of his career in Brescia, the capital city of a province that was one of the most active cultural centres among the Venetian possessions on the Italian mainland. Politically subject to Venice between 1426 and 1797, Brescia retained a considerable amount of artistic and social independence, which was aided by its proximity, as a border territory, to the duchies of Milan and Mantua. The book therefore includes some discussion of music in Brescia during the late seventeenth century in the context of the whole of northern Italy.

Finally, there is the Vinaccesi family itself. Since it belonged, both in Brescia and Venice, to the citizenry—the social class immediately below the nobility—information on it from contemporary records is fairly abundant. In addition to its intrinsic interest, this information can tell us a good deal about how our composer saw his place in the world and how he planned his career. In the seventeenth and eighteenth centuries personal career strategies were subordinated to wider family strategies and cannot be evaluated in isolation from them. The chronicle of the Vinaccesi family, which I have tried to reassemble in outline, is the book in which Benedetto consciously inscribed his life.

The present study is organized along conventional lines. A chapter introducing the Vinaccesi family is followed by three dealing specifically with the life of the composer Benedetto. A final biographical chapter relates briefly the not uneventful life of the other members of the family in Brescia and Venice during the eighteenth century. The second part of the book contains five chapters discussing, genre by genre, Benedetto's compositions and a final assessment of his achievement. Appendices provide family trees, transcriptions, quotations in the original languages (which, for ease of reading, I normally give in English in the main text), and a short catalogue of Vinaccesi's extant works.

The research that led to the writing of this book was supported by the British Academy, which awarded me a Research Readership during the academic years 1990–1 and 1991–2, and the Gladys Krieble Delmas Foundation, which made a generous grant towards the expenses of my research in Italy. In addition, the British Academy made a grant towards a short period of study in 1992 at the Bibliothèque Nationale, Paris, and, with a final, very substantial award, helped to meet the book's production costs. I have also to thank the University of Liverpool and my colleagues in the Department of Music for looking so tolerantly on my absence from normal duties and, indeed, facilitating my work in many ways.

The successful completion of my book depended heavily on two 'support systems'. The first was my family. The second was that circle of fellow musicologists and historians working in cognate areas whose advice or practical help I have cause to seek so frequently. I owe special debts of gratitude to Olga Termini, whose continuing work on the Pollarolo and Pescetti musical families intersects with mine at so many points, and

Carlo Vitali, whose encyclopedic knowledge in the linguistic, literary, and musical domains remains for me an object of wonder. Colin Timms had the patience to read my drafts and comment on them. I dedicate this book to him not simply as a recompense (insufficient, indeed) for this thankless task but also out of admiration for his contributions to the study of Italian vocal music and in celebration of our long friendship. Paul Everett, with whom I frequently collaborate on Vivaldian projects, did me the honour of computer-setting the music examples. May I be forgiven for simply listing alphabetically my other informants, critics, and helpers: Jane Baldauf-Berdes, Enrico Careri, Victor Crowther, Emidio De Felice, Norbert Dubowy, Jonathan Foster, Jonathan Glixon, Wolfgang Reich, John Roberts, Faun Tanenbaum, and Gastone Vio. Finally, a special word of thanks to Dr Girolamo Marcello, who allowed me to consult his family archives, and to Don Stefano Olivetti and Don Emilio Magrinello in Brescia, who granted me access to the parish archives of Sant' Alessandro, San Clemente, and Sant'Afra.

M.T.

Liverpool
1993

Contents

List of Plates
(between pages 180 and 181)

1

The Vinaccesi Family

VINACCESI is not a common Italian surname. It does not appear in
Emidio De Felice's authoritative *Dizionario dei cognomi italiani*,[1] and I
have not encountered it in telephone directories, the most accessible
repository of unusual surnames. Its most likely derivation is from *vinaccia*
(plural *vinacce*), the lees left after wine-pressing.[2] A *vinaccese* is a person
who works in some way with the *vinacce*, and *vinaccesi* is simply the plural
form found as a variant in so many Italian surnames. The spelling with
two Cs, 'Vinaccesi', is the most correct according to the canons of standard Italian, and was accordingly adopted by the better-educated members
of the composer's family (including Benedetto himself in later years), but
spellings with only one C, which reflect the lack of sounded double conso-
nants in many north Italian dialects, are very common, as are such variants as 'Vinacese' and 'Venacese'. Wills from the fifteenth century latinize
the surname as 'De Vinacesibus'.

By a curious stroke of fortune, we possess two synoptic accounts of the
family's early history. The first appeared as the preamble to a eulogy of
Fortunato Vinaccesi (1631–1713), the famous *erudito* living in Brescia.
This touching portrait was penned soon after Fortunato's death by his
friend Giulio Antonio Averoldi, who submitted it to the *Giornale dei letterati d'Italia*, which published a shortened (and sanitized) version.[3] The
source of Averoldi's information on the early history of the Vinaccesi family was, as the writer himself discloses, a printed book in Fortunato's possession (which has unfortunately not come to light). The second account,
entitled simply 'Memoria', was included among the set of documents

---

[1] (Milan, 1978). I am grateful to the author for confirming, in private correspondence, the surname's rarity and suggesting to me its etymology.

[2] *Vinaccia* also exists in its own right as a surname. A family of Neapolitan mandolin-makers by
this name achieved prominence; one member, Pasquale, created *c*.1835 the design of the modern man-
dolin.

[3] The Brescian nobleman Giulio Antonio Averoldi (1651–1717) is best known for his guide to
paintings in Brescia published there in 1700 as *Le scelte pitture di Brescia additate al forestiere*. The
original full version of the eulogy of Fortunato Vinaccesi remained in manuscript among Averoldi's 22
vols. of 'Miscellanee' until it was published in Brescia in 1889 under the title of *Elogio di Fortunato
Vinaccesi* to celebrate a wedding in the Averoldi family. A brother of the bridegroom, Giovanni
Averoldi, was responsible for the dedication of the vol. and presumably also for editing the text and
supplying the accompanying notes. The abridged version, containing some extra information on
Fortunato's literary activity, appeared in the *Giornale dei letterati d'Italia*, 16 (1713), 493–6.

published as a record of the lawsuit brought against Benedetto's son Pietro
Antonio in the 1740s by his third wife, Giovanna, who was seeking to
recover her dowry in connection with the annulment of their marriage.[4]
This aide-mémoire had originally been compiled by Pietro Antonio in
order to impress his bride-to-be, a general's daughter, with the distinctions
gained by his family; the point of adding it to the published documentation was, it seems, to reinforce the image of Giovanna as a deceived wife.

Averoldi devotes a mere paragraph to recording Fortunato's ancestry:

The Vinaccesi family, of noble blood, drew its origin from the city of Prato in
Tuscany (as one may read clearly in a printed book that Signor Fortunato showed
me on several occasions). Because of civil disturbances Nicoluccio Vinaccesi left
Prato and came to Venice, where he settled in 1374. His talent and judicious valour being recognized immediately, he was admitted to the Venetian citizenry and
sent to Rhodes as a consul. His descendants moved to Brescia, where, likewise
accepted into the citizenry, they have up to the present maintained undiminished
the lustre and credit of the family through the honourable employment of shop-
keeping, while their tree, no longer bearing fruit, is drying up.[5]

The description of the Vinaccesi family as 'noble', not to be taken in
the strictest sense of the word, reflects the unusual situation of the early
Italian communes, in which wealth derived from mercantile activity could
be regarded as equivalent to that derived from feudal possessions.
Averoldi's sketch, while accurate enough in regard to Fortunato's branch
of the family, which traced its descent back to a natural son of Filippo
Vinaccesi (born *c*.1521), does insufficient justice to the main, 'legitimate'
branch descended from Filippo's younger brother Bernardino (born
c.1540), whose members were active in Venetian government service
rather than commerce. Similarly, the imminent extinction of the family, to
which Averoldi refers with his picturesque metaphor of a shrivelled tree,
refers accurately only to Fortunato's branch, not to the main branch as
represented by the composer Benedetto in Venice.

The family chronicle in the 'Memoria', much more extensive, deserves
quotation in full:

Among the most illustrious of the families that have made Etruria the equal of
any other Italian province by virtue of the nobility and glory bestowed on them
by their antiquity, their meritorious deeds, and the honours they have acquired,
one may include that of the Vinaccesis, which flourished from the year 1269 in
the city of Prato, where it was rewarded with the highest honours and became
related to the most noble families, as one may see from nos. 2 and 3 [referring to
enclosures that were unfortunately not reproduced in the 'Memoria']; and

[4] The 'Memoria' occupies pp. 6–7 of *Stampa della Signora Marchesa Giovanna Miseroni ora consorte del Signor Conte Paolo Sormani* [Venice, 1745], preserved in Venice, Archivio di Stato (hereafter *I-Vas*), Inquisitori di Stato, Processi civili 1743–1746, Busta 1030, n. 50.

[5] *Elogio di Fortunato Vinaccesi*, 8. For a complete transcription of the document see App. B.1.

although one sees from no. 4 that the Vinaccesi family, like other leading families of Prato, was employed in commerce, this was normal in those days, when the profession of merchant was exercized above all by noble families.

One reads that this Vinaccesi family was a notable benefactor of the Dominican order (no. 12) as well as of another order, the first having been given the site for the building of a monastery, and the second having been presented with a piece of land of considerable value in the year 1306 (nos. 12, 13, and 24).

Speaking of togas [i.e. persons entitled to wear a toga, such as senators], we find that Guidolotti de Vinaccesi, and in 1317 Guglielmo, were elected procurators and governors of the city of Prato, and that Bellato Vinaccesi was a former governor in Avignon.

In the year 1388 the house of Vinaccesi, already enjoying noble status in Prato, was admitted, in addition, to the citizenship of Florence and membership of the Florentine nobility, as evidenced by nos. 38, 39, and 40, in which the Vinaccesi family is always referred to as 'nobile patrizia fiorentina', and in subsequent years it was always recognized as such, obtaining from the city prominent titles and positions reserved for Florentine nobles, such as that of Prior of the Supreme Magistracy, which Nicolussio [= Nicoluccio] Vinacese became in 1470 (no. 71).

The Vinaccesi family subsequently married into the most prominent Florentine families and in 1446 proved the quarter of the Religion of Malta [the Knights Hospitallers of St John]. In 1585 *Cavaliere* Francesco, having proved the quarters of the Medici and Vinaccesi families, donned the habit of a Knight of Malta (no. 81).

The Vinaccesi family is seen also to have contracted alliances with the houses of Dini and Capponi, two leading Florentine families, and in 1509 to have married one of its daughters into the ruling house of the Medici, who have for several centuries been grand dukes of Tuscany (nos. 81 and 82).

Having moved from Florence to the capital city of Venice, the most noble Vinaccesi family, admitted to the Venetian citizenry but maintaining its noble rank, survives today in the person of the Illustrious Pietro Vinaccesi, who has been made and declared a count by the most serene house of the Gonzagas still reigning in Guastalla, as shown by the certificate, in whose lengthy text the aforesaid most serene house of the Gonzagas affirms its attachment to the house of the Vinaccesis, that is, to the Illustrious Signor Conte Pietro and his forebears, etc.

Finally, there is the Vinaccesi coat of arms, shown on many old and new monuments in the form depicted in the Book [the book to which Averoldi referred?], and which the family seeks to have inspected and approved as its official heraldic emblem.[6]

Despite its wealth of reference to attached documents (whose genuineness can of course no longer be verified), the 'Memoria' is obviously extremely tendentious in its interpretations, even where the facts themselves are true. At all costs, Pietro Antonio is to be portrayed as noble and identified as a descendant of those family members who earned high

---

[6] See n. 4 above and App. B.2. In heraldry 'proving the quarter' of an aristocratic family means establishing that a grandparent belonged to it.

distinctions. For this reason, the Florentine branch of the family is discussed at length, while the Brescian branch, which had been continuously resident in that city for over two centuries when the document was compiled, is passed over in total silence. Pietro Antonio even has the Vinaccesis emigrate from Florence to Venice at a conveniently vague point in time, whereas we know from Averoldi and corroborative documents that they came directly from Prato long before many of their distinguished Florentine relatives were born. Even the title of count is suspect. By only implying, not stating explicitly, that it was from the Gonzaga ruling house of Guastalla (rather than the Gonzagas of Mantua or Castiglione delle Stiviere) that he received his title, and by citing his forbears ('predecessori') in addition to himself—which opens up the possibility that it was not him but one of them (perhaps even his father, the *cavaliere* Benedetto) who earned it—Pietro Antonio seems suspiciously evasive.

The coat of arms to which the 'Memoria' refers survives in a crude pen-drawing accompanying the entry for 'Vinaccesi' in a manuscript preserved in the library of the Museo Civico Correr, Venice.[7] This anonymous eighteenth-century source contains genealogies and historical annotations relating to the families making up the *cittadinanza originaria* (i.e. the officially registered citizenry of Venice) similar to those compiled for the Venetian patriciate by Marco Barbaro and his continuers. The entry itself is startlingly brief, consisting merely of the uncompleted sentence 'Venero dà . . .' (They came from . . .). Most probably, the removal of the Vinaccesis to Brescia in the early sixteenth century had created a hiatus in the record of the family that defeated the best efforts of the compiler. The drawing appears to show a lion rampant holding a snake.

It will not have escaped notice that both accounts mention, from different generations, a Nicoluccio Vinaccesi. This is a suitable point at which to discuss the system by which our family allotted given names to its members—a system that today can indeed prove vexatious to the writer who wishes to distinguish between different individuals but occasionally aids the researcher intent on establishing the relationship between them. There is no universal naming practice followed in Italy in the early modern age; however, one notes among the lower classes a tendency to be influenced by fortuitous factors such as the name of the saint on whose day the child is born (hence, for example, Antonio *Lucio* Vivaldi, born on 4 March 1678, the feast of St Lucius, Pope and Martyr), but among their social superiors a desire to use a small group of Christian names as a set of 'badges' recurring over and over again through the generations as if to

---

[7] Venice, Museo Civico Correr (hereafter *I-Vmc*), Ms. Gradenigo 83, 'Cittadini veneziani', iv, fo. 635.

symbolize family continuity. This practice applies mainly to males, since the choice of female given names suitable for commemoration in later generations is constantly widened through marriage, but it also operates to a small extent on the female side as well.

The constant principle is that sons never take the name of their father but are named after their grandfather or an uncle. This sometimes gives rise to sequences where two names alternate through several generations. Such patterns are clearly visible in the series of family trees making up Appendix A (from which the following identification numbers are taken). One encounters, for example, the sequences Francesco (5)—Filippo (11)— Francesco (12)—Filippo (15)—Francesco (26) and, later on, Francesco (53)—Lodovico (59)—Francesco (65)—Lodovico (67). Several female names are 'twinned' with male names borne by siblings, as witness Lelio (27) and Lelia (29), Giulio (35) and Giulia (36), Fortunata (37) and Fortunato (39, prematurely deceased, then 43). It is noticeable that Primo (25), a first-born but illegitimate son, inaugurates a branch of the family (shown in Appendix A.3) in which the traditional given names are abandoned in favour of an alternative set, as if to prevent confusion with the legitimate line. This branch also adopts the 'twinning' principle in another guise by naming actual twins after the two patron saints of Brescia, Faustino (40) and Giovita (41). Perhaps the most individual name in the whole set of tables is that of Fortunato's elder brother Vinaccese (42), derived synthetically from the surname after the fashion of Galileo Galilei and Speron Speroni.

This discussion of names is intended to make one important point: that the Vinaccesis, throughout the period in which we shall meet them, had a strong consciousness of their unity as a family—almost a collective ethos. When we consider the composer Benedetto or any other member, we must look at him not only as an individual with aspirations of his own but also as a person destined by his particular position within the family structure for a role not necessarily of his own choosing.

Our prime source of information on the first Venetian period of the Vinaccesis—that is, the period running from their arrival in Venice from Prato in 1374 (if Averoldi is to be believed) to their departure for Brescia at some point after *c.*1517 and before 1534—is the collection of manuscript notes on Venetian citizen families collected by the local historian Giuseppe Tassini (1827–1899), author of the famous book *Curiosità veneziane* first published in 1863. These notes, preserved in the Museo Civico Correr, are largely the fruit of Tassini's diligent studies in the Venetian State Archive.[8] I have been able to find and evaluate a few of

---

[8] *I-Vmc*, Ms. P.D. 33 D 76, 'Notizie storiche e genealogiche sui cittadini veneziani'.

the original documents to which he refers, but most await rediscovery. In
his entry for 'Vinaccesi' Tassini writes:

> From Tuscany. They erected many buildings, especially in the parish of Santi
> Apostoli, and, according to the chronicles, pursued their activity in Venice from
> 1355.
>
> 1431 Citizenship granted to Francesco, son of Raffaele Vinaccesi from Prato res-
>   ident in [the *contrada* of] San Casciano.
> 1449 Confirmation of the same citizenship, in which Vinaccesi is stated to be res-
>   ident in [the *contrada* of] San Giovanni Grisostomo.
>
> [Tassini then sketches a family tree basically identical with that shown in
> Appendix A.1, except that Giusti (10) and Nicoluccio (1) do not appear.
> Annotations provide the information that Raffaele (3) drew up his will in 1492
> and was buried in [or by] the church of San Giovanni Grisostomo and that Elena
> (8), from the *contrada* of San Marziale, drew up her will in 1520, with Alvise
> Nadal as her notary, and was buried in [or by] the church of Corpus Domini.]
>
> 1464 Griselda Vinaccesi, wife of Giacomo Pierleoni, has a mortuary inscription
>   placed by her husband in [the church of] Santi Giovanni e Paolo.[9]

It is noteworthy that Tassini places the arrival of the family in Venice
almost twenty years earlier than Averoldi. The 'citizenship' to which he
refers in connection with Francesco denotes the socially elevated stratum
of *cittadini originari*. This 'caste', hardly more numerous than the patriciate itself, supplied Venice with its civil service and was headed by a *can-
celliere grande* who ranked second only to the doge in the republic's
hierarchy, at least in ceremonial terms. To qualify for membership of the
cittadinanza originaria and become inscribed in the 'Silver Book' (the
counterpart of the patriciate's 'Golden Book') an aspirant had to satisfy
four criteria: to have been born in Venice, to be legitimate by birth, to
have had parents and grandparents who practised no mechanical art, and
not to have been convicted of any offence.[10] Like the *popolani* (members
of the general population), the citizens had no voting rights in any of the
councils of state. In certain periods, especially during wars that drained
the republic's exchequer, it was possible for wealthy citizens to buy their
way into the nobility, just as it was always possible for patricians to forfeit
their nobility and be relegated to the *cittadinanza* as a result of marriage
to a spouse of a lower class.[11]

The reason for the confirmation of Francesco's citizenship in 1449 is
presumably that in 1431 he was still a minor. No dates of birth for any of
the members of the family included in Appendix A.1 are known, but

---

[9] Tassini, 'Notizie storiche', v. 90–1. See App. B.3.

[10] M. Ferro, *Dizionario del diritto comune e veneto* (Venice, 1778–81), iii. 189–90; G. Dolcetti, *Il
'Libro d'Argento' dei cittadini di Venezia e del Veneto* (Venice, 1922–8), i, 'al lettore'.

[11] Male patricians who married daughters of citizens passed on their nobility to their children, but
this did not happen when the sexes were reversed.

Filippo (11), Francesco's son, cannot have been born much after 1450 if he was the husband of that name mentioned in the will of a Chiara Vinaccesi, who dictated it on 22 November 1477.[12] The wills of married female members of the family from this period provide surprisingly little information about the Vinaccesis; they are mainly concerned with the inheritance, after the wife's death, of her dowry, which often reverts to her family of origin. Besides that of Chiara we have those of Giovanna, widow of Filippo Vinaccesi (1427), Agnola or Angela (1427), widow of Matteo Vinaccesi, Cassandra (1479), possibly the wife of Benedetto (whose will of 1478 also survives), and Elena (1520).[13] From the fact that the Vinaccesis have acquired property in several parishes, and from the size of their legacies to charity, one gains the impression of a prosperous and fecund family.

Elena's will is the last known record of any Vinaccesi in Venice until the composer Benedetto's arrival there in 1698 or 1699. It appears that the whole family—at any rate, that part of it which was producing children—uprooted itself to settle in Brescia. In the Brescian municipal census (*estimo*) of 1534, the return is completed by Francesco Vinaccesi (12), who reveals that his father, Filippo (11), is no longer alive (by using 'fo [fu] di', rather than plain 'di', to introduce the patronymic) and describes himself as a citizen of Venice and Brescia.[14] Nevertheless, the likelihood is that it was Filippo who emigrated, together with his two sons Francesco and Raffaele (13). Tassini's family tree certainly supports this conclusion, since it breaks off precisely when it reaches Filippo's generation. The family must have arrived in Brescia after 1517, since it submitted no return to the *estimatori* for the census of that year. We lack information on the reason for the move, but in view of the careers followed by Filippo's descendants, the best guess is that he entered the service of the Venetian government in Brescia, perhaps as a book-keeper or provisioner (suitable posts for someone with a mercantile background).

Brescia belongs to a chain of north Italian cities (Turin, Ivrea, Como, Bergamo, Verona, Vicenza, Treviso, Udine) stretching out along the North Italian plain at or close to the foot of the Alps. It was therefore an important staging post for travel between eastern and western parts of

[12] *I-Vas*, Cancelleria Inferiore, Miscellanea Testamenti, notai diversi, Busta 27, n. 2545.

[13] The location of the wills is as follows (all in *I-Vas*, Sezione notarile, Testamenti): Giovanna—atti notaio Marco Tagliapietra, Busta 995, n. 7 (10 Nov. 1427); Agnola—Busta 995, n. 40 (same date); Cassandra—Busta 995, n. 87 (18 Jan. 1479); Benedetto—atti notaio Girolamo Bonicardi, B. 68, n. 52 (30 Nov. 1478); Elena—atti notaio Alvise Nadal, Busta 740, n. 102 (29 Dec. 1520). Cassandra's will is dated 18 Jan. 1478 in accordance with the old Venetian calendar, which advanced the year on 1 Mar. instead of the preceding 1 Jan. I have not added Filippo, Matteo, and Benedetto to the family tree in App. A.1, since their relationship to the other family members is uncertain.

[14] Brescia, Biblioteca Queriniana, Archivio Storico Civico (hereafter *I-BRq*, ASC), Registro 249, Polizze d'estimo in ordine cronologico dall'anno 1517 all'anno 1734 e in ordine alfabetico, Fascicolo VIA 1534. See also n. 19, below, and App. C.1.

northern Italy and between Italy and the Alpine passes. Only 76 miles distant from Milan, lying to the East and very slightly to the North, Brescia fell, in 1337, under the sway of the Visconti dynasty of Milan, from which it rescued itself in 1426 by voluntarily acceding to the Venetian Republic, of which it and its territory remained a province until the extinction of Venice as a sovereign state in 1797. The *dominante* (Venice) was considerably further away than Milan—121 miles, in fact—and the republic wisely ruled Brescia with a light hand. In the middle of the eighteenth century the English traveller Thomas Nugent observed:

The inhabitants of this town and province are better used by the *Venetians* than their other subjects, probably because, as it once was a part of the *Milanese*, were they ill used, they might think of returning to their old masters.[15]

The historical city of Brescia—rectangular, almost square, in basic outline—was surrounded by a wall that followed the line of the ring road of the modern city. On the hill known as the Cidneo towards the East of the northern boundary of the city stood the heavily fortified citadel (Nugent mentions a nickname for it: the 'Falcon of Italy'). Like many such castles in medieval Italian cities, it served a dual purpose: to defend the city against external aggression and to dominate the city in situations of internal unrest (as occurred, notoriously, in 1849, when the Austrians crushed the uprising known as the 'Ten Days'). Outside the city walls the Venetians established a defensive strip, one mile in width, completely void of buildings and human settlement. This had the unfortunate effect of separating Brescia from its so-called *Chiusure* (literally, 'Enclosures') a cordon of small agricultural colonies extending outwards from the city for two or three miles, and in which many inhabitants of the city had landholdings. About the city itself Nugent has this to say:

The houses are well built, with abundance of squares, and large well paved streets, which are kept very clean by the streams of the neighbouring *Alps*. The town is very populous, and the inhabitants industrious and rich, having a very great trade in linen, cheese, and iron-work, but particularly in swords and firearms, which employ a great number of gunsmiths, esteemed the best in *Italy*.[16]

Nugent caught the city at a happy moment when its population had stabilized, after the mid-seventeenth century, at between 30,000 and 40,000. Its high point had been at the beginning of the sixteenth century, when its inhabitants numbered about 65,000, but wars and plagues periodically reduced the population, which had even fallen to a mere 5,000 just before the start of Venetian rule.

Brescia's importance as a manufacturing centre extended to the realm of musical instruments, for during the sixteenth and seventeenth centuries

---

[15] T. Nugent, *The Grand Tour* (London, ²/1778), iii. 161.   [16] Ibid., 160.

the city boasted makers of lutes, viols, and violins to rival Cremona. Of these the best known are Gasparo Bertolotti (1540–1609: called 'da Salò' to show his provenance from the 'second city' of the Brescian territory) and his pupil Giovanni Paolo Maggini (*c*.1581–*c*.1632). For two centuries beginning in the mid-fifteenth century the Antegnati family, based in Brescia, were Italy's leading organ-builders.

During the entire period of Venetian domination Brescia laboured under a harmful—and to us today, almost incredible—restrictive practice: the whole of its produce for export had to be channelled via Venice, adding to costs but enriching the merchants of the *dominante*. Constitutional protest was impossible, since even the Brescian nobility had no role to play in the government of the State, whose directives were enforced at local level by ministers (*rettori*) appointed from the ranks of the Venetian nobility: a *podestà* (chief magistrate), a *capitano* (military commander), and two *camerlenghi* (treasurers). In order to prevent the formation of coalitions between these officials and local interest-groups (and also, no doubt, to mitigate the boredom of Venetian nobles who, through the accident of a ballot, had to serve in the provinces), the *rettori* were replaced at regular intervals. Depite these efforts to integrate it within the Venetian State, Brescia retained some of the characteristics of a frontier society. One sign of this is its monetary system. After 1426 Brescia retained its traditional money of account, the *lira di planeti* or *lira imperiale*, although the Venetian *lira di piccoli* came to be used alongside it.[17] However, the coins in actual circulation included a very high proportion minted outside the Venetian State; the Milanese scudo and philip were especially common.

The city was divided administratively into four quarters (Santo Stefano, Sant'Alessandro, San Giovanni, and San Faustino). These were further divided into a total of 18 *quadre*, or city wards. San Faustino contained 8 *quadre* (one of which covered the settlement of Mompiano South of the city), San Giovanni 6, Sant'Alessandro 2, and Santo Stefano also 2. The wards belonging to Santo Stefano were known as Cittadella Vecchia and Cittadella Nuova respectively. Cittadella Nuova was the administrative heart of the city. It included the Duomo (cathedral)—both the original rotunda and the Duomo Nuovo built to replace it in the seventeenth and eighteenth centuries—the Broletto, which was a complex of buildings to the North of the new cathedral mostly housing Venetian officials and their dependants, and, a little to the West of it, the Palazzo della Loggia, seat of the city administration (and today still functioning as the town hall).

---

[17] A money of account is the common accounting unit into which the value of all coins, whether fixed or 'floating', can be reduced. The Venetian 'ducat current' (*ducato corrente*) was equivalent to 6 *lire di piccoli* and 4 *soldi* (a *soldo* was a twentieth part of a *lira*) but to only 3 *lire di planeti*. The latter was thus more than twice as valuable than its Venetian counterpart.

There was a certain amount of rivalry between the state (Venetian) and civic (Brescian) administrations as each tried to encroach a little on the prerogatives of the other.

Unlike in Venice, where the city ward (*contrada*) was coextensive with the parish of the same name, the twelve parishes of Brescia freely crossed the boundaries of the *quadre*.[18] That of the Duomo itself was partly in Cittadella Nuova, partly in Cittadella Vecchia. Whereas the last-named *quadra* contained three parishes in addition to its portion of that of the Duomo, a single church, San Giovanni Evangelista, had to serve the fourth, fifth, sixth, and seventh *quadre* of San Faustino. Some of the parish churches were under diocesan clergy, others under religious orders, who possessed in addition numerous non-parochial churches, monasteries, nunneries, and *luoghi pii* (hospices, residential homes, etc.). Many churches possessed their own *disciplina*, or fraternity of devout laymen. Then, as today, Brescia was a singularly pious city, in which the religious dimension—in music as in the other arts and humanities—dominated all others.

Many aspects of the life of the Vinaccesis in Brescia can be gleaned from their census returns. The city periodically conducted an *estimo*, or census, of property-owners as a basis for their taxation. Such *estimi* were carried out in 1517, 1534, 1548, 1568, 1574, 1588, 1627, 1630–4, 1637, 1641, 1653, 1661–7, 1687, and 1720–37.[19] Heads of property-owning families had to submit to the *estimatori* a document (*polizza*) providing specific information. Having identified himself, the respondent had first to itemize his dependants, including servants (with their wages) as well as family members. It was appropriate to list even a *cavalcatura*, a team of horses and their equipment. The *polizze* give the age of all males, but for females the age is often not supplied, although it is normal to show whether they are married or single. Real estate owned by the family in Brescia and elsewhere in its territory is listed. Its value is shown by quoting the rent it

[18] The parishes were: Duomo, Sant'Afra, Sant'Agata, Sant'Alessandro, San Clemente, Santi Faustino e Giovita, San Giorgio, San Giovanni Evangelista, San Lorenzo, Santa Maria Calchera, Santi Nazzaro e Celso, and Santo Zeno.

[19] The completion of a census usually took more than one year, and the quoted dates are those under which documents are stored. The Archivio di Stato di Brescia contains in the section 'Polizze e petizioni d'estimo' (hereafter *I-BRas*, PPE) a set of boxes housing the census returns for 1641. Those for the Cittadella Nuova *quadra*, in which the documents for Francesco (53) and Raffaele (30) Vinaccesi appear, are in Busta 13. Returns for the other census years are preserved in *I-BRq*, ASC. They have been reordered so that the returns from every census year for a given short segment of the alphabet are contained within a single box, which separates the returns for the different years into separate folders (*fascicoli*). There are in fact two separate series of boxes (Registri 139 and 249), which in principle contain duplicate copies of all returns, although some survive today only in one. To complicate matters further, some returns also exist in duplicate *within* a single box. So a reference in the abbreviated form '*I-BRq*, ASC, Registro 249, Fascicolo VIA 1568' denotes the folder labelled 'VIA 1568' contained in the appropriate box ('VIA-VIR') belonging to the series 'Registro 249'. Individual *polizze* can be identified by the name of the respondent (who may also be the writer, though many householders employed secretarial assistance), the *quadra*, and the number given to the document by the clerks of the census office. App. C.1 tabulates the census returns of the Vinaccesi family.

commands, actual or notional, or, in the case of landed property, the size of the holding and the type and quantity of the produce. Property rented by members of the family or purchased over a period through a kind of mortgage known as a *livello* is described, and the ordinary place of residence of family members is given.[20] It is often possible to pinpoint on a map the location of a house or shop, since co-ordinates at the four points of the compass are always supplied; that is, the respondent names the street or the owner of the property bounding it to the North (*a monte*), South (*a mezzo dì*), East (*a mattina*), and West (*a sera*). Outstanding credits and debits are listed, as well as *pretensioni*, or claims to property awaiting the outcome of litigation. Traders give estimates of the value of their stock and their cash in hand. As in tax returns throughout the ages, credits are minimized and debits maximized. For instance, in his census return presented and sworn on 27 July 1641 Raffaele Vinaccesi (30) notes that his eldest son Giulio (35) is banished (as a judicial punishment) but supported financially by the family; he remembers to add, 'it will also cost a lot of money to release him [from the banishment]' (ne converra anco spendere grossa somma di danari a liberarlo).[21] Similarly, Filippo Vinaccesi (15) observes in his return submitted on 3 February 1574 that the house he owns in Contrada delle Bassiche, rented out to various poor men, brings in an average of 50 *lire di planeti* a year but—and here he goes into considerable detail—urgently needs repairs that could cost ('potria importar') 800 *lire*.[22]

The ages given for family members in these census returns need to be accepted only with some reservation. The date of submission of the return as entered by the clerk often differs significantly from that by which the census as a whole is identified. For example, the *polizza* of the brothers Giovita (41) and Fortunato (43) Vinaccesi presented on 18 November 1657 belongs to the '1653' census.[23] Even more frequently, the submission date precedes the official census date. The return of the same Giovita and Fortunato for the '1687' census is dated as early as 29 December 1685, although some later property acquisitions were declared on 28 February 1687.[24] In no instance is it possible to determine from the *polizza* itself how many days, weeks, or even months in advance of the date of submission the respondent wrote down the ages of his dependants, though one

[20] Because of the prohibition of usury under canon law, the payment of interest that a *livello* entailed had to be effected under cover of a fiction, namely that the mortgagee (*livellario*) had first sold the property to the mortgager (*livellatore*), who then sold it back to him at a higher price, allowing him to pay by annual instalments. *Livelli* could be perpetual, fixed-term, or for the duration of the life of the *livellatore*. See Ferro, *Dizionario*, vii. 39–42.

[21] *I-BRas*, PPE, Busta 13, Estimo civico del 1641, Cittadella Nuova, n. 152.

[22] *I-BRq*, ASC, Registro 249, Fascicolo VIA 1627–37, Cittadella Nuova, n. 193.

[23] *I-BRq*, ASC, Registro 139, Fascicolo VIA 1653, San Faustino Ottava, n. 27.

[24] *I-BRq*, ASC, Registro 249, Fascicolo VIA 1687, Sant'Alessandro Prima, n. 119.

would not imagine that a long time normally elapsed. In a few cases, where it has been possible to find a record of baptism (sometimes including a birth date), there exists a ready means of checking the accuracy of the ages in the census returns.[25] The general picture (that can never be assumed to apply in individual cases) is that ages for young children, especially infants, are accurate, but that the standard of accuracy declines in an almost arithmetical progression as their years increase. We are dealing with a society in which meticulous attention was paid to the calculation of money, weights, and measures, but where there was rarely a need to place a person on one side or another of an age-divide. When such a need arose, as, for example when he or she was contemplating marriage, the parish priest could provide the required documentation.

Unfortunately, even when the age in years of a person is known with certainty, the year of birth cannot be determined without external corroboration. If we find, in a *polizza* of 1627, that Francesco (53) Vinaccesi is aged '41' (i.e. has completed 41 years), his year of birth can be either 1585 or 1586. Only the fortunate discovery of a record of Francesco's baptism, on 23 April 1585, settles the question.

Despite the lack of precision in dating the birth of most family members, the census records provide an almost complete family tree for the Brescian Vinaccesis between the time of their arrival in Brescia and the end of the seventeenth century, discounting any children whose birth and death occurred between consecutive censuses. This family tree (shown in Appendices A.2–5) exemplifies the typical 'strategy for prosperity' of a property-owning family in early modern Italy. There were three components of this strategy. The first, and most important, was to prevent dispersal of the family patrimony through having to divide it up among several heirs. This was achieved by ensuring that in any generation only one son married and produced children. The sequence Filippo (11)—Francesco (12)—Bernardino (24)—Francesco (53)—Lodovico (59) conforms to this pattern. The apparent exceptions to it can be explained by special factors. As illegitimate sons, Primo (25) and Vincenzo (50) are excluded from the patrimony and thus free to establish their own lines—which they do on exactly the same principle as the main, legitimate line. The composer Benedetto's younger brother, Francesco (65), also has a family, but the children start arriving only *c.*1700, when Benedetto, having made his home in Venice, has forfeited his right to be the sole source of continuity for the legitimate branch of the family in Brescia. (Besides, Francesco, whose mother was different from Benedetto's, had a responsibility to provide her with an heir to her dowry.) The appearance of three younger, legitimate brothers (or perhaps half-brothers) of Primo appears

---

[25] Details of baptisms, deaths, and marriages of members of the Vinaccesi family living in the parishes of Sant'Alessandro, San Clemente, and Sant'Afra are given in App. C.2.

to violate the principle, but it is noteworthy that none of them carries the line further; we learn from the census return of Francesco (26) in *c*.1584 that he and his brother Giulio lived with their uncle Bernardino, which means that they did not establish a separate household.[26]

The policy of allowing only one son in each generation to become a parent was fraught with great risk. For what happened if the marriage proved infertile, if plague struck, or if all the children were females? The last fate was in fact suffered by the fourth generation of the line founded by Vincenzo (50), which thereupon became extinguished. At least, the Vinaccesi family sought safety in numbers by allowing 'parent' members to have a good number of children including several males—as witness the eleven children of Francesco (12)—rather than stopping after the birth of the first male child, as some Venetian noble families did. The perils of such a radical policy were pointed out by the genealogist Pompeo Litta in connection with the eminent Giustiniani family 'da San Salvatore' to which the author of the famous psalm paraphrases set by Benedetto Marcello belonged.[27] Drawing perhaps too facile a moral, Litta noted, after sketching the biography of Girolamo Ascanio Giustiniani (1753–1787):

He was the only male child, just as his father and grandfather had been, in consequence of the custom among Venetian patricians to cease having children as soon as a male heir was produced. The need to stay rich was the driving force, but this contributed not a little to the extinction of the oldest patrician families and thus to the fall of the Republic.[28]

The second component of the strategy was to safeguard the interests of the non-marrying males (particularly of those who did not enter the priesthood) by establishing a family trust (*fidecommisso*).[29] The essential requirement of a family trust was that all the property governed by it was inalienable: it could not pass out of the hands of the family through sale or gift. In Venetian territory males alone could inherit, generally in equal shares, real estate (houses, farms, etc.), but both males and females had a claim on 'movable' property (furniture, table linen, etc.). That the Vinaccesis practised such an arrangement is obvious from the census returns, in which individual male members of the family are often seen to own specified fractions of houses and other property.

[26] *I-BRq*, ASC, Registro 139, Fascicolo VIA 1568–95, Cittadella Vecchia, n. 87.

[27] The *Estro poetico-armonico* (pub. 1724–6) was the work of an earlier Girolamo Ascanio Giustiniani (1697–1749). This family had the custom—common among the Venetian patriciate—of transmitting the same two names (Girolamo, Ascanio, or, more generally, both combined) from father to son, thus suggesting a 'reincarnation' of the same family essence in each generation. Contemporary beliefs regarding the heritability of blood made this practice seem quite logical.

[28] Pompeo Litta and continuers, *Famiglie celebri italiane*, xlviii/78, 'Giustiniani di Venezia' (Milan, 1840), table ix. See App. B.4.

[29] See Ferro, *Dizionario*, v. 180–204.

The third component concerned the female side. Dowries had to be settled on daughters who married (including those who became 'brides of Christ'). These dowries were their personal property, to be passed on to their children, and were in that sense charges on the family wealth. It was therefore important to attempt to gain dowries from incoming brides that equalled or surpassed those that went out.

Several habitations and shops of the Brescian Vinaccesis can be identified. Another set of documents in the Archivio di Stato provides, for the years 1641 and 1646, useful supplementation to the information in the *polizze d'estimo*. These documents belong to the series 'Estimi e catasti' (Censuses and Registers), in which the clerks of the *Estimatoria* list all properties according to location, noting their owners and tenants.[30] The co-ordinates for each property, described earlier, can often be linked together to form a chain guiding the researcher to fixed points such as intersections of streets or squares, in this way enabling him to determine the precise location of the building. Many of the original names of streets and squares have been superseded, even when they survive today (which they normally do, since most of the city centre, despite the demolitions wrought by Mussolini's town planners, retains its historical outline), so it is necessary to consult an old plan. An almost ideal source of reference is provided by the *Mappa napoleonica*, a set of large handwritten maps showing eight different zones of the city that was prepared *c*.1816.[31]

The earliest known dwelling occupied by the family in Brescia—from 1533 or earlier—lay in the middle of the block today known as Via dei Musei, 29–29a–29b, and containing the Ufficio Provinciale Elettorale. The stretch of Via dei Musei in question was formerly known as Broletto Longo (it flanks the Broletto palace on the northern side), and the square that it abuts on the West side, today Piazza Tito Speri (named after the hero of the 1849 uprising), is the former Piazza dell'Albera. This property, sandwiched between apartments inhabited by officials and soldiers of the Venetian government, was obviously capacious as well as occupying a 'prime site'; Bernardino (24) valued it at 900 *lire di planeti* in 1548. Because this property, which served as the *casa dominicale* of the 'legitimate' branch of the family, had been purchased directly from the 'Ducal Camera', it was exempt from taxation by the municipality, a point reiterated painstakingly in successive census returns. Eventually, before 1641 (and probably before 19 March 1639, when Emilia (62), Bernardino's granddaughter, was baptized in the parish of Sant'Alessandro), it reverted

---

[30] One series of 'Estimi e catasti', dating from 1641, lists the residents of each *quadra*, noting their property-holdings elsewhere in the city. A complementary series, prepared in 1646, lists the houses themselves for each *quadra*, zone by zone.

[31] *I-BRas*, Mappa napoleonica, Registri 68–75.

to the Camera Ducale, which suggests that it was held under a long lease rather than outright.[32]

Already by 1574 Bernardino and his brothers owned a property in the Contrada delle Bassiche (so-named also today) in the western quarter of the city, San Giovanni. This was the old, decrepit building rented out periodically to old men that was mentioned earlier. It was still in the family's hands in 1588 but must have been given up soon afterwards, as it does not appear in subsequent census returns.[33]

A smaller house, situated in the Contrada di San Clemente (today the stretch of Via Agostino Gallo lying between Via Carlo Cattaneo and Via Trieste), was in the possession of Giulio (28) Vinaccesi by 1585, and may have served as the separate house (and shop?) of his father Filippo (15). It was rented out to his uncle Bernardino, who must have commenced occupation in or just before that year, since Bernardino's second son, Francesco (53), but not his first son, Lodovico (52), was born there. By 1614 Bernardino, now its owner, was letting it out to a stranger. In 1686 the composer Benedetto also had an address in the parish of San Clemente, but because the house in the Contrada di San Clemente is not mentioned in intermediate census returns, one assumes that it was given up and that Benedetto's habitation was different.[34]

The parish archive of San Clemente records the baptism on 24 June 1626 of Lelia, the daughter of a certain Piero Vinaccesi and his wife Alessandra who do not appear there in any other connection.[35] The Piero in question can hardly be Bernardino's elder brother of that name, who was born *c.*1534 and took holy orders (in 1588 we find him living separately in a house in the Contrada di San Faustino, which is today the part of Via San Faustino between Vicolo Manzone and the ring road). One thinks next of Primo's son Pietro (33), whose age certainly fits, but in Primo's census return of 1627 this Pietro is listed without mention of a wife and daughter.[36] Besides, the given name 'Lelia' belongs to the repertory of Bernardino's branch rather than Primo's. So the likelihood is that this Piero was a younger relative of Bernardino—possibly a grandson of his brother Filippo, or even a son of his brother Benedetto (21), who is known to have married. Whether this Piero resided in the house in the

---

[32] *I-BRas*, Estimi e catasti, Registro 70, Estimo delle case di Cittadella Nuova, n. 62. *I-BRq*, ASC, Registro 139, Fascicolo VIA 1568–95, Cittadella Vecchia, n. 87. *I-BRq*, ASC, Registro 249, Fascicoli VIA: 1734, Cittadella Nuova; 1548, Cittadella Nuova, n. 24; 1588, Cittadella Vecchia, n. 203; VIA 1627, Cittadella Nuova, n. 197. Brescia, Archivio parrocchiale di Sant'Alessandro, Nascite III (1617–64), fo. 149ᵛ.

[33] *I-BRq*, ASC, Registro 249, Fascicoli VIA: 1627–37 [but dated 1574!], Cittadella Nuova, n. 193; 1588, Cittadella Vecchia, nn. 203 and 576.

[34] *I-BRq*, ASC, Registro 139, Fascicolo VIA 1614–19, Cittadella Nuova, n. 22. *I-BRq*, ASC, Registro 249, Fascicoli VIA 1588, Cittadella Vecchia, n. 203; 1687, Cittadella Vecchia, n. 254.

[35] Brescia, Archivio parrocchiale di San Clemente, Battezzati I (1541–1647), fo. 129ᵛ.

[36] *I-BRq*, ASC, Registro 249, Fascicolo VIA 1627, Cittadella Nuova, n. 179.

Contrada di San Clemente or at a different address in the same parish is yet another question.[37]

After the loss of the house in Broletto Longo it appears that the legitimate descendants of the first Bernardino moved into rented accommodation, perhaps an indication that the family's financial situation was less comfortable than before. Francesco's daughter Emilia (62) was born, as we saw, in the parish of Sant'Alessandro in 1636. But the family evidently moved on before long, since her younger brother Pietro was born elsewhere *c.*1640, and Francesco's census return of 1641 was filed under Cittadella Vecchia. From the time of his second marriage in 1673, if not earlier, Emilia's elder brother Lodovico (59) was living in the parish of Sant'Afra in the *quadra* of Sant'Alessandro Seconda. In 1686 Lodovico and his younger brother Bernardino (61) were renting for 50 *scudi* (a fairly high sum: about 170 *lire di planeti*) a house in the Tresanda (or Contrada) dei Padri Capuccini, probably the present-day Via Gezio Calini, which formerly continued eastwards beyond Via Antonio Callegari to the city perimeter.[38]

The older Bernardino's illegitimate son Vincenzo (50) had to find his own accommodation. In 1630 he was occupying a rented house in Cittadella Vecchia, in the Contrada della Piazzola del Novarino, which led from the South-East corner of the Piazzola del Novarino (today Piazza del Foro) to the Contrada d'Ercole (today Via Carlo Cattaneo) along the route of the present-day Via Agostino Gallo. The rent was quite high—23 *lire di planeti*, 10 *soldi* per annum—but income from both main branches of the Vinaccesi family must have eased the burden. From the estate of his father Bernardino, Vincenzo had received a settlement of 1,000 *lire* payable as a *livello* from the legitimate heirs at the rate of 50 *lire* per annum, while his cousin Primo was paying him a similar *livello* of 10 *lire* 5 *soldi* (or 5 per cent of a capital of 205 *lire*) as dowry for his wife Apollonia. This subsidy shows that the Vinaccesis still regarded themselves as a united extended family, despite the different legal and economic position of legitimate and 'natural' sons and their descendants. When Vincenzo died some time before 1641, it was his half-brother Francesco who acted as guardian to his children Maria (71) and Geronimo (72). In the census of 1653 Geronimo has moved to an unidentified house in Cittadella Nuova, where he rents a house for only 32 *lire* 16 *soldi* annually. This is no symptom of poverty, however, but merely reflects the fact that he is still a young man. When, at the age of 58, he submits his cen-

[37] Because of the uncertainty of this Piero's relationship to the other Vinaccesis, he, his wife, and his daughter have been omitted from the family trees in App. A.

[38] *I-BRq*, ASC, Registro 249, Fascicolo VIA 1687, Sant'Alessandro Seconda, n. 163. *I-BRq*, PPE, Busta 13, Estimo civico del 1641, Cittadella Vecchia, n. 27. Brescia, Archivio parrocchiale di Sant'Afra, Matrimoni IV (1653–74), 17 June 1673. A *tresanda* or *tresandello* is the same as a *vicolo* (alley).

sus return in 1685, his rise in the world is evident, since he is now renting an obviously larger house in Cittadella Nuova for 121 *lire* and in addition pays the municipality rent of 60 *lire* for a house (in which also to conduct business?) on the Piazza del Duomo (today Piazza Papa Paolo Sesto) and another 124 *lire* to enable his son Vincenzo (74) to hold a stall 'sotto Loggia' (i.e. in the forecourt of the Palazzo della Loggia).[39]

But the economically most successful branch of the family was unquestionably that founded by Primo, and this is reflected in its houses. In his first census return, of 1588, Primo lists no houses in his possession, although he refers to a former shop 'at the sign of the lobster' ('al gambaro'). In 1597, however, he bought from the Venetian authorities the ground floor ('un fondo di casa terraneo') of a house in the Contrada di Broletto, the street leading diagonally out of the North-West corner of the Piazza del Duomo. This house seems to have stood on the North side of the street (today Via Cesare Beccaria, numbers 13 upwards) facing Strada Nuova (Via Cesare Beccaria, numbers 1–11), which leads off it into the Piazza della Loggia. This house, too, was exempt from local taxation. It remained in the hands of Primo's descendants until at least 1685, when his grandsons Giovita and Fortunato listed it.[40]

In 1627 Primo was also renting from the municipality a house with a shop in Strada Nuova itself, for which he paid 300 *lire di planeti* annually. This street, whose appearance is largely intact today, has been the object of special study by historians of town planning.[41] It is a rare example, for the cities of the Veneto, of a planned street conceived by a municipality as an economic investment. The thirteen terrace houses in it, seven on the North side and six on the South, were to earn money for the city by being rented out to traders, at the same time having the beneficial effect of concentrating the commercial life of Brescia in this central area. The construction of Strada Nuova took place in the early 1550s. Its planned nature is evident from the manner in which it strikes out in a straight line from its junction with the Contrada della Broletto towards the centre of the Palazzo di Loggia on the far side of the square.

Primo's house was the fourth along, proceeding from the West on the South side: today Via Cesare Beccaria, 6. In 1632 the property, which included a courtyard with a fountain, was pawned to Primo for 2,700 *lire*

[39] *I-BRas*, PPE, Estimo civico del 1641, Busta 13, Cittadella Vecchia, n. 27. *I-BRq*, ASC, Registro 139, Fascicolo VIA 1687, Cittadella Nuova, n. 74. *I-BRq*, ASC, Registro 249, Fascicoli VIA: 1630–34, Cittadella Vecchia, n. 42; 1661–67, Cittadella Nuova, n. 189.

[40] *I-BRas*, PPE, Busta 13, Estimo civico del 1641, Cittadella Nuova, n. 152; Estimi e catasti, Registro 70, Cittadella Nuova, n. 71. *I-BRq*, ASC, Registro 249, Fascicoli VIA: 1588, Cittadella Vecchia, n. 276; 1627, Cittadella Nuova, n. 179; 1630–34, Cittadella Nuova, n. 84; 1653, Cittadella Nuova, n. 12; 1661–67, Cittadella Nuova, n. 70; 1687, Sant'Alessandro Prima, n. 119.

[41] *I-BRq*, ASC, Registro 249, Fascicolo VIA 1627, Cittadella Nuova, n. 179. On the history of the Strada Nuova see Ugo Soragni, 'La Strada Nuova di Brescia', in Carlo Pirovani (ed.), *Lombardia: Il territorio, l'ambiente, il paesaggio* (Milan, 1981–2), ii. 153–68.

di planeti by the city, which reserved the right to redeem it at a future date. This unusual arrangement was not followed in the case of the other houses in Strada Nuova, which remained rented. In 1677 the municipality reclaimed the property.[42]

In 1641 Primo's daughter-in-law, Teodora, had a half-share (the other was owned jointly by her husband Raffaele, his brother Pietro, and her sister Lucia) in a row of three houses in the Contrada di Sant'Antonio (the stretch of the modern Via Cairoli running between the Contrada delle Bassiche and Via Pace). At some point before 1657 these were sold off. This is an example of the complicated fractions of ownership that could arise with property subject to family trusts or otherwise divided equally among children.[43]

After the loss of the house in Strada Nuova, the brothers Giovita, Vinaccese, and Fortunato moved to a rented house in the Contrada di Sant'Alessandro, which includes the part of the present-day Via Moretto running eastwards from Via Pietro Bulloni up to the church of Sant'Alessandro and the first part of Corso Cavour going North from that point. The rent of 50 *scudi* per annum (equivalent to almost 170 *lire di planeti*) suggests a large property. The house must have been occupied by the family until at least 1736, when Vinaccese's son Raffaele (44), a priest, died. If Gaetano Vinaccesi (98), who died in the same parish (Sant'Alessandro) in 1756, was a relative, the residence of Primo's descendants in the house may have been longer.[44]

For their shop the three brothers rented a property on the Piazza del Duomo, where their cousin Geronimo also worked.[45]

A vital factor in the economy of the family was its holdings on the land. In an age when insurance against loss had not come into being, long-term investment in land must have seemed more attractive than investment in buildings or movable property, for whereas a house could be burnt down or valuables stolen, land was virtually immune to permanent destruction. As town dwellers forbidden by their status as citizens to practise any mechanical art, the Vinaccesis could not, obviously, turn themselves into agriculturalists, but by employing *massari* (farm managers) and letting out pieces of land to *mezzadri* (tenant farmers), they were able to ensure that the land they acquired in the territory of Brescia yielded a

---

[42] *I-BRas*, Estimi e catasti, Registro 2, Estimo civico del 1641, Cittadella Nuova, n. 230. *I-BRq*, ASC, Registro 249, Fascicoli VIA: 1630–34, Cittadella Nuova, n. 84; 1687, Sant'Alessandro Prima, n. 119.

[43] *I-BRas*, PPE, Busta 13, Estimo civico del 1641, Cittadella Nuova, n. 152. *I-BRas*, PPE, Busta 13, Estimi e catasti, Registro 36, Estimo civico del 1641, San Giovanni Terza, n. 304. *I-BRq*, ASC, Registro 249, Fascicolo VIA 1653, Cittadella Nuova, n. 12.

[44] *I-BRq*, ASC, Registro 249, Fascicolo VIA 1687, Sant'Alessandro Prima, n. 119. Brescia, Archivio parrocchiale di Sant'Alessandro, Nascite IV (1664–1702), and Defonti II (1658–1702), III (1702–56), and IV (1756–1773), *passim*.

[45] *I-BRq*, ASC, Registro 249, Fascicolo VIA 1687, Sant'Alessandro Prima, n. 119.

good income. In his census return of 1548, Francesco (12), still only one generation removed from Venice, declares 66 *piò* (the local measure of land) in the settlements of Offlaga and Manerbio to the South and 12 *piò* in Rebuffone, part of the rocky terrain to the North-East of the city aptly known as 'I Ronchi' (The Stony Slopes). The first holding is worked by tenant farmers, the second by a farm manager.[46] That the main branch of the family took great interest in the development of its landed property becomes evident when we consider the return submitted by Francesco (53) in 1641, in which the Offlaga and Manerbio holdings have increased to 105 *piò*, the Rebuffone holdings to 26 *piò*.[47] Primo and his descendants were involved much less actively with the land, though one notices a little property in the *Chiusure* in Primo's returns for 1632 and 1641 and various pieces of land arriving as dowries later on.[48]

The census returns provide disappointingly little information on the occupations followed by the Vinaccesis. Perhaps this is to be expected. One's status as a citizen derived from a quality of being rather than doing, from unearned as much as earned wealth. Few occupations open to members of the citizenry were 'full-time' in the modern sense of excluding parallel occupations or taking up the whole of the working day. No doubt, most family members derived their living from a number of sources. Even those who were less successful as individuals could expect a 'trickle down' of wealth from their more successful relatives. It is certainly not with a sense of any shame that more than one family member enters 'senza esercizio' (without occupation) in his return.

The first pointer to an occupation arrives in the return of Filippo (15) dated 3 February 1574, in which he estimates the value of his stock-in-trade in (unspecified) merchandise ('traffega in mercantia') as 1,200 *lire di planeti*.[49] His first-born, illegitimate son Primo also plies the merchant's trade. In 1588 his stock is described as 'marchantia de mazzaro [mercanzia di massaro]'(valued at 800 *lire*), in 1632 as 'mercantia di mezzadro' (5,000 *lire*).[50] The meaning of these expressions is not entirely clear, but the business seems to be in stock and seed for tenant farmers and farm managers, perhaps also in agricultural implements. Of the commercial activity of Primo's grandsons we will speak in the next chapter. Meanwhile, at least two of Filippo's other sons, Benedetto (21) and Bernardino (24), moved into Venetian government service. An account-book of *Camerlengo*

---

[46] *I-BRq*, ASC, Registro 249, Fascicolo VIA 1548, Cittadella Nuova, n. 24.

[47] *I-BRas*, PPE, Busta 13, Estimo civico del 1641, Cittadella Vecchia, n. 27.

[48] *I-BRas*, PPE, Busta 13, Estima civico del 1641, Cittadella Nuova, n. 152. *I-BRq*, ASC, Registro 249, Fascicolo VIA 1630–34, Cittadella Nuova, n. 84. The dowry of Paola Rebusca, wife of Primo's grandson Vinaccese (42), included property in Provelle (Fascicolo VIA 1687, Sant'Alessandro Prima, n. 68).

[49] *I-BRq*, ASC, Registro 249, Fascicolo VIA 1627–37, Cittadella Nuova, n. 193.

[50] *I-BRq*, ASC, Registro 249, Fascicolo VIA 1588, Cittadella Vecchia, n. 276.

Vendramino for the years immediately following 1592 makes intermittent reference to them. From the context one gathers that they are book-keepers concerned, among other things, with the provisioning of the garrison.[51] Perhaps they held exactly the same post as Bernardino's son Francesco, who describes his position in 1641 as that of a *contadore* (accounts clerk) in the Camera Fiscale.[52] This was the revenue department of the Camera Ducale situated inside the Broletto palace (as one entered the Broletto from the Piazza del Duomo the Camera Fiscale was on the left; its counting-room, the Camerino del Denaro, faced the piazza).[53] Francesco quotes his annual salary as 48 ducats, or 144 *lire di planeti*. This is not especially high for a non-manual occupation and suggests that his office was no more than middle-ranking. Later in the century we find Geronimo (72) describing himself as a 'servitore della Illustrissima Città', but with no hint of what kind of service he performed for the municipality.[54]

There is some evidence that in Brescia the family strove to better its level of education. Francesco's son Piero (22) reports in his census return for 1568 that he is studying in Padua, presumably at the famous university. In his return for the same census his elder brother Filippo reports the expense, 150 *lire di planeti* a year, of keeping his 8-year-old son Francesco (26) at the 'accademia nelle casse [case] del Signor Giovanni Battista Ceruta nella tresanda di Boni' as well as that of having his three other sons (Primo, Giulio, and Lelio) taught grammar, and one of them also writing, for all of which he has to pay their tutor 30 *lire* per annum.[55]

It was Primo's descendants who gave the family its greatest intellectual lustre—at least, until the composer Benedetto came along. His grand-daughter Ottavia (38), through her marriage to Pasquino Dotti, gave birth to the great satirical poet Bartolomeo Dotti (1651–1713), whom we will encounter in another connection later on. Ottavia's younger brother Vinaccese (42) acquired the title of 'Dottore', although it is unclear whether his qualification was in medicine or law. It was, of course, another brother, Fortunato (43), who made the family name famous. But of him we will speak at length in the next chapter.

[51] *I-Vmc*, Ms. P.D. C1409/3, 'Quarto memoriale principiato a 7 dicembre 1592 del Clarissimo Signor Camerlengo Vendramino'. The entries for Benedetto and Bernardino span the years 1594–7. I am grateful to Jonathan Glixon for drawing my attention to this source.

[52] *I-BRas*, PPE, Busta 13, Estimo civico del 1641, Cittadella Vecchia, n. 27.

[53] Shown in *I-Vas*, Dispacci Rettori Brescia, Busta 18, disegno 8, reproduced as fig. 173 in Soragni, 'La Strada Nuova di Brescia', 154.

[54] *I-BRq*, ASC, Registro 139, Fascicolo VIA 1687, Cittadella Nuova, n. 74.

[55] *I-BRq*, ASC, Registro 139, Fascicolo VIA 1568, Cittadella Nuova, nn. 45 and 47.

2

Benedetto Vinaccesi

The Brescian Years

AFTER so much chapter and verse concerning more remote members of his family, it is chastening to have to admit that the exact date and place of the composer Benedetto's birth remain unknown. We know in which parishes his father Lodovico (59) was living after his second marriage (to Lucia Galvani on 17 June 1673) and third marriage (to Caterina Goffi on 30 June 1689), but not in which parish, or even *quadra*, he lived with his first wife, whose name is likewise a blank. The information doubtless survives, but it is hard to know which parish archive to consult first.

There exist, however, two dated documents in which the composer's age in years is given. By superimposing the time-frames implied by each, we can narrow down the period during which the birth must have occurred to that between 1 June and 25 December 1666—on the assumption, naturally, that both documents state Benedetto's age correctly.

The first document is the census return submitted by Benedetto to the Brescian authorities on 31 May 1686. This gives his age as 19.[1] The other is the notice of his death in the parish archive of San Severo, Venice, of which a shortened version appeared also in the *Necrologia* of the Provveditori alla Sanità.[2] Here his age is stated to be 'about 53' ('d'anni 53 in circa'—the *Necrologia* omits 'in circa', presumably in the interest of brevity rather than accuracy).

We know nothing about the occupation of his father Lodovico, who was born *c*.1630 and must have died between 30 June 1689, date of his third marriage, and *c*.1714, when the *Catastico di Venezia* prepared for the *estimo* of 1711 was completed (Benedetto's entry in the register of San Severo describes him as 'quondam Lodovico').[3] It is virtually certain that neither Lodovico nor his younger brother Bernardino, with whom he lived, was a merchant, since otherwise we would have seen a declaration of the value of their stock and cash in hand in their census returns. In all

---

[1] *I-BRq*, ASC, Registro 139, Fascicolo VIA 1687, Cittadella Vecchia, n. 254.

[2] Venice, Archivio parrocchiale di San Severo, Registro dei morti 1715–1756, opening 16. *I-Vas*, Provveditori alla Sanità, Busta 914, Necrologio 1719, 25 Dec. 1719.

[3] *I-Vas*, Dieci Savi sopra le decime di Rialto, Busta 428, Catastico di Venezia, Estimo del 1711, San Severo, n. 195.

probability, Lodovico continued in the tradition of his father Francesco, working for the local representatives of the Venetian government.

The only information that we have about Benedetto's early years comes from an entry for him in Leonardo Cozzando's *Libraria bresciana*. Cozzando (1620–1702) was a Servite friar who before his retirement to the convent of the order in the nearby small town of Rovato had been a professor of philosophy at the sister convent of Sant'Alessandro in Brescia.[4] During his retirement he published, in 1694, two notable reference works on Brescia. The first, entitled *Vago e curioso ristretto profano e sacro dell'historia bresciana*, is a cross between a historical guide to the city and a record of famous Brescians.[5] It contains notes on several dozen musicians under such headings as 'Cantori', 'Sonatori d'organo', 'Maestri di cappella', 'Fabbricatori di organi', and 'Scrittori di musica'. The second book, *Libraria bresciana*, is a celebration of Brescian 'erudition', particularly in the literary sphere.[6] Here only a handful of musicians appear, and the criterion for their inclusion seems to be less their musical distinction than their high social status: all are clerics or members of the citizenry.

In 1694 Benedetto was aged only about 28, and his mention in Cozzando's work seems almost premature. However, a special factor may have played a part. Cozzando owed a debt of gratitude to Benedetto's cousin Fortunato, who, as a free-lance dealer in books, had obtained for him in Brescia works that were unfindable in Rovato. He refers to his helper as 'the Most Illustrious Signor Fortunato Vinaccesi, who spared no effort to search the bookshops of Brescia to see if any [books needed by Cozzando] could be found, and who gave me some [as a present]'.[7] The link can only have been strengthened by the fact that Fortunato was a member of the *disciplina* of Sant'Alessandro, hence an adherent of the Servites. In the circumstances, to sing the praises of his helper's kinsman must have been, for Cozzando, an apt way of returning past favours.

He writes as follows on Benedetto:

Benedetto Vinaccesi, Cavaliere, was noted from his early years for his good looks and love of singing and playing instruments. This led him to attend the school of Signor Don Pietro Pelli, a secular priest blessed with great virtues but also a gifted singer and performer on various instruments, and he profited greatly from

---

[4] See the biography of Cozzando in *Dizionario biografico degli Italiani*, xxx (Rome, 1984), 551–2.

[5] Leonardo Cozzando, *Vago e curioso ristretto profano e sacro dell'historia bresciana* (Brescia, 1694). The book is divided into two parts, respectively 'profana' and 'sagra', but has continuous pagination.

[6] *Libraria bresciana, prima e seconda parte nuovamente aperta dal M. R. P. maestro Leonardo Cozzando, Servita Bresciano* (Brescia, 1694). This work, too, is laid out in two parts with a continuous pagination.

[7] Ibid., i. 17: 'il M[olt]o Illustre Sig. *Fortunato Vinaccesi*, che non hà punto mancato di far ogni inquisitione per le Librarie Bresciane, se qualch'uno rinvenirne poteva, e di parecchi son stato favorito'.

his instruction, as is evident from the works he has published [of which Cozzando appends a list].[8]

Pelli was one of the leading church musicians of his time in Brescia. He was born in the city *c*.1619.[9] In 1671 he became *capo musico* (equivalent to *maestro di cappella*) at the Duomo.[10] He also served as musical director to the Accademia degli Erranti, Brescia's foremost learned society. In 1680 he gave up the first post, and in 1681 the second, on account of old age, but in 1687 we find him still active as *maestro di cappella* of the little church of the Madonna del Mercato al Lino next to the old linen market.[11] He has been claimed as the teacher of the composers Carlo Francesco Pollarolo and Giovanni Battista Quaglia.[12]

From Pelli Benedetto undoubtedly received a good grounding in the *stile antico*, the neo-Palestrinian style dubbed by Monteverdi the 'prima prattica', or 'first practice'. Because of Pelli's obviously wide interests (not all organists showed an interest in playing 'various instruments' or frequented secular *accademie*), Benedetto's musical education will not have stopped at the *stile antico*. Certainly, the seeds of his later career as an organist good enough to win one of the two principal organist posts at San Marco, Venice, must have been sown during this period.

For a more general cultural stimulation Benedetto had no need to look further than the salon of his famous cousin. At this point it will be opportune to return to the *Elogio* by Giulio Averoldi and learn more about Fortunato.[13]

Fortunato was born on 9 September 1631. Having received his education in Brescia, he decided at the age of 26 to spread his wings and embark on a kind of 'Grand Tour in reverse' (whereas northern Europeans travelled to Italy in order to further their knowledge of classical antiquity, Italians were likely to venture North of the Alps in pursuit of a greater understanding of the modern sciences). He visited Holland, England, and parts of Spain and France as well as almost all of Italy. His longest stay was in Holland, where he learned Greek, French, Spanish,

---

[8] Ibid., ii. 235–6. See App. B.5.

[9] *I-BRq*, ASC, Registro 226, Fascicolo PE 1630–34, Sant'Alessandro Prima, n. 199.

[10] Olga Termini, 'Organists and Chapel Masters at the Cathedral of Brescia (1608–1779)', *Note d'archivio per la storia musicale*, NS 3 (1985), 81.

[11] *I-BRq*, ASC, Registro 475, 'Estimo dal [sic] 1687', Cittadella Vecchia, n. 70. This vol. is a register of tax payments received.

[12] For Pollarolo see Maria Teresa Rosa Barezzani *et al.*, *La musica a Brescia nel Settecento* (Brescia, 1981), 32; for Quaglia see Giuseppe Brunati, *Dizionario degli uomini illustri della Riviera di Salò* (Milan, 1837), 119. Cozzando, however, claims that Quaglia's teacher was Francesco Turini (*Vago e curioso ristretto*, ii. 245). Caution must always be exercised in accepting as fact teacher–pupil relationships claimed in older—and not only older—literature, since these are so often based on inference rather than documentary evidence.

[13] Transcribed in full (except for editorial footnotes) as App. B.1.

Dutch, English, and a little Hebrew and German.[14] In the tradition of a 'universal savant', he mastered many other branches of knowledge, becoming expert in mathematics, geography, and cartography. He took an informed interest in painters and painting, collecting canvases with discernment. He was an equally keen bibliophile who turned his love of books to good account by acting as an agent for those seeking to obtain rare or inaccessible works (as we saw in the case of Cozzando).

Prior to his departure on his travels, Fortunato was a keen collector of ancient coins and medals. This was an interest that did not survive his period of absence from home. The reason for his abandonment of his hobby makes such a good and scandalous tale that we will tell it in Averoldi's words:

Returning after six years and two months to breathe his native air, and wishing to hold in his hands again those splendid relics of antiquity, he became extremely perturbed at his first sight of them and forsook his intention—nor ever again (as he told me repeatedly) did he cast a glance at his medals or allow anyone else to look at them. The cause of his discomfort was that his brothers [Giovita and Vinaccese] had too readily and obligingly allowed a prelate, contrary to his instructions, to gain access to the box containing those medals; this prelate had relieved Signor Fortunato of the inconvenience of having to make a careful choice [of what to collect] by helping himself to the best of them without so much as a 'by your leave'.

In confidence—and no one else must know this—I will reveal who the prelate was. He was Cardinal Pietro Ottoboni [great-uncle of the homonymous cardinal, Corelli's protector], our own bishop who later became Pope under the name of Alexander VIII. Having learnt of this collection of medals, he dressed himself in a short black habit and, as dusk was falling, betook himself to the house of the Vinaccesis, where he asked to see them. In their bafflement the brothers told him that the absent owner had forbidden this, but they were unable to deny the wishes of so eminent a prelate. The visitor stayed for several hours, admiring and handling the medals, and with a practised and understanding eye placed those that took his fancy in a handkerchief, saying as he departed, 'I will enjoy these for the love of them', prior to adding them to his own collection.[15]

Fortunato found many recreations to replace the one he had lost. Averoldi tells us that he played the recorder marvellously ('sonava a meraviglia di flauto') and also played the 'leuto alla francese' (i.e. a lute tuned, in the French manner, to the *nouveau ton*) and the guitar. His main new enthusiasm, however, was lens-grinding—the profession of Spinoza. His

---

[14] Cozzando (*Vago e curioso ristretto*, i. 99) includes Fortunato under the 'Professori di varie lingue, e traduttori dal Greco in Latino'.

[15] The abridged version of the *Elogio* published in the *Giornale dei letterati d'Italia* tactfully omits this passage, which would certainly have given offence to the younger Pietro Ottoboni, a prominent benefactor of the literary world. In a footnote, Giovanni Averoldi makes the tart comment: 'Ottoboni's high-handedness as Cardinal of Brescia explains perfectly his nepotism as Pope' ('La *disinvoltura* dell'Ottoboni Vescovo di Brescia spiega perfettamente il nepotismo dell'Ottoboni Papa').

lenses were used for spectacles, telescopes, and other optical instruments. They were sought after all over Europe and fetched high prices.[16]

Delighting in the company of other educated people, Fortunato opened a salon where *conversazioni* could be held. The house where he lived, not far from the church of Sant'Alessandro, was too distant for the purpose, so he found a suitable room in the city centre. Averoldi implies that the room was acquired specially for the purpose, but one would guess that it belonged to the house owned by the descendants of Primo in the Contrada di Broletto, which is certainly very central. Averoldi writes that no learned foreigner—nor any painter, musician, or craftsman—passed through Brescia without visiting Fortunato's salon. The biographer states proudly that on 14 May 1685 he himself brought there Jean Mabillon (1632–1707), the Benedictine monk famous for his pioneering work on diplomatics (*De re diplomatica*, 1681).[17] Another visitor, introduced by Averoldi on 29 March 1686, was a 'Monsieur Vaillant', almost certainly identifiable with Jean Foy-Vaillant (1632–1706), a noted numismatist. A few days later Averoldi brought along a man he describes as 'il celebre Carlo Patino'; this must be the Frenchman Charles Patin, another numismatist, albeit one more famous for his travel writings.[18]

According to Averoldi, Fortunato disliked lending out his books (except to Averoldi himself!), since he feared that they would be lost, mutilated, or soiled. Of course, the fact that he traded in books must also have influenced his attitude towards lending. Although not an author in his own right, Fortunato earned money and intellectual credit by editing, and seeing through the press, several works by others. His greatest achievement in this area was to edit for publication the *Memorie bresciane* of Ottavio Rossi, which appeared in 1693.

His death on 25 November 1713 came soon after an attack of apoplexy. He was buried in the chapel of the Virgin in the church of Sant'Alessandro, the place reserved for members of its *disciplina* (no burial inscription for him exists there today).

It is easy to see connections between the interests of Fortunato and those of his young cousin, who must have frequented his salon. The most

[16] Averoldi observes that Fortunato never made a pair of spectacles for himself even though he had bad sight. The minuteness of Fortunato's handwriting as seen in his surviving letters suggests myopia.

[17] Mabillon briefly records his meeting with Fortunato in his *Museum italicum seu collectio veterum scriptorum ex bibliothecis* (Paris, 1687–9), i. 22, describing our subject as 'a certain merchant, but [*and the nuance introduced by this conjunction needs no comment*] versed in many languages and knowledgeable about books' ('mercatorem quidem, sed qui multas linguas & libros callet').

[18] Since Averoldi was himself interested in old medals, as Mabillon (*Museum italicum*, i. 22) confirms, the presence of two experts on this subject among the visitors he took to Fortunato's salon is easily explained. Numismatics, particularly when applied to medals and coins of the ancient world, united the pleasures of a hobby with the studies of a classicist and historian; for that reason, it enjoyed a great vogue among the erudite of that time and numbered even the great Apostolo Zeno among its adherents.

obvious link is painting. We know from Benedetto's will that he possessed a large collection of canvases, and the inventory taken of the paintings owned by his son Pietro Antonio, many of which were probably inherited from him, reveals a collector's eye—and a collector's appetite.[19] As we shall learn below, one of the witnesses at his wedding was a painter.

Since the recorder and the 'leuto alla francese' were instruments that during the seventeenth century were cultivated mostly North of the Alps—one thinks of the works of Jacob van Eyck (*c.*1590–1657) for the first and of Denis Gaultier (1603–72) for the second—Fortunato will probably have learnt his skills on them in Holland or another northern country. It will be remarked later that Benedetto, in some of his early works, shows clear signs of French influence. Fortunato's transalpine repertory is not likely to have been the only source of this influence, which pervaded all the courts of northern Italy, but one cannot discount its effect altogether. At all events, the music heard by Benedetto in the salon of his cousin must have been a good antidote to the fare provided at the school of Pietro Pelli.

Perhaps Fortunato's most important legacy to Benedetto was not specific but general. One notices in all the latter's compositions a certain intellectual quality, a willingness to conceive a work in an individual way that, while not taking him to the farthest shores of *bizzarria*, can certainly lay claim to boldness. Knowledge of Fortunato and his distinguished company can only have stimulated the budding musician's curiosity and built up his self-confidence as an artist.

In 1685 Benedetto, aged no more than 19, married a slightly younger woman named Veronica Illuminati. The details of the ceremony are recorded in the marriage register for San Clemente, the bride's parish:

27 December 1685

Signor Benedetto Vinaccese, son of Lodovico Vinaccese, to Donna Veronica, daughter of the late Don Francesco Illuminati, my parishioner, having been granted a dispensation from the customary publications [banns] and permission to marry at any time and in any place; they have contracted marriage on the word of those present, with myself, Father Tomaso Fenarolo, curate of San Clemente in Brescia, officiating, in the house of the Very Reverend Don Giovanni Terrallio, my parishioner; present as witnesses the aforesaid Reverend Don Giovanni, Signor Apollionio Tartaro, and Don Pietro Antonio Erazzio [or 'Enazzio'?], a Cremonese painter residing in Brescia.[20]

The reason for the dispensation is almost certainly explained by the birth of the couple's first son, Lodovico Tito, around April 1686. The

---

[19] *Stampa*, 86–8. See App. B.33.
[20] Brescia, Archivio parrocchiale di San Clemente, Matrimoni I (1566–1705), fo. 121ᵛ. See App. B.6.

Illuminatis were certainly a citizen family, but not one habitually resident in Brescia, since they presented no census returns there. They were probably so-called 'cittadini rurali' who lived in one of the many small settlements in Brescian territory. As her dowry Veronica brought a parcel of land in Rocca Franca, a *borgo* for which the 1687 census listed only two property-owning families.

On 31 May 1686 Benedetto, who, following traditional practice, had moved to his new wife's parish, submitted his census return, whose text reads as follows:

Declaration by me, Benedetto, son of Signor Lodovico Vinacese, son of the late Signor Francesco, a citizen of Brescia living in [the parish of] San Clemente.

I, Benedetto Vinacese, the above-named, aged 19 years
Veronica Luminati, my wife, aged 18 years
Lodovico, my son, aged one month

Property in the territory of Rocca Franca

I possess a piece of land, arable, planted with vines, and irrigated, in the above-named territory in the Contrada di San Rocco [also] called 'Il Gerone' described in the general census of the Magnificent City [of Brescia] for 1641 and listed in the register for Rocca Franca at number 3, first entry, under the name of the late Giovanni Battista [Il]luminati, son of the late Bartolomeo; which piece of land borders to the East the high street, to the South the former property of the Signori Alovisio and the Rovati brothers, now owned by Count Giacomo Sovardo, to the North a lane, and to the West the property of Count Cesare Martinengo, having the area of four piò.

Which piece of land has been assigned to me as the dowry of my above-named wife by her mother Donna Barbara, widow of Don Francesco.

[Officially dated '1686: 31 Maij']^{21}

As a 'gentleman', hence by definition a *dilettante*, Benedetto had no need to secure—and may at first have been dissuaded by his family from seeking—a salaried post as a musician. The first hint of any such position comes from the title-page of his first published work, a set of six *Suonate da camera a tre* that appeared in 1687 from the Venetian music publisher Giuseppe Sala.[22] The text of this title-page runs:

---

[21] See n. 1, above, and App. B.7.

[22] Karlheinz Schlager (ed.), *Einzeldrucke vor 1800* (Kassel, 1971- , ix. 98)) lists the collection as 'V 1577' and records surviving examples, both complete, in Wiesentheid, Bibliothek der Grafen von Schönborn-Wiesentheid, Nr. 136, and Oxford, Bodleian Library, [Ms.], Mus. Sch. E. 554. Incipits of the first movements and details of the title, tempo marking, and time signature of all movements are given in Fritz Zobeley, *Die Musikalien der Grafen von Schönborn-Wiesentheid: Thematisch-bibliographischer Katalog*, pt. 1: *Das Repertoire des Grafen Rudolf Franz Erwein von Schönborn (1677–1754). Teil i: 149 Drucke aus den Jahren 1676 bis 1738* (Tutzing, 1967), 124–5. Transcriptions of the title-page, dedication, preface, and concluding table of contents appear in Claudio Sartori, *Bibliografia della musica strumentale italiana stampata in Italia fino al 1700* (Florence, 1952–68), ii. 176–7, which identifies the publication as '1687(l)'. Sartori's transcription of the dedication omits eight words (from 'formar' to 'purgato') in error.

VIOLINO PRIMO [*etc.*] / SUONATE / DA CAMERA / A TRÈ / Due Violini Violoncello,
& Cembalo. / *Di Benedetto Vinacese Maestro di Capella dell'Ecc: Sig:* / D. FERDI-
NANDO / GONZAGA / PRENCIPE DI CASTIGLIONE &c. / DEDICATE AL MERITO SUBLIME
/ *Dell'Eccenlentissima* [*sic*] *Signora Dona* / LAURA PICCA / GONZAGA PRENCIPESSA /
DI CASTIGLIONE &c. / [decorative emblem] / IN VENETIA, MDCL XXXVII. / Appresso
Giuseppe Sala.

Before we consider Vinaccesi's relationship to the prince of Castiglione,
his employer, and the princess, his wife, to whom the set was dedicated, it
will be useful to answer three questions. Why should an organist have
chosen to make his début as a composer before a wider public with a collection of works for string ensemble? Why should Vinaccesi not have
obtained a post with a Brescian noble family rather than with the rulers of
a small principality sandwiched between Brescian and Mantuan territory?
And finally: why should he have elected to publish his sonatas in distant
Venice?

The first question is easily answered at a practical level, though less sat-
isfactorily explained in theoretical terms. In Italy, as in most of Europe,
the organ—even the small, portable type of organ that was so much in
vogue—was regarded as an instrument for use in churches, not one to be
cultivated by amateurs in a domestic, recreational setting. Hence the market for organ music was virtually limited to professional organists. Yet this
did not of itself prevent, in the first half of the seventeenth century, the
publication of numerous collections of toccatas, canzonas, variations, cantus firmus settings, and many other types of composition for the solo
organ medium by such acknowledged masters as Frescobaldi and Merulo.
However, in the whole of the second half of the century Italian organ
music could boast no composer of European stature, and the literature for
the instrument retreated into a kind of ghetto, enjoying less prestige than
before and exciting little public attention. It had also reached a stylistic
impasse, uncertain whether to imitate the increasingly 'free-voiced' style
of harpsichord music or to maintain strict part-writing and the contrapuntal rigour that traditionally went with it. The few published collections of
organ music to have survived from this period include a high proportion
of anthologies, itself a sign of the lack of any dominating figure.[23] In contrast, the genre and medium of the trio sonata—a sonata in three contra-

---

[23] A representative anthology from the end of the century is that collected by the organist Giulio
Cesare Arresti and published in Bologna *c.*1690 as *Sonate da organo di varii autori.* The 18 single-
movement 'sonatas' (which are, however, often divided into distinct sections) comprise works by
Pietro Andrea Ziani and Carlo Francesco Pollarolo from Venice; Giovanni Battista Bassani from
Ferrara; and Bartolomeo Monari, Giovanni Paolo Colonna, and Arresti himself from Bologna, besides
a number that are anonymous or by little-known composers. Only Colonna's sonata is comparable in
quality of invention and workmanship with, say, a contemporary canzona by Buxtehude, and it is
significant that this master, though trained as an organist, chose to make his greatest effort not in
organ music but sacred vocal composition, where the artistic return was greater.

puntal parts supported by continuo—stood right in the mainstream of musical activity. A composition of this kind allowed the composer to establish his credentials as a contrapuntist while at the same time setting his music before a broad, international public made up of amateur as well as professional musicians. No wonder that so many composers chose to make their first published opus a set of trio sonatas, especially after Corelli, in his influential series of publications from 1681 onwards, had won even greater prestige for the genre.[24]

The answer to the second question tells us something important about the cultural life of the Veneto. The major cities of the Venetian republic, not excepting the *dominante* itself, differed from the majority of similar centres in north and central Italy by not having a courtly society of the conventional kind. Music was placed at the service of institutions (church, municipality, opera-house) rather than individuals. When prominent citizens or members of the local nobility required professional musicians for a particular purpose—to celebrate, say, a wedding or the entry of a daughter into a convent—they were engaged on an *ad hoc* basis. No private individual set himself up as the head of a court that could include among its regular members a group of household musicians, even a whole orchestra, on the model of Cardinal Ottoboni in Rome. The census returns of the Brescian nobility bear this statement out. Even the senior branch of the Gambara family (to a member of which, Annibale, Vivaldi was to dedicate his Op. 1 trio sonatas in 1705) included among the seventy-three members of its *servitù* listed in 1687 not a single musician, if one may discount two trumpeters, whose function was arguably ceremonial rather than musical.[25] Naturally, the nobility of the Veneto patronized and supported musicians in an informal way—the Gradenigo family of Venice even took Antonio Lotti under their wing while he was still a boy—but that is not really the same thing. This rather unusual situation meant that musicians desiring to hold a court position had to go outside the Veneto. In the 1690s Albinoni, from Venice, entered the service of the duke of Mantua, while in 1718 his fellow citizen Vivaldi also joined the Mantuan court (by now subject to an imperial governor, Prince Philip of Hesse-Darmstadt). Caldara went successively to Mantua, Rome, and Vienna; Lotti to Dresden.

---

[24] During the 1680s the following 11 Italian composers besides Vinaccesi published trio sonatas as their Op. 1: Arcangelo Corelli (1681), Alessandro Ziani (1683), Giovanni Bononcini (1685), Giovanni Pietro Franchi (1685), Carlo Fedeli (1685), Giuseppe Torelli (1686), Carlo Andrea Mazzolini (1687), Carlo Antonio Marino (1687), Giovanni Battista Borri (1688), Domenico Zanatta (1689), and Giovanni Maria Ruggieri (1689).

[25] *I-BRq*, ASC, Registro 64, Fascicolo GAL 1687, Cittadella Vecchia, n. 418 (return by Lucrezio and Marc'Antonio Gambara, dated 28 Feb. 1687). Lucrezio's son Annibale (1682–1709), to whom Vivaldi dedicated his sonatas, was a patron of the singer Girolamo Soave, who is described as 'virtuoso del conte Annibale Gambara' in the cast-list of *Il Decio* (Udine, Teatro Mantica, 1705), but it is doubtful whether the latter was a salaried member of his household staff.

The choice of Sala (*c.*1642–1727) as publisher was virtually pre-ordained. Although many cities of the Veneto had general publishers, none except Venice itself possessed music publishing houses. In the closing years of the seventeenth century Sala held a near-monopoly of music publishing in the *dominante*, becoming the publisher of first resort for the whole of the Veneto. In this period (which was, however, soon to end) music publishers did not often take a controlling hand in the development of their catalogue like their modern counterparts. They acted in the first instance as printers for those composers who chose to entrust their manuscripts to them, and in the second as retailers and distributors of the published work. The financial risk was borne, as in a modern private publication, by the composer himself, who might hope, however, to recoup his costs by dedicating the work to a person of quality in the expectation of receiving the customary *regalo* (gratuity).

Similarly, the choice of Laura Pico della Mirandola (the form 'Picca' is an elegant feminization of the surname) as dedicatee of his Op. 1 must have occurred naturally to Vinaccesi, given his service with her husband, the prince of Castiglione delle Stiviere. We do not know how or when he acquired this post of *maestro*, which was probably exercised *in absentia* through the regular provision of compositions, since, as we saw, he was still resident in Brescia in 1687, the year of the work's publication.

Benedetto's path to this post may have been smoothed by the association that already existed between the rulers of Castiglione and his three merchant cousins. From surviving correspondence (1659–73) of the brothers Giovita, Vinaccese, and Fortunato with officials of Ferdinando Gonzaga's court we gain an insight not only into the nature of their business but also into the close, albeit unequal, relationship between the upper nobility and their suppliers of luxury goods—for the brothers were apparently no longer dealing in 'mercanzia di mezzadro' like their grandfather Primo. Let us first quote, by way of example, from a letter that Giovita sent on 10 October 1672 to Guglielmo Corradini, who appears to have been some kind of court chamberlain.

I have received your kind letter of 9 inst. containing payment for the two books sent to you by Signor Fortunato, my brother.

The latter has drawn my attention to the advance [payment] for the items made to order for Her Excellency the Princess by command of His Excellency the Prince, my master, in connection with which we request satisfaction at his earliest convenience; with which matter I close by kissing your hands most cordially.[26]

---

[26] Mantua, Archivio di Stato, Archivio Gonzaga di Castiglione delle Stiviere, Busta 253/5, n. 101. See App. B.8.

A letter to Corradini from Fortunato himself, dated 12 February 1671, sheds further light on the business relationship.

I have received from His Excellency's Councillor the 54 *lire* that you sent me as payment in advance for six months' supply of the *avvisi*, which sum I had already remitted to my friend in Venice.

This friend has already sent me by post 7 *lire* 10 *soldi* to cover the *barzino* and the *carnovale*; payment is outstanding only for the two pelerines [a kind of mantle worn by women], which cost 3 *lire* and for which we have not received reimbursement, perhaps through an oversight on your part.

Payment for the collars of Her Excellency the Princess can follow at your convenience.[27]

The *avvisi* were weekly or monthly news-sheets, generally handwritten, that were produced in Venice. From the many copies that survive, we can see that they fulfilled most of the functions of a newspaper, reporting on political, diplomatic, military, ceremonial, and cultural events, as well as the usual disasters and curious happenings of every kind. The meaning of *barzino* and *carnovale* (literally, 'carnival') eludes me, but it would appear that they were kinds of garment like the pelegrines (*peregrine*) and collars mentioned further on.

The history of the Gonzaga dynasty in Castiglione delle Stiviere was chequered, to say the least.[28] In 1574 Emperor Maximilian II made Ferrante Gonzaga *marchese* of Castiglione, which, like neighbouring Mantua, was an imperial fief. Ferrante died in 1586 and was succeeded by his second son, Rodolfo, since his eldest son Luigi (posthumously San Luigi Gonzaga) had become a Jesuit, thereby forfeiting his right of succession. In 1592 Rodolfo's uncle Alfonso, the lord of Castelgoffredo, a small territory adjoining Mantua, was assassinated. Rodolfo was implicated by some in the murder, since it was known that Alfonso was on the point of disinheriting him. Eight months later Rodolfo himself was assassinated while visiting Castelgoffredo. Mantua took the opportunity to lay claim to the territory, which it eventually obtained in 1602.

Meanwhile, Rodolfo was succeeded by his younger brother Francesco, who in 1612 was elevated from the rank of marquis to that of prince. On his death in 1616 he was succeeded by his son Ferdinando (I). For two more generations the succession was orderly, passing in 1675 to Francesco's cousin Carlo and in 1680 to Carlo's son Ferdinando (II), Benedetto's patron.

This second Ferdinando proved a scandalously bad ruler, since right

[27] Mantua, Archivio di Stato, Archivio Gonzaga di Castiglione delle Stiviere, Busta 253/5, n. 102. See App. B.9.
[28] For the history of Castiglione delle Stiviere and its ruling Gonzaga dynasty, see Bartolomeo Arrighi, *Storia di Castiglione delle Stiviere sotto il dominio dei Gonzaga* (2 vols., Mantua, 1853–4). With the addition of a 3rd vol., by Emilio Ondei, this work is available in a modern reprint (Mantua, 1968).

from the start he treated his principality as a personal patrimony to be exploited for his private benefit. He instituted a general ban on hunting (except by the court), acquired a monopoly over the most profitable local industries, exacted heavy duties on essential commodities, and forced his subjects to accept payment in his debased, non-convertible coinage. When he decided to widen the *piazzetta* of his castle, he demolished the private houses standing on the site without compensating the owners properly. At the instigation of his wife Laura (whom the chronicler Arrighi describes, without giving details, as 'a woman even worse than him'), he decided to create an artificial lake on which she could go boating. To do this he had to divert water from the river Albana and other mountain streams. Despite warnings of the risk of flooding some areas and dessiccating others, he went ahead. The worst prognoses were confirmed: a breach in the protective earthworks occurred on 27 October 1689, and enormous flood damage ensued.

Responding to an appeal from Ferdinando's subjects, the emperor asked the prince to curb his excesses, but without result. On 23 December 1691 the Castiglionesi rose and drove him out. Through pressure from the emperor (who was bound to support his right to rule, impeccable in dynastic terms), Ferdinando was able to return in 1693 from his exile in Milan and reoccupy his castle. It took several years, however, before he was reconciled with his subjects, although a *modus vivendi* was eventually found. Soon afterwards, however, Ferdinando committed an even greater error by supporting the French cause (as the Mantuan Gonzagas also did, with a similar result) during the War of the Spanish Succession. Castiglione changed hands several times in the course of the war but in 1706 was ceded definitively to Austria. For his disloyalty Ferdinando was deprived of his fief and went into a second exile, this time in Venice, where he died in 1723.

History does not tell us what kind of court life was enjoyed at Castiglione delle Stiviere under Ferdinando. One would assume that it reproduced, in miniature, that of neighbouring states such as Mantua and Modena. Francesco's first exile must have disrupted it greatly, and it may be significant that Vinaccesi's Op. 2, published in 1692, makes no mention of his former post, which probably lapsed during all the turmoil.

Little can be learnt from Vinaccesi's letter of dedication to Laura Pico della Mirandola, which goes through the familiar, convoluted motions of lauding the musical sensibility of the dedicatee while disparaging the talent of the author:

Most Illustrious and Excellent Princess,

Your Excellency, adorned with such rare and distinguished qualities, will in no way risk your enviable reputation, on which you rightly pride yourself, if, blessed in addition with an understanding not unequal to your most noble inclination towards, and good taste in, music, you do not disdain to accept with a kindly indulgence this first, unripe fruit of my truly little study and small aspiration to proficiency. I nourish the desire, which impels me strongly to bring my plea before Your Excellency, to win myself some great honour—if not as much as I would like, then at least as much as I am capable of achieving—hoping one day to have a further opportunity to make myself known.

Your Excellency's

Most humble, devoted, and obsequious servant
Benedetto Vinacese
[see Appendix B. 10]

Vinaccesi paid a further tribute to his benefactress's good taste by heading the fourth sonata 'al buon gusto di S. E.', though this is perhaps one of those compliments that are intended to reflect back on the person having the perspicacity to make them.

At the end of the table of contents in the partbook for first violin Vinaccesi appended a second note to the reader in which he stated that if the sonatas were well received, he would publish his second opus, consisting of church sonatas ('la Seconda Opera, che sarà da Chiesa, e di differente studio'). In 1692 he was to honour this promise, but not before an exceptional opportunity had caused him to rush into print an entirely different collection, which he labelled 'Op. 3'.

This third opus, published out of sequence, is one of the works listed by Cozzando, who calls it '*Il consiglio delli amanti, overo Cantate da Camera, à voce sola*. In Venetia 1688. Al Serenissimo gran Prencipe Ferdinando III di Toscana'. (See Appendix B.5.) No example of the print is known to survive today, but the existence of the work is confirmed by its listing in the sale catalogue of the estate of the Dutch bookseller Nicolaas Selhof (1759), a sad monument to the perishability of old editions of music.[29] In the Selhof catalogue, where it is given the lot number 1657, the collection is described as '*Ben. Vinacese*, il Consiglio degl'-Amanti, o vero Cantate amorose a Voce Sola, Libro primo, opera terza'.

It was precisely in this year, 1688, when Grand Prince Ferdinando, son of the reigning Grand Duke Cosimo III of Tuscany, paid a visit to Venice, which he reached on 19 January. He stayed there for fifty days, choosing to remain *incognito* (i.e. with an ostensible rank lower than his true one, a device that enabled protocol to be bypassed and gave the visitor to Venice greater freedom to take his pleasures). Vinaccesi may

---

[29] The complete catalogue is reproduced in facsimile in Alec Hyatt King, *Catalogue of the Music Library, Instruments and Other Property of Nicolas Selhof, Sold in The Hague, 1759* (Amsterdam, 1973). The appearance in this catalogue of a number of published works of which all trace has otherwise been lost is discussed in Michael Talbot, 'Vivaldi in the Sale Catalogue of Nicolaas Selhof', *Informazioni e studi vivaldiani*, 6 (1985), 57–63.

have had an opportunity personally to meet the grand prince on his passage through the Veneto to or from the capital, since Brescia often served as a staging-post on such journeys. There was a special reason why it was appropriate to dedicate a third opus to Ferdinando. The grand prince was expected one day to succeed his father Cosimo and become Grand Duke Ferdinando III. In anticipation of this event (which was not to be, since Ferdinando died in 1713, Cosimo in 1723), he was often referred to as 'Ferdinando III'. Certain composers played on this prospect by pointedly dedicating their third opus to him. Giuseppe Torelli appears to have started the fashion in 1687 with his *Sinfonie*, Op. 3; Vinaccesi was next, in 1688, and Albinoni, Gentili, and Vivaldi followed suit in 1701, *c.*1706, and 1711 respectively. The opportunity to flatter Ferdinando in this way was really too good to miss, since he was seen as the future ruler of one of the most powerful independent states of Italy as well as a prominent benefactor of the arts (his patronage of Alessandro Scarlatti and, briefly, Handel is well known).

In the preface of his Op. 2 sonatas, addressed to the 'Dilettante Amorevole', the composer explains that the anticipation of his second opus by his third was due to a 'supremo comando', as if to imply that it was Ferdinando's insistence rather than his own ambition that dictated it. We have no means of establishing the truth on this point, but one suspects that the publication and dedication of Vinaccesi's Op. 3 was an act of opportunism comparable with Vivaldi's dedication of his Op. 2 sonatas to King Frederik IV of Denmark (1709)—an attempt to steal the show by reacting quickly to the presence, at short notice, of an important foreign visitor.

It is worth noting here, in passing, that an important Brescian musician exactly contemporary with Vinaccesi also dedicated a volume of cantatas to Ferdinando, possibly on the same occasion.[30] This was Paris Francesco Alghisi (1666–1733), who was to become organist at the Duomo in 1701 and served earlier as *maestro di cappella* at the church of Santa Maria della Pace. The parallels between the two men are striking. Both Vinaccesi and Alghisi sprang from established citizen families (Alghisi, too, is admitted to Cozzando's *Libraria bresciana*), enjoyed a broad liberal education, were trained as organists, dabbled briefly in opera, and composed both instrumental music and church music. The main differences between them were that Vinaccesi was an innovative, Alghisi a conservative, composer, and that whereas the latter returned from his early sojourn in Poland to settle permanently in his native Brescia, the former emigrated in mid-career.

The title-page of Op. 2, which like Op. 1 (and, one suspects, also Op. 3) was entrusted to Sala, reads as follows:

[30] Cozzando's *Libraria bresciano* (ii. 288) contains a biography of Alghisi slightly longer than that for Vinaccesi. The vol. of cantatas in question, no longer extant, is described there as 'Al Sereniss. Gran' Prencipe di Toscana *Ferdinando Terzo* un' libro di Cantate, stampato in Bologna'.

ORGANO / SFERE / ARMONICHE / Overo Sonate da Chiesa à due Violini, con Violoncello, / è [*sic*] Parte per l'Organo / CONSAGRATE, / *All'Illustrissimo Signor Conte* / ALEMANO GAMBARA / Feudatorio di Pratalbuino, Milzano, Gambara, Corulone, &c. / *DAL CAVALIER* / *Benedetto Vinaccesi* / OPERA SECONDA / [publisher's emblem of King David playing the harp] / IN VENETIA. Da Gioseppe Sala. 1692[31]

The dedicatee, Count Alemanno Gambara (born *c*.1647), belonged to a minor branch of this prominent Brescian noble family and lived in the Contrada d'Adamo in the *quadra* of San Faustino Sesta. His census return for 1687 shows him to have maintained a fairly modest household with far fewer servants than those employed by his cousins in Cittadella Vecchia.[32] One infers from the letter of dedication that this Gambara was a keen amateur musician:

My Most Illustrious and Respected Lord and Master,

To the true temple of glory, to the most venerable likeness of honour, to the most exalted conception of the most revered greatness, to Your Most Illustrious Lordship, the *Harmonic Spheres* of my notes come to prostrate themselves, victims to my ambition and sacrifices to my duty. They appear under this title not because they presume to compare themselves with those sovereign melodies that pass all human understanding, but because when they are brought together under our [Brescian] skies, where Your Most Illustrious Lordship shines as the brightest star, and are tuned to the most sonorous tone of your fame, they cannot fail, like *spheres*, to enrapture the most delicate hearts and the most devout souls with your great merit. I, who can claim to be foremost among these in broadcasting my obsequious respect, can presume also to be the first to hope to see appreciated by the most kindly spirit of Your Most Illustrious Lordship these bow [literally, plectrum] strokes, which, having been privileged to rise, with [other] similar fantasies, to the ears of Italian rulers, cannot appear dissonant to your hearing, which has been continually purified by the praises of someone who is now voluntarily laying before you, as before any great potentate, the feelings arising from his own humble state. May Your Most Illustrious Lordship allow me to make this proud boast, for the great variety of sounds that I am consecrating to you is matched by the multitude of my submissive duties [towards you], and the cadences of a profound servitude are the resting-place of the glorious honour that I profess in calling myself

Your Illustrious Excellency's

> Most humble, devoted, and obligated servant
> Benedetto Vinaccesi.
> [see Appendix B.11.]

---

[31] Schlager (ed.), *Einzeldrucke vor 1800*, ix. 98, gives the collection the identification number 'V 1578'. All that survives of this publication is an *Organo* partbook in Venice, Biblioteca Nazionale Marciana (hereafter *I-Vnm*), Mus. 264; both violin parts and the cello part are lost. Sartori, *Bibliografia della musica strumentale italiana*, i. 568–9, transcribes the title-page, dedication, preface, and table of contents, and identifies the publication as '1692(e)'.

[32] Alemanno Gambara's census return for 1687 is preserved in *I-BRq*, ASC, Registro 64, Fascicolo GAL 1687, San Faustino Sesta, n. 71.

The 'Italic rulers' ('Italici dominanti') to whom Vinaccesi refers are presumably those of Castiglione delle Stiviere. One cannot help feeling that Alemanno Gambara is a dedicatee *faute de mieux*. Had Vinaccesi still enjoyed the patronage of Ferdinando Gonzaga, this prince would surely have been the natural choice for the dedication of this second opus, after the first had been offered to his wife.

Despite, or perhaps because of, the tortuous syntax and strained imagery of this dedication (which can be appreciated fully only in the original language), one senses the composer's effort to appear a man of wider culture than his status as a musician would imply. It is symptomatic that the informal spelling 'Vinacese', used in Op. 1, has now been replaced by the more educated 'Vinaccesi'. Too little is known about the background to such dedications to make it certain that a ghost-writer was not employed, but in Vinaccesi's case the need for one must be doubted. The classical allusions continue in the preface, which is much more substantial than that introducing Op. 1:

Dear Music-lover

In the present circumstances where my third [published] work is appearing under the opus number '2', I would not like to be blamed for the order, which was decreed by a supreme command, but I would crave indulgence for the transgressions of my instruments. Rather than making themselves heard in a church, they invite you into a place where errors are more easily forgiven and where the performer may more comfortably conceal with the mantle of his protector those defects that may be discovered by modern Aristarchs of this kind, among the small numbers of whom there are ears of Syracuse larger than a mountain. I remind him [the performer] that tyrants have recourse to them [ears of Syracuse] in order to commit injustices, and that these ought not to be able to rail against the Spheres without being called impious; and I would rather call you pious and well-disposed, wishing you happiness. [see Appendix B.12.]

Aristarch of Samothrace (*c*.217–145 BC) was a literary critic noted for his thoroughness whose name became in later times, unfairly, a byword for pedantry and small-mindedness. He is very often invoked in the dedications and prefaces of musical works published around this time (for instance, in the dedication of Vivaldi's Op. 1). Altogether more recondite is the reference to 'ears of Syracuse'. More commonly known as the 'Ear of Dionysius', the 'Ear of Syracuse' was the narrow opening above a certain stone-quarry near Syracuse in Sicily where convicts were sent to work; it was popularly supposed that the tyrant Dionysius I (*c*.430–367 BC) was able to listen through the 'ear' to the talk of the convicts. Vinaccesi's point seems to be that listening can be so close as to be indecent.

In the second sentence of his preface the composer refers to the custom of performing church sonatas, *sonate da chiesa*, actually in church—only to suggest, rhetorically rather than literally, that their shortcomings make them unworthy of such an exalted place. In the seventeenth, as distinct from the early eighteenth, century it is fairly rare for sonatas to come with the actual label 'da chiesa' attached; even Corelli's Opp. 1 and 3 did not carry it in their original Italian editions. However, we know that all sonatas that were conceived abstractly without invoking the world of the dance were considered proper for use in church as an accompaniment to worship: as introductory or concluding music, and even as commentaries to, or substitutes for, parts of the liturgy.[33] Vinaccesi's remark reminds us that even in Italy—more so, of course, in protestant northern Europe—so-called church sonatas could be used for purely recreational purposes in a domestic context. Significantly, in northern Europe, and perhaps also in Italy, instrumental parts called 'Organo' (the usual description of the continuo partbook in church sonatas) were commonly considered suitable for any keyboard instrument, including harpsichord.[34] In these circumstances, the distinction between 'church' and 'chamber' at a functional level falls away, and we are left with merely a stylistic difference.

In this publication, and in the libretto of his first known oratorio, *Gioseffo che interpreta i sogni*, which dates from the same year (1692), the composer is accorded for the first time the title of 'Cavalier', which is equivalent to a knighthood. We do not know which ruling house conferred this honour on him, and whether it was his musical accomplishments or his *gentilezza* (or a combination of both) that earned him it. The Gonzagas of Castiglione delle Stiviere (or their relatives who governed Mantua and Guastalla), Ferdinando of Tuscany, and—for reasons we shall shortly see—the Este family of Modena naturally spring to mind as possible bestowers of the title, but all this is speculation. What is certain is that the Venetian State itself was not responsible. One of its similar titles, the *cavaleriato della stola d'oro* (Order of the Golden Fleece), was reserved for nobles, while the other, the *cavaleriato di San Marco*, could be awarded to commoners for meritorious or valorous service. At least one musician, the singer Nicola Grimaldi (Nicolino), was awarded the second title (1705). However, in the official documents of San Marco Vinaccesi nearly always appears without a prefatory 'Cav.' (or 'Kav.', as the Venetians preferred), a sign that his title, having been conferred by a foreign state, was not

---

[33] The various functions of the ensemble sonata within church services in 17th- and 18th-cent. Italy are described at length in Stephen Bonta, 'The Uses of the *Sonata da chiesa*', *Journal of the American Musicological Society*, 22 (1969), 54–84.

[34] Sébastien de Brossard writes in his *Dictionnaire de musique* (Paris, 1703), 'Les Italiens se servent ordinairement du mot *Organo*, pour marquer la *Basse-Continuë* chiffrée', and there are many cases in northern European publications of the 18th cent. where a reference to 'cembalo' occurs in a partbook designated *Organo*. What remains uncertain is to what extent the Italians themselves used 'organo' in this wider, generic sense.

officially recognized (needless to say, the same documents never mention Grimaldi without giving his title).

The Selhof catalogue lists under Vinaccesi's name a set of 'Suonate da Camera a Tré, doi Violini, Violoncello e Cembalo, opera quarta, parte prima'.[35] While this catalogue is not free from simple errors of the most basic kind, the information on this lost Op. 4 rings true, particularly in view of the designation 'parte prima', which recalls the 'libro primo' of Op. 3. Presumably, Vinaccesi in both cases published only half the complete collection, hoping for a later opportunity to bring out the complementary half. The presence of an obbligato cello, following the precedent set by his Op. 1 sonatas, is another sign that the attribution is correct, since in the 1690s this feature was still a rarity in chamber, as opposed to church, sonatas.

It is a sad state of affairs that of the four collections of music by Vinaccesi published before 1700 only one should have survived complete and only two in any form at all. One would guess that the print run of each was very short—perhaps only a few dozen examples. There is one hint in both Op. 1 and Op. 2 that Vinaccesi was economizing on cost. It was more normal than not for the composer to have a special block cut in order to show the dedicatee's coat of arms on the title-page just above the imprint. Neither opus includes this coat of arms: Op. 1 has a simple 'off the peg' decoration, while its sequel features Sala's own typographical emblem (a seated King David playing the harp), which is more often found in reprints issued on the publisher's own initiative. The low number of examples printed, and the consequent quick exhaustion of the stock, could also explain why Sala's general music catalogue of 1715, which includes several collections published by him during the 1680s and 1690s, contains no items by Vinaccesi other than his motets of 1714.[36]

In the 1690s the focus of Vinaccesi's activity switched for good to church music. It is possible that his endeavours in the area of secular chamber music failed to win him recognition, compelling a change of tack, but equally possible that his sonatas and cantatas were all along a 'sideline', more visible today by virtue of their publication but in fact always a subsidiary enterprise. The first sign of his aspirations as a church musician comes in his application, with four others, for the post of organist at the Duomo, which became vacant at the end of 1689 following the move to Venice of the incumbent, Carlo Francesco Pollarolo. Brief details of the election are given in the minutes of the Deputati Pubblici, the city councillors, of Brescia.[37] The post was publicly advertised through the posting

---

[35] King, *Catalogue*, no. 881.

[36] Sala's catalogue is transcribed in Oscar Mischiati, *Indici, cataloghi e avvisi degli editori e librai italiani dal 1591 al 1798* (Florence, 1984), 339–44.

[37] *I-BRq*, ASC, Registro 854, Atti dei Deputati Pubblici 1688–95, opening 62. See App. B.13.

of handbills ('furono esposte le cedole') on 31 December. On 2 January 1690 Vinaccesi and Paris Francesco Alghisi (via his brother Giovanni) made application. They were joined on 4 January by Bernardo Borgognini and Orazio Pizzamiglio (via an intermediary, Angelo Bofino) and on 5 January by Bartolomeo Antegnati.

On the face of it, this was not impossibly strong competition. Alghisi, of course, had the advantage of gentle birth and the experience of service at the royal court of Poland, but could not be said to be a celebrity outside Brescia. Borgognini was evidently a composer strong enough, like Alghisi and Vinaccesi himself, later to receive a commission from a Venetian opera-house (for *La Nicopoli*, at San Fantino in carnival 1700), but otherwise hardly less obscure than Pizzamiglio or Antegnati.[38]

But between 5 January and 10 January, when the Deputati Pubblici voted, a much stronger challenger entered the lists. This was Giovanni Battista Quaglia (*c.*1625–1700), *maestro di cappella* at Santa Maria Maggiore, Bergamo, and a man of great experience and reputation as both an organist and a composer. Since the minute-book of the Deputati Pubblici does not record Quaglia's application in its usual way (which is to give the date, followed by 'Comparse il Sig. . . .') but simply appends his name beneath the others, one has the suspicion that he was 'headhunted'. At all events, Quaglia triumphed in the election, presumably without there having been any audition.[39]

In the realm of composition the first hint of Vinaccesi's new direction occurred two years later, when his lost oratorio *Gioseffo che interpreta i sogni* was performed at the Este court in Modena.[40] Under Duke Francesco II (1660–94), who succeeded his father Alfonso IV in 1662 but remained under the regency of his mother Laura Martinozzi until 1674, oratorio was cultivated in Modena with particular enthusiasm. The usual site of performances was the oratory of San Carlo rotondo behind the ducal chapel of San Vincenzo. Between 1681 and 1694 a minimum of four

[38] Borgognini must have settled in Venice, for in 1702 we find him employed as a *mansionario* (a priest reciting Mass for the soul of a benefactor) at the Ospedale della Pietà. It was in fact none other than Vivaldi who took over from Borgognini the *mansioneria* of Lucrezia Trevisan Memmo in Sept. 1702.

[39] *I-BRq*, ASC, Registro 854, opening 64.

[40] Cozzando (*Libraria bresciana*, ii. 235) calls this work 'l'Oratorio di Gioseffe il casto'. This is not the title of the work as it appears either in the printed libretto, preserved in the Biblioteca Estense, Modena, or in the inventory of the music collection of Francesco II ('Repertorio de libri musicali si manuscr. come stamp. di S. A. S.') in the Archivio di Stato, Modena, which appears to take its titles directly from the musical sources themselves. The whole inventory is transcribed in Elisabeth J. Luin, 'Repertorio dei libri musicali di S. A. S. Francesco II d'Este nell'Archivio di Stato di Modena', *Bibliofilia*, 38 (1936), 418–45: 421–36. References to the protagonist as 'Gioseffo il Casto' are, however, present in the libretto (one occurs in the very first sentence of the *Argomento*), and it is not inconceivable that Cozzando took the title from a manuscript libretto or an informal description. Andrea Valentini, *I musicisti bresciani* (Brescia, 1894), 107, and derived sources have 'Gioseppe il casto'.

oratorios were given each year—as many as thirteen are recorded for 1689.[41] Although the Modenese court had its own poets and musicians, the desire for quantity, and perhaps also variety, led it increasingly, after 1680, to commission librettos and musical scores from the leading practitioners of both arts in Italy. (One writes 'commission' somewhat loosely, for since poet and musician often hailed from the same city (in the case of Tommaso Bernardo Gaffi's *La forza del divino amore* of 1691, they were the same man), one wonders how often oratorios were sent speculatively, without prior commission, to Modena in the hope of a performance and the appropriate *regalo*.)

The names of external composers (*forastieri*) whose oratorios were performed at Modena in the 1680s and 1690s read like a roll-call of musical celebrity. From Rome there were Flavio Lanciani, Giovanni Lorenzo Lulier, Alessandro Melani, and Bernardo Pasquini; from Bologna, Giovanni Bononcini, Giovanni Paolo Colonna, Pietro Degli Antonii, Giacomo Antonio Perti, and Giovanni Battista Vitali; from Venice, Marc'Antonio Ziani and Giovanni Legrenzi; from Ferrara, Sebastiano Cherici and Giovanni Battista Bassani; from Naples there was Alessandro Scarlatti; from Genoa, Alessandro Stradella; from Parma, Francesco Antonio Pistocchi. To have been able to join this select company, many of whose members were specialists in oratorio, Vinaccesi must have impressed as a composer.

His literary collaborator for *Gioseffo*, Giovanni Battista Neri, was a Bolognese *dottore* who, in the closing two decades of the seventeenth century, produced several librettos for both operas and oratorios. The eight known opera librettos begin with *Il Gige in Lidia* (Bologna, 1683) and end with *L'enigma disciolto* (Reggio Emilia, 1698)—an early version of the last-named text was probably set, as we shall learn later, by Vinaccesi. *Gioseffo che interpreta i sogni* (1692) was the second of two oratorio librettos for Modena, being preceded by *La profezia d'Eliseo* (1686), for which Colonna wrote the music.[42]

In 1694 Vinaccesi provided Modena with a second oratorio: *Susanna*. The subject was very familiar to the court, since Stradella's oratorio *La Susanna*, first given in Modena in 1681, had been revived there in 1692.[43]

[41] A list of oratorios performed at Modena during this period is given in Victor Crowther, 'Alessandro Stradella and the Oratorio Tradition in Modena', in Carolyn Gianturco (ed.), *Alessandro Stradella e Modena: Atti del Convegno internazionale di studi, Modena 15–17 dicembre 1983* (Modena, 1985), 59–62.

[42] Neri's libretto for *Gioseffo che interpreta i sogni* received new settings from Antonio Caldara and Francesco Conti in 1726 and 1736 respectively. Neri was also a prolific writer of texts for cantatas.

[43] From Francesco Caffi, *Storia della musica sacra nella già cappella ducale di San Marco in Venezia dal 1317 al 1797* (Venice, 1854–5), i. 359, comes the incorrect information that *Susanna* was performed in Brescia rather than Modena—a statement that has led some modern lexicographers, beginning with Carlo Schmidl (*Dizionario universale dei musicisti* (Milan, 1938), ii. 656), to play for safety and hypothesize performances both in Modena and Brescia. Barezzani (*La musica a Brescia*, 31) even

It is not impossible that Vinaccesi, who probably visited Modena in order to attend the performance of his first oratorio, heard Stradella's work on that occasion and decided to write a work on the same subject—though one must take care not to assume unthinkingly that it was the business of the composer rather than the librettist (who, after all, is the first to set down his thoughts) or, indeed, the patron to determine such things.

This time, Vinaccesi had as his literary collaborator Giovanni Battista Bottalino (or Bottalini), a prominent member of the Accademia degli Erranti in Brescia who became its vice-secretary in 1673 and subsequently its principal secretary.[44] The composer may have come into contact with Bottalino earlier via Alemanno Gambara, for whose wedding in 1676 the poet provided an epithalamium, his first known literary work. Bottalino wrote the texts of three operas performed in Brescia: *La Venere travestita* (1678) and *Il Roderico* (1684), both of which were given at the city's public theatre, that of the Accademia degli Erranti, and *Jarba impazzito*, performed in the private theatre (*teatro domestico*) of Teofilo Martinengo in 1687.

It appears that, contrary to the more common practice for dramatic works, it was the composer rather than the poet who on this occasion assumed responsibility for presenting the new work to the patron, Francesco II. Both the printed libretto of *Susanna* and its manuscript copy-text preserved in the Modenese State Archive unambiguously identify Vinaccesi as the person who dedicated it to the duke (in Chapter 8 we will examine further the relationship between the libretto and the score).

Modena may have beckoned to Vinaccesi as a place of future opportunity and reward, but he remained active at a local level. It is more than likely that he held the post of organist at some local church. In 1694 he appears for the first time in the records of Santa Maria della Pace. This was the church and oratory of the Philippine fathers in Brescia. Following their acquisition in 1683 of a palace belonging to the Colleoni family, the Philippines moved to the new site and instituted a vigorous musical life.[45] Up to 1700, when he was appointed organist and *capo musico* to the Duomo, Paris Francesco Alghisi served as *maestro di cappella*. His regular musicians initially consisted of five solo singers, three string players, and

suggests the Philippine church of Santa Maria della Pace as the locale of the Brescian performance, which is ruled out in any event by the fact that in 1694, as we shall learn, Vinaccesi was paid by the Chiesa della Pace not for an oratorio but for music manuscript paper.

[44] Caffi errs again by calling the poet 'Bettolino', a form that later reappears in several musical dictionaries beginning with Luigi Ferdinando Tagliavini's article on Vinaccesi in Friedrich Blume (ed.), *Die Musik in Geschichte und Gegenwart* (13 (1966), cols. 1651–2). A short account of Bottalino as a writer appears in Giovanni Maria Mazzuchelli, *Gli scrittori d'Italia*, (Brescia, 1753–63), ii. 1877–8.

[45] On the musical life of the Chiesa della Pace see esp. Barezzani, *La musica a Brescia, passim*, Olga Termini, 'Vivaldi at Brescia: The Feast of the Purification at the Chiesa della Pace (1711)', *Informazioni e studi vivaldiani*, 9 (1988), 64–74, and Michael Talbot, 'New Light on Vivaldi's *Stabat Mater*', *Informazioni e studi vivaldiani*, 13 (1992), 23–38.

an organist (later, as was happening in churches all over Italy around this time, the string ensemble grew from 'chamber' to 'orchestral' dimensions, although the number of singers remained unchanged). The father in charge of music, the *prefetto della musica*, disposed, in addition, of a generous annual allowance for 'miscellaneous expenses' (*spese straordinarie*); these ranged from simple consumables such as violin strings to fees paid to composers of new works, from manuscript or printed copies of music to extra musicians engaged for important festivals.

The payment to Vinaccesi on 10 May 1694 is entered among the *spese straordinarie* for 1694 in the 'Libro per la musica 1694–1726', the church's special account-book for music covering the stated period.[46] But the service provided is unexpected and rather puzzling: he is paid three *lire di piccoli* for supplying two quinternions of pre-ruled music-paper.[47] Did Vinaccesi perhaps run a business in music-paper, following in his family's mercantile footsteps? Or did he merely divert to the Chiesa della Pace a portion of the paper he bought and used for his own purposes? Elsewhere in the account-book the supplier of music-paper is not named, and there is nothing to suggest that he was, or was not, Vinaccesi.

There happens to be another entry for 10 May 1694, immediately preceding the one described. This records the payment of 5 *lire* and 12 *soldi* to Troian Carpanino for several copies and scores of the Magnificat ('per più copiature, e Partiture di Magnificat'). Carpanino is one of the better known music copyists of the time; he settled in Venice around the turn of the century and after a short career as a comic singer established himself there as a full-time copyist.[48] These Magnificats could have been Vinaccesi's own—which would provide an explanation for his supplying the music-paper—and this hypothesis is strengthened by an entry for 4 January 1696, in which the *prefetto* notes that 4 *lire* and 2 *soldi* have been paid 'to Troiano for a Magnificat by Vinaccesi sold to me and a score of a *De Profundis*' ('a Troiano per un Magnificat del Venacesi vendutomi, et una Partitura d'un De Profundis').[49] This is the last entry concerning Vinaccesi in the book. These entries are important not so much for their demonstration of a link between Vinaccesi and the *cappella* of the Chiesa

---

[46] *I-BRas*, Fondo di religione, Busta 49, 'Libro per la musica [1694–1726]', fo. 7ᵛ.

[47] A quinternion (Italian: *quinterno*) is a gathering of 5 folded sheets, which in quarto format (the usual format for Italian music paper) yields 20 folios.

[48] Carpanino sang a *parte buffa* (Grino) in the pasticcio *L'Erginia immascherata* (Venice, San Fantino, autumn 1710) and appeared in the comic intermezzi performed with Giovanni Maria Ruggieri's *Armida abbandonata* at Santo Stefano, Ferrara, in carnival 1711; he also took the comic role of the Satyr in *Gli amici rivali* (Venice, San Fantino, carnival 1715), a retitled version of Pollarolo's *L'enigma disciolto* mentioned earlier. He was the copyist of the operas performed at the Grimani theatres of San Giovanni Grisostomo and San Samuele in 1730: see Venice, *I-Vnm*, Ms. it. XI–426, 8 (= 12142, 8). His younger relatives or descendants Gerolamo and later Carlo Carpanino carried on the business.

[49] *I-BRas*, Fondo di religione, Busta 49, fo. 13ᵛ.

della Pace—which was obviously a casual one of short duration concerned solely with the supply of music and music-paper—as for establishing that he was by then already composing sacred vocal works on liturgical texts. It is a pity that no 'Libro per la musica' for the period preceding 1694 has survived, since he may well have contributed to the church's repertory at an earlier stage.[50]

Two further oratorios, both lost, bring to a close what we know of Vinaccesi's musical activity in Brescia. The first, *Il cuor nello scrigno*, was written in 1696 for the annual celebration by the Accademia dei Disuniti of Cremona on 13 June of the feast of their spiritual protector, St Anthony of Padua. This society was founded in 1675 by Francesco Arisi (1657–1743), a noted jurist and man of letters who served it variously as secretary and president.[51] Between 1677 and 1705 Arisi personally supplied the librettos of six oratorios connected with this feast: *La tirannide soggiogato* (1677), *Il disinganno della gelosia* (1678), *L'eresia avvelenata* (1680), *L'innocenza sprigionata* (1683), *Il cuor nello scrigno* (1696), and *Il plauso degli elementi* (1705). The libretto of the 1696 work was printed in Milan.[52] There is no reason, of course, to suspect a performance in Milan on that account, since it was common for the librettos of dramatic works performed in smaller centres to be printed in the nearest large city. Totally mystifying, however, is Sven Hansell's statement in the *New Grove* that *Il cuor nello scrigno* was given in Venice, in the church of Santa Maria della Fava, on 4 March 1696.[53] There is no evidence that Vinaccesi had any connection with Venice before 1698, and to have performed this work, whose subject is so clearly the saint of Padua, on the feast of St Lucius Pope and Martyr would seem to defy all logic.[54]

The final oratorio is *Li diecimila martiri crocefissi*, on the subject of the ten thousand soldiers who were said, according to legend, to have been crucified on Mount Ararat. It was given in 1698 on the occasion of their feast, 22 June. The sponsor of the performance was Count Francesco Martinengo, and it may well be that the private theatre (that of Teofilo Martinengo) in which Bottalino's *Jarba impazzito* had been heard in 1687

[50] The subsequent account-book covering the years 1727–45 survives, however, in the archive of the Philippines in Brescia.

[51] On the Accademia dei Disuniti see Michele Maylender, *Storia delle accademie d'Italia* (Bologna, 1926–30), ii. 204–7. Biographies of Arisi can be found in Mazzuchelli, *Gli scrittori d'Italia*, i. 1086–92, and the *Dizionario biografico degli italiani*, iv (Rome, 1962), 198–210. The best list of Arisi's numerous literary works is that provided by the same author in his own *Cremona literata* (Parma and Cremona, 1702–1741), iii. 59–65.

[52] The libretto survives in the Library of Congress, Washington. In *Cremona literata* (iii. 60) Arisi gives the libretto the date of 1704, which is probably a mistake rather than a reference to a later performance of the oratorio.

[53] (London, 1980), xix. 780–1.

[54] Doubt is cast on a Venetian performance of *Il cuor nello scrigno* also in Denis and Elsie Arnold, *The Oratorio in Venice* (London, 1986), 17, where the authors point out that the accounts of Santa Maria della Fava make no mention of the work.

served as its place.[55] The poet, Aurelio Paolini, was another local figure, who had earlier written the libretto of an opera, *L'Artaserse*, performed in Brescia in 1684.[56]

In the *computisteria* (household accounts) of the court of Cardinal Pietro Ottoboni in Rome we find a reference, in a bill for copying dated 15 March 1697, to a work described as 'La Pastorale intitolata chi e causa del suo mal Pianga se stesso'.[57] Since this is the exact title of a pastoral opera by Vinaccesi whose score is preserved in the Bibliothèque Nationale, Paris, there is a very good possibility that this is the composition in question.[58] The title is in fact a variant of one first employed by the librettist-cum-composer Filippo Acciaiuoli for a wholly unrelated comic opera produced in Rome in 1682, *Chi è cagion del suo mal pianga sé stesso* (the words mean: 'He who is the cause of his own misfortune should blame only himself'). Unexpectedly, it is not Acciaiuoli's work but only Vinaccesi's that derives the moralistic title, following a very common practice, from a *sentenza* forming the last line of the libretto. The chances that the libretto of the second opera was set more than once are not high, for it does not appear to have been published (a situation acceptable to the local censors, provided that the performance was held on private premises)—and in any case, the pastoral subgenre was not very widely cultivated. Moreover, the probable identity of the librettist provides a link to Vinaccesi. In 1698 a new version of the libretto adapted for the public stage (it includes an extra character, a comic satyr) was produced at Reggio Emilia under the title of *L'enigma disciolto* and with music by C. F. Pollarolo.[59] The dedication of the libretto was made not by the author himself but by the impresario, who identifies him, in a note to the reader placed after the cast-list, as G. B. Neri, with whom Vinaccesi collaborated on *Gioseffo che interpreta i sogni*. It remains unclear whether Neri was responsible for the original text, the adapted version, or both, but the coincidence remains significant. Of relevance, too, is the fact that Vinaccesi is known to set one cantata text by the cardinal's father, Antonio Ottoboni. Provisionally, therefore, we can equate the work performed in Rome with the pastoral opera surviving in Paris. It is not

[55] Barezzani, *La musica a Brescia*, 31, suggests that this oratorio, too, was performed at the Chiesa della Pace, but the hypothesis lacks all credibility, since the libretto states that it was Martinengo who commissioned the performance. The count also wrote the dedication of the libretto (to the *podestà* and *capitano* of the city).

[56] Ibid., 41.

[57] Hans-Joachim Marx, 'Die Musik am Hofe Pietro Kardinal Ottobonis unter Arcangelo Corelli', *Analecta musicologica*, 5 (1968), 151. I am grateful to Norbert Dubowy for bringing this source to my attention.

[58] Paris, Bibliothèque Nationale (hereafter *F-Pn*), Vm.⁴ 13. Nothing is known about the provenance of this manuscript score except that it was acquired before the Revolution but was not among the volumes donated to the royal library by Sébastien de Brossard in 1725.

[59] Example consulted: Bologna, Civico Museo Bibliografico Musicale (hereafter *I-Bc*), libr. 6301.

totally certain that the performance itself was sponsored by Ottoboni, since the leading Roman patrons often ordered copies of works given in the residences of other members of their circle, although that is the most likely possibility. Whether Vinaccesi travelled to Rome to supervise the performance is a question that for the moment cannot be answered.

Not long afterwards our composer moved to Venice, for all practical purposes severing his artistic links with Brescia, although most of his children stayed behind. In his native city he had been a biggish fish in a small pool. Now he was to try his luck in one of the largest and most competitive 'pools' in the whole of Italy.

3

Benedetto Vinaccesi

The Venetian Years, i. The Ospedaletto

T HE earliest evidence of Vinaccesi's presence in Venice so far uncovered is a report in the handwritten news-sheet *Pallade veneta* for the week ending 29 November 1698 that on 25 November he composed, and presumably also directed, the music for the patronal festival of the convent of Santa Cattarina.[1] By that time he must already have been installed as *maestro di coro* at the Ospedale (Ospitale) dei Poveri Derelitti ai Santi Giovanni e Paolo, known more simply as the 'Ospedaletto', or 'little hospital'. Surviving documents from the Ospedaletto agree that 1698 was the year of his appointment but do not give the month or day.[2] This year has to be interpreted *more veneto*, opening on 1 March 1698, modern style. It would, of course, be helpful to know the date when Vinaccesi's predecessor, Giovanni Paolo Biego, gave up the post. Since death or incapacity were obviously not the reason—Biego lived on until 1714 and remained fully active at the ducal church of San Marco—the best likelihood is that at the annual ballot of the Ospedaletto's *proviggionati* (salaried staff) held on the customary date, 2 February, Biego failed in 1698 to obtain the necessary four-fifths of the votes cast by the governors and thus was voted out of office.

We saw that at the Duomo of Brescia the closing date for applications came only a few days after the vacancy was announced, a procedure that obviously placed non-local applicants at a distinct disadvantage. San Marco was accustomed to act with similar urgency when filling its senior musical posts. In both cases it seems that the administrators were not willing to tolerate a long interregnum merely in order to have a stronger field from which to choose. In the Venetian *ospedali grandi*, the four great charitable institutions (the word 'grandi' distinguishes them from the large number of smaller and more highly specialized similar institutions in the city), the tempo of the appointment process was usually more relaxed. The reason was probably that whereas a *capo musico* or *maestro di cappella*

---

[1] fo. 3, transcribed in Eleanor Selfridge-Field, *Pallade veneta: Writings on Music in Venetian Society, 1650–1750* (Venice, 1985), 231.

[2] Venice, Archivio storico IRE (hereafter *I-Vire*), Der. G. 1.48, Fascicolo 'Musica', Inserti 1, 8, and 45.

employed by a church functioned not merely as a 'house' composer but also as the director of all musical performances (whether by beating time or playing the organ), a *maestro di coro* at one of the *ospedali grandi* was first and foremost a composer. True, the contracts of these *maestri* obliged them in theory to take rehearsals, attend performances, and give tuition a specified number of times per week, but their absences were easily covered by senior members of the *coro* themselves or one of the external *maestri* in its service. New repertory could *in extremis* be commissioned and purchased from any composer willing to supply it, whether or not prior links with him existed. This explains how the Ospedale della Pietà managed to survive without an effective *maestro di coro* between 1713 and 1719.[3]

The manner of choosing a *maestro di coro* was at the Ospedaletto a matter only of custom, not of constitutional procedure. In a memorandum submitted to the governors on 20 September 1743 by its three officers responsible for music, the *deputati sopra le figlie*, the history of making appointments was reviewed.[4] Both Biego in 1688 and Vinaccesi in 1698 had been chosen in open competition by means of *prove*, which might have been either practical auditions or written tests. However, Vinaccesi's successor, Antonio Pollarolo, whose resignation provided the occasion for the memorandum, had been appointed in 1716 by direct invitation, and the *deputati* recommended that head-hunting should continue to be the method employed since, as they argued, the best candidates would not wish to expose themselves to the risk of public humiliation if, in the event, the post went to someone less distinguished following bargaining behind the scenes. The *deputati* mention that on one unspecified occasion candidates were asked to submit compositions for inspection, but there is no way of knowing whether this refers to the 1698 competition.

Only one report in which *deputati sopra le figlie* of the Ospedaletto assess candidates for the post of *maestro di coro* has survived in full, although the extant minute-books of the institution make many references to such reports, sometimes quoting extracts from them. The document in question refers to the *concorso* of 1766, following the failure of *maestro* Antonio Gaetano Pampani, first appointed in 1747, to secure re-election that year (Pampani, incidentally, wished to be a candidate for the post he had been forced to vacate, but the governors ruled against him).[5] Since the Ospedaletto, like San Marco and, indeed, the generality of Venetian

---

[3] Francesco Gasparini departed in Apr. 1713 on a leave that was intended to last only six months but in the event became permanent. His successor, Carlo Luigi Pietragrua, was appointed in Feb. 1719.

[4] *I-Vire*, Der. G. 1.48, Inserto 45. The corresponding entry in the minute-book (*Notatorio*) for 1732–48 (Der. B. 11, opening 195, 23 Sept. 1743) is transcribed in Jolando Scarpa (ed.), *Arte e musica all'Ospedaletto* (Venice, 1978), 120–1.

[5] *I-Vmc*, Ms. Cicogna 3079, 'Carte Ospedaletto', Fascicolo 5, transcribed as App. B.14.

institutions, was an extremely conservative body that liked to find
justification for any action by reference to a precedent (or, failing that, to
the practice at comparable institutions), even a source dating from as late
as 1766 can shed light on the procedure through which Vinaccesi went
nearly seventy years earlier.

The *deputati* first report that the candidates for the post of *maestro di
coro* (as well as those of *maestro di solfeggio*, *maestro di maniera*, *maestro di
violino*, and *maestro di violoncello*, which were being advertised concurrently) were asked to submit an application within thirty days of the posting of the notices. It was then the duty of the *deputati* to find out,
through making enquiries, as much as possible about the morals and abilities of each candidate. Although candidates were free to submit whatever
they pleased in support of their application, there was, it appears, no
audition or other kind of *prova*. The emphasis on moral rectitude should
not surprise us in the light of the fact the *maestro di coro* was destined, in
his employment, to deal with musicians exclusively of the female sex (discounting external *maestri*), to whom he was allowed personal access only
under the most rigorously controlled conditions.

The *deputati* frankly confess their inability to pass value-judgements on
the music written by the candidates, their own impressions being subjec-
tive and those of outside informants being partisan. They therefore propose merely to state how well the compositions of each candidate have
been received in Venice. The first name mentioned belongs to Tommaso
Trajetta, whose letter of application has provided them with a few personal details and a brief career history, which they pass on. They point
out that his operas have won great acclaim and can find no blot against
his character. Apparently, the second candidate, Salvatore Perillo, did not
even provide a letter of application—his name may have been proposed by
a proxy. The *deputati* merely record his sound morals and the success of
two of his comic operas in Venice. The third and last candidate was
Gregorio Sciroli, like his rivals a Neapolitan opera composer; he is discussed in a few lines in a manner similar to Trajetta.

In the election, held on 8 June 1766, it was Trajetta who triumphed.[6]
What amazes, however, is the lack of rigour—in modern parlance one
would call it the amateurishness—of the selection process. One appreciates
the dilemma of the *deputati*, faced, like so many lay committees throughout history, with a situation in which the only expert judges were partial
and the only impartial judges inexpert. But the information provided by
the report is so thin, even within its limited terms of reference, as to be
almost risible. In the event, Trajetta's very clear-cut victory—he obtained
almost as many positive votes as the other two together—probably

[6] *I-Vire*, Der. B. 13, Notatorio 1763–74, 129 ff, partially transcribed in Scarpa, *Arte e musica
all'Ospedaletto*, 73–4.

stemmed from the greater popularity of his operas rather than any achievement in the realm of sacred music. No doubt, lobbying by patrons also played its part.

Because of the *prova* that formed part of the 1698 competition, Vinaccesi probably underwent a stiffer test than this. What the report just described does indicate, however, is that unless the conditions of the *concorso* had changed by 1766, he had ample time to make application directly from Brescia. It took six days for mail from Venice to reach Milan (thus less time to reach Brescia, which was a staging post on the way).[7] This would have allowed an informant to send word from Venice of the vacancy and given the composer the chance to send in a well-considered application long before the thirty days had expired. Very likely, he was still living in Brescia when *Li diecimila martiri crocefissi* was performed there on 22 June 1698. At all events, there is no reason to suppose that he moved to Venice before his appointment at the Ospedaletto was confirmed.

The terms of his employment cannot be ascertained directly from the minute-books of the governors' meetings, the *notatori*, since all volumes for the period 1605–1732 are lost. Fortunately, however, many of the supporting papers relating to music that were tabled at the meetings (they were read out to the assembled governors by the officer known as the *fattore*) have survived.[8] They include draft resolutions, reports, memoranda, petitions, accounts, financial projections, and lists of various kinds. The draft resolutions, whether adopted or defeated, were normally written into the minute-books as they stood, and many of the other types of document refer to or quote from the minutes. With their help, one is able to form a picture of musical life during the 'blank' period that, for all its incompleteness, shows the main outlines.

We learn from an entry in an aide-mémoire of late 1730, a chronological list of the *maestri di coro* and other salaried music masters employed at the Ospedaletto up to that time, that Vinaccesi was engaged under the same conditions as his predecessor Biego.[9] The duties of the latter are

---

[7] Postal communications between Venice and other major centres are described on p. 393 of the 1724 edn. of the *Guida de' forestieri per succintamente osservare tutto il più riguardevole nella città di Venezia*. This celebrated guide-book, whose original author was Vincenzo Coronelli (1650–1716), was first published in 1698 (1697 *more veneto*) and went through no fewer than forty edns.

[8] 116 documents ('inserti') from the period 1676–1796 are preserved in *I-Vire*, Der. G. 1.48, Fascicolo 'Musica'. Several are transcribed in Scarpa, *Arte e musica all'Ospedaletto* (to avoid confusion it should be mentioned that when that vol. was published in 1978, the documents were included in the section Der. G. 2. instead of Der. G. 1 as in the more recent general catalogue of the archive (Giuseppe Ellero, *L'archivio storico IRE: Inventari dei fondi antichi degli ospedali e luoghi pii di Venezia* (Venice, 1984)). Another collection of similar loose papers, most dating from the later 18th cent., is *I-Vmc*, Ms. Cicogna 3079, 'Carte Ospedaletto', Fascicoli 1 and 5.

[9] *I-Vire*, Der. G. 1.48, Inserto 1. This *aide-mémoire*, reproduced as a plate by Scarpa, was prepared in connection with a request by Antonio Pollarolo for an ex-gratia payment towards his music copying expenses (for which his contract made him liable). A list of the *maestri di coro* and other teachers of music, largely based on information in this document, is included as App. C.3.

summarized in the preceding entry. The *maestro di coro* had to teach singing and give instruction in instrumental performance (for both Biego and Vinaccesi this must have involved primarily keyboard instruments) four times a week. He had to accompany on the organ at all festivals—thus by implication not on ferial days—and attend during the whole of Lent, when services with 'figural' music (i.e. *canto figurato* as opposed to simple plainsong, or *canto fermo*, and harmonized plainsong, or *falsobordone*) took place in the church of the Ospedaletto virtually every day. It was also his duty to provide the *coro* regularly with new compositions, taking on himself the expense of obtaining music paper and the labour of copying out the score and parts.

His basic annual salary was 200 ducats current (1,240 *lire*), paid out of the general account, or *cassa grande*. If the method of his payment followed the pattern of later *maestri*, he will have received 50 ducats each quarter on production of an affidavit from one of the *maestre* (the senior women in charge of the *coro*) confirming his satisfactory performance of his duties and listing the new compositions supplied in the previous period. It appears that at the Ospedaletto contracts with *maestri* normally ran for three or six years, although the incumbents always needed to have their posts reconfirmed by a four-fifths majority at the annual ballot of employees held in February.[10]

Vinaccesi may also have benefited from an important perquisite that later *maestri di coro* certainly enjoyed: one third of the proceeds from the hiring out of chairs (called *scagni* or *careghe*) to the visitors attending services. The number of these chairs, which could be hired for about one *lira*, rose from 230 to 330 in 1748 and reached a peak of 480 in 1767. At the four *ospedali grandi* the income from chairs was a barometer, first, of the relative popularity of their respective *cori* (and *maestri di coro*) and, second, of general public interest in sacred music. Disadvantaged among its sister-*ospedali* in certain ways, as we shall see later, the Ospedaletto sometimes fared badly in the competition to attract an audience (for such we should call the congregation). In 1744, obviously during a lean period, the *deputati sopra le figlie* estimated the annual income at only 30 ducats (186 *lire*);[11] but in 1770 the sum was more respectable and perhaps also more typical, totalling around 1,023 *lire*.[12] Potentially, at least, the *scagni* provided the *maestro di coro* with a useful supplement.

To assess the standard of life and degree of social status implied by a salary of 200 ducats, one must bear in mind that like most church posts at the time, that of *maestro di coro* at a Venetian *ospedale* was not conceived

---

[10] In contrast, appointments at the Ospedale della Pietà were permanent, though subject to annual reconfirmation. In practice, all tenure at the *ospedali* was precarious.

[11] *I-Vire*, Der. G. 1.48, Inserto 42.

[12] *I-Vmc*, Ms. Cicogna 3071, Fascicolo 1, 'Conteggi per mantenimento figliuole'.

as a full-time post debarring the holder from another employment or from free-lance activity. In relative terms, of course, the post of musical director was much more demanding of time and effort than that of a simple teacher of singing or of an instrument, which is partly why the salary differential was so great; as against the 200 ducats earned by the *maestro di coro* at the Ospedaletto in Vinaccesi's time, a *maestro di violino* or *maestro di canto* could expect to earn only 40 or 50 ducats (see Appendix C.3). Whereas several of the ordinary teachers managed to hold down the equivalent post at two, or even three, of the *ospedali*, commuting from one to the other in order to give their lessons, no *maestro di coro* is known ever to have served more than one *ospedale* concurrently.[13] No doubt, none of the *ospedali* would have tolerated for long a situation where its musical director was assisting a rival institution, but even if this had not been so, the similarity of the calendar and daily routine at all four *ospedale* churches would have made it physically impossible for a single person to hold the senior post at more than one. On the other hand, a few *maestri di coro* managed simultaneously to hold a *maestro* post at San Marco. The most successful of them was Antonino Biffi (1667–1732), who headed the *coro* of the Mendicanti from 1700 to 1730 and the *cappella* of the ducal church from 1702 until his death. Vinaccesi's successor at the Ospedaletto, Antonio Pollarolo (1676–1746), served the ducal church as *primo maestro* from 1740 to 1746, but the practical difficulty of fulfilling both obligations, which was probably aggravated by old age, caused him to retire from the first post in 1743.[14] Earlier, both Antonio Pollarolo and, before him, his father Carlo Francesco (*c.*1653–1723) had successfully combined the post of *vice-maestro* at San Marco with the directorship of the *coro* at the Incurabili and the Ospedaletto respectively. The participation of members of the *cappella ducale* in the musical life of the *ospedali* increases as one goes down the hierarchy.

The possibilities for free-lance activity outside the main institutions were truly immense. Although some church musicians held aloof from opera, most—including many who were clerics—plunged whole-heartedly into it. The instrumentalists among them, protected from unlicensed competition by the privileges of their guild, the *Arte de' sonadori*, were recruited into opera orchestras; the singers joined the chorus or took minor roles—indeed many of the leading singers at San Marco were able

---

[13] A report from the *deputati sopra le figlie* dated 5 Sept. 1733 (*I-Vire*, Der. G. 1.48, Inserto 48) refers to an attempt to enlist Giovanni Porta, the highly successful *maestro di coro* of the Pietà, as the Ospedaletto's 'maestro di composition', with the sole task of composing new works and attending their rehearsal (but not, presumably, their performance). The idea evidently came to nothing, but the reasons for its abandonment are not made clear. Perhaps the Pietà itself vetoed the proposal.

[14] Pollarolo's petition for retirement on a pension (undated, but 1743) is preserved in *I-Vire*, Der. G. 1.48, Inserto 13, transcribed in Scarpa, *Arte e musica all'Ospedaletto*, 126–7. The governors approved the request on 19 Aug. 1743, awarding him a pension of 40 ducats for the rest of his life.

to obtain leave of absence to perform on the stage outside Venice, this being the price for retaining them.[15] For those able to compose, lucrative commissions for new scores beckoned, and the most adventurous of all tried their hand, riskily, at operatic financing and management. An organist-composer such as Vinaccesi could expect to be invited to preside over the music for the patronal festivals of churches without a permanent *cappella* or choirmaster; this could entail composing the music, hiring the musicians, and directing the performance. (We have already encountered him doing this in 1698 at the convent of Santa Cattarina.) Then there were cantatas and instrumental works to be written for the *accademie* of the nobility, and serenatas for special celebrations.

These 200 ducats constituted, therefore, a stable but not necessarily preponderant element in Vinaccesi's domestic economy, which must have included, besides a share of the family income from landed property, occasional fees from many sources. He was certainly sufficiently well off within a few months of his arrival in Venice to move into good rented accommodation. The civic property register of 1711 records that he is living in a house (or set of apartments—the term casa is used very loosely) rented for 80 ducats per annum from the nobleman Marin Zorzi I.[16] The entry also notes that his occupation of the house began on 1 March 1699. It is easy to identify the approximate location of the house, which was situated in the parish of San Severo on the 'far' side (relative to the parish church) of the Ponte del Tagliapietra, or stone-cutter's bridge (today known as the Ponte dei Greci). This area is centred on the modern Salizada Zorzi; the Palazzo Zorzi, listed first among the houses 'giù del Ponte del Taglia Pietra', stands at the angle of this street and the Rio di San Severo. In the seventeenth and eighteenth centuries this zone was the heart of Venice's Greek community, whose church, San Giorgio dei Greci, lay close by. Many of Vinaccesi's immediate neighbours were in fact Greek merchants. The composer lived in one of the more expensive houses in the neighbourhood; the register shows that apart from the palazzo Zorzi, which was rented out to other nobles at 650 ducats, *case* in the immediate vicinity fetched between 20 and 86 ducats.

---

[15] The operatic activity of many singers in the *cappella ducale* is examined in Olga Termini, 'Singers at San Marco in Venice: The Competition between Church and Theatre (*c*1675–*c*1725)', *[RMA] Research Chronicle*, 17 (1981), 65–96.

[16] *I-Vas*, Dieci Savi sopra le decime di Rialto, Busta 428, 'Catastico di Venezia: estimo del 1711', San Severo, no. 195. The register for this parish must have been completed at the end of 1713 or the beginning of 1714, since a tenancy beginning as late as 20 Oct. 1713 (for no. 186) is noted. Since Vinaccesi died in the same parish in 1719, it is likely that he remained in the same house until his death. The significance of the 'I' following the given name of Marin Zorzi is that in this patrician family, as in certain others, all male siblings were given the same name (I being the eldest, II the next, and so on), either in order to comply with the wishes of a testator or to distinguish the branch of the family in question from others with the same surname. In daily life, of course, each son would be known by a different, informal name.

In order to evaluate Vinaccesi's work at the Ospedaletto, we have to go more deeply into the nature of this institution and find out the ways in which it was similar to, or differed from, the other three *ospedali grandi*. The first question to ask, however, is why it was in Venice rather than elsewhere that such unusual organizations came into being.

The answer undoubtedly lies in Venice's peculiar nature as a 'sacral' state—that is, a society in which the temporal power invested itself with religious functions distinct from, though coexisting with, those of the Universal Church represented by the papacy.[17] The historical roots of this fusion of the sacred and secular arm lie in eastern Christianity; the Venetian doge can be seen as the last example of a *basileios*, or priest-king. In a functional sense, Venice's religious autonomy could be likened to that of England during the early years of the Reformation, for the point at issue was not doctrine, nor in any important sense ritual, but authority. It is true that the diocese of Venice, which comprised the ducal church itself and four other churches (San Giacomo di Rialto, Santi Filippo e Giacomo, San Gallo, and San Giovanni Elemosinario), employed a liturgy that at certain points diverged from the Roman rite, but the sacral function of the State was upheld no less vigorously in the diocese of Castello, whose head was the patriarch of Venice, and the dioceses of the *terraferma*. The conflict of authority between Rome and Venice is dramatized by the five papal interdictions, the last and most bitter occurring in 1606–7. Where a *modus vivendi* was achieved, it was Rome that made the concessions. A typical case is the Venetian Inquisition, established in 1547. Its three lay members were all Venetian patricians, while one of the three clerics was the patriarch of Venice, invariably also a Venetian nobleman. Its constitution therefore gave the republic an inbuilt majority, enabling it to decide for itself how liberally (or otherwise) to treat non-Catholics and free-thinkers.

Further, the whole mythologized history of Venice was permeated by events of religious significance. The miraculous foundation of the city on 25 March 421, the theft from Alexandria of the relics of St Mark in 829, the naval victory over the Turks at Lepanto in 1571: all were interpreted as the unfolding of a divine plan. The very improbability of the city's laborious and ingenious construction over an archipelago, its envied mercantile success, and its acquisition of an empire that, uniquely for the Old World during the Christian era, owed its existence mainly to maritime power seemed to mark Venice out as a city favoured by Providence,

---

[17] The uniquely sacral nature of Venice is discussed, with particular reference to the *ospedali* and their *cori*, in Jane L. Baldauf-Berdes, *Women Musicians of Venice: Musical Foundations, 1525–1855* (Oxford, 1993), 19–29 and *passim*. This recent book, based on the same author's doctoral thesis, is by a long way the most comprehensive and penetrating study of the *ospedali grandi* so far written, and I gratefully record here my huge indebtedness in these pages to its factual information and original insights.

almost a 'City of God' in the Augustinian sense. Its situation at the 'cutting edge' of Christendom's conflict with Islam in the eastern Mediterranean reinforced its sense of being both a missionary and an exemplary society. Many rituals of State, such as the doge's annual 'wedding to the sea' on Ascension Day, synthesized the sacred and the secular so perfectly that it would be hard to determine where one realm ended and the other began.

Since public welfare was by tradition (and by the choice of its providers) the responsibility of the religious sphere, most European states took little direct part in its organization and financing during the medieval and early modern periods. In the case of Venice, however, it was precisely the sacral nature of the State that caused it to supervise, co-ordinate, regulate, and (mostly by indirect means) maintain a comprehensive welfare system unmatched, at the time, in scale and efficiency. This was a system that evolved piecemeal over several centuries. It allowed for great variation in the government of the various institutions and was, by modern standards, untidy in its details. It owed its existence more to the acts of individual philanthropists, whose work the State subsequently facilitated, than to consciously planned civic initiatives, though the latter were not altogether absent. And yet: by a process resembling natural selection the system expanded until it addressed all major social needs, and each institution found its own niche within the whole.

In the vast secondary literature on the four *ospedali grandi*, emphasis is usually laid on their similarities, as if they were as alike as, say, English comprehensive schools under the same education authority.[18] It is true that their *cori* (which constituted their public face) were remarkably similar in size, composition, and level of attainment—a uniformity that their rivalry and fear of falling behind tended to encourage—but this sameness concealed important differences in the 'clientele' served by each *ospedale*. In a sense, focusing our attention on the *cori* at the expense of the wider institution falsifies the overall picture and even belittles the achievement of those *ospedali* with a narrower base of recruitment for their *coro* (the Ospedaletto and the Incurabili) in matching the musical accomplishments of those more favoured (especially the Pietà). A thumbnail sketch of each institution in turn will bring out these contrasts.

The oldest of the four was the Ospedale di San Lazzaro e dei Mendicanti ('the Mendicanti'), founded by 1182 as a refuge for beggars, lepers, and wandering crusaders. Originally, its government was entirely in the hands of the diocese of Castello, but in 1479 the state entrusted its management to an independent lay body, leaving the patriarch with

[18] An example of an account that 'homogenizes' the *ospedali* in this manner (I single it out merely because it is deservedly admired and much quoted) is Denis Arnold, 'Orphans and Ladies: The Venetian Conservatoires (1690–1797)', *Proceedings of the Royal Musical Association*, 89 (1962–3), 31–47.

authority over its religious affairs alone. The governing body (the *pia con-gregazione*, in the language of the time) eventually came to have 40 members, divided between nobles and citizens. In 1595 the Mendicanti was turned into a general-purpose charitable institution with a heterogeneous population that included beggars, orphans, widows, invalids, retired workers, and the patrician elderly. In that year it moved into a new building close to the Ospedaletto on the Fondamente Nuove in the *sestiere* of Castello. Its separate church, San Lazzaro, was completed in 1634 to a design by Vincenzo Scamozzi. Its total population seems to have been the largest after the Pietà; in 1715 a French visitor, the comte de Caylus, estimated it (perhaps with a little exaggeration) at 800.[19] The residents were segregated rigorously according to sex after the fashion of a 'double' monastery. Although the potential intake of the Mendicanti, in view of the large number of categories of resident, was very large, a restrictive admissions policy kept the numbers stable.

The second-oldest was the Ospedale della Pietà. It was founded in the late 1330s by a Franciscan friar from Assisi, Fra Pietro, and came under the jurisdiction of the state in 1353. The State retained authority, via the diocese of Venice, over its religious affairs, though its religious services followed the Roman, not the Venetian, liturgy. Its resident population consisted almost entirely of foundlings—infants abandoned by their parents and deposited, usually under cover of night, in a specially provided niche on the outside wall. In 1727 the governors estimated the number of annual admissions as 500.[20] Clearly, it was impossible, even with a high rate of infant mortality, to accommodate such large numbers in the institution's buildings in Venice; and it became the practice to board out infants with peasant families on the *terraferma* in the hope, not often fulfilled, that they would eventually be adopted. So although the Pietà had responsibility for several thousand souls, only a proportion—typically, about 800–900—lived in Venice at any one time. Its governing board comprised forty nobles. As a State institution in the full sense, the Pietà enjoyed the privilege of having as its protector the doge himself; it was the only *ospedale* to receive an official ducal visit every year, on Palm Sunday. In 1436 a law dating back to 1375 that required notaries drawing up wills to remind testators to leave money to charity was amended to include a mention of the Pietà by name.[21] In 1475 the Pietà moved to its final site on the Riva degli Schiavoni slightly to the East of the ducal

[19] Caylus, comte de [Anne-Claude-Philippe de Tubières de Grimoard de Pestels de Lévis], *Voyage d'Italie, 1714–1715*, ed. Amilda-A. Pons (Paris, 1914), 96–7.
[20] *I-Vas*, Ospedali e luoghi pii diversi, Busta 630, Fascicolo 5, fo. 3ᵛ, quoted in Diana E. Kaley, *The Church of the Pietà* (Venice, [1980]), 13.
[21] The wills of all the Venetian Vinaccesis include the obligatory question of the notary and the testator's response. It was not difficult—indeed, it was the most common outcome—to avoid making a charitable bequest or endowment by simply pleading poverty.

palace along the waterfront. Its first chapel was established in 1528–9, its second in *c*.1640. Its third place of worship, which survives today as Santa Maria della Visitazione (or della Pietà), was erected in 1745–60 to a design by Giorgio Massari.[22]

The Incurabili and the Derelitti (Ospedaletto) were both products of the reforming zeal of the Counter-Reformation. The first was established officially in 1522 by a group of nobles associated with the Compagnia del Divino Amore in response to the rapid spread of syphilis, the 'incurable' disease *par excellence*. It later came to accommodate four entirely different types of resident: the sick (including syphilitics), reformed prostitutes (*convertite*), a quota of thirty-three orphaned boys, and a quota of seventy girls from noble and citizen families, for whom it served as a boarding-school, or *conservatorio*. Reckoning together the male and female sections, which were divided as at the Mendicanti after the fashion of a double monastery, its population totalled around 500. The institution was sited on the Fondamente delle Zattere near the Chiesa dello Spirito Santo in the *sestiere* of Dorsoduro. Its church, San Salvatore, was designed by Jacopo Sansovino and finally consecrated in 1600. Unlike the churches attached to the other *ospedali*, this was located within the main building itself. The State appointed the twenty-four governors, divided equally between nobles and citizens, but ecclesiastical jurisdiction was held by the patriarch, representing the diocese of Castello. Its seventy female boarders—the only statutory residents at any of the *ospedali* who could not be classed as 'needy'—gave the Incurabili a slightly higher social status than its sister-institutions.

Finally, the Ospedaletto. Its foundation in 1528 followed closely on a famine on the *terraferma* that drove large numbers of destitute people to seek sustenance in the capital and coincided with the enactment of Venice's first poor laws. Once again, its founders—a lawyer and two merchants—were adherents of the Compagnia dello Divino Amore; among its first governors was the Venetian nobleman Girolamo Miani (later to be canonized as St Girolamo Emiliani), the founder of the Somaschian order. It was a private lay institution whose administration by a board of 50 governors, who included both nobles and citizens, was independent of the state and whose church, entrusted to six Somaschians (three of whom were laymen), was subordinate to neither the diocese of Venice nor that of Castello. As at the Incurabili and the Mendicanti, the intake was strikingly mixed. The institution's main function was as an orphanage for 125 girls and forty boys. To be admitted, a child normally had to be no younger than 6 and no older than 10, to have lost both its father and its mother (in the parlance of the time, any child without a father could be classed as

---

[22] Notwithstanding the fact that Vivaldi last supplied the Pietà with compositions in 1740 and died the following year, publicity insists today on calling Massari's church 'La chiesa di Vivaldi'.

an 'orphan', which is why the apparently tautological phrase *orfano di padre e di madre* is so often used instead of plain *orfano*), to be of legitimate parentage, and to enjoy good health. Then there were forty sufferers from skin diseases (*tignosi*), other sick people (*febbricanti*), and a floating population of itinerants such as pilgrims who were offered hospitality for three days. Its able-bodied stable population was therefore rather low: certainly under two hundred, including juveniles. The buildings of the Ospedaletto occupied a narrow strip of land stretching from the Calle di Barbaria delle Tole, close to the church of Santi Giovanni e Paolo, all the way to the Fondamente Nuove and the lagoon. The four-storey main building, which housed the *figlie*, stood on the Barbaria delle Tole separated from the Ospedaletto church, Santa Maria dei Derelitti, by a narrow *calle*; however, the upper floors of the residence communicated with choir-lofts in the church, as a list of rooms in the former (undated, but *c*.1770) confirms.[23] The original church was built soon after the founding date, but a generous legacy from the draper Bartolomeo Cargnoni, who died in 1662, permitted Baldassarre Longhena to redesign the façade, which was reconstructed in 1674; the high altar was refashioned soon after.

Contemporary reports and modern literature alike say very little about the male residents of the *ospedali*. The reason is that orphans and foundlings, who were almost the only able-bodied persons among them (the rest were elderly or infirm), left in adolescence after a brief education and perhaps some basic vocational training to enter the world of employment. In theory, their female counterparts could have followed a similar path to become domestic servants or seamstresses. However, to have cast them off before they reached full adulthood would have shown scant regard for their moral welfare. Further, the institution would then have had the impossible choice of leaving them undowered, so condemning them to a life of poverty and insecurity, or providing a dowry that had not been earned.[24] All the *ospedali* resolved this problem by retaining their *figlie* well into adult life. Some were permitted to marry, take the veil, or simply leave—but only after they had first generated income for the

[23] *I-Vmc*, Ms. Cicogna 3079, Fascicolo 1.
[24] In the late 17th cent. the Ospedaletto provided those of its *figlie* who left to marry with a dowry of 250 ducats (this sum included 100 ducats from Bartolomeo Cargnoni's bequest). In addition, leavers were allowed to take the personal possessions stored in their *cassa* and any money they had inherited during their wardship. They had to sign an undertaking that a third of the dowry would be returned to the Ospedaletto if they died childless. *Figlie* who became nuns received a dowry of 300 ducats, adjustable upwards or downwards according to the particular requirements of the convent they were to enter. At some point before 1776 the dowry of *figlie* entering wedlock was raised to 300 ducats, removing the differential. Other *ospedali* were, it seems, less generous: in 1780 the Pietà was offering its wards 200 ducats plus 50 ducats worth of household goods, while the Mendicanti in 1767 could grant only 137 ducats.

institution by performing a prescribed term of service.[25] Many chose to remain residents for the rest of their lives, in their later years becoming part of a cadre of *maestre* and elderly women named *donne savie* (wise women) or *discrete* (prudent ones) collectively responsible for teaching, supervising tasks, and keeping order.[26] The senior administrator in the internal female hierarchy, the prioress (*priora* or *superiora*), was usually a resident who had worked her way up through the *coro*. There was an ironic twist to this situation in that those *figlie* most likely to come to the attention of the outside world and have their hand sought in marriage— the star performers among the *figlie di coro*—were also those whom the institution was least pleased to lose, since they earned it money and prestige. It therefore often happened that an *ospedale* delayed the departure of a favourite *figlia di coro* by interpreting the rules as strictly as possible.

The daily regime of the *figlie* at the Ospedaletto is described in its regulations (*Capitoli et ordini*) first set out in 1567–8 and periodically revised.[27] *Mutatis mutandis*, it characterizes the life of the female residents at all four *ospedali grandi*. In spring and summer the *figlie* were allowed to spend seven hours in bed; in autumn and winter, eight. They rose at the sound of a Hail Mary and collectively recited the Miserere, De Profundis, and Salve Regina. Having dressed in silence, they proceeded to the oratory, prayed, returned to make their beds, and spent half an hour cleaning before going to their appointed places of work. While working, they were to recite the Office of the Blessed Virgin (on Sundays adding that of the Holy Spirit) and say prescribed prayers for the living governors and governesses. On Mondays and Thursdays they had to recite Vespers for the dead in memory of deceased governors; on other days they said prayers for the Fathers (the resident Somaschians), the prioress, and the *figlie di casa*. They interrupted their morning shift only to attend Mass. Lunch was taken at *ore* 14 (ten hours before nightfall) in summer, *ore* 20 (four hours

---

[25] At the Ospedaletto members of the *coro* had to serve for ten years after completing their apprenticeship to become entitled to a dowry.

[26] The demography of the female section of the Ospedaletto shows how few *figlie* were able—or willing—to take advantage of the opportunity to leave the institution after completing their obligatory service. In 1770 the 128 *figlie* included no fewer than 30 who were aged 50 and over (one had reached the age of 80!). This information is found in a document (*I-Vmc*, Ms. Cicogna 3079, Fascicolo 1, 'Figliole descritte nelli perdoni con parte di Congregazione') identifying those *figlie* who, on reaching the age of 50, qualified for *perdoni*, i.e. indulgences obtained by visiting specified churches in the city. The age at which *figlie* retired from active work in the *coro* or in a *laboratorio* depended on individual circumstances. For instance, in 1770 a 62-year-old, Catterina Ruspante, was still singing in the choir, while a 53-year-old *violone*-player, Andriana Galeotti, was already retired (*I-Vmc*, Ms. Cicogna 3079, Fascicolo 1, 'Figliole di coro').

[27] A handsome manuscript copy of these regulations ('Capitoli et ordini per il buon governo del Pio Hospitale de Poveri Derelitti appresso Santi Giovanni e Paolo di Venetia . . .') is preserved in *I-Vire*, Der. A. 5. The regulations take account of revisions up to 1668. The section concerning the *figlie* is found on openings 13–22. In 1668 (1667 *more veneto*) the *Capitoli et ordini* were published; two reprints (1681 and 1704) are also known.

before nightfall) in winter. It was signalled by the ringing of a bell, on hearing which the *figlie* were to kneel in front of the cross and say a Pater Noster and an Ave Maria. They entered the refectory as they had entered the chapel for Mass: processing two by two and singing a psalm or hymn. Quasi-monastic rules governed their eating; they had to remain totally silent, rapping on the table with a knife if they needed anything. At the end of the meal they sang a Te Deum. They were then allowed about half an hour of free time in their dormitories before returning for the afternoon shift at their workplace. Their labour was now accompanied by the recitation of the Vespers and Compline of the Blessed Virgin and Litanies for all the living and dead governors, interspersed with spiritual songs. At *ore* 22 (two hours before nightfall) in summer and at the appropriate later time in winter they said Matins while continuing to work. In Lent they recited the Seven Penitential Psalms. At sunset in summer (later in winter) they finished their tasks and went first to the oratory and then to supper, which they ate under the same conditions as lunch. Supper was followed by a quarter-hour of silent prayers. The *figlie* then returned to their dormitories, where the duty monitor for the week (*settimaniera*) recited the Miserere and the De Profundis. The dormitory doors were locked and the time for sleep arrived. From the age of 12 upwards *figlie* were assigned a bed of their own; younger girls slept two to a bed. To inhibit what the regulations call 'immoderato affetto' a light was left on all night.

On paper at least, discipline was severe. The *figlie* were not supposed to form close-knit groups of friends ('far camerate') or talk secretly among themselves. They had to be kind to one another—on pain of punishment. The prioress and governesses carried out random inspections of the boxes containing each resident's personal property in order to prevent the *figlie* from keeping forbidden objects. Minor breaches of discipline were dealt with by penitences and mortifications, public or private; for serious transgressions a *figlia* could be sent to the Ospedaletto's own prison and kept on a diet of bread and water.

The *figlie* had very limited contact with the outside world. At the Ospedaletto visitors were limited to close relatives, and visiting times to Sunday afternoons. All conversations between a *figlia* and her visitors had to be held in the hearing of *maestre* and *discrete*. In its zeal to build a wall between itself and the outside world, the Ospedaletto expressly forbade its ex-residents to revisit their former home, fearing, perhaps, that they would entice others away. No younger female resident could go out of the institution, however briefly, without the governors' permission and a *discreta* as chaperone. The seclusion of the *figlie* was maintained even during their annual outing (*ricreazione*), which invariably took them, in the company of the governors and governesses, to one of the less inhabited islands of the lagoon, far from the public eye.

Particular care was taken to shield the *figlie* from the opposite sex. Only by special permission were men, who included the music masters, allowed to visit their building; access to the upper floors, containing their dormitories, was even harder to obtain. In the adjoining church the singers and players in their choir-lofts were efficiently screened by means of grilles and gauze from the members of the congregation.

This regime, which to us today appears horrifically over-restrictive, was in no sense regarded as excessive at the time. It arose, first, from the application of a 'rule' modelled on those of female religious communities (hence hardly extraordinary) and, second, from the sincere belief that the inculcation of a strong work-ethic and diligent religious observance were the best service that a charitable institution could offer its beneficiaries. Conversely, compliance with them gave the latter a means of showing appropriate gratitude towards those who had rescued them from a life of penury or worse. That conditions at the *ospedali* were perfectly acceptable by contemporary standards can be seen from the fact that the Ospedaletto, the Mendicanti, and the Pietà all followed the example of the *conservatorio* at the Incurabili by admitting a small number of fee-paying female pupils, boarding or non-boarding, from well-to-do homes.[28] Nor should we forget, when passing judgement, that life must have been humanized by a thousand little accommodations and circumventions of which the rules give no inkling.

The *ospedali* certainly spared no effort to use their *figlie* to raise money and so pay, in part, for their keep. The children were regularly sent on alms walks around the city, escorted by senior residents. These processions gave the general public a chance to recognize the distinctive uniform of each *ospedale*: white (symbolizing virginity) for the Ospedaletto; red (charity) for the Pietà; blue (faith) for the Incurabili; purple (mourning) for the Mendicanti. The adult residents assigned to the workshops (*labo-ratori*) practised traditional 'feminine' skills such as embroidery and lace-making.

Productive work was organized around the system known as the *tasca*. Cognate with the English words 'task' and 'tax', the *tasca* was a fixed quota of work defined not by the hours worked or the quantity of articles produced but by the value of the latter when sold at prices fixed by the administration. According to the regulations each adult *figlia* had, notionally, to earn about 11 or 12 *soldi* a day (with small variations according to season and the type of article produced). Since there were approximately 200 working days in a year (Sundays and festivals being free of work), each *figlia* subject to the *tasca* could be expected in the course of a year to 'pay' into the coffers of the Ospedaletto over 100 *lire*, of which a third

---

[28] At the Ospedaletto such students, called *figlie di spese*, cost their guardians 30 ducats a year. They were not allowed to become full members of the *coro* but could perform as supernumeraries.

was retained in a special fund set up for the benefit of the *figlie* them-selves.

In the eighteenth century the system went into decline for two main reasons: the goods produced became less popular, hence less lucrative, and a growing number of *figlie* obtained exemption from the *tasca*. These exemptions were used by the administration as a means of persuading women to accept special responsibilities (*cariche*) such as assisting the *maestri* or escorting the children on their alms walks. Members of the *coro*, who had to attend lessons and take part in rehearsals and perfor-mances, were naturally also eligible for exemption. In 1755 nine members were fully exempt and fifteen more were relieved of half the *tasca*, result-ing in a notional loss of earnings by the institution (at the new, lower rate of 40 *lire* per head per annum) of 660 *lire*.[29] Ten years later the *deputati sopra le figlie* had to confess, in a report to the governors, that income from the *tasca* had averaged only 178 *lire* 5 *soldi* over the previous decade; since the value of the women's work hardly sufficed to pay the *tasca*, they were seeking exemption by any means possible.[30] In 1770, when the Ospedaletto, now under great financial stress, considered reducing the statutory number of *figlie* from 125 to 100, it found that of the 126 *figlie* in residence only 23 were subject to the *tasca*: 41 were exempt as mem-bers of the *coro*, 44 as former or current holders of *cariche*, and 18 as chil-dren.[31]

The musicians of the *coro* formed a privileged and valued elite within the female section. However, we would be mistaken to believe that the expenditure on music by the Ospedaletto or any of its sister-institutions was motivated by a desire to educate the *figlie* or enrich their cultural life for the sake of those ends themselves (indeed, so little did the *ospedali* care for the personal development of their *figlie di coro* that before a mem-ber of the *coro* left the institution, she had to give a written undertaking never again to display her musical skills in public). There was certainly a desire to serve God through music and show that the city's opera-houses did not have 'all the best tunes', a sentiment absolutely consonant with the idea of sacral Venice. Then there was what we would today call a 'public relations' function, since the musical accomplishments of the *coro* could advertise to the public at large the institution's success at harnessing the talents of its wards and keeping them from idleness. But the overrid-ing concern was, as usual, money. It was vital for the continued existence of an *ospedale* to obtain bequests and endowments, beside which the income from *scagni* and the *tasca* was small beer. Music in the institu-tion's church was, so to speak, a thanksgiving in advance for such

[29] *I-Vire*, Der. G. 1.48, Inserto 96.
[30] *I-Vmc*, Ms. Cicogna 3079, Fascicolo 5, report dated 20 Dec. 1765.
[31] *I-Vmc*, Ms. Cicogna 3079, Fascicolo 1, 'Figliole di coro'.

benefits. A characteristic form of endowment was the *mansioneria*, in which a benefactor left money to the institution in return for the saying of Masses for his or her soul. Each *ospedale* maintained a staff of beneficed priests (*mansionari*) to carry out the testators' wishes. In 1680 the Ospedaletto retained eight clerics for this purpose; by 1704 their number had climbed to twenty-seven.[32]

So music was a means rather than an end. We know from the governors' minute-books at the Ospedaletto and the other *ospedali* how stringently the principle of cost-benefit was applied. Were it not for the competition between the four institutions, one could well imagine that more than one of them would have been tempted in hard times to abandon the struggle to maintain its *coro* (the Ospedaletto actually suspended musical activity altogether between 1647 and 1655, before the *cori* had become so institutionalized that such drastic action was unthinkable). The less populous *ospedali* (which really means all except the Pietà) often had difficulty in keeping up the numbers in their *cori* and sometimes had to make exceptional admissions in order to maintain the flow of recruits.

The *cori* of the four *ospedali grandi* came into existence through a process of incremental development in the late sixteenth century; that of the Ospedaletto was established formally in 1577. The first permanent *maestri di coro* of whom we have knowledge were appointed in the early seventeenth century (see Appendix C.3 for a list of the Ospedaletto's *maestri* from 1612 onwards). The number of active members of each *coro* (i.e. discounting *figlie* still in training and supernumeraries) was, at least notionally, fixed. In 1624 the membership of the Ospedaletto's *coro*, like that of the Incurabili, was pegged at thirty-three, symbolizing the years in the life of Jesus.[33] The number fluctuated in subsequent years. If Vinaccesi's petition of 1713 is to be believed, it had sunk to twenty at the time of his appointment.[34] He claimed, however, to have raised it to forty, and this number (to which we must add the operator of the organ bellows) appears to have remained stable until the *coro*'s dissolution following the fall of the Venetian Republic in 1797.

The census of the *figlie* dating from the year 1770 that was mentioned earlier in connection with the *tasca* provides us with a breakdown of the members of the *coro* of the Ospedaletto in that year. Twenty-one are singers (though the four oldest are no longer active), presumably divided fairly equally between sopranos and contraltos. The remaining twenty members comprise seven violinists, three violists, four cellists (one inactive), three players of the *violone* (one inactive), two organists, and one

[32] Baldauf-Berdes, *Women Musicians*, 76.

[33] Ibid., 126. The *coro* at the Pietà was larger, its members officially numbering at least 42 around 1745. That of the Mendicanti was still more numerous but included many part-timers.

[34] See n. 54, below.

bellows-operator. Wind instruments are conspicuously absent, though it is possible that some string players 'doubled' on them.[35] It seems that the human and financial resources of the Ospedaletto were kept at full stretch merely to maintain a respectable string band.[36] Conditions at the Incurabili were similar; at the Mendicanti, a little better. But only the Pietà, especially during its period of association with Vivaldi (1703–40), put great effort into developing its orchestra and winning a name for instrumental performance. This it did almost to excess: no court orchestra of the time could boast such a varied instrumentarium containing real rarities such as the *viola inglese*, the *viola d'amore*, the clarinet, and the chalumeau.

The internal organization of all the *cori*, in which musical and disciplinary functions went hand in hand, was pyramidal. At the apex stood a *maestra di coro* responsible for the singers, and her instrumental counterpart. Below them was a corps of *maestre* and *sottomaestre* responsible for elementary tuition. Next came the ordinary active members of the *coro*. The bottom of the pyramid was provided by the girls in training and the reserves. It suited the governors both ideologically (in support of the prevailing ethos of diligence) and economically (in terms of cutting costs) to maximize the self-sufficiency of the *coro*, so that it could, at least in the short term, function without external aid apart from the supply of new compositions by the *maestro di coro*. But realism compelled them to supplement these efforts with expertise drawn from outside. In their more thoughtful moments the governors recognized the stagnation and the perpetuation of bad habits that could result from what the *deputati sopra li figlioli e figliole* of the Ospedaletto described in 1739 as the 'privata scuola delle figlie'. [37]

The external *maestri* were thus in the unenviable position of being treated as a necessary evil. Their fate was delicately balanced. If their efforts failed to bear fruit, they would be dismissed or fail to secure reappointment at the next annual ballot. If they were too successful, on the other hand, it would be argued that the *figlie* whom they had trained were

---

[35] A memorandum from the *sopraintendente alla musica*, Francesco Corner, dated 15 Apr. 1716 (*I-Vire*, Der. G. 1.48, Inserto 15, transcribed in Scarpa, *Arte e musica all'Ospedaletto*, 109–11) lists among the *maestre* a certain 'Anna Maestra di Violino, et Oboè', who must have been a pupil of the oboe teacher introduced at Vinaccesi's request. Did she, perhaps, have students of her own who maintained the tradition? The distribution of players between the different instruments must have varied from period to period. It is hard to imagine that in Vinaccesi's day the Ospedaletto did not have performers on the lute and theorbo, which for a long time remained popular continuo instruments in Venice.

[36] Some idea of the effort can be gleaned from an annotated list of 113 *figlie* drawn up by an unnamed governor *c.*1770 (*I-Vmc*, Ms. Cicogna 3079, Fascicolo 5). This names several *figlie* who formerly sang or played an instrument but gave up of their own volition or else found their entry to the *coro* blocked.

[37] *I-Vire*, Der. G. 1.48, Inserto 35, transcribed in Scarpa, *Arte e musica all'Ospedaletto*, 113–16.

capable of acting in their stead, and their employment was then placed equally in jeopardy. The instability of the situation caused both parties— the teacher and the institution—to look for short-term advantage. For the teacher, a post at an *ospedale* was merely one of many irons in the fire— desirable but not indispensable; for the institution, a *maestro* represented, however unrealistically, a stop-gap addressing a temporary need. At the Ospedaletto the funding of these posts varied. Depending on circumstances, they were paid out of the main account (*cassa grande*), a separate music account (*cassa della musica*), or the private coffers of benefactors.

Appendix C.3 lists the Ospedaletto's *maestri* from the earliest times to the middle of the eighteenth century. The first known teacher other than the *maestro di coro* was an unnamed violinist appointed in 1662. During the directorship of Antonio Pollarolo (1716–43) three violin-teachers were appointed at different times. They included Carlo Tessarini, a noted composer from Rimini, and from 1733 Antonio Martinelli, best known for his activity at the Pietà after Vivaldi's departure.[38] Under Vinaccesi a cello-teacher, Giacomo Taneschi, was appointed for a few years on two occasions. More teachers of this instrument followed under Pollarolo and his successors. Between 1716 and 1722, exceptionally, the Ospedaletto employed a separate *violone*-teacher, Camillo Personé. It waited until 1715 before appointing its first teacher of *solfeggio*, a discipline that embraced the rudiments of music, plainsong, and singing in the strict style. The same year also saw the first appointment of a *maestro di maniera*, whose job was to coach advanced singers in the florid style derived from operatic practice. Both vocal posts continued, with the usual interruptions, into the second half of the century.

Whenever possible, the Ospedaletto 'doubled up' posts. Most *maestri di coro* up to and including Pollarolo were organists who gave tuition in organ-playing, which removed the need for a separate teacher. Pollarolo's successor Porpora, however, had previous experience as a teacher of singing. The governors reacted to this new situation by combining his post with that of *maestro di maniera* and paying the *maestro di solfeggio*, Girolamo Brunelli, to carry out the duties of organist and organ-teacher. Martinelli taught both violin and cello (doubtless also viola and double-bass) from the outset, besides composing instrumental works for the Ospedaletto's repertory. His position, in fact, was comparable with Vivaldi's old post of *maestro de' concerti* at the Pietà.

It is not possible to give more than a general picture of the place of music in services at the *ospedali*. Much useful information is contained in

---

[38] Martinelli, who also taught at the Mendicanti, is a figure important enough in the musical life of Venice in the mid-18th cent. to merit investigation. One wonders whether he was a relative (a son?) of the Martinelli, a converted Jew employed as a violinist by the company of comedians headed by Giuseppe Imer, whom Goldoni encountered in 1735.

books for the tourist such as the *Guida de' forestieri*, and contemporary diaries and news-sheets. Further, the survival of extensive fragments of the repertory of the Ospedale della Pietà in the Fondo Esposti at the Conservatorio di Musica 'Benedetto Marcello' in Venice gives a clear idea of the musical requirements of at least one *ospedale*. But the variable structure of the church year and the unrestricted freedom of each institution to choose whether to employ plainsong or 'composed' music for any individual liturgical item make detailed description risky. All four *ospedali* employed *canto figurato* regularly in their Sunday services (Mass and Second Vespers) and also those held on Saturday, the Vigil of Sunday (First Vespers, Compline, Lauds). All had to observe the mandatory feasts, called *feste di precetto*, which were celebrated throughout the Venetian state. Four major feasts—Christmas, Easter, Whitsun, and Corpus Domini—were celebrated with an Octave; that is, the seven days following the feast proper employed the same liturgy. Each *ospedale* singled out from the *feste di precetto* a small number of feasts to which, by custom, it attached especial weight. These comprised the patronal festival (at the Ospedaletto, the Assumption of the Blessed Virgin Mary on 15 August), the anniversary of the church's dedication (at the Ospedaletto, the feast of St Anthony of Padua on 13 June), and a few more. All Marian feasts, which naturally had special significance for communities of girls and women, were celebrated with much pomp. During Lent, music was offered almost daily—opportunely, when the opera-houses were all shut. To some extent, the *ospedali* responded to the social calendar of the Venetian nobility. It is noticeable that musical activity slackened off during the two *villeggiature* (in summer, from 13 June until the end of July; in autumn, from 18 October to 11 November), when a large part of the nobility repaired to their estates on the mainland.

It has been stated that the *ospedali* co-ordinated their Sunday services so that 'clashes' of important events were avoided.[39] This may have been the case during certain periods, and would certainly have been to the advantage of music-loving governors, who often served on the board of more than one *ospedale*.[40] The overall impression, however, is of intense competition, particularly during major festivals such as Easter and Christmas.

The compositions required from a *maestro di coro* do not seem to have varied much between institutions. New works were usually introduced at a major festival, when a large congregation could be expected, and thereafter remained in the repertory for some while until superseded in their turn. For Mass, settings of the first three sections of the Ordinary (Kyrie,

---

[39] Baldauf-Berdes, *Women Musicians*, 132.

[40] One example is Antonio Ottoboni, a procurator of St Mark who served on the boards of the Ospedaletto and the Pietà from 1701.

Gloria, Credo) were needed. In the period we are considering the last two sections of the Ordinary (Sanctus, Agnus Dei) seem always to have been left in plainsong. The Credo was often treated independently from the Kyrie–Gloria pair, which is sometimes described in its own right as a 'Messa', paralleling the tradition of the *Missa brevis* cultivated in Lutheran music.[41] The Proper was never set. Up to two motets (a term used here in the technical sense of a setting of a non-liturgical text) were required for a solemn Mass. It is not certain whether the *figlie di coro* participated in Mass on ferial days. At the Ospedaletto, for example, the contract of service of the six Somaschian priests obliged them to officiate at eight Masses each week—although this was not necessarily in the church itself.

Of all the services, Vespers demanded the most music. The unchanging items were the response *Domine ad adiuvandum me festina* at the start of the service and the canticle, the Magnificat. A Vesper service employs a sequence of five psalms. Eleven different sequences were needed to cover all the festivals of the church year celebrated at the *ospedali*, according to information in a contemporary handbook for members of the congregation.[42] Four psalms—*Dixit Dominus, Confitebor tibi, Domine, Laudate pueri*, and *Beatus vir*—belonged to eight or more of these sequences (the first is in fact the opening psalm of all 11); at the other extreme came three psalms—*Beati omnes, In convertendo*, and *Domini probasti me*—needed for only one feast or type of feast. As one would expect, the frequency with which psalms were set to music bore some relationship to how frequently they could be used. At least one new setting of the *Dixit Dominus* would be *de rigueur* every year, while an *In convertendo* might have to wait its turn. It was common for composers to set a complete psalm-sequence as a cycle of five works that, though varied in scoring, were tonally congruent with one another and exploited the same thematic ideas. In practice, however, it was rare to hear more than two or three sung during one service (the remainder could be left in plainsong). For example, the diarist Pietro Gradenigo records having heard at the Ospedaletto on Whitsunday (25 May) 1760 three psalms (*Beatus vir, Laudate pueri, In exitu Israel*) newly composed by *maestro* Pampani; these were repeated on the remaining two days of the triduum.[43]

There are few surviving examples of settings of Vesper hymns (the Fondo Esposti does, however, preserve a few examples of the *Ave maris stella*, for Marian feasts, the *Veni creator spiritus*, for Whitsunday, and the *Pange Lingua*, for Corpus Domini), and it appears that plainsong normally

[41] Significantly, Porpora's list of compositions produced for the Ospedaletto in 1744 (*more veneto*) cites a 'Messa' and a 'Credo' as separate items. See n. 51, below.

[42] Antonio Groppo [publisher and probable compiler], *Salmi che si cantano in tutti li vesperi dei giorni festivi di tutto l'anno dalle figliuole nelli quattro ospitali di questa città* (Venice, 1752).

[43] *I-Vmc*, Ms. Gradenigo 67, Notatori Gradenigo, vi, fo. 20ʳ.

sufficed. Settings of the antiphons intoned before and after each psalm are completely absent. In compensation, up to two motets were normally sung at solemn Vespers.

The service of Compline, which follows Vespers, has a structure of four fixed psalms—*Cum invocarem, In te, Domine, speravi, Qui habitat in adjutorio*, and *Ecce nunc benedicite*—and a canticle, *Nunc dimittis*. All five texts were frequently set, sometimes as a complete cycle, in a manner that generally appears more intimate, less striving for effect, than that found in contemporary Vesper music.

Lauds, though originally a morning service, were, like the preceding Matins, often celebrated 'by anticipation' in the early part of the night, so becoming, in effect, a prolongation of Compline. The repertory of the *ospedali* includes settings of the canticle at Lauds, *Benedictus Dominus*, and—in great quantity—the four Marian antiphons, each proper to its season, that end the service.[44] From the feast of the Purification on 2 February until Holy Saturday the prescribed antiphon is *Ave Regina coelorum*; this is succeeded by *Regina coeli laetare* (up to the first Saturday after Whitsunday), *Salve Regina* (up to Advent), and *Alma Redemptoris Mater*. A few settings also exist of the Miserere (Psalm 50/51), which was sung at Lauds during Lent, and with especially solemnity at the conclusion of Tenebrae in Holy Week.

A few extra liturgical items should be mentioned for sake of completeness: the hymn Te Deum, used on occasions of rejoicing (military victories, births, etc.); Litanies for the Novena of Christmas; lessons and settings of the Passion for Holy Week; the responsory of St Anthony of Padua, *Si quaeris miracula*.

Besides motets, the non-liturgical compositions a *maestro di coro* might be expected to produce included oratorios and sacred dialogues. The Mendicanti, in 1667, was the first *ospedale* to put on an oratorio; it was followed in 1677 by the Incurabili and in 1683 by the Pietà. The Ospedaletto held back, perhaps for reasons of economy, until 1716, when the first of four oratorios written for it by Antonio Pollarolo appeared.[45] Earlier, however, the Ospedaletto had witnessed Christmas pastorals,

---

[44] Although they were, strictly speaking, part of the liturgy of neither Vespers nor Compline, Marian antiphons were commonly used as the closing musical item in both. In the 18th cent. they were almost invariably set in the style of solo motets, 'customized' for individual singers. This largely explains why so many alternative settings were required by the *ospedali*: to have written only one new antiphon per season would have restricted the performance of the text to a single singer, which was clearly an impossibility.

[45] Pollarolo's oratorios *Sacrum amoris novendiale* (1716), *Rosa inter spinas* (1717), and *Sterilis faecunda* (1717) are known from their librettos. The existence of a lost fourth oratorio can be inferred from the list of Pollarolo's works for the Ospedaletto drawn up in 1730 (see n. 48, below). If this was another work written in the early part of Pollarolo's career at the Ospedaletto, it would appear that oratorio went into hibernation there from *c.*1717 until 1755, which is the date of the next known oratorio, Pampani's *Messiae praeconium carmine complexum*.

which were probably similar in structure to dramatic cantatas (sere-natas).[46]

Purely instrumental music also was required for services: as an intro-duction, conclusion, or background 'commentary', and also in alternation with sung portions of the liturgy.[47] In this sense, a good proportion of Vivaldi's concertos and sonatas originated as 'sacred' music, even if, in most cases, the music was interchangeable with that heard in secular sur-roundings. Before the *ospedali* appointed *maestri de' concerti* like Vivaldi or Martinelli who took over responsibility for writing instrumental works, such music was written perforce by the *maestro di coro*. Giovanni Legrenzi's letter of resignation to the governors of the Ospedaletto, writ-ten *c.*1676, mentions 'sonate da arco' (pieces for strings) and 'sonate da tasto' (pieces for keyboard, probably organ) among the vocal compositions supplied to the institution.[48] Vinaccesi, too, probably had to provide instrumental works alongside the vocal ones.

In the contracts drawn up with their *maestri di coro* the governors at the *ospedali* tried to specify, broadly, how many compositions, and of what type, the former should produce in the course of a year. Occasionally, they were over-optimistic. In a list of obligations (*incombenze*) of the *maestro di coro* approved by the governors of the Pietà on 6 July 1710 the requirement is for at least two Masses and two cycles of Vesper psalms (probably with the response and canticle) respectively for Easter Sunday and the patronal festival, the Visitation of the Blessed Virgin Mary on 2 July. Further, the *maestro di coro* had to supply two new motets every month and carry out whatever other assignments, particularly in connec-tion with Holy Week, the governors might choose to give him.[49] In prac-tice, however, the output of a typical *maestro di coro* was smaller—or rather, more diverse—than these official obligations suggest. The surviv-ing fragments in the Fondo Esposti show that between 1727 and 1737 inclusive *maestro* Giovanni Porta composed eleven Vesper cycles—thus only one a year—and four Masses. On the other hand, he produced two complete Compline cycles and much music for Lauds, including votive

---

[46] The issues of the *Pallade veneta* for Dec. 1687, 7 Jan. 1702, and 3 Jan. 1705 contain reports of the performance of pastorals at the Ospedaletto. The last two were composed by Vinaccesi, the first probably by Carlo Grossi. See the annotated transcriptions in Selfridge-Field, *Pallade veneta*, 198, 234, and 260. Pollarolo contributed three more between 1716 and 1730.

[47] The most comprehensive account of the role of instrumental music in Italian churches during the baroque period remains Bonta, 'Uses of the *Sonata da Chiesa*'.

[48] *I-Vire*, Der. G. 1.48, Inserto 8, transcribed in Scarpa, *Arte e musica all'Ospedaletto*, 124–5.

[49] *I-Vas*, Ospedali e luoghi pii diversi, Busta 689, Notatorio H, fo. 136, transcribed in Remo Giazotto, *Antonio Vivaldi* (Turin, 1973), 363–4. In 1733 the same conditions were in force at the Pietà, to judge from a report of the *presidenti* and *deputati sopra le figlie* of the Ospedaletto dated 5 Sept. 1733 (*I-Vire*, Der. G. 1.48, Inserto 31); this report concerned an attempt—in the event, unsuc-cessful—to secure Porta's services as *maestro di composition*, which was the reason for noting his oblig-ations to the Pietà.

antiphons. The file of *parti* (draft resolutions) voted on at the governors' meetings includes a list of works by Porta for the year 1729 (*more veneto*) accompanying a report on the service provided by him and his colleagues on the music staff during that year. The compositions include no Mass movements and only three psalms but are raised to a respectable number by 6 antiphons, 22 motets, an *Ave maris stella*, and a serenata; the last work was probably written in honour of some eminent foreign visitor to the Pietà.[50] It is interesting to see that a later list of obligations of the *maestro di coro* at the Pietà (*c*.1745) reduces the annual quota of Vesper and Mass settings to one each, a more realistic requirement.

A similar list exists for Nicola Porpora's first year of service (1744 *more veneto*) at the Ospedaletto. This list accompanied a petition of Porpora to the governors requesting (in the event, successfully) that the cost of copying out new compositions should not be borne by the *maestro* himself but be absorbed, as at the other three *ospedali*, by the institution.[51] He quotes from his terms of service the annual obligation to write one Vespers plus motets and antiphons. His productivity is very impressive: for Holy Week he has provided a Miserere, a Mass (Kyrie and Gloria), a Credo, and four motets; for Easter, three settings of the *Regina coeli* and three more motets; for Ascension Sunday, a complete Vesper cycle with four motets and four settings of the *Salve Regina*; for Christmas, four psalms, four motets, and four settings of the *Alma Redemptoris Mater*.

Even more interesting is the list of compositions by Antonio Pollarolo in the first fifteen years of his appointment (1716–30) prepared by the *deputati sopra le figlie* of the same institution as a supplement to a report dated 10 December 1730.[52] This report was in response to a petition submitted by the *maestro di coro*. Pollarolo, too, felt the injustice of having to pay out of his own pocket for the materials needed to copy his compositions but stopped short of making the same bold demand as Porpora. Instead, he referred back to Vinaccesi's tenure of the post (1698–1715), during which time his predecessor had on five different occasions received *ex-gratia* payments totalling 145 ducats in recognition of this expense.[53] The purpose of the list, prepared by the senior *maestra di coro* as a summation of the separate lists submitted at regular intervals, was to give an overall impression of the music by the supplicant that had already been copied into parts *gratis*. Three hundred and eighty-two works are mentioned; they comprise 95 psalms for Vespers and Compline, 73 antiphons,

---

[50] *I-Vas*, Ospedali e luoghi pii diversi, Busta 658, 'Parti'.

[51] *I-Vire*, Der. G. 1.48, Inserti 49 and 50.

[52] *I-Vire*, Der. G. 1.48, Inserti 22 and 23. Inserto 23, the list, is reproduced in Ellero, *L'Archivio storico IRE*, 200.

[53] The payments to Vinaccesi are recorded as 30 ducats on 30 Nov. 1699, 30 ducats on 16 Apr. 1703, 30 ducats on 4 Aug. 1707, and 25 ducats on 27 Apr. 1711; a fifth payment of 30 ducats (*c*.1715?), needed to bring the total up to 145 ducats, is omitted by an evident oversight.

5 *dialoghi a più voci*, 4 oratorios, 3 pastorals, 3 Masses, 9 lessons for Holy Week, 1 Passion for Good Friday, 4 settings of the Miserere, and 185 motets. It is interesting that motets account for almost half the listed compositions; they were composed by Pollarolo at an average rate of about one a month.

We come now to consider Vinaccesi's contribution to music at the Ospedaletto. It is unfortunate that so little of the musical repertory of the Ospedaletto has survived. Until the institution itself, from Porpora's time onwards, assumed responsibility for preparing copies of the parts, which entailed having the *maestri* deposit their scores in the archive, the conservation of its music was haphazard. Even so, the yield from the second half of the eighteenth century is disappointingly meagre. Some performances of works are reported in the *Pallade veneta*, but obviously only very selectively. We are lucky, however, to possess a petition dated 29 May 1713 that Vinaccesi presented to the governors.[54] This was an application for retirement on a pension, and in it the composer reviewed his achievement since his appointment.

Before we discuss this letter, however, we should delve back into the previous history of *maestri di coro* at the Ospedaletto. As Appendix C.3 shows, the first such *maestro* of any real eminence was Giovanni Rovetta (*c.*1595–1668), appointed in 1635. At the time of his appointment Rovetta, a former singer, was *vice-maestro* under Monteverdi at San Marco; in 1644 he was made *primo maestro*. He is described by one writer as 'one of the most talented composers of the second rank to exploit the concertato style of northern Italy'.[55] Unfortunately, none of his surviving music is connected for certain with his activity at the Ospedaletto.

In 1655 Rovetta was succeeded by Massimiliano Neri (*c.*1615–66). An organist at San Marco and, concurrently, the church of Santi Giovanni e Paolo close to the Ospedaletto, Neri acquired his greatest fame through instrumental music, although some motets survive. His departure in 1663 left a void that was filled only in 1670 when Giovanni Legrenzi (1626–90) arrived. Gifted, versatile, and ambitious, Legrenzi could not be held for long; in 1676 he 'moved across' to the Mendicanti, and his progress continued with his appointment to San Marco as *vice-maestro* in 1681, *primo maestro* in 1685. His letter of resignation[56] hints at a lack of success in the practical management of the *coro*, although this may be just a pretext invented to conceal the real reason for his departure.

Under Legrenzi's successor, Carlo Grossi (*c.*1634–88), music at the

---

[54] *I-Vire*, Der. G. 1.48, Inserto 8, transcribed in Scarpa, *Arte e musica all'Ospedaletto*, 124–5, and as App. B.15.

[55] Jerome Roche, article 'Rovetta, Giovanni', in *New Grove Dictionary of Music and Musicians*, xvi. 279.

[56] See n. 48, above.

Ospedaletto began to rise in public esteem. Grossi was both an organist—Neri's successor at Santi Giovanni e Paolo—and from 1666 a bass singer at San Marco. His compositions were gracious and melodious. He was fortunate in acquiring for the Ospedaletto the superb vocal talent of a singer, nicknamed 'la Vicentina', to whom we shall return at the end of this chapter. Grossi was succeeded by Paolo Biego (died 1714), who had the previous year been appointed to one of the *organetti*, or auxiliary organs, at San Marco. Biego is a cipher: documents of the Ospedaletto say nothing about his period of tenure and remain silent even about the reason for his departure. He was evidently something of a composer, since between 1682 and 1689 he wrote three operas for the Venetian stage. If Vinaccesi was correct in stating, as we saw earlier, that at the time of his arrival the *coro* could muster only twenty active members, it would appear that under Biego a period of serious decline set in.

The petition submitted by Vinaccesi points, as one would expect, to a record of diligence and effectiveness. There is, however, an undercurrent of defensiveness that hints at difficulties and criticisms. Here is its text:

Illustrious and Most Excellent Sirs, Pious and Venerated Congregation,

Having spent fifteen years in the service of this pious and venerated congregation as music master to its daughters [*figlie*], I, Benedetto Vinaccesi, must finally turn my thoughts to attaining peace of mind and to the just desire that another person assume this burden, which in many different ways is much heavier than one would think. It was my destiny to be chosen in 1698 for this post, in competition with candidates of great talent and fame, by a majority of votes.

I have sought to make myself not wholly unworthy of such an honour by attending regularly in order to take these *figlie*, as one might put it, as far as their natural talent allowed—which God has not willed to let me find equal to my desires or to the good fortune of another similar *pio luogo* [*ospedale*], where it seems that an atmosphere of favour is somehow more easily obtained. It was I who suggested to the late most excellent Signor Giovanni Francesco Pisani that the organ should be rebuilt and the choir decorated and gilded, and His Excellency, supporting my most devoted recommendations, took the matter in hand at his own expense, generous of spirit as ever, and produced the result that one sees today. Not only did I arrange for the purchase of instruments with money from benefactors, but on several occasions I also brought about the engagement of teachers of the violin, oboe, and *viola* [cello] solely at their [the benefactors'] expense. When first appointed, I found the *coro* numbering not more than 20 *figlie*, including *maestre*, singers, and instrumentalists. I am now leaving it doubled in strength and numbering 40, not counting a few *figlie* who are currently being trained in order to enlarge it still further. During this time my pen has produced, in the service of the *coro*, over 450 compositions of various kinds—a quantity that has not been matched by several of my honourable predecessors combined over a longer period of years. These works, whatever their nature, will remain useful for their purpose and will perhaps earn some modest approval from a connoisseur of this art, if fate ever allows him to hear them. On Sundays and feast-days throughout the year I have been present at performances by the *coro* and have played the organ, exceeding the duties laid down in my terms of employment, provided that I have not been prevented from doing so by my duty to the Most Serene Prince [the doge] as organist of the ducal *cappella* of San Marco or by my participation, as organist or *maestro*, in solemn functions elsewhere in the city. For all that, I am comforted by the thought that I have never, on any account, failed in the duty and compliance that I owed and professed—and will always profess—towards so distinguished a congregation and its exalted presidents, having perhaps expected that I would experience greater success but certainly not greater zeal in the performance of my service to it. So I humbly beg you to reward generously my diligent and conscientious labours, carried out over such a long period, by graciously allowing them to cease herewith, so that, by choosing a new *maestro* in place of me, you will grant me rest and make me worthy to receive with redoubled gratitude, as I divest myself of this responsibility, that same magnanimous bounty that was accorded to me, well in excess of my deserts, when I took it up.

1713. 29 May

Presented at the venerable congregation [meeting of the board of governors] to the noble presidents on the same day and read out by me, Giacomo Aliprandi, *fattore*.

And the resolution submitted by the most excellent presidents was put to the vote with the following result:

For	6	
Against	15	rejected
Undecided	2	

The heavy defeat of the presidents' motion is all the more striking, since it gave unequivocal support to Vinaccesi's request. Its text ran:

Having performed assiduously the laborious duty of *maestro* to this *coro* of ours for the long period of fifteen years, and justly wishing to enjoy peace of mind and repose at his advanced age, *Kavalier* Benedetto Vinaccesi asks this venerated congregation to grant him the favour of an honourable retirement; therefore the presidents move that, as an act of kindness, his request be granted and that it be accompanied by a token of recognition for his deserving ability and wise, careful, and very upright service.[57]

It was perhaps unwise of the presidents to draw attention, by speaking of Vinaccesi as 'avanzato nell'età', to a fact that contradicted this description: in 1713 the composer was no older than 47. The disfavour to which his petition delicately alludes may have led the governors to begrudge him a pension. Or they may simply have been unwilling for economic reasons to pay a pension of, say, 40 ducats (the sum awarded to Pollarolo in 1743) on top of the salary of the next *maestro*.

---

[57] *I-Vire*, Der. G. 1.48, Inserto 9, transcribed as App. B.16.

Whatever the reason for this refusal, Vinaccesi's eventual departure, just over two years later, occurred in circumstances at which we can only guess. We learn of it, in passing, from the same memorandum, dated 20 September 1743, in which the *deputati* review the selection procedure.[58] The date was 24 June 1715; on the very same day a new acting *maestro di coro*, whose name is not given in the document, was appointed. The retirement—or dismissal—must obviously have been prepared in advance for the new appointment to be immediate. Perhaps Vinaccesi, following a common practice of the time, passed over his duties to a substitute, with whom he shared his salary. What is surprising is that the change-over occurred neither at the time of the annual ballot on 2 February nor at the halfway point in the Venetian year, when it was customary for the governors to consider proposals for adjustments in salaries. Once again, economic factors may have been at work, as we shall see shortly.

The small amount of evidence found in other sources confirms the pattern of activity described by Vinaccesi. On 1 July 1702 the *Pallade veneta* commented approvingly on the gilding of the organ case, noting the great expense of the operation.[59] We have already mentioned the presence of cello and oboe teachers for short periods during Vinaccesi's tenure of his post, although it is not clear in what way their appointment reflected well on him, since their salaries were not paid out of his pocket. Perhaps the credit that he claims is merely that of having perceived a need and acted on it. His boast of having composed more than several of his predecessors combined (Legrenzi, Grossi, and Biego?) during a shorter period rings true, although Pollarolo, with 382 compositions in his first 15 years, and Pampani, with over 400 in his 20 years of service, would later run him quite close.[60] A few reports of performances at the Ospedaletto of new compositions by him appear in the *Pallade veneta*. On 7 January 1702 we read of a pastoral, presumably of his composition, in which 'the cradle hymns sung there by angels rang out so gloriously that the listeners imagined themselves to be in Bethlehem'.[61] On 5 March 1704, the Vigil of the feast of Saints Perpetua and Felicity, a new Compline of his was introduced.[62] A new Vespers for the feast of St Michael Archangel (celebrated in Venice as a *festa di precetto* on the fourth Sunday in September) is recorded for 28 September 1704.[63] Another Christmas pastoral, to words

---

[58] See n. 4, above.

[59] Selfridge-Field, *Pallade veneta*, 240. Photographs of the organ showing its ornamental case appear in Scarpa, *Arte e musica all'Ospedaletto*, and Giuseppe M. Pilo, *La chiesa dello 'Spedaletto in Venezia* (Venice, 1988). The instrument itself was rebuilt within the existing case in 1751 by Pietro Nachini.

[60] The petition from Pampani in which this figure appears is minuted in *I-Vire*, Der. B. 13, 'Notatorio 1763–1774', 120 (12 May 1766).

[61] Selfridge-Field, *Pallade veneta*, 234.

[62] Ibid. 240.   [63] Ibid. 257.

by *dottor* Pietro Palliani (*recte*, Pariati?), was given in the week ending 3 January 1705.[64]

Vinaccesi's explanation of his forced absences took for granted the understanding of the governors that when his duties to the Ospedaletto clashed with those to the ducal church, the latter had to take precedence. Doubtless, the governors disliked this competition for his services but were too accustomed to the situation to think ill of it. Their reaction to his free-lance activity in other Venetian churches may not have been so tolerant, although such occasional work for churches and convents that had no permanent *cappella* of their own was in Venice a normal practice which, by enhancing the reputation of the *maestro*, could indirectly aid the purposes of his employing institution. The *Pallade veneta* mentions his composition of the music for the funeral, on 28 June 1702 at the church of the Angel Raphael, of the uncle of its *piovano* (parish priest).[65] Two days earlier Vinaccesi had composed 'dolcissime compositioni' for the feast of Saints John and Paul, but it is unclear from the report whether this was for the Ospedaletto or another church.

There are two interesting references to occasional music provided by Vinaccesi for San Salvatore (not the church of the Incurabili but the monastic church of this name close to the Rialto) in letters written by a certain Don Girolamo Desideri to Giacomo Antonio Perti, *maestro di cappella* at the basilica of San Petronio, Bologna.[66] Desideri, whose task it evidently was to make the practical arrangements for solemn occasions at San Salvatore, asked Perti for help in recruiting a male soprano or alto singer for the function accompanying the taking of the veil by a Venetian noblewoman in September 1704.[67] If none was to be found in Bologna, he should try Modena. The music was to be by Vinaccesi, 'famoso compoitore, e d[e]i primi di questo paese'. On 5 July 1710 Desideri wrote again to Perti with a similar request.[68] This time, a male soprano or alto was needed for the church's patronal festival, the Transfiguration of the Lord on 6 August. To make the engagement seem more attractive, Desideri mentioned the good possibility that the singer would be recruited for the next season's operas in Venice, or for the patronal festivals of the convents of San Lorenzo (on 10 August), for which Pollarolo (Carlo Francesco?) was to write the music, and Santa Maria della Celestia (on 15 August), where Francesco Gasparini was to officiate. He describes Vinaccesi, Pollarolo, and Gasparini as 'tre de' primi virtuosi di questa dominante'.

[64] Selfridge-Field, *Pallade veneta*, 260. Between Jan. 1705 and Sept. 1710 no issues of *Pallade veneta* are extant, hence the absence of references to Vinaccesi during this period.

[65] Ibid. 240.

[66] My knowledge of the letters from Desideri to Perti comes from transcriptions kindly made for me by Carlo Vitali.

[67] *I-Bc*, P.146.168.   [68] *I-Bc*, P.145.80.

The most interesting instance of a contribution by Vinaccesi, as an external *maestro*, to a local religious function is perhaps his participation alongside four other composers in the Octave held at the church of Santi Giovanni e Paolo from Christmas Day 1712 to New Year's Day 1713 in celebration of the canonization, on 22 May 1712, of Pius V (Michele Ghislieri), the architect of the victory at Lepanto.[69] On each day after the first there was specially composed music, preceding or following panegyrics delivered by famous preachers. On 26 December Ferdinando Antonio Lazzari, the *maestro di cappella* at the Frari, supplied Vespers. The next day it was Vinaccesi's turn to compose (and, one assumes, also direct) Vespers. On 28 December a Mass by Francesco Gasparini was performed. On 29 December the Mass was by Lorenzo Baseggio, a local organist-composer who was also active as a printer. Marco Martini, a former *maestro di coro* at the Mendicanti (in 1699–1700), provided the music for New Year's Eve. The ceremonies were rounded off on 1 January with a Te Deum by Andrea Paulati, the church's own *maestro di cappella*.

Of one thing we can be certain: under Vinaccesi's leadership the *coro* of the Ospedaletto enjoyed one of its most stable periods. The decades that followed were to witness a long series of crises triggered by economic, artistic, and personal factors that often became intertwined. It will be instructive briefly to follow the history of the *coro* from 1715 into the second half of the century.

Vinaccesi was the last *maestro di coro* of the Ospedaletto whom one could describe as a church musician with only a subsidiary interest in opera. If we ignore the anonymous and apparently unsuccessful master who replaced him in 1715 and move straight to Antonio Pollarolo, appointed by simple nomination on 2 March 1716, we encounter a musician who attempted, with some success, to keep a foot in both camps without prejudice to either. The administration of the *coro* changed at this point. One particular *deputato sopra le figlie*, Francesco Corner, was made sole superintendent of music for three years and given charge of a special *cassa della musica* funded from the *scagni* and by private benefactors, of whom he himself was the most prominent. The start of the new regime was auspicious: Corner appointed teachers of *solfeggio*, *maniera*, violin, cello, and double-bass on three-year contracts. A minor drama occurred at the beginning of 1718 when Corner threatened to resign since other governors were questioning his sole right to manage the *coro* (this included choosing the singers of solo parts and meting out rewards and punishments).[70] The storm passed, and in 1718 Pollarolo's salary, previously only 150 ducats, was raised to the 'historical' level of 200 ducats. The

[69] *I-Vmc*, Ms. Cicogna 3255/I/34, fos. 7–12.
[70] *I-Vire*, Der. G. 1.48, Inserto 15, transcribed in Scarpa, *Arte e musica all'Ospedaletto*, 109–11.

arrangement continued as before in 1719–21, except that the payment of Pollarolo's salary reverted to the *cassa grande*.

In 1722 the *cassa della musica* was abolished, and the management of the *coro* returned to the *deputati sopra le figlie* as a whole. All the auxiliary teachers were removed from the payroll, and it was suggested that in future the senior *figlie di coro* could teach solfeggio, leaving the *maestro di coro* himself to take charge of *maniera*. The need for a violin teacher was accepted, but other stringed instruments were also to be taught by competent *figlie*. The Ospedaletto stumbled along in this manner until 1727, when it once again recognized the need to engage external teachers, only to discard them in 1730. The reason for the non-reappointment of the teachers (with the significant exception of the *maestro di maniera*, Pietro Scarpari) was that the governors felt that the same result could be attained without the additional cost if the *maestro di coro* and the *figlie* merely put their shoulders to the wheel (this emphasis on good discipline as a solution to most ills runs like a leitmotive through the governors' deliberations). In 1733 Pollarolo failed to achieve re-election, and during the year of his absence (he was reinstated in 1734 under the old conditions) the Ospedaletto employed Bartolomeo Cordans as interim *maestro*, while it toyed inconclusively with the idea of appointing Johann Adolf Hasse or Giovanni Porta as the permanent replacement. Already at this stage the governors were concerned about the state of the *coro*; they were becoming increasingly aware that the problem was too deep to be solved simply by 'throwing money' at it in the shape of extra teachers. But they glimpsed a possible solution only dimly.

Greater understanding informed the discussion in 1739, when the *deputati sopra le figlie* produced a closely argued report on the 'decadence' of the *coro*.[71] A key element in their analysis (which mentions many other factors) was that musical style had undergone great change in recent times, so that, stuck in its old ways, the *coro* was now offering the public fare that it found unpalatable. The change to which they referred was the one that musicologists today identify as the advent of the melody-dominated *galant* style, which reached Venice via opera in the mid-1720s, spearheaded by young composers (Leo, Vinci, Porpora, etc.) trained in the Neapolitan conservatories. Venetian composers of an older generation such as Vivaldi, Albinoni, and Antonio Pollarolo copied, up to a point, the *galant* style—in order to retain the favour of the public, they had to join what they could not beat—but they found it hard to enter wholly into its spirit and write as a Neapolitan would have done (it was the generation of Galuppi that finally accomplished this).

Something of what the new style represented is conveyed by the anony-

---

[71] *I-Vire*, Der. G. 1.48, Inserto 35, transcribed in Scarpa, *Arte e musica all'Ospedaletto*, 113–16.

mous preface to a collection of motets sung at the Ospedaletto published in 1772. This espouses fully the 'operatic' values of the newer style but acknowledges that its introduction into church music was achieved against bitter opposition. The relevant passage runs:

But perhaps it would not stray too far from the truth to ascribe the blame [for the primacy of secular, theatrical music] to that dismal, weak, inconclusive manner, inadequate to express the variety of great concepts contained in sacred psalmody, with which music was treated in churches during the centuries before ours; for which reason, men, bored with the similarity produced by that plainness of style, sought to enjoy the pleasures of so divine an art wherever foolish scruples allowed it to express itself in the most brilliant guise [i.e. in the opera-houses]. The enormous error of such a practice was overcome little by little by reason, which, strengthened by divine authority, made us aware that the incomprehensible majesty of the Lord whom we worship in our temples is not lessened by music of the most spirited, harmonious, and lively kind. Excellent practitioners of that art who in the course of the present century had to write for the sanctuary [church] attempted to sow the first seeds that would restore it to its original magnificence; but they soon ran into an impetuous torrent of opposition that, inspired by a zeal unilluminated by religion, considered that the holiness of the place had been profaned by the apt liveliness of the expression.[72]

Behind the smug Enlightenment-speak of this preface lies an accurate historical assessment of a change of attitude in Italy towards the style of religious music—a change brought to a head around 1730 by the rapid and unopposed triumph, in the secular sphere, of the Neapolitan composers and their followers throughout the peninsula. The crisis of the Ospedaletto in the 1730s, reflecting a general crisis at all the *ospedali* around the same time, was perhaps not due simply to Pollarolo's antiquated style and the old-fashioned manner of singing handed down to each other by the *figlie di coro*; it may, paradoxically, have arisen equally from the opposition by partisans of the old, unreconstructed style of church music to the efforts by the *coro* to modernize itself. In other words, Pollarolo, in a period of transition, may have have fallen between two stools, pleasing neither one side nor the other.

Another, more damning report by the *deputati sopra le figlie* on 13 May 1743 sounded the warning bell for Pollarolo, who quickly petitioned for retirement. Even before this happened, preparations were under way for a change of outlook. From September 1742 Nicola Porpora was teaching singing to a few *figlie* without payment, but doubtless with an eye on the succession. When the time came in late 1743 to choose the new *maestro*, he was virtually unopposed—the only other candidate was the ageing Albinoni (1671–1751), whose small involvement with sacred vocal music,

---

[72] *Raccolta di cose sacre che si soglion cantare dalle pie vergini dell'ospitale dei Poveri Derelitti* (Venice, 1772), 3–4. See App. B.17.

in which he had enjoyed little success, dated back to his youth. Porpora drove a hard bargain with the governors over conditions of employment but proved as successful at his job as he had been earlier at the Incurabili (1726–33) and the Pietà (1742–3). However, he abruptly resigned from his six-year contract after only three years, pleading the need to return to Naples in order to look after his family but in reality intending to seek his fortune in Dresden.

Porpora's brief period of service is a turning-point. It marks, first, the start of the dominance of Neapolitan composers at the Ospedaletto, which in this respect followed the trend of the other *ospedali* (but not of San Marco, which remained to the last a refuge for 'native' Venetian musicians). Second, it signals the ascendancy of a type of composer for whom a church post was only an adjunct to a career spent largely in the opera-house. His successors—Pampani (1747–66), Trajetta (1766–8), Sacchini (1768–73), and Anfossi (1773–81)—were all cast in this mould.

Although the musical atmosphere in which Vinaccesi worked at the Ospedaletto was clearly more 'churchly' in character, one important factor affecting the work of his successors already existed in his time: the existence of favourite *figlie di coro*, mostly singers, whom the public adored and flocked to hear. Such stars among the wards of the *ospedali* completely overshadowed their *maestri* in the public eye—a natural situation in an age when the 'composing' function was viewed, generally speaking, as subordinate to the 'performing' one. Vinaccesi had the good fortune to work at the Ospedaletto during the latter part of the career of a singer who was by far the most eminent musician its *coro* produced in the whole of its existence: Angela Albieri, universally known as 'la Vicentina'.

Albieri, who, as her nickname implies, came from Vicenza, was the first of a small number of girls to be admitted, by virtue of their talent, to the Ospedaletto and its *coro* notwithstanding regulations. In her case, the irregularity was that her mother was still alive. At the time, she was living in the house of the Foscarinis in the *contrada* of Santa Ternita, having probably been adopted as a protégée by this distinguished noble family.[73] She was admitted on 27 March 1667 and after training emerged as both the only performer of special note at the Ospedaletto and the most famous singer in the whole of Venice. The *Pallade veneta*, ever given, as a propagandistic organ, to hyperbolic praise of things Venetian, goes to the limits of its eloquence in praising her. In the issue of February 1687 (we are speaking here of the monthly printed journal that preceded the handwrit-

---

[73] The custom among Venetian nobles of taking musically gifted children into their household has been insufficiently studied. Other musicians who enjoyed this kind of patronage in their youth were: Francesco Cavalli, who exchanged his original surname Caletti for that of his protector; Faustina Bordoni, to whom the Boldù family of San Barnaba gave shelter; and Antonio Lotti, a protégé of the Gradenigo family of Santa Giustina.

ten news-sheets) reference is made to 'a stylish and skilful singer called la Vicentina who, if she were not so young, would make us wonder whether it was she who in the first hours of the world's existence taught nightingales how to sing and produce trills, embellishments, and warbles (the writer uses the semi-technical terms *trillo, gorgia*, and *battere della voce*)'.[74] The visiting elector of Bavaria, Max II Emanuel, was among those who heard her perform a motet. In June 1687 the journal reports a commemorative service at the Ospedaletto on the anniversary of a particularly destructive fire in the city. Here la Vicentina 'unleashed that heavenly tongue to such welcome effect that her voice provided compensation of a hundred *doppie*, in the hearts of her listeners, for the damage that the greedy flames had caused'.[75] The plaudits continue in this vein. In 1693 she captivated the crown prince of Denmark, later Frederik IV;[76] for the traveller François Maximilien Misson, the 'Vicentin songster of the Hospitalettes' was 'a little charming creature'.[77]

She inevitably appeared among the names of *ospedale* musicians given in Coronelli's *Guida de' forestieri*. In the 1700 edition the section on noteworthy *figlie di coro* runs:

The [singers and instrumentalists] among the *figlie* of the four *ospedali* are very celebrated. Cecilia, Apollonia, and Coccina sing with much acclaim at the Incurabili; likewise, Vienna, Cecilia, Antonina, and la Turchetta at the Mendicanti, where Barbara plays the organ and the oboe very well; at the Ospedaletto la Vicentina is famed for her singing; at the Pietà Barbara la Jamosa, for her playing of the archlute.[78]

The same entry for Albieri occurs in subsequent editions up to at least 1713. In the edition for that year some of the surrounding material has been changed, which suggests that if revision in the case of la Vicentina had been needed—if, say, she had retired, died, or left the institution—this, too, would have been carried out. However, with the *Guida de forestieri* one can never tell: even in the 1724 edition Vinaccesi, dead for more than four years, is still named as *maestro di coro* at the Ospedaletto. If she was the normal age (6–10) when admitted, Albieri would have been in her fifties in the 1710s, therefore probably approaching the end of her career as a soloist.

So it seems that Vinaccesi's departure in 1715 marked the end of a distinct and not inglorious chapter in the history of the Ospedaletto—an

[74] Selfridge-Field, *Pallade veneta*, 155–6.
[75] Ibid. 172–3. Selfridge-Field also reproduces (p. 357) the text of an adulatory sonnet in Venetian dialect addressed to la Vicentina by Bartolomeo Dotti, whose imagery makes the most of the 'angelic' connections of her first name.
[76] Frederik Weilbach, *Frederik IV's italiensrejser* (Copenhagen, 1933), 22.
[77] François Maximilien Misson, *A New Voyage to Italy* (London, 1695), i. 191–2. Misson's journey was made in 1688.
[78] Coronelli, *Guida de forestieri* . . . (Venice, 1700), 27. See App. B.18.

episode dominated by a single singer of uncommon talent who shouldered almost the entire burden of maintaining its musical reputation. He may have secretly envied her fame, so much more conspicuous than his, but in practical terms she was undoubtedly a godsend to him.

4

Benedetto Vinaccesi

The Venetian Years, ii. San Marco

IT would be remarkable if Vinaccesi did not already entertain at the time of his appointment to the Ospedaletto, if not even prior to his application for that post, the idea of one day joining the *cappella* of the ducal church (unofficially, the 'basilica') of San Marco. He would have been aware of the success of Carlo Francesco Pollarolo, who after leaving Brescia, as we saw, in 1689, obtained the post of second principal organist at San Marco in 1690 and two years later was promoted to *vice-maestro*. Pollarolo, too, held the post of *maestro di coro* at one of the *ospedali*, the Incurabili, though it remains uncertain whether this appointment preceded or followed those that he held at the basilica.[1]

While waiting for his chance to fill a senior musical post at San Marco—there was obviously no question, given his social origin and the distinction of his post at the Ospedaletto, of his joining the rank and file—Vinaccesi tried his luck at opera. He harboured, it seems, no particular inclination towards the musical theatre, which he may well have despised for its subservience to public taste and the whims of singers. Nor did he ever betray the slightest interest in operatic management, a sphere of activity that many musicians willingly embraced. However, there was no way in which, given his ambition, he could remain in Venice and ignore operatic composition completely. To have done so would have suggested one of two things, both unhelpful to his career aspirations: either that he had principled objections to the operatic genre or that he doubted his ability to achieve success in it. Although Venetian operatic life was dominated around 1700 by a handful of composers (Pollarolo was now among them), they were far from establishing a 'closed shop'. The six theatres that regularly presented opera clamoured for new works, giving frequent opportunities to musicians of even quite humble standing, such as singing teachers, organists, or violinists, to receive commissions for scores. The appointment of Vinaccesi, an outsider, to the Ospedaletto in

---

[1] Reference works concur in describing Pollarolo as being in post 'by' 1696. Alone of the *ospedali*, the Incurabili has no surviving minute-books or collections of papers relating to this period that would enable the date of such appointments to be ascertained more precisely.

1698 must have made the Venetian public curious to learn more about his talent as a composer outside the confines of church music.

He had hardly been given time to put down roots in Venice before he was invited to provide the music for the first carnival opera at the theatre of San Salvatore. This theatre, named in conventional fashion after the parish in which it was situated, was the property of the Vendramino family, who leased it season by season to an impresario willing to take the financial risk in the hope of making a profit.[2] In Venice a carnival season ran from St Stephen's day (26 December) to the evening of Shrove Tuesday, thus normally for between seven and eleven weeks. It was preceded, in some opera-houses, by an autumn season beginning in early October and ending in mid-December (a decree of the Council of Ten in 1699 made the closure of all theatres during the Novena of Christmas compulsory).[3] During the carnival season it was normal to present two operas one after the other (not in alternation, as was the practice on the London stage at this time). Since the number of visitors to Venice reached its highest point some way into the new year, and since, also, the company of singers engaged for the season could be expected, given the hectic conditions, to be better prepared for the second opera than the first, the latter was by convention the less prestigious commission, hence the one more likely to be offered to a novice composer. Both the autumn opera of 1698 and the two carnival operas of 1699 (counting the period 26–31 December as part of the following year) at San Salvatore introduced new composers to the Venetian stage: the autumn work was Giovanni Bononcini's highly successful *Camilla, regina de' Volsci*, first produced in Naples at the end of 1696; the first carnival opera was Vinaccesi's *L'innocenza giustificata*; the second carnival opera was Giuseppe Aldrovandini's *La fortezza al cimento*, a new work by an established composer who had achieved success with his operas in his native Bologna and elsewhere.

The librettist for the operas of both Vinaccesi and Aldrovandini was Francesco Silvani, a Venetian secular priest who between 1682 and 1716 provided 38 librettos for the opera-houses of his native city. Silvani's merits as a dramatic poet were a matter for dispute, as we shall see in

---

[2] A collection of accounts relating to the San Salvatore theatre during the period 1703–25 is preserved in *I-Vmc*, P. D. C1409/4. While these confirm that the brothers Andrea (b. 1657) and Alvise (b. 1668) Vendramino entrusted the management of their theatre to independent impresarios, most of the information in this source is of only marginal interest to students of opera, since after 1700 San Salvatore was used almost exclusively for spoken comedy.

[3] Whereas spoken comedy played at Venetian theatre from early Oct. onwards, the start of the operatic autumn season was usually delayed until mid-Nov., when the Venetian nobility had returned from its second *villeggiatura* (vacation) on the mainland. No more than one opera was normally programmed for this season, which was commonly regarded as a 'run-up' to carnival. For all administrative purposes, autumn and carnival formed in effect a single season, since the personnel (impresario, singers, scenery-painters, etc.) engaged for the first were usually retained for the second.

Chapter 8, but by 1699 he was already a prominent literary figure with whom it was undoubtedly advantageous to collaborate. In the foreword of the libretto to *L'innocenza giustificata* Silvani pays the customary tribute to his musical partner: 'turning to you, generous reader, I ask for a benign indulgence towards these poor verses of mine, brought to life by the remarkable talent of Sig. Cavaliere Benedetto Vinacese, who, on this first occasion that his notes have graced the Venetian stage, has given you ample proof of his profound understanding [of the operatic genre] and the fertility of his imagination' ('e rivoltomi à te, Lettore Generoso, ti prego onorare del tuo benigno compatimento queste povere mie rime, che ritroverai animate dalla Virtù singolare del. Sig. K. Benedetto Vinacese, che in questa sua prima uscita sovra le Venete Scene con le sue note, ti da un gran saggio del suo profondo intendimento, e della fertile bizarria delle sue Idee').[4]

There is little doubt that Vinaccesi achieved at the very least a respectable success with his first opera. It was revived, wholly or largely with his original music, at the Teatro del Falcone, Genoa, in autumn 1699 (under the new title of *Carlo, re d'Allemagna*), at the court theatre of Mantua in carnival 1700, and in Crema, near Cremona, in 1701.[5] Much of Vinaccesi's music, especially the recitative, may have been retained for a production at the Teatro Ducale, Milan, in 1711. From 1712 onwards the librettos for productions of Silvani's drama, which now goes under an ever-increasing number of alternative titles (in addition to the two already mentioned, we encounter *L'innocenza difesa*, *La Giuditta di Baviera*, *Carlo il calvo*, *Carlo calvo*, and *Feraspe*), identify as the composer a succession of other persons (Giuseppe Orlandini, Luca Antonio Predieri, Stefano Andrea Fiorè, Alessandro Scarlatti, Fortunato Chelleri, Conrad Friedrich Hurlebusch, Nicola Porpora, and Antonio Vivaldi); it is probable that most of these men produced substantially new settings of the libretto (allowing, of course, for the *bricolage* endemic in Italian baroque opera).[6]

Since the libretto of 1699 contains no cast-list (this feature becomes general in Venetian opera librettos only after about 1700), the means by

---

[4] The preface ('Benignissimo, e Giustissimo Lettore') occupies pp. 11–14 of the libretto; the reference to Vinaccesi occurs on p. 14.

[5] The nature of a production of the opera (as *Carlo, re d'Allemagna*) in Florence at the Teatro del Cocomero in Jan. 1700 has yet to be determined. The likelihood is that it represents an offshoot of the same performance tradition as the productions in Genoa, Crema, and Mantua, but was somewhat modified to suit local taste. In Robert L. and Norma W. Weaver, *A Chronology of Music in the Florentine Theater 1590–1750: Opera, Prologues, Finales, Intermezzos and Plays with Incidental Music* (Detroit, 1978), 186–7, the librettist is identified in error as Giacomo Maggi (the person who signed the dedication of the libretto of the Genoese production, probably as impresario). The usefulness of the discussion of the opera by Weaver and Weaver is limited by the fact that the authors do not equate *Carlo, re d'Allemagna* with *L'innocenza giustificata*.

[6] Silvani's libretto and its settings are discussed in greater detail in Ch. 8. See also App. C.4, which tabulates the productions of operas based on it between the years 1699 and 1740.

which Vinaccesi's first opera achieved diffusion must remain conjectural. One suspects, however, that the singer Ubaldesca Salvi Sironi, whose nickname was 'La Pisanina', had a key role. By at least 1698 she had entered the service of the duke of Mantua; in that year she wrote the dedication for the librettos of two operas performed in Cremona, *L'Enone gelosa* and *L'idea del valore e della costanza*, which suggests that she acted on occasion as an impresario.[7] The librettos for the productions in Mantua (1700) and Crema (1701) of *L'innocenza giustificata* were signed by a certain Giacomo Sironi, whom one takes to be Ubaldesca's husband (Salvi being her maiden name), perhaps serving as her surrogate. The libretto for the Milan production of 1711 suggests that the Sironis were also involved with the revival of the opera in Genoa (1699), since one of its aria texts is found only in the Genoese libretto of 1699 (another exists only in the Mantuan libretto of 1700, while a further two numbers go back directly to the Venetian libretto of 1699).[8] Although one might conclude from this that the Milanese libretto was a compilation from all three earlier printed versions, a more likely explanation is that all the early productions of *L'innocenza giustificata* belonged to a single performance tradition based on a common stock of performance material. What is implied by this description is that when adjustments to the literary text or the music were made in response to the needs of a specific production, the new versions were retained afterwards for possible use on another occasion but—and this is the important point—did not supersede the earlier versions definitively.[9] If this analysis is correct, the chances are high that the Sironis were also involved with the original Venetian production and that in Genoa. The pattern of interconnections observable in the early librettos also provides justification for the claim made earlier that Vinaccesi's music continued to be used up to 1711 (no libretto other than the first cites his name).

A chance reference in a letter establishes, at least, that this was the music used for the production in Mantua. Ubaldesca Sironi's connection with the court of Ferdinando Carlo II has already been noted. After carnival 1699, as subsequent librettos attest, Silvani, too, was made a *servitore*

---

[7] Ubaldesca Sironi also dedicated two librettos for the anonymous opera *L'Elvira regnante* (Cremona, Teatro Aliberti, carnival 1697, and Vicenza, Nuovo Teatro di Piazza, carnival 1699). Her involvement, here and in *L'innocenza giustificata*, in successive productions of the same opera suggests strongly that she was the 'guardian' of the performance material, another pointer to her role as impresario.

[8] The numbers in question are 'Non sempre è dolce' (Gilade—Genoa: II, 15; Milan: II, 11), 'Su, guerrieri, a l'alta impresa' (Berardo—Mantua: II, 15; Milan: II, 13), 'Convien legarti' (Gilade—Venice: III, 8; Milan: III, 8), and 'Al seren di sì bel giorno' (*a 6*—Venice: III, 10: Mantua: III, 10).

[9] Vivaldi's autograph scores in the Biblioteca Nazionale, Turin, show not only how ready the composer was to make cuts, additions, and substitutions but also how much care he took to enable a future user to revert to the unamended text if circumstances demanded this. Composers and poets did not confuse change with improvement.

of the duke, who is known to have visited Venice during that season and must have attended the opera at San Salvatore.[10] Mantua was therefore a logical destination for Silvani's new drama.

The letter in question was sent by Stefano Frilli, a singer in the service of the grand princess of Tuscany, to Giacomo Antonio Perti in Bologna. It is dated 29 December 1699, at Mantua. The relevant passage runs:

The work to be performed is *La Giuditta*, produced last year at San Luca [the alternative name of the San Salvatore theatre] with music by *Cavaliere* Vinaccese; if this does not succeed in driving away his [presumably the duke's] melancholy, I hope, at least, that it will not be found displeasing. The dress rehearsal is tomorrow evening.[11]

Vinaccesi's next opera is surrounded by an element of mystery. We learn of it from a letter sent by the composer to Georg Friedrich, the margrave of Brandenburg-Ansbach, in October 1702. One gathers that this was a covering letter accompanying a score of the 'drama pastorale' to which the composer refers. The letter is written in a calligraphic hand that is not the composer's own.

Most Serene Highness,

The august mind of princes has always been seen to incline towards artistic accomplishment; emboldened by this thought, I have presumed to set before Your Most Serene Highness this very feeble product of my pen, which I composed with no other object than that it might serve to entertain you, now that it has pleased you to rest for a while from your martial exertions, with which you are filling your exalted name with glory. I know that the flight that I am attempting is hazardous, but I know too that the mind of Your Highness is familiar with the sounds not only of military trumpets but also of the instruments of Apollo, and that you encourage and protect swords and pens with equal magnanimity like a true Maecenas of the arts. My idea was to cast this pastoral drama in a light vein and make as few demands as possible regarding the number of characters and stage sets, so that at your least command it will be able to appear with ease before Your Most Serene Highness's eyes and give you delight. To ask you to look on it with favour would be too great an insult to the gracious clemency of Your Highness, who, as a hero in the service of glory, sees in the minuteness of the offering only the immensity of the heart of the offerer, who, if he does not bring as much as he ought, at least gives as much as he can. In presenting to Your Most Serene Highness this imperfect product of my invention, I am

[10] Ferdinando Carlo's frequent visits to Venice are recorded in Harris S. Saunders, 'The Repertoire of a Venetian Opera House (1678—1714): The Teatro Grimani di San Giovanni Grisostomo', Ph.D. diss. (Harvard University, 1989), 16. Remarkably, Silvani retained his position under Prince Philip of Hesse-Darmstadt, the governor installed by the Austrians after the duke's expulsion.

[11] *I-Bc*, P.145.19. I am grateful to Carlo Vitali for bringing the letter to my attention. The extract is transcribed in App. B.19. In the Mantuan production Frilli took the part of the *primo uomo* Berardo.

respectfully presenting my whole self in most profound veneration, in order to be able to receive from your supreme generosity the right to style myself

Your Highness's

Venice, 6 October 1702

> Most humble, devoted, compliant, and respectful servant
> Benedetto Vinaccesi[12]

Margrave Georg Friedrich was a most suitable recipient for a short Italian opera. He had succeeded to his title at the age of only 16 in 1694. Like many German courts of the time, that of Ansbach was open to both French and Italian, besides native German, artistic influence.[13] The accession of Georg Friedrich saw a significant tilt towards Italian musical culture. In 1696 the celebrated Bolognese singer and composer Francesco Antonio Pistocchi was made Kapellmeister. He was soon joined by another Bolognese luminary, Giuseppe Torelli, who was appointed leader of the orchestra. Between 1697 and 1700 Pistocchi composed two operas and a serenata for the court theatre, but from 1701 onwards the frequent absence of the margrave on military campaigns—he fought on the side of the emperor against the Bavarians and French—seriously disrupted musical life. Pistocchi and Torelli themselves left Ansbach during this uncertain period. The margrave's return to Ansbach between campaigns in 1702 is what Vinaccesi describes as his 'rest from military exertions'.

The composer's letter makes it clear that the pastoral opera was no commissioned work but one submitted speculatively; the last sentence hints at Vinaccesi's desire to receive an official appointment, perhaps as a non-resident court composer. It is possible that Vinaccesi had already met Georg Friedrich in Venice, for few were the high-ranking nobles of northern Europe who did not—particularly when young—pay visits to the capital of pleasure. Another prior connection is suggested (but no more) by the presence of Stefano Frilli in the cast-list of Pistocchi's pastoral opera *Narciso* (Ansbach, March 1697); because of their wide travels, operatic singers were excellent informants and intermediaries.

The description in the letter of the main features of Vinaccesi's opera makes one wonder whether it is identical with the pastoral opera *Chi è causa del suo mal pianga sé stesso* performed, as we saw, in Rome at the Ottoboni court in 1697.[14] In the first place, it would be unlikely, though of course not impossible, that Vinaccesi wrote more than one pastoral opera, given the comparative rarity of the subgenre. Then the composer's

---

[12] This letter is preserved in Staatsarchiv Nürnberg, Geheimregistratur Bamberger Zugang, Rep. 103a III Nr. 111. I am grateful to Norbert Dubowy for bringing it to my attention. It is transcribed as App. B.20.

[13] A short account of musical life at Ansbach under George Friedrich is contained in Günther Schmidt, *Die Musik am Hofe der Markgrafen von Brandenburg-Ansbach* (Kassel, 1956), 67–72.

[14] See the discussion of this work in Ch. 2.

emphasis on the small number of singing parts fits the Paris score, which calls for only four singers, uncommonly well. This score seems, at any rate, to be of north European origin, to judge from the paper (large in dimensions and without a visible watermark), the style of musical hand-writing, and, especially, the many mistakes in the underlaid text, which leave one in no doubt that the scribe was more familiar with French than with Italian.[15] French must certainly have been a language much employed in their daily life by members of the Ansbach court (not for nothing did the Italians habitually style Germans 'Monsù'!). If Vinaccesi sent the autograph score of *Chi è causa del suo mal pianga sé stesso* to Ansbach, the Paris score could have been a primary (i.e. first-generation) copy, whereas to have been based on the Roman performance, it would presumably have had to take as its exemplar an Italian primary copy that somehow found its way North of the Alps—a more complicated and thus less likely scenario.

Whether the opera, whatever its identity, was actually staged at Ansbach must remain in doubt, since no record of a performance survives. The margrave took to the field again in early 1703 and was killed near Regensburg on 29 March—an event that naturally put paid to any hopes of a court appointment that Vinaccesi may have entertained. Yet if we are right to discount a direct connection with the Roman performance of 1697, the character of the Paris score suggests strongly that the work it contains was at least considered for staging, for it is a calligraphic, appar-ently professional, copy that would not have been made without a definite end in mind: if it is not material for a projected performance, it must be the souvenir of one that had previously taken place. But if Vinaccesi knew that, following Georg Friedrich's death, the chances of a performance of the opera at Ansbach were small, there would have been nothing to pre-vent him from sending the same work elsewhere—even to France itself, where the cult of Italian music was already beginning to spread beyond small circles of enthusiasts. One has to admit that in the final analysis, the relationship between *Chi è causa del suo mal pianga sé stesso* and the Ansbach project remains tantalizingly elusive.

Shortly after despatching his pastoral opera to Ansbach, Vinaccesi must have started work on his second—in the event, his last—opera for Venice. This was *Gli amanti generosi*, on a text by Giovanni Pietro Candi, which opened at the little theatre of Sant'Angelo on 5 January 1703.[16] The librettist was a citizen of Padua who, in comparison with Silvani, wrote dramatic poetry only infrequently.[17] Like San Salvatore, the Sant'Angelo

---

[15] One symptom of this linguistic confusion is the occasional rendering of the hard C sound by 'qu' instead of 'c' or 'ch'.   [16] Selfridge-Field, *Pallade veneta*, 162.

[17] Candi's four known opera librettos are: *La forza delle passioni* (Padua, Teatro Obizzi, summer 1696); *Gli amanti generosi* (Venice, Sant'Angelo, carnival 1703 and, as *Idaspe*, Venice, San Giovanni

theatre, which was the joint property of the Marcello and Cappello families, was run on a commercial basis by impresarios. As before, Vinaccesi found himself sandwiched between the more experienced composers of the autumn and second carnival operas (Antonio and Carlo Francesco Pollarolo respectively).

From Candi's preface ('Generoso Lettore') one gathers that Vinaccesi was a rather reluctant participant in the enterprise. The paragraph in which the poet acts, no doubt by prior agreement, as a mouthpiece for his collaborator is, *faute de mieux*, the clearest statement of Vinaccesi's artistic outlook that we possess.

For his part, the *Signor Maestro* wishes to state that he undertook the composition of the music for this drama only in order to comply with a request from the directors of the theatre that he was unable to refuse, notwithstanding his firm intention to write no more music for operas; he lets it be known, further, that in many arias he has followed the taste of the public rather than his own inclination.[18]

Perhaps Vinaccesi let his underlying antipathy to opera show too clearly in this work, for it was never revived, and no arias from it are known to have been copied out for collectors. The libretto can hardly have been at fault, since in 1705 it was set again for Naples by Francesco Mancini. In 1710 Mancini's score travelled to London, becoming, under the new title of *Idaspe fedele*, the fourth Italian opera to be produced at the Queen's Theatre. In 1730, as *Idaspe*, it finally returned to Venice in a new setting by Riccardo Broschi, the brother of the famous castrato Farinelli.

Although 1703 marks the end of Vinaccesi's short flirtation with opera, he retained an involvement with secular vocal music, at least for a short while, through his solo cantatas and dramatic cantatas (serenatas) for several voices. We read in the *Pallade veneta* for 2 and 9 September 1702 of a serenata to words by Silvani performed on 3 September in the newly erected clubhouse (*casino*) of a society of nobles situated on the Fondamente Nuove behind the riding-school (*cavallerizza*).[19] The two singers were Francesco De Grandis and Tomaso Fabris, both noted soloists, and it is interesting to see how the writer of the report seems to view the whole occasion mainly as a contest of skill (*virtuosa gara*) between them. With an optimism typical of this news-sheet he observes that a downpour which had occurred two hours before the start of the performance was an attempt by the deities represented in the serenata (allegorical and mythological characters are favoured by this genre) to clear the air. In reality, the rain was probably a great inconvenience, since

Grisostomo, carnival 1730); *Il tradimento premiato* (Venice, Sant'Angelo, autumn 1709), *L'inimico generoso* (Bologna, Teatro Malvezzi, carnival 1709).

[18] The preface occupies pp. 5–6 of the libretto. Extract transcribed as App. B.21.

[19] Selfridge-Field, *Pallade veneta*, 241–2.

when serenatas were given in Venice, situated in a lagoon and criss-crossed with canals, it was normal to place either the performers or their audience in the open on the water.

In 1704, shortly after his appointment to San Marco, Vinaccesi joined the small number of Venetian composers who had an opportunity to supply music for serenatas sponsored by members of the foreign diplomatic community. Because of Venice's strict laws prohibiting social contact between members of her government (i.e. the entire patriciate and non-noble members of her civil service) foreign diplomats in Venice led a very enclosed existence, relying mainly on each other for company. They sustained, in miniature, a 'courtly' mode of life similar to that practised in most states but absent from their host community. One kind of event that an ambassador was obliged to celebrate with a *festa*, into which a serenata might appropriately be inserted, was a birth occurring in the family of his sovereign. On 21 July 1704 the French ambassador Joseph-Antoine Hennequin, Seigneur de Charmont, threw open his *palazzo* to mark the birth of Louis, duke of Brittany (1704–10), who was the first child born to the duke of Burgundy, Louis XIV's grandson, and thus a possible future king. The *festa* included a serenata for four voices, *Sfoghi di giubilo* (Outbursts of Joy), for which Pietro (an Italianized version of Pierre?) Robert, the ambassador's secretary, wrote the words, and Vinaccesi the music.[20] The four allegorical characters in the serenata were La Gloria, La Virtù, La Fede Pubblica, and Il Genio della Francia; their parts were sung by Tomaso Fabris, Stefano Romano, Catterina Inverardi, and Maddalena Giustiniani.

This work was mentioned by Caffi, who claimed that the music was subsequently sent to Paris and performed at court there and that it earned Vinaccesi his title of *cavaliere*.[21] Although it is logically possible for our composer to have had the same title bestowed on him at different times by different courts, it seems a far-fetched idea. As we shall see below, this author fell victim to slips with great ease; in addition, he had an unfortunate propensity to draw elaborate (and, too frequently, erroneous) inferences from simple facts. That *Sfoghi di giubilo* reached Paris is less implausible, especially since ambassador Hennequin was recalled later in 1704, but here again one suspects embroidery. Elsewhere, Caffi makes exactly the same claim about the serenata, *Il concilio de' pianeti*, written by Albinoni for the birth of the dauphin in 1729—namely that it was performed in Paris after its première at the residence of the French ambassador to Venice—and again no supporting evidence has been found.[22]

---

[20] The libretto is preserved in *I-Vnm*, Misc. 3420.35.
[21] Caffi, *Storia della musica sacra*, i. 359–60.
[22] Id., 'Storia della musica teatrale in Venezia' (MS notes), *I-Vnm*, Cod. it. IV–747/4 (= 10465), fo. 39ʳ.

In his book on Brescian musicians Andrea Valentini reproduced the information given by Caffi very inexactly.[23] For instance, the duke of Brittany was made the son instead of the great-grandson of Louis XIV, and the monarch himself became king of France and Novara instead of France and Navarre. Valentini's most serious slip, however, was to give the serenata the title *Gli sponsali di giubilo* (The Wedding of Rejoicing), for many subsequent writers have taken this to be a separate composition and listed it accordingly. The *New Grove* even suppresses *Sfoghi di giubilo* in favour of this phantom work.

The *Essai sur la musique ancienne et moderne* of Jean Benjamin La Borde, whose note on Vinaccesi is extremely complimentary ('un des plus grands Maîtres de son tems . . . il a joui dune brillante réputation'), suggests that he was a composer particularly in demand for occasional music ('c'était à lui qu'on avait recours dans les occasions importantes').[24] Most likely, this is another piece of embroidery, though one should not forget that La Borde (1734–94) was born early enough to have had the chance to meet persons acquainted with the composer during his lifetime and so to receive information not transmitted via any written record. But the fact remains that no serenata or other occasional work by Vinaccesi later than 1704 is recorded, and the simplest conclusion is perhaps the correct one.

Vinaccesi's first opportunity to advance his career as a church musician arrived in February 1702, when he competed for the post of *primo maestro* at San Marco. It may seem a little odd that he should have applied out of the blue for the senior musical post at the basilica, but this happened to be the first suitable vacancy that occurred, his choice being limited, effectively, to the positions of *primo maestro*, *vice-maestro* (also called *secondo maestro*), and first and second organist. Doubtless, he entertained few illusions about the likelihood of his success but was determined to set down a 'marker' for the future. To understand the situation at San Marco in all its complexity, it is necessary to examine the inner workings of the ducal church and the organ of state, the Procuratia de Supra, that governed it.[25]

Of all the Venetian State magistracies, that of the procurators of St Mark (*procuratori di San Marco*) had the highest standing after the doge's inner cabinet, the *serenissima signoria*. Indeed, this office was more highly coveted than any other save the dogeship, since, like the latter (for which it customarily served as a preparation), it was held for life, whereas membership of the *signoria*, as of all other magistracies, lasted for only a fixed period. To become a procurator of St Mark, a patrician had to have a dis-

[23] Valentini, *I musicisti bresciani ed il Teatro Grande* (Brescia, 1894), 108.

[24] Jean Benjamin de La Borde, *Essai sur la musique ancienne et moderne* (Paris, 1780), ii. 242.

[25] 'Procuratia de Supra' is the Venetian dialectal form preferred in official documents; the Italian (Tuscan) equivalent is 'Procuratoria di Sopra'.

tinguished record of service to the State as a provincial governor, ambassador, or similar high-ranking official.

The magistracy had been created in the ninth century after the theft from Alexandria of the reputed relics of St Mark and the building of the basilica named after him. It had three divisions: the Procuratia de Supra, responsible for the administration and maintenance of the ducal church and its treasure, the State archives and library (the aptly named Biblioteca Marciana), and the adjacent Piazza and Piazzetta; the Procuratia de Citra, concerned with the administration of wills and legacies pertaining to the near side of the Grand Canal; and the Procuratia de Ultra, which carried out a similar function for the far side of the Grand Canal. Each procuracy had three statutory members (*procuratori ordinari*) elected by the Senate when a vacancy arose; these had the right to occupy the nine magnificent apartments in the Procuratie Nuove running along the South side of the Piazza (where, today, the Museo Civico Correr is housed). Then there was a variable number of supernumerary members (*procuratori estraordinari*) elected from time to time by the Senate either on account of their merit alone (*per merito*) or in recognition of their gift of at least 20,500 ducats to the State (*per denaro*).[26] The supernumerary procurators easily outnumbered the statutory ones; in 1672 they totalled twenty-six.[27] For administrative purposes, their existence was a boon, since with their participation the three procuracies each had enough members—upwards of a dozen—to form a governing board of sufficient size.

The Procuratia de Supra, whose business meetings were held, generally on Sundays, throughout the year (excluding the two *villeggiatura* periods), had responsibility for over two hundred employees. Just over twenty of them were concerned with central administration and the responsibilities of the procuracy lying outside the ducal church itself (see the table in Appendix C.5). The organizational ladder descended from the pair of highly paid chief administrators (*gastaldi*), one overseeing day-to-day finances of the church and the other managing legacies, to the lowly refuse-remover and dog-shooer. As always seems to be the case in such hierarchies, the most highly paid posts were also the ones most generously endowed with perquisites, one example being the annual Christmas bonus shown in the table.

The bulk of the employees, however, were attached to the ducal

---

[26] Sometimes the 'merit' belonged not to the recipient of the honour himself but to another member of his family, as in 1689, when Antonio Ottoboni was made a procurator of St Mark and a *cavaliere* immediately after his uncle Pietro became pope as Alexander VIII. A complete list of procurators of each type appointed up to 1752 appears in [Giovanni Meschinello], *La chiesa ducale di S. Marco* (Venice, 1753–4), ii. 81–119. Meschinello's 3-vol. work, apparently little consulted by music historians, is a mine of information on the history, physical structure, and hierarchy of the basilica.

[27] This figure comes from Alexandre Toussaint Limojon de Saint-Didier, *La Ville et la république de Venise* (Paris, 1680), 162, quoted in Selfridge-Field, *Pallade veneta*, 330.

church, whose members are tabulated in Appendix C.6. Of the established posts, 94 were for clergy, 74 for musicians, and 11 or more for support staff (teachers of the choristers, churchwardens, etc.). The clergy were headed by the *primicerio*, who as head of the diocese of Venice enjoyed the privileges of a bishop. The tier immediately below him comprised a master of the choristers (called *maestro di coro* or *maestro di cerimonie*), 2 sacristans, and 24 canons (of whom 14 were honorary, since they held posts elsewhere in Venice). At the base of the clerical hierarchy came the 24 junior choristers (*chierici* or *zaghi*), in training at the ducal seminary, the Seminario Gregoriano, at Sant'Antonio di Castello, and the 30 *giovani di coro* into whose ranks they hoped to climb when fully qualified. It was these choristers who, together with the stipendiary canons, were responsible for the singing of plainsong in the basilica, in which they were instructed by a *maestro di canto*.

During the period under discussion the musical establishment comprised, besides the four senior positions mentioned earlier, 36 singers and 34 instrumentalists.[28] However, although the notional number of *cappella* members in each division was fixed, their disposition according to voice-type or instrument was not. This allowed the *primo maestro*, subject to the approval of the procurators, to modify the composition of the *cappella* in response to its needs and, more especially, changes in style and taste that affected its musical repertory. One serious obstacle to change persisted, however. A position in the *cappella ducale* was a 'job for life', barring a serious misdemeanour or incapacity through illness (in which case a musician would be likely to be granted retirement on a generous pension). This meant that, in theory at least, the restructuring of the *cappella* could proceed no faster than the rate of 'natural wastage' permitted. The only times when a sweeping rather than incremental change could be implemented were when the membership of the *cappella* was allowed to rise above the norm or, conversely, when it was allowed to sink below the norm through a temporary 'freeze' on the filling of vacancies.

The table shown as Appendix C.7 illustrates this complex situation. In 1685 the newly appointed *primo maestro*, Giovanni Legrenzi, obtained the approval of the procurators for a model orchestra.[29] It included 'choirs' of strings and brass (assigning the cornetts to the last category), besides the inevitable theorboes for the continuo line and the traditional bassoon, one of whose tasks was to give the note for tuning. One is struck by the preponderance of violas (11) over violins (8). This reflects the characteristic

---

[28] These totals remained unchanged until the approval in 1765–6 of Galuppi's plan, which provided for the reduction of the singers to 24 (with 6 per part) and the instrumentalists to 35 (12 violins, 6 violas, 4 cellos, 5 double-basses, 4 flutes doubling oboes, 4 horns doubling trumpets).

[29] *I-Vas*, Procuratia de Supra (hereafter PdS), Registro 147, Decreti e Terminazioni 1675–90, fo. 209ᵛ (21 May 1685).

form of scoring for strings in the late seventeenth century, when the violas were often divided into two (*alto viola* and *tenore viola*), sometimes even three (with *canto viola*), parts. Legrenzi's layout allows both the strings and the five-part choir of cornetts and trombones either to double the voices or to pursue a *concertato* dialogue with them on equal terms, which corresponds perfectly to the usage of the generation before Vivaldi.

The plan already foresaw no function for the existing harpist and implied a switch of emphasis away from disparate continuo instruments towards extra strings—in other words, towards a more 'orchestral' conception (in baroque terms) where richness of tone enjoyed a higher priority than variety of timbre. During the period 1685–90, in Legrenzi's eagerness to implement his plan, extra players were taken on without much regard for the occurrence of vacancies.[30] By 1690 the instrumentalists had climbed to a record number, 48, and the procurators intervened to stop the proliferation.[31] On 6 August 1690, the very day—significantly—on which they appointed a new *primo maestro*, Giovanni Battista Volpe, they instituted a freeze on new appointments, subject to carefully debated exceptions. During the period leading up to the next major review, in 1714, the policy generally held, although a major exception occurred in 1698, when an oboist, Onofrio Penati, joined the *cappella*. No doubt, there was considerable pressure to appoint a player of the newly fashionable oboe (which had first appeared in Venetian opera in 1692 and whose qualities the procurators had been able to appraise *in situ* in 1696, when Penati had been one of the supernumerary musicians engaged for the Christmas services of 1696); Penati's appointment was possibly eased by the fact that he became concurrently one of the doge's four *piffari*, wind-players employed for ceremonial purposes.[32]

In 1714 the *primo maestro* of the day, Antonino Biffi, was instructed to draw up a list of serving personnel, which survives.[33] Then on 13 May

---

[30] On p. 119 of her article 'The Viennese Court Orchestra in the Time of Caldara', in Brian Pritchard (ed.), *Antonio Caldara: Essays on his Life and Times* (Aldershot, 1987), 115–51, Eleanor Selfridge-Field has provided a valuable table giving membership statistics for the orchestra at San Marco from 1679 to 1720. The table needs to be interpreted with care, however, since it does not state at what point during each year the 'snapshot' is taken (several changes of personnel often occurred during the course of one year). There is often, too, some doubt about the date when musicians ceased to be members of the *cappella*. To illustrate: Giovanni Battista Vivaldi, the composer's father, was granted one year's leave in Sept. 1729, but there is no record either of his continued presence in the orchestra after his return (he died in 1736) or of his retirement or dismissal.

[31] The various decisions of the procurators regarding the *cappella* and recruitment to it in the period 1685–1714 are recapitulated in a memorandum entitled 'Relazione circa lo stato della capella di S. Marco' submitted by the *cassiere* (the procurator in charge of finance) on 13 Mar. 1714; it is copied into the minutes for that day in *I-Vas*, PdS, Registro 152, Decreti e terminazioni 1713–21, fo. 26.

[32] The duties of the *piffari* are set out in an undated document, 'Obbligazioni delli piffari', which lists 19 functions during the year in which they have to participate (Venice, private collection of Dr Girolamo Marcello, Cod. 167.17).

[33] *I-Vmc*, Ms. Gradenigo 173, Chiesa di San Marco, fo. 287ᵛ. The members of the *cappella* listed by Biffi appear again in a list of all the personnel attached to the ducal church in the same year (1714)

the procurators decided on the nature of the thirteen posts to be filled in order to bring the instrumentalists, whose number had sunk to twenty-one, up to the statutory strength. As a matter of principle, they resolved not to appoint any more players of the bassoon, the trombone, or the theorbo, all instruments that, in their words, were 'no longer in use' (although three of the *cappella*'s theorbists, two of its trombonists, and a cornettist, all appointed in the previous century, lingered on, secure in their posts). The addition of thirteen players on 9 December 1714 gave the orchestra the configuration shown in the second column of the table.[34] The orchestra now has a shape typical of the late Baroque. Violins (13) outnumber violas (7), a proportion reflecting the growing tendency to reduce the number of viola parts to one (*alto viola*), though one must also bear in mind that players could, and doubtless sometimes did, switch between the two instruments when the occasion demanded. The wind 'choir' is now defunct for practical purposes, leaving the trumpet and oboe to serve as occasional obbligato instruments.[35]

Little had changed by the end of 1720, when the composition of the orchestra was reviewed again, except that the last cornettist, a theorbist, and a trombonist had gone.[36] The eight vacancies filled by the procurators on 15 December all went to string players, the violas making up some of the ground lost to the violins in the previous review. It is interesting to see for the first time a numerical majority of double-basses over cellos, since this fondness for sixteen-foot tone, an Italian peculiarity, was to persist into the classical period and even beyond.[37] The same proportions in the bass section are found in a specification for the orchestra dating from around the middle of the eighteenth century; with its paired oboes (doubling flutes?) and trumpets (doubling horns?) and its single bassoon, this formula looks tailor-made for the early symphonic repertory.

The distribution of voices among the singers, albeit an essentially simpler question, proved equally difficult to manage over the same period. As their memorandum of 13 May 1714 states, the procurators made a decision on 23 April 1686 to have nine singers in each of the main vocal

prepared for an unknown purpose by Damiano Donati, the 'maestro delli chierici' (a synonym for *maestro di grammatica*), in 1774 (*I-Vmc*, Ms. Cicogna 801).

[34] *I-Vas*, PdS, Registro 152, fo. 30.

[35] The general structure of the San Marco orchestra in 1714 (discounting its 'superannuated' instruments) corresponds very closely, allowing for its greater number of strings, to that of the Ospedale della Pietà around the same time, for which Vivaldi wrote such works as his two settings of the Gloria (RV 588 and 589). Doubtless, the musical directors at the various institutions in Venice kept a very close eye on what their opposite numbers were doing—and all ultimately took their cue from public taste, which was heavily conditioned by what was heard in the opera-house.

[36] *I-Vas*, PdS, Busta 10, Decreti in originale 1716–20, Fascicolo 32 (1720).

[37] One cannot, of course, discount the possibility that cellists could also play double-bass and vice versa. The quoted figures make the assumption that, in accordance with normal Venetian usage around 1700, 'violone' refers exclusively to the contrabass instrument and not to the ordinary bass violin or an instrument of intermediate size.

ranges. On 1 August 1686, when they examined how the singers were made up, they discovered to their dismay that the proportions were very far from the desired state: the tenors numbered 13, the basses 10, the altos 7, and the sopranos only 6. In the period leading up to the review of 1714 they overdid the correction; Biffi's list contains 11 active sopranos, 10 tenors, 8 basses (including a baritone), but only 3 altos. The replacement of the dominance of the tenor voice by that of the soprano voice may in part have been a response to changes in choral practice (if, for example, divided tenor parts became less common than divided soprano parts), but one suspects that the preference of late baroque taste for high voices, expressed in operatic casting and the vocal specifications of solo cantatas and motets, was the root cause. We must remember that at San Marco none of the singers were boys: the sopranos and some of the altos were castratos, the remaining altos being falsettists. All of them therefore possessed as musicians the level of maturity and experience that would make them eligible for an operatic part, and several of them—above all, the sopranos—were indeed active in opera.[38] The numerical preponderance of sopranos may even have been intended as an insurance against depletion caused by absences during operatic seasons. It may be significant that when appointments to the four vacancies were made on 9 December 1714, the opportunity to bring the altos as close as posssible to the target figure of nine was not taken; one of the four singers elected was another soprano. At the time of the review in 1720 the proportions were still not quite right, but this time the procurators used the shortfall of six singers to produce, through their new appointments, a perfect symmetry.

Throughout this episode one detects a lack of grip on events by the procurators, which is symptomatic of their somewhat 'hands-off' approach. They were able to take good advice on musical questions from their *primo maestro*, to react swiftly to serious crises, and to follow the rule-book meticulously. What they were unable to do, however, was to monitor a situation effectively and assess how faithfully their policies were being implemented. To a much greater extent than the minute-books suggest, the *cappella* must have ordered its affairs in its own way, while the procurators chose not to look too closely.

This spirit of tolerant acquiescence seems also to have marked the disciplinary system at San Marco. As early as 1324 the Procuratia de Supra created the office of monitor (called *appuntador* after the points, 'punti', deducted for disciplinary offences).[39] This was one of several offices within the Procuratia de Supra whose holders were in a position to enjoy extra perquisites, and in consequence it had to be bought from the State

---

[38] The extraordinarily active participation by the singers of the basilica in opera (and not only in Venice itself) is documented and discussed in Termini, 'Singers at San Marco in Venice'.

[39] The *appuntador* (Tuscan: *appuntatore*) system was widespread in Italian *cappelle*.

in a competitive auction and was subject to a *decima* of 30 per cent. Assisted by two duty monitors, who served for two months and were responsible for the clerics and musicians respectively, the *appuntador* distributed his penalty points according to a strict tariff. The larger the salary (in 1700 that for a singer ranged from 25 to 100 ducats, that for an orchestral player from 15 to 50 ducats), the severer the penalty.[40] The most common infringements of discipline punished in this way were lateness at services and unauthorized absence. When salaries were paid, every two months, the appropriate deductions were made, and the *punti* were redistributed with a typically Venetian ingeniousness that gave small incentives to those who helped to maintain good discipline without tempting them too much to invent offences among their colleagues in order to reap the benefit: half the amount was shared out among those members of the *cappella* who had incurred no penalty points (described as 'i più diligenti'), a quarter went to the *appuntador* himself, and the remaining quarter reverted to the *cassa* of the procuracy.

On paper this looks an impressively efficient and equitable system. But when one examines individual cases of *cappella* members who are known to have had important outside interests that took them away from the ducal church, one sees that the rule-book was not always followed or that, at the very least, decisions were not recorded in the proper manner. G. B. Vivaldi, who often accompanied his asthmatic son on his travels, is a good case in point. On 23 November 1702 the *cassiere*, Antonio Ottoboni, authorized him to take leave for three months.[41] In theory, this was *ultra vires*: one day's absence required simply the permission of the *primo maestro*, an absence of up to one month that of the *cassiere*, but any longer absence the approval of the procurators as a whole. The minutes remain silent on the matter. Then Vivaldi senior failed to draw his pay on 30 June, 27 September, and 26 November 1718 (a proxy collected the arrears on his behalf on 13 January 1719); he also missed several further payments between 1720 and 1724.[42] The absences during 1718–20 are almost certainly connected with Antonio's presence in Mantua as director of secular music (*maestro di cappella da camera*), to the imperial governor, Prince Philip of Hesse-Darmstadt. Yet all these absences, too, seem to have needed not even the permission of the *cassiere*. One concludes that a lot of informal covering for absentees took place and that the formulaic precision

---

[40] The minimum salary for an instrumentalist (15 ducats) may seem very miserly, especially when one considers that in 1791, after many decades of only low inflation, a simple gondolier could earn ten times as much in a year (see Thomas Martyn, *A Tour through Italy: Containing Full Directions for Travelling in that Interesting Country* (London, 1791), p. xix), but one must take into account the essentially part-time nature of the job and the many opportunities to earn extra money through occasional engagements.

[41] *I-Vas*, PdS, Registri 211, Mandati e licenze 1694–1712, 23 Nov. 1702.

[42] *I-Vas*, PdS, Registri 40 and 41, Libri di scontro 1708–19 and 1719–27, *passim*.

and self-congratulatory sententiousness of the San Marco documents mask a much more relaxed human environment.

The attendance required from the musicians was laid down in fairly minute detail in prescriptive tables issued at intervals during the period 1517–1761. These have been transcribed and studied exhaustively by James Moore and need only be summarized here.[43] The heaviest demands were made on the singers, though in some cases the full complement was not required. In a memorandum of complaint submitted to the procurators in 1653 the spokesman for the singers calculated the number of services (*obbligazioni*) in a single year as 525, to which 80 extra obligations had been added since the plague of 1630.[44] The players had fewer obligations, since a proportion of the services were 'senza instrumenti'. It remains unclear whether the players participated in services described in the tables as 'a capella'. Whereas in modern usage *a cappella* denotes performance by unaccompanied voices, in the baroque period it referred to a style of performance without independent instrumental parts, leaving open the possibility of instrumental doubling. It is interesting to note that on six occasions during the year when the singers were not present (the sung portions of the service being taken by the choristers in plainchant) the instrumentalists were required to contribute a 'suonata dopo l'epistola' at Mass.

The duties of the two principal organists ('first' and 'second' organists as they were often called, depending on whether they performed at the larger or smaller instruments placed opposite one another in the apse) were different again. In principle, they had to be present at the same times as the singers, but there were numerous exceptions, particularly during Lent (when the use of instruments was mostly prohibited) and whenever the latter performed 'fuori coro'. This expression is difficult to interpret. Taken literally, it means 'outside the choir'. If by 'choir' the rubric refers to the part of the church East of the iconostasis (the roodscreen surmounted, Byzantine fashion, by icons)—in other words, the sanctuary—the area 'fuori coro' must include the *pergola* or *bigonzo*, the large octagonal platform (still standing) just beyond the inconostasis in the South transept.[45] This was precisely the location of the singers during

---

[43] *Vespers at St. Mark's: Music of Alessandro Grandi, Giovanni Rovetta and Francesco Cavalli* (2 vols., Ann Arbor, Mich., 1981), 282–308 and *passim*. Moore's brilliant study centres on the peculiar Marcian liturgy for Vespers and the repertory written for it in the early 17th cent. but provides a better general introduction to music at the basilica than any other single modern source. Its bibliography encompasses most of the vast secondary literature on San Marco and includes a very useful list of relevant primary sources.

[44] *I-Vmc*, Ms. Cicogna 3118/46–7.

[45] The *bigonzo*, filled with about a dozen singers, is illustrated in a pen-and-ink drawing by Canaletto made in 1766 and used as a cover-illustration for the present book. The importance of the *bigonzo* for the performance by unaccompanied voices of *salmi spezzati* (which, although polychoral, did not require the two *cori* to be separated spatially) is brought out in David Bryant, 'The *cori*

performances described as 'a capella'. The non-participation of the organs—at least, of the main organs—in performances where the choir was installed in the *bigonzo* makes good acoustic sense, since the co-ordination of musicians on opposite sides of the iconostasis would have been problematic. The organists had a handful of extra obligations on occasions that did not require the singers, and for the three Tenebrae services at the end of Holy Week the duty organist had to uphold the ban on the use of his normal instrument during Passiontide by exchanging it for the spinet. The saving grace for the organists was that during most of the year they served singly in alternate weeks. Both were required at the same time only when the rubrics specify 'con organi' (in the plural), which includes many, but not all, of the solemn occasions when the doge attended.

The basilica also employed, at the annual salary of 12 ducats, one or two auxiliary organists (sometimes called 'third' and 'fourth' organist respectively). Their status in the hierarchy was ambiguous. On one hand, they do not appear in lists of the establishment of the ducal church; in that respect, they have the status of 'casual' employees equivalent to the organ-tuner or the extra musicians brought in at Christmas. On the other hand, lists of musicians drawn up by the *primo maestro* take their membership of the *cappella* for granted. It seems that before 1645 their use was irregular. Between 1645 and 1720 both posts were regularly filled, but after Alvise Tavelli's promotion to the second principal organ in 1720 the 'fourth' post was discontinued for good.[46]

The auxiliary organists were required for those relatively few services described in the rubrics as 'con palchetti'. These *palchetti* were the two raised niches (often termed *nicchie* in documents) at the angle of the two sides of the sanctuary and the respective transepts.[47] The one on the South side overlooking the *bigonzo* is identified in documents as 'dalla

spezzati of St Mark's: Myth and Reality', in Iain Fenlon (ed.), *Early Music History, i. Studies in Medieval and Modern Music* (Cambridge, 1981), 165–86.

[46] In Biffi's list of Dec. 1720 both *organetti* were described as vacant, since the other auxiliary organist, Agostino Bonaventura Coletti, was absent from his post. At that very time a new instrument for the *palchetto* on the South side was being completed by the builder Felice de Beni, using 18 pipes from its predecessor. This was the organ to which Coletti returned and which was later inherited successively by Antonio Coletti (a younger relative acting as his substitute?), Giovanni Francesco Brusa, Angelo Cortona, Alessandro Maccari, and Carlo Faggi. In 1730 the *organetto* on the North side was scrapped. See *I-Vas*, PdS, Busta 78, Processo 183, Fascicolo 1, Organi di chiesa, quire 3, and Registro 153, Decreti e terminazioni 1721–35, fo. 126ᵛ (23 July 1730).

[47] Caffi and later writers seem to have assumed that the 'palchetti' were structures different from the 'nicchie', but the estimates tendered by the two organ-builders Felice de Beni and Ubaldo Corloni for the construction of the new *organetto* in 1720 (preserved in Busta 78, see n. 46, above) show that the terms were synonymous: Corloni writes of an 'organo nel palchetto', Beni of the second *organetto* 'dalla parte della Santissima Croce'. Given the advantages of the *nicchie*, with their openings on two sides, and their positioning at almost the same height as the main organs, it would have made no sense to relocate the portable organs. This equation of 'palchetto' and 'nicchia' needs to be borne in mind when rubrics such as 'con tutti gli organi, palchetti et instrumenti' are interpreted.

parte della Santissima Croce', its counterpart on the North side as 'dalla parte della Madonna'. The great virtue of these niches, which could each accommodate a portable organ and a few players or singers, was that they faced in two directions: through one opening into the sanctuary and through the other into the transepts and nave.[48] They were thus suitable for use on whichever side of the iconostasis the main body of musicians was performing.

As the rubrics make clear, the performers were asked to group themselves in many different ways according to the nature of the service and the forces involved. At least seven different possible 'zones' for the performers can be identified. First, there were the two choir-lofts surrounding each of the principal organs (these are the areas described in documents as 'negli organi'). Then there were a pair of extra galleries immediately below them, except that these were often occupied during the most solemn services by distinguished members of the congregation and so became unavailable.[49] Next, there were the two *palchetti*; an anonymous painting of 1690, which offers a view of the South side of the sanctuary during an elaborate function, shows a small gallery occupied by three singers and a theorbist underneath the *palchetto*, but it is unclear whether this is a permanent structure.[50] Finally, there was the capacious *bigonzo*. The traditional position of the *primo maestro* was in the North organ-loft by the larger main organ (presumably, the *vice-maestro* attended the second organ), but he, too, must have been mobile to some extent in order to give effective direction in every situation.

It was into this complex, self-absorbed institution that Vinaccesi ventured to step early in 1702. *Primo maestro* Giovanni Domenico Partenio had died on 18 February 1701 at the age of 67.[51] On this occasion the procurators, contrary to their normal habit, took their time over appointing a successor. They began by writing to Venetian ambassadors abroad, hoping for a suitable recommendation. Perhaps they sensed the lack of a truly strong internal candidate. When this produced no effect after nearly a year (whether because no ambassador could find anyone to recommend or because the men proposed were found wanting, the minute does not say), the procurators decided to advertise. The text of the advertisement itself has not survived, but it must have closely resembled, *mutatis*

---

[48] The organs in question possessed, like the two principal organs, only one manual, but they disposed of a smaller number of ranks and registers. The estimates from both Beni and Corloni assume the presence of four eight-foot ranks, each with 41 pipes. In the early 17th cent. the portability of one *organetto* was frequently put to the test, since it was an instrument borrowed for special occasions from the ducal seminary.

[49] Sandro Dalla Libera, *L'arte degli organi a Venezia* (Venice, 1962), 29.

[50] Reproduced in Moore, *Vespers at St. Mark's*, 108.

[51] Gastone Vio, 'I maestri di coro dei Mendicanti e la Cappella Marciana', in Maria Teresa Muraro and Franco Rossi (eds.), *Galuppiana 1985, studi e ricerche: Atti del Convegno internazionale (Venezia, 28–30 ottobre 1985)* (Florence, 1986), 95–111: 101 n.

mutandis, the one issued for the post of organist after Cavalli's promotion to *primo maestro* in 1668:

The Most Serene Prince [the doge] makes known by order of the Most Illustrious and Excellent Procurators of St Mark *de Supra*

that all those who intend to compete for the post of organist to the church of San Marco in place of Master Francesco Caletto called Cavalli, who has been elected *maestro* in the *cappella* of the same, have to appear in the procuracy belonging to their Excellencies [i.e. the Procuratie Nuove] and make written application, for they [the procurators] intend at their next meeting, in accordance with normal practice, to proceed to the election for the post of the said organist etc.

[posted on] the notice-board [literally, the stone] at San Marco
[and] the notice-board at the Rialto

1669 [1668 m.v.]: on 18 January this was published on the steps of San Marco and of the Rialto by me, Carlo Finesti, the *comandador* of the said procuracy[52]

Since the death of Monteverdi in 1643 all successful candidates for the post of *primo maestro* had been either serving *vice-maestri* or organists of the *cappella*—a pattern that was destined to continue all the way to the extinction of the republic (and the *cappella*) in 1797. It was only natural, therefore, that the two internal candidates were the holders of such posts. By good fortune, we possess today the letters of application submitted by both. It was not the custom of the procurators, perhaps mindful of the sensibilities of the losers, to have such letters copied into the minutes, but a few survive in the Venetian State Archive in its collection of 'Decreti in originale', the papers read out at their meetings.

The more obvious applicant of the two was Carlo Francesco Pollarolo, *vice-maestro* since 22 May 1692. Pollarolo had in fact put his name forward for the senior post a week before his election as *vice-maestro* but had withdrawn before a vote was taken, perhaps on the advice of backers among the procurators who persuaded him to keep his powder dry and settle for the lesser but more certain honour (though his letter claims a nobler motive). In the several months that had elapsed since Partenio's death Pollarolo had gained the opportunity to prove his worth as leader of the musicians, which perhaps explains why the letter makes only a fleeting reference to his abilities. He writes in his own hand, somewhat untidily, but his apparent artlessness conceals a certain cunning. By drawing attention to his length of service, to the fact that his predecessor served as *vice-maestro* prior to his elevation (a precedent was always a good argument at San Marco), and to his children (including a virtual promise of future service in the *cappella* by his son Antonio), Pollarolo proposes criteria that favour him uniquely. Even the seemingly overdone use of religious language towards the end has its purpose. As a layman, Pollarolo knew him-

---

[52] *I-Vas*, PdS, Busta 91, Processo 207, Organisti, fo. 45ʳ. Transcribed as App. B.22.

self to be at a disadvantage, for of Monteverdi's five successors up to 1702, only one, Cavalli, had not taken holy orders. He is therefore at pains to convince the procurators of the depth of his piety. As is normal in such letters, two words are rarely shunned when one would do.

Most Illustrious and Excellent Lord Procurators *de Supra* and Most Merciful Patrons,

Prostrate at the feet of Your Excellencies are the age, the toils, the family, and, may I say, the reputation of myself, Carlo Francesco Pollarolo, your most reverent and faithful servant and subject. Having spent thirteen years in the employment of the ducal [literally, royal] chapel of San Marco, thereby abandoning my native city and employment, and having produced a son born and raised in the ardent hope of living and dying in that service, I bow before the greatness of Your Excellencies and offer a prayer, which will not be news to you, that by your most merciful grace I will be permitted to progress from *vice-maestro* to *maestro*. This promotion, which was granted to my predecessor eleven years ago (when out of respect for seniority I withdrew my application) might serve me as an example and give me cause for hope, if my feelings of obedience and loyalty did not remind me that it is in the hands of Your Excellencies alone that my destiny, the well-being of seven children of both sexes, and, what concerns me most, my reputation and standing, which are dearer to me than life itself, are placed. At such a critical juncture I kneel before the revered and venerated grace of Your Excellencies, and as its child I implore to be made worthy of it, not by invoking the proofs [of my ability] I have already given, but by appealing to the lofty, benign judgement of this sanctuary itself, which a great many years ago made me *vice-maestro*; and I would be committing the sin of ingratitude if, in this hour of need, I did not call on that august body that saw fit to promote me to the next-highest rank that its supreme benificence can award. I place my trust humbly in this [grace] and on account of it beg, with my mouth lowered to the ground, for the ultimate perfection of this same benificence, since in the last resort, just as with God one grace is the foundation of another, so, too, when I fall at the feet of Your Excellencies, who stand in place of God, your having invested me ten years ago with the title of *vice-maestro* will serve to give me consolation through the abundance of your mercy. I thank you.[53]

If Pollarolo's letter adopts a distinctly pleading, almost desperate, tone, that of his main rival oozes confidence. It is written professionally in a special type of calligraphic hand that sets out to imitate print and at first sight could be mistaken for it.[54] The second candidate was Antonino Biffi, a man about fourteen years Pollarolo's junior. Fresh from his ordination as a priest, Biffi had joined the *cappella* on 6 July 1692 as an alto. Almost immediately (on 13 July 1692), he was called to step into the shoes of

[53] *I-Vas*, PdS, Busta 6, Decreti in originale, Fascicolo 13 (1701), 5 Feb. 1701 (1702 m.v.). Transcribed as App. B.23.

[54] A well-known example of this 'print-like' style of handwriting is the manuscript catalogue of operas produced in Venice (1741, continued to 1767) prepared by the publisher Antonio Groppo: *I-Vnm*, Cod. it. VII–2326 (= 8263).

Antonio Lotti, who had recently become second organist. The function
vacated by Lotti was an exceptional one not allowed for in the plan of the
cappella. It arose from the coincidental fact that one of the auxiliary
organists, Paolo Biego, was also a bass singer on whom fell the special
duty to act as the 'basso del maestro'. This entailed joining the *primo maestro* in the North organ-loft. When this happened, Lotti was assigned to
Biego's instrument. His salary of 30 ducats, which Biffi inherited, might
seem a little excessive, but one gathers from the latter's letter of application that the supernumerary organist was sometimes directed by the *maestro* to take over at one of the main organs if the incumbent was absent,
an altogether more responsible task carrying with it the implication that
first Lotti, then Biffi, were being 'groomed' for eventual service as a principal organist. On 21 March 1700 Biffi had become *maestro di coro* at the
Mendicanti, a sure sign that his star was rising.

In his letter he plays ruthlessly to his strengths, taking every advantage
of the procurators' respect for precedent. He declares his support for the
practice of appointing men in holy orders and, to rub the point in (and if
possible discredit his rivals), claims to have concerned himself solely with
sacred music.[55] He refers to lucrative offers, turned down, to serve foreign
princes and to his diligent and obedient work as a composer and organist.
Even his post of *maestro di coro* at the Mendicanti, not yet two years old,
is pressed into service, for he finds three earlier *primi maestri*, including
Partenio himself, who had held that position at the time of appointment.

Most Illustrious and Excellent Lord Procurators *de Supra*,

I, Antonino Biffi, a native of this city and the servant and most humble subject of
Your Excellencies, venerate, as an auspicious prelude to my greatest good fortune,
the age-old custom of this most august and wise assembly to confer the signal
honour of being *maestro* of the *cappella* of the ducal church of San Marco on
someone holding the title of priest in order that a sacred place and a pious office
should be matched with a person in holy orders. The constancy of this most
exemplary principle, which has proved its worth over the centuries and has been
unfailingly observed in successive elections in the past, lends courage to my most
humble [!] confidence as I bring myself before the greatness of Your Excellencies
to beg for this position, both because I am a priest and because I have always
applied my feeble efforts exclusively to sacred functions in churches or to the
teaching of the girls in the *ospedali*. I have not taken advantage of any of the
other opportunities [to write and direct music] that might have come into conflict
with this firm principle of mine. For this reason I have refused to bind myself to
foreign princes, even though they have repeatedly made attractive offers to me
and promised much money, since I regard it as a greater reward than any mere
payment to have the honour of serving my revered prince in this ducal *cappella*
and as *maestro* to the esteemed *coro* of the Mendicanti. In this connection I may

---

[55] Biffi did not spurn secular music altogether, however, for some cantatas by him have survived.

draw attention to the service that I have provided for ten years as a contrapuntist [i.e. composer] and organist without ever failing in my duties and, indeed, with the satisfaction of having uncomplainingly obeyed the commands of the *maestri*, who used my prompt willingness to assist to fill the gap when any of the players of the principal organs was absent. So the punctiliousness that I have always shown during my far from short service and my well-regarded compositions for the Ospedale dei Mendicanti, which three of my predecessors, Reverend[s] Nadal Monferrato, Legrenzi, and Partenio, served on their way to this estimable title, give me hope that I will win the generous votes of Your Excellencies, which I most humbly implore, promising, if successful, to carry out the duties of the post exactly as I have done those of my present service to the church. May God, to whom I have always devoted my feeble labours, lead the minds of Your Excellencies to elect the man who is willing, with the most punctiliousness, and is able, with the most diligence, to carry out the great work of the state *cappella* unimpeded by other tasks and responsibilities, and, if I am elected, may he give me the grace of his assistance, on which I call, to enable me to perform well, for His greater glory and the better service of Your Excellencies, that office which, abject and prostrate, I beg from the grace and greatness of mind of each of Your Excellencies. I thank you etc.[56]

Unfortunately, the letter of application of the third candidate, Vinaccesi, has not survived. It is difficult to imagine what he could have said on his own behalf that would have stood comparison with Biffi's, or even Pollarolo's, statement. His sonatas and oratorios for Brescia and his one opera already written for Venice would have been at best irrelevant, at worst a debit against his name. Only his service at the Ospedaletto would have counted in his favour, and Biffi could claim a connection with an *ospedale* that enjoyed closer historical links with the basilica.

On 5 February the procurators assembled to make their decision. What happened is recounted in the minutes.

5 February 1701 [m.v., therefore 1702]

The post of *maestro* to the *cappella* of the ducal church of San Marco, [previously] held by Reverend Giovanni Domenico Partenio being vacant, it is necessary to proceed to the election of another man, who, by virtue of his own skill, ability and proven experience, is a competent and suitable person to hold such a distinguished position and is held in a regard commensurate with the reputation and function of the same ducal *cappella*. However, since the Most Illustrious and Excellent Lord Procurator our *cassiere* has written to the courts [i.e. to Venetian ambassadors attached to foreign courts] without the desired result, and since, after the customary notices have been posted for the information of those who might wish to be candidates, we are informed by our *comandador* Angelo Carminati that those whose names are listed below have made application, we will proceed to a vote. The successful candidate will be instructed to carry out conscientiously and precisely all the duties associated with this post and will be entitled

---

[56] Source as n. 53, above. Transcribed as App. B.24.

to the provisions and emoluments enjoyed by the same late *maestro* Partenio. The successful candidate will forfeit all other payment [as a member of the *cappella*] but receive the usual salary pertaining to the above post of *maestro*.

Sig. Don Antoni[n]o Biffi	For	9	
	Against	5	
Sig. Benedetto Vinaccesi	For	3	Sig. Don Antoni[n]o Biffi elected
	Against	11	
Sig. Carlo Pollarolo	For	8	
	Against	6[57]	

So that was that: our composer came a poor third, blackballed by eleven procurators. For Vinaccesi, the worst aspect of the result was that the election produced no chain-reaction creating immediate vacancies lower down the ladder, since Biffi's post as organist was not an established one.

But his chance came sooner than he may have feared. On 18 March 1704 the player of the first principal organ, Giacomo Filippo Spada, handed in a doctor's note and the following letter:

Most Illustrious, Most Excellent Lord Procurators *de Supra*,

The vigilant and punctilious service that I, Giacomo Spada, first organist of the ducal church of San Marco, have rendered in the performance of the task entrusted to me by the revered authority of Your Excellencies has always been well known; equally well known has been the devotion with which I have always, from the depths of my soul, striven to sacrifice all my efforts, and my very life, to the glorious satisfaction of Your Excellencies and the regal service of the prince. Now that my health has been consumed by the continual and unceasing labours required by my most demanding employment, and that I have been advised by the opinion of the doctors who attend me to take a rest in my native parts [Faenza], where I will breathe an air that suits my temperament, I beg the charity of Your Excellencies kindly to grant me leave of about four months and allow me to be replaced in the meantime, for the services that require me, by my pupil Alvise Tavelli, the most able person known to me, without any extra charge to Your Excellencies, so that, having drawn fresh strength from this brief repose, I will be able to continue to sacrifice myself, with my spirit ever more lively and fervid, in perpetual submission to the revered commands of Your Excellencies, whose grace I most humbly worship and desire.[58]

Without dissension, the procurators acceded to his request. But their action came too late, for when the four months were nearly up, during the week ending 19 July, Spada died.[59] The mechanism for electing his replacement was set in motion, but before that happened, Antonio Lotti,

[57] *I-Vas*, PdS, Busta 150, Decreti e terminazioni, 1700–7, fo. 23(bis)ʳ. Transcribed as App. B.25. By rendering Biffi's first name as Antonio instead of Antonino, the minutes commit an error that has persisted up to the present day.

[58] *I-Vas*, PdS, Registro 211, mandati e licenze 1694–1712, fo. 54ᵛ. Transcribed as App. B.26.

[59] Selfridge-Field, *Pallade veneta*, 253.

the second organist, put in the traditional request by holders of his post to be allowed to move in the meantime to the vacant first organ. Although the two posts of organist were nominally equal in status, as they were in salary, it is clear that custody of the larger organ brought a certain prestige to the incumbent, either because of the size and power of his instrument or because of his proximity to the *maestro di cappella*.[60] The procurators agreed to this request on 17 August.[61] When the election took place on 7 September, there were four candidates: Andrea Paulati, Alvise Tavelli, Giovanni Marco Martini, and Vinaccesi.

As the recommended pupil of the outgoing organist and a priest, Tavelli might have been expected to be the favourite. La Borde extols his qualities both as an executant ('un des meilleurs Organistes que l'on ait connu') and as a composer ('très habile compositeur').[62] But if this is not idle word-spinning, it must at least be qualified by what we learn from Caffi, who took much of his information from a later Venetian organist-composer, Anselmo Marsand (1769–1841).[63] According to Marsand, Tavelli was, technically speaking, an outstandingly good organist but conducted his personal life in a highly eccentric manner, destroying most of his compositions after their first performance and refusing to maintain a fixed domicile.

Paulati (also called Paulato) was another internal applicant. He had been an alto in the *cappella* since 1692—evidently a good one, since his salary was raised to the maximum for a singer of 100 ducats in the following year—and is recorded by Coronelli as the *maestro di cappella* at Santi Giovanni e Paolo already in 1700. In 1689 he had dedicated his Op. 1, a set of ten *Cantate a voce sola*, to Antonio Ottoboni, just after the latter had been made a procurator of St Mark. It is unlikely, however, that Ottoboni was greatly impressed, since these are short-winded, uninspired pieces.[64]

Another priest, Marco Martini, who, like Paulati and Vinaccesi, was to be a contributor to the celebrations at Santi Giovanni e Paolo in 1712 marking the canonization of St Pius V, was a violinist in the *cappella*

[60] Eleanor Selfridge-Field has suggested that the second organ was used only on occasions when both organs were required and that, therefore, the second organist played the first organ during those weeks when it was his turn to be in attendance (*Venetian Instrumental Music from Gabrieli to Vivaldi* (Oxford, 1975), 11). The proprietary attitude taken by the San Marco organists towards their designated instruments belies this hypothesis. The second organists Volpe, Spada, and Lotti would surely not have been so keen to be reassigned officially to the first organ if they would have played it nearly half the time in the normal course of events. It is much more likely that the other musicians rearranged themselves according to which organist was on duty.

[61] *I-Vas*, PdS, Registro 150, fo. 62ʳ.

[62] *Dictionnaire de la musique ancienne et moderne*, iii. 237–8.

[63] Caffi, *Storia della musica sacra*, i. 361–3.

[64] Sébastien de Brossard's catalogue of the music donated by him to the French king (*F-Pn*, Rés. Vm.⁸ 21) pointedly refrains from commenting critically on Paulati's cantatas—a case of condemnation through silence.

ducale, appointed in 1684. He had been elected *maestro di coro* at the Mendicanti on 31 May 1699 but had absented himself for an unknown cause in early 1700 after having had his request to resign refused. His dismissal on 21 March 1700 coincided with Biffi's appointment there.[65] How much weight the procurators would lay on this curious episode hung in the balance.

For the appointment of principal organists at the basilica there was an established test of ability that obviated the need for submitting an elaborate letter of application.[66] The first part consisted of opening a choirbook and finding at random the beginning of a Kyrie or a motet; this was then copied out and given to the contestant, who had to go to the vacant organ and improvise a strictly contrapuntal fantasia on the given subject 'as if four singers were performing'. For the second part, the contestant was given a piece of plainsong, similarly chosen at random, and instructed to treat it as a *cantus firmus* in each of four voices in turn, making sure to keep the accompanying parts complex and to include 'fughe' (here probably in the common contemporary sense of florid runs rather than imitations). Finally, the choir was to sing a verse from an unfamiliar composition, which the contestant had to imitate and respond to, both in the same mode ('in tuono') and in a different mode ('fuori di tuono').

On 7 September 1704 the procurators delivered their verdict. In the words of the minute:

7 September 1704

The usual notices having been posted for an organist at the ducal church of San Marco to replace Antonio Lotti, who has taken over the responsibility of the late Don Giacomo Filippo Spada, those whose names appear below have made application. Following their submission to the usual tests, a secret vote was taken by the following Most Illustrious and Excellent Lord Procurators [their names are listed], and Master Benedetto Vinaccesi was elected, as shown by the voting figures below, his duties, salaries, and perquisites being the same as those enjoyed by his predecessor as organist, Antonio Lotti.

Andrea Paulati	Yes	9
	No	7
Alvise Tavelli	Yes	6
	No	10
Giovanni Marco Martini	Yes	9
	No	7
Benedetto Vinaccesi	Yes	10
	No	6[67]

[65] Scarpa, *Arte e musica all'Ospedaletto*, 172.

[66] The tests for organists are described in an undated manuscript preserved in *I-Vas*, PdS, Busta 91, Processo 207, Organisti, fo. 1[r].

[67] *I-Vas*, PdS, Busta 150, fo. 62[v]. Transcribed as App. B.27.

By a whisker, our composer had acquired a job for life. There is no reason to suppose that he owed it to anything other than a good showing in the tests, but one wonders whether Ottoboni, concurrently a governor at the Ospedaletto, acted as his advocate. As we shall see later, Vinaccesi set at least one of Ottoboni's cantata texts, which implies some degree of social contact, and the latter was almost a neighbour, since his palace abutted the Rio di San Severo not far from the Palazzo Zorzi.

The perquisites (*utilità*) of the post mentioned in the minute were seemingly neither numerous nor especially lucrative. We know of two such extra payments that came Vinaccesi's way during his fifteen years at the second organ. One was the fee of 4 ducats paid to him, as duty organist, on 10 June 1707 for accompanying the singing of Tenebrae on the spinet.[68] By the law of averages, he will have received this bonus on seven or eight occasions. The other payment—made, coincidentally, on the following day—was for playing the organ at the church of San Nicolò di Lido on Ascension Day, in connection with the annual ceremony named after the *bucintoro*, the doge's ceremonial boat. This fee of 7 *lire*—little more than a ducat current—is recorded in a receipt made out by the composer himself (reproduced as Plate 3), which is the only specimen of his handwriting so far uncovered, apart from the signature on his will.[69] The two organists doubtless earned it an approximately equal number of times over the years.

With one important exception, Vinaccesi's service as organist at San Marco was totally uneventful right up to his death. No absences or disciplinary infringements are recorded—nor are any commendations. Since Biffi and Lotti remained in their posts all this time (Pollarolo had managed to pass on his title to his son Antonio shortly after his failure to become *primo maestro*), we cannot know whether Vinaccesi had now reached the summit of his ambitions within the basilica.

The official duties of an organist provided little scope for composing music for the repertory of the *cappella ducale*. The composition of new works on liturgical texts (psalms, canticles, sections of the Mass, antiphons, etc.) was strictly the province—the prerogative, one might say—of the *primo maestro*. Exceptionally, the organist in attendance on Christmas Eve had the prescribed task of composing the Kyrie for the Mass which, by virtue of a special privilege granted by the pope, was celebrated at San Marco two hours after nightfall.[70] In general, the best hope for aspiring composers among the ordinary members of the *cappella*, from *vice-maestro* downwards, was to dedicate a collection of pieces, either

---

[68] *I-Vas*, PdS, Registro 39, Libro di scontro 1701–8, 10 June 1707.

[69] *I-Vas*, San Nicolò di Lido, Busta 8, Perg: 'Pollizze e ricevuti dell'anno 1707', Organisti di San Marco. I am grateful to Gastone Vio for bringing this source to my attention.

[70] On the composition of the Kyrie see *I-Vmc*, Ms. Gradenigo 173, Chiesa di San Marco, fo. 295^r. The information on the papal privilege comes from Franz Haböck, *Die Kastraten und ihre Gesangskunst: Eine gesangsphysiologische, kultur- und musikhistorische Studie* (Stuttgart, 1927), 172.

published or manuscript, to the procurators in the expectation that they would receive a gratuity (called *regalo* or *ricognizione*) and that the music would be added to the archive of the *cappella* and become part of its active repertory.

In early 1714 the procurators were presented with a set of four printed partbooks containing fourteen motets for two or three voices with organ, the composition of their second organist. On the title-page of each volume they could read:

CANTO [similarly ALTO., BASSO., and ORGANO.] / MOTETTI / A DUE, E TRE VOCI. / *Del K: Benedetto Vinaccesi* / Organista della Serenissima Ducal Capella / DI SAN MARCO / CONSAGRATI / A GL'ILL.:^{mi} ET ECC:^{mi} SIG:^{ri} / PROCURATORI / DE SUPRA / CASSIERE / *L'Illustrissimo, & Eccellentissimo Signor* / PROCURATOR / DANIEL DOLFIN / PRIMO / IN VENETIA Da Gioseppe Sala. MDCCXIV. / Si Vendono à S: Gio: Grisostimo [*sic*]. All'Insegna del Rè David. / CON LICENZA DE SUPERIORI.

Turning a page, they would have come to a letter of dedication, followed by a short preface, both quoted below in translation:

MOST ILLUSTRIOUS AND EXCELLENT LORDS

To the sublimity of the august name of Your Excellencies I most respectfully consecrate these feeble musical products of my pen, which appear in print expressly for the use of the most serene ducal *cappella*. My offering is justified because, after I have been admitted solely through the generosity of Your Excellencies to the honour of serving in it [the *cappella*] as an organist, to it alone belongs everything that may emerge from my small talent, nothing of my own remaining in me. Further, I most humbly beg Your Excellencies not to behold the insignificance of my poor oblation, which falls far short of the immensity of my debt, but to render it worthy by your magnanimous approval, and I am right to hope that this will be so, since God himself, of whom you are the living images on earth, looked with equal favour on the precious gifts of kings and the rustic tributes of shepherds. I bow to kiss your glorious purple [robes] and in the most profound submission dare to declare myself

Your Excellencies'

Most humble, devoted, respectful, and reverent servant
BENEDETTO VINACCESI

SKILFUL READER

These sacred duets and terzets of mine have been published for the sole use of the ducal [*cappella*] of San Marco. To explain this work it is enough to consider the place where they are to be performed. I am certain of your benevolent approval and hope that there is no truth in the saying

Taci[tus] [Dialogue on] Orat[ors] The human vice of malignity always holds old things in esteem, things of today in scorn.[71]

---

[71] The original text of the dedication is given in Michael Talbot, 'The Marcian Motets of Benedetto Vinaccesi', in Franco Rossi and Francesco Passadore (eds.), *Giovanni Legrenzi e la Cappella*

Although the dedication is on the surface little more than a compilation of formulas that we have already encountered in many similar documents, a little decoding is needed to bring out its full significance. When Vinaccesi writes that the motets, cast in the form of sacred duets and terzets, are for the exclusive use of the ducal *cappella* he is not descending to mere flattery: they are indeed conceived, textually and musically, in a way that made them difficult, at the time, to employ anywhere else (in Chapter 10 we shall provide evidence for this statement). When he speaks of the 'insignificance' (*picciolezza*) of his offering, he is in fact drawing the reader's attention towards its very considerable size—the soprano part contains 71 pages of music, each with eight staves. The quotation from the *Dialogus de oratoribus* of Tacitus (written in around AD 100) not only attempts to place Vinaccesi, in contrast to most of his fellow musicians, in the ranks of the classically educated but also alludes to the genuinely novel character of the works, which we shall examine later.

A familiar enough motif, though, is the combination of the words 'worthy' (*degno*) and 'approval' (*gradimento*) towards the end of the dedication. This is the conventional veiled request for a *regalo*. Convention, too, demanded that the procurators do the expected thing. But they had to be reminded of the going 'tariff' for such offerings, and to that end a memorandum was prepared, listing all relevant entries in the minute-books from 1670 onwards.[72] The table below summarizes its content.

Date	Composer	Position	Type of Work(s)	Reward
1670, 31 Jan.	Monferrato	*vice-maestro*	printed motets; 2 Masses and a Magnificat (MSS)[a]	120 ducats
1676, 19 Mar.	P. A. Ziani	organist	3 MSS of his works	100 ducats
1682, 11 Jan.	Monferrato	*primo maestro*	motets[b]	medal worth 100 sequins
1689, 10 July	Legrenzi	*primo maestro*	responses for Holy Week (MS)	silverware worth 200 ducats
1698, 22 July	Lotti	organist	a cappella Mass (MS)	50 ducats

[a] Monferrato's *Motetti concertati*, Op. 17 (1669).
[b] Monferrato's Op. 18 (pub. 1681).

A resolution awarding Vinaccesi the very reasonable sum of 100 ducats was drafted, in words borrowed as far as possible from the earlier resolutions, and passed without opposition at the meeting of the procurators on 19 March 1714. Its text runs:

Ducale di San Marco (Florence, forthcoming). Vinaccesi slightly misquotes the observation of Tacitus, which should properly read 'Vitio autem malignitatis humanae vetera semper in laude, praesentia in fastidio esse' (*Dialogus de oratoribus*, 18.3). I am grateful to Jonathan Foster for locating this quotation.

[72] *I-Vas*, PdS, Busta 9, Terminazioni in originale, Fascicolo 26 (1714), 19 Mar. 1714. The memorandum omits, perhaps unintentionally, to mention the award of a medal worth 50 ducats to the bass Carlo Grossi on 1 Oct. 1684, for unspecified compositions.

Our Benedetto Vinaccesi, for the past ten years an organist in the ducal church of San Marco, having dedicated to this procuracy a collection of motets for several voices intended for use in the same church, the Most Illustrious and Excellent Lord Procurators, whose names appear below [these names follow], have decided, in token of their approval of his praiseworthy efforts, to give him once and for all from the *cassa della chiesa* [the general account] 100 ducats current.

Yes 9   No 0   Undecided 1   Carried[73]

In an almost unbelievable comedy of errors, Vinaccesi's offering of motets and its reward have given rise to some extraordinary misinterpretations in secondary literature. Caffi set the ball rolling with a pair of simple slips: he stated that the meeting at which the *regalo* was awarded took place on 19 June (instead of March) 1714, adding that this occurred in the year of Vinaccesi's appointment (instead of almost ten years later).[74] The revised edition of the *Biographie universelle* of Fétis compounded the error in 1870 by stating that on that occasion Vinaccesi's salary was raised to 300 ducats (whereas the 100 ducats were quite expressly a once-and-for-all payment).[75] The most curious mistake, however, was made by Giovanni Tebaldini, the *maestro di cappella* of the Basilica del Santo in Padua (from 1894) and a former *maestro* of the Schola Cantorum at San Marco itself. To Tebaldini belongs the credit for having been the first musician in modern times to recognize the great merit of Vinaccesi's music, of which he performed extracts in concert with the Cappella Antoniana. But he identified the works dedicated to the procurators not with the printed volumes but with around thirty so-called 'motets' by Vinaccesi preserved in manuscript in the Biblioteca Antoniana, Padua. These are extracts, generally single movements, from longer compositions; most (but not quite all) are taken from the motets published in 1714. In Tebaldini's annotated catalogue of the music in the Biblioteca Antoniana these thirty fragments themselves become the 'muda di motteti' to which the procurators referred.[76] Few twentieth-century discussions of Vinaccesi's music, not excluding such authoritative reference works as the *New Grove* (1980) and the *Dizionario della musica e dei musicisti* (1983–8), fail to reproduce one or more of the above mistakes.[77]

Vinaccesi reportedly had two pupils during his period at San Marco. One was Nicolò Domenico Turri, who was elected *maestro di canto* to the

---

[73] *I-Vas*, PdS, Registro 152, fo. 16ʳ. Transcribed as App. B.28.

[74] Caffi, *Storia della musica sacra*, i. 360.

[75] *Biographie universelle des musiciens et bibliographie générale de la musique* (Paris, ²/1868–70), viii. 353.

[76] *L'archivio musicale della Cappella Antoniana in Padova* (Padua, 1895), 117–19.

[77] The transmission of these errors up to the present day offers a salutary caution to those who place their trust in older secondary literature. Ironically, information from the minutes of the procurators is so easy to extract, since, although the vols. have no index, marginal summaries lead one swiftly to each item.

choristers in 1707 and again (presumably after a break in service) in 1713.[78] The information comes from Caffi, who rarely identifies his sources but is usually correct in such matters.[79] The other was a minor German musician, Friedrich Georg Dieterich (born 1686), who, according to Johann Mattheson, studied keyboard-playing (*Clavierspielen*) and composition (*Setzkunst*) with him.[80] Dieterich thus joins Handel, Heinichen, Stölzel, Pisendel, and Hasse as a member of that large band of German musicians who were sent by their patrons, or went on their own initiative, to Italy in the early eighteenth century in order to perfect their skills.

The last known reference to Vinaccesi's activity as a composer dates from 12 September 1716, when the *Pallade veneta* reported his composition of 'musica esquisitissima' for the feast of the Translation of the Body of St Zachariah (father of St John the Baptist), celebrated at the Venetian convent of San Zaccaria on 6 September

During the last week of November 1719 Vinaccesi fell ill and took to his bed. On 20 December he called for a notary, Andrea Sandei (Sandelli in Tuscan), and dictated his will, which runs as follows:

I, Benedetto Vinaccesi, son of the late Lodovico Vinaccesi, wishing to dispose of my affairs, particularly since I am ill and confined to bed, have instructed Sig. Andrea Sandei to write this, my last will and testament, as my confidant prior to my presenting it to him as a notary for its validation.

First, prostrating my mind and heart before the cross of Christ, I pray to him, by the power of his most precious blood shed for my sake, to give succour to this poor soul of mine in its last moments through his holy grace and to lead it into the port of salvation through his infinite mercy. In doing which, I implore the intercession of the Blessed Virgin Mary, my advocate, and all my guardian saints.

As my fortune is very small and my family, in times gone by, was always very large, despite which I have given five children to the church, to God's glory, I declare that I have agreed to avail myself, for the sake of the necessary ceremonies, of certain capital sums inherited by Signora Veronica, my consort, as shown in official documents and contracts. However, I intend, order, command, and wish that all my movable effects, wherever they may be [inserted above: organ, clothes, and linen for my use], are, and shall be understood as being, the property of the same Signora Veronica, in payment for what I owe her as described above, and that she shall be allowed, in any event, to dispose of them as she wishes, since I know well that they will be insufficient to repay her fully, which is why I ask her to accept what I have in recompense for the greater sum that she deserves.

I further declare that all the pictures in the room on the first floor next to the staircase of my house, and a few others by various modern painters hanging in other rooms, belong to Sig. Giacomo Ganassoni, to whom they must be returned on request.

[78] Turri's two appointments are recorded in *I-Vas*, PdS, Registro 151, fo. 12[r] (24 Sept. 1707) and Registro 152, fo. 8[v] (13 Dec. 1713).
[79] *Storia della musica sacra*, ii. 51.   [80] *Grundlage einer Ehren-Pforte* (Hamburg, 1740), 52.

I make my son Pietro the universal heir of the residue comprising everything that I possess or is owing to me, asking him to live in holy fear of God and to conduct and govern himself well, and imploring Heaven to add its celestial blessing to my own as a father.

And I wish this to be my last will and testament, to God's glory.

[*own hand*] Affirmed by me, Benedetto Vinaccesi[81]

The unpretentious dignity of this document is perhaps a better guide to Vinaccesi's real character than the convoluted, flattering letters written to dedicatees, governors, or procurators. It breathes simplicity and seriousness. One need not infer from the beginning of its fourth paragraph that Vinaccesi was in straitened circumstances at the time. The transfer of his personal effects to his consort (note the use of this term instead of 'wife', so as to draw attention to the separation of property) in return for her payment for his funeral was probably a conventional device aimed at simplifying accounts and perhaps also at reducing the inheritance tax, five per cent of the value of the estate, payable to the magistracy of the Inquisitore all'Acque. Nothing else is left to Veronica in the will, since the dowry she brought at the time of her marriage remains intact and to some extent safeguards her future.

The mention of an organ among the composer's possessions and the evidently large collection of pictures (only one part of which, we infer, belongs to Ganassoni) remind us of his profession and his other great interest. No Giacomo Ganassoni appears in the *polizze d'estimo* of Brescia for the years 1661 or 1687, but one would be surprised if this man were not a member of the wealthy merchant family of that name active in that city from the fourteenth century and numbering two painters, Giorgio and Giovanni Battista (both working in the sixteenth century), among its members.[82] It is highly likely that Vinaccesi maintained links as a matter of course with Brescian *cittadini* living in Venice, since emigrants from the various provincial centres, just like those from cities outside the Veneto, tended to band together for common advantage.

After the will had been drawn up in the presence of two witnesses (one of them the same Ganassoni), the notary, following the correct legal procedure, sent them out while he read it aloud in private to the testator.[83] It was probably at this point that Vinaccesi thought of making specific mention of his organ, clothes, and linen, and had the insertion added. Then the witnesses returned and the notary completed the formalities, remem-

---

[81] *I-Vas*, Sezione notarile, Testamenti, Busta 606, Andrea Sandelli, no. 48. Transcribed as App. B.29. I am grateful to Olga Termini for informing me of the existence of this will.

[82] *Enciclopedia bresciana* (Brescia, 1982), v. 94–5.

[83] Venetian law concerning wills is explained exhaustively in Ferro, *Dizionario del diritto comune e veneto*, x. 250–69.

bering to ask the standard question concerning a possible legacy to one of the four *ospedali grandi* and especially the Pietà. Like thousands of others before him, Vinaccesi pleaded poverty but good intentions. The entire procedure is described in the *rogito* (formal attestation) entered by the notary on the last page of the bifolio containing the will:

In the name of the eternal God, amen, in the year 1719 from the Incarnation of Our Lord Jesus Christ, registered at the Rialto as number 12 on Wednesday 20 December. Sig. *Cavalier* Benedetto Vinaccesi, son of the late Lodovico Vinaccesi, by God's grace sound of mind, sense, and intellect, though ill and bed-ridden, has presented to me, Andrea Sandei, Venetian Notary, at his home in this city in the parish of San Severo, in the presence of the undersigned witnesses, this unsealed document, which he has identified as his last will and testament written out by me, the notary, as his confidant. The witnesses having been sent out, it was read to him in privacy as the law requires, and he made me add certain things, as shown, and signed it. The witnesses having been called back, he presented it to me again, confirming its correctness in all its parts and as it stands. He asked me to deposit it in the Cancelleria Inferiore [the magistracy where one copy of every will was kept] for safe keeping, so that, in the event of his death, I should take it, open it, execute it, and roborate it, according to law. When I, the notary, asked him whether he would leave anything to the four *ospedali*, and especially the Pietà, or other places or works of charity that I mentioned by name, he replied: If I had [anything to give], I would leave a bequest with all my heart. [*closing formula*]

[signed] I, Don Pietro Barozzi, son of the late Giovanni Battista Barozzi, witnessed the above-mentioned presentation, being summoned and sworn [to silence].

I, Giacomo Ganassoni, son of the late Andrea Ganassoni, was a witness as shown opposite [in Barozzi's declaration], being summoned and sworn.

On Christmas Day Vinaccesi died. We find in the parish registers of San Severo the following entry:

25 December 1719

Sig. *Cavalier* Benedetto Vinaccesi, son of the late Lodovico Vinaccesi, aged about 53, ill with fever and a constriction of the chest for thirty days. Doctor: Tosi. His wife will have him buried with the full chapter in attendance.[84]

Slightly abbreviated, the same notice was copied into the civil necrology.[85] The stated symptom, 'a constriction of the chest' (*strettezza di petto*), is ostensibly the same as that from which Antonio Vivaldi suffered all his life. Its associated complaint has been convincingly identified, in Vivaldi's case, as bronchial asthma, but there is no reason to accept the

[84] Venice, Archivio parrocchiale di San Severo, Registro dei morti 1715–1756, opening 16. Transcribed as App. B.30. I am grateful to Gastone Vio for transcribing this entry on my behalf.

[85] *I-Vas*, Provveditori alla Sanità, Busta 914, Necrologio 1719, 25 Dec. 1719.

same diagnosis for Vinaccesi, given the vagueness of the description and the primitive state of medical science in his day.

On 30 December the notary proved the will, making a note of this under the signatures of the witnesses.

Showing their usual lack of sentimentality about deceased servants, the procurators attended to practicalities and elected Vinaccesi's successor on 7 January 1720. The only person to respond to their advertisement was Alvise Tavelli, who received the unanimity of votes cast. In the minute, the procurators noted that he was to have 'all the duties, salary, and perquisites enjoyed by the aforesaid late Benedetto Vinaccesi, organist'.[86]

---

[86] *I-Vas*, PdS, Registro 152, fo. 105^r.

5

The Later Vinaccesis

EVEN though none of Benedetto Vinaccesi's descendants, so far as we know, made a career in music, their story holds enough interest to deserve a rapid account taking the family up to the end of the eighteenth century.

Benedetto's will speaks of five 'figli' who followed a religious vocation. This word was translated as 'children' rather than 'sons', since in Italian it can mean both, and although we have no knowledge of any female children born to him, one of the five children to whom he was referring could conceivably have been a girl born after his move to Venice. We know of six sons born in Brescia, of whom at least four, perhaps five, survived infancy. Their dates of birth or baptism are all extractable, with varying degrees of precision, from Benedetto's census return in 1686 and from baptismal records at San Clemente (see Appendix C.2). In order of birth (the bracketed numbers refer to names in Appendix A.6), they are:

1. Lodovico Tito (81), born in April or May 1686
2. Antonio Francesco Diego (82), baptized on 18 November 1687
3. Amerigo Emanuel Gaetano (83), baptized on 21 January 1691
4. Filippo (84), baptized on 6 June 1692
5. Giovanni Francesco (85), born *c.*1685, died on 31 July 1697
6. Pietro Antonio (86), baptized on 10 February 1697.

Only the youngest of these, Pietro Antonio, is known for certain to have come with Benedetto to Venice. It appears that he was the son 'earmarked' for marrying and carrying on the family line, while his elder brothers entered the religious life. Perhaps all the sons except Pietro Antonio, who was still an infant, were left behind in Brescia to complete their education.

By a curious chance, the names of three sons who entered the Scolopian order have come down to us. The Scolopians, founded by the Spaniard Giuseppe Calasanzio in 1597 and recognized by the pope in 1621, were pioneers in the provision of free education for the children of the poor—their name comes from the *scuole pie* ('pious schools') they set up throughout Catholic Europe but particularly in Italy.[1] In 1784 they

---

[1] The importance of the Scolopians to Bolognese musical life is discussed in Sergio Durante, 'Alcune considerazioni sui cantanti di teatro del primo Settecento e la loro formazione', in Lorenzo Bianconi and Francesco Degrada (eds.), *Antonio Vivaldi: Teatro musicale, cultura e società* (Florence, 1982), 427–81.

boasted no fewer than 218 houses. Their educational philosophy was out-standingly progressive for the time, promoting the use of the vernacular, admitting a broad range of subjects including music and the sciences, and attempting to maintain discipline through persuasion rather than punish-ment. The fathers also took an interest in the literary arts, founding a society that they called the Accademia Mariana. This became an affiliate, or 'colony', of the Roman Arcadia on 8 November 1703. Unlike most of the Arcadian colonies, which were geographically based, the Accademia Mariana had no fixed seat but existed wherever its Scolopian members happened to find themselves.

Once admitted to Arcadia, the members of the Accademia Mariana became beneficiaries of the excellent record-keeping of the parent organi-zation. Three Vinaccesis are among its early members listed in the *Onomasticon* of Arcadians published in 1977.[2] One was Father Benedetto di Sant'Antonio di Padova, called in Arcadia Sindalio Fenicunteo and in secular life Antonio Vinaccesi: he is almost certainly to be identified with Antonio Francesco, the second son. Lagiaco, alias Father Amerigo di Santa Veronica, whose secular name is given as Amerigo Emanuele, is obviously the third son. The original first name of Delmisto, alias Father Luigi di San Filippo Benizi, is not stated, but he can hardly be other than Filippo, the fourth son, in view of the name he chose in religion. This leaves two out of the five *figli* unaccounted for. One may have been the first-born, Lodovico, and another a child born in Venice.

One of these Scolopian Vinaccesis left his mark before he died, at a tragically early age. In the third volume of *Notizie istoriche degli Arcadi morti* (1721) there appears a touching obituary of him by Father Niccolò Maria di San Domenico (Euristene Aleate), a fellow 'shepherd' in the Colonia Mariana.

BENEDETTO DI S. ANTONIO DI PADOVA

Benedetto di S. Antonio di Padova, born in Brescia of noble parents belonging to the house of Vinaccesi, lived for only ten years in the Scolopian order, but won a reputation and an admiration, both in the sciences and in letters, that another person (to be honest) would not have gained after many long years of strenuous activity. His literary endeavours were so unrelenting that they robbed him of almost all his hours of sleep and reduced his spirits and humours to such a point that he began to suffer a very acute and continual headache, from which he died on 4 October 1716 in his father's house in the city of Venice, where he had gone, on his doctors' advice, to seek the benefit of the air. He was buried in the distin-guished church of the nuns of San Lorenzo. He was mourned by his relatives and also by the whole of our colony, which called him Sindalio Fenicunteo and was hoping to see him become a famous writer on old manuscripts, towards which

---

[2] Anna Maria Georgetti Vichi (ed.), Gli Arcadi dal 1690 al 1800: *Onomasticon* (Rome, 1977), 76, 153, 234.

end he had already composed a solid and well-fashioned Lenten sermon and given evidence of his striking talent in various panegyrics delivered in Rome, particularly in the patriarchal basilica of the Vatican, and in an Advent sermon that earned him much credit when he sent it to the distinguished collegiate church [basilica] of Santa Maria in Trastevere.[3]

Sure enough, the parish archive of San Severo records his death. The day of death is given there as 5 October rather than 4 October. Such discrepancies are not uncommon in Italian records; they often arise from the fact that the end of the social day, which continues past the hours of daylight into the evening, is the beginning of the next calendar day according to the traditional Italian system of time-keeping (*ore italiane*).

5 October 1716

The Very Reverend Father Don Benedetto di S. Antonio di Padova, son of the Sig. *Cavalier* Benedetto Vinaccesi, aged around 29, ill already for one month, from fever and head pains. Visited by the Excellent [doctor] Coen. His father will have him buried with the full chapter in attendance.[4]

Benedetto's youngest son and universal heir, Pietro Antonio (also called Pierantonio), had a much longer and still more eventful life. He married young: his considerably older first wife, Caterina Zanforti (born in 1690 or 1691), drew up her will on 1 June 1719 after taking to bed with a fever in the middle of the previous month.[5] The marriage seems to have been childless, for Caterina stipulated that her mother should recover her entire dowry after her death. She died on 25 June 1719.[6] The couple were living at the time in the parish of Santa Ternita in the *sestiere* of Castello, not far from the husband's paternal home.

The earliest information we have about Pietro Antonio's career is the letter he presented on 30 March 1724 to the Procuratia de Supra, asking to be elected formally to one of the two *gastaldie*, which he had bought for an undisclosed sum from the nobleman Nicolò Manin on 2 January of that year.[7] The two posts of *gastaldo* at San Marco were among a number of public offices (another was the *appuntadore* at San Marco) that since 1636 had been offered for sale to the highest bidder by the magistracy of the Cinque Savi sopra gl'Offizi.[8] At the time of the purchase the office

[3] Giovan Mario Crescimbeni (ed.), *Notizie istoriche degli Arcadi morti* (Rome, 1720–1), iii. 52–3. Transcribed as App. B.31.

[4] Venice, Archivio parrocchiale di San Severo, Morti 1715–1756, opening 6. Transcribed as App. B.32. I am grateful to Gastone Vio for transcribing this entry on my behalf.

[5] *I-Vas*, Sezione notarile, Testamenti, Busta 17, Pietro Grigis, no. 26, 1 June 1719.

[6] *I-Vas*, Provveditori alla Sanità, Registro 914, necrologio 1719, 25 June 1719.

[7] *I-Vas*, PdS, Registro 153, Decreti e terminazioni 1721–35, fos. 43ᵛ–44ʳ.

[8] The discussion of the post of *gastaldo* to the Procuratia de Supra and of Pietro Antonio Vinaccesi's tenure of it is based on the following documents in *I-Vas*, PdS: Busta 7, Fascicolo 16 (1704), 13 Dec. 1704; Busta 11, Fascicolo 36 (1724), 30 Mar. 1724; Registro 41, 2 Aug. 1724; Registro 42, 3 July 1728; Busta 69, Processo 152, Fascicolo 1, fo. 50, and Processo 153, Fascicolo 4, fos. 1 and

had to be registered in the name of a person—the purchaser himself or a nominee—who would be its official 'registered owner' for the duration of his life. The ownership was subsequently transferable, but the life on which it was based was usually not. This turned the office into a sort of annuity: against his expected annual earnings a purchaser had to weigh the number of years that would elapse before the original holder died. It was originally possible, with approval from the employing institution, to have the office carried out by a substitute. This practice proved so common that it gave rise to serious abuse, since one person could buy a number of different offices and place them all in the hands of substitutes, over whom he exercised no control. In 1709 the Senate voted to put an end to the employment of multiple substitutes.

From around that year, too, comes an interesting break-down of the average annual earnings of a *gastaldo* of the Procuratia de Supra. His fixed earnings comprised the salary of 200 ducats (of which 60 ducats were deducted at source as a *decima*), the Christmas bonus (5 ducats), the free occupancy of a house in the Procuratie Vecchie (the row of apartments on the same side of the Piazza as the clock), whose annual rent was assessed at 160 ducats, a servant's house (worth 5 ducats), and 20 ducats from the legacy of a certain Zuanna (Giovanna) Barbaro. His commissions on business transactions gave him about as much again, leaving him, according to the calculation, with a surplus for the average year of 469 ducats 16 *grossi*. If the cost of purchasing the *gastaldia* was within the normal range of 3,500–4,000 ducats, every year that passed would enable the holder to recoup at least a tenth of his initial outlay.

The *gastaldia* to which Pietro Antonio succeeded was originally sold, for a cost of 3,620 ducats 23 *grossi*, to Angelo and Benedetto Ricci (or Rizzi) on 25 February 1679. It was purchased on behalf of Benedetto Ricci's son Marc'Antonio (then aged 23), who became its first holder. On 13 July 1687 the Procuratia de Supra agreed to repossess the office from Ricci in annual instalments and itself become the owner. The circumstances were exceptional: the Ricci family was about to buy itself into the nobility (during the war against the Turks in the Peloponnese, large sums were raised for the exchequer by opening the Golden Book to approved newcomers). This act would debar Marc'Antonio Ricci from continuing as *gastaldo*, since the post was open only to *cittadini originari*. The exercise of the office on behalf of the Procuratia de Supra passed to Andrea Rossini, who had been acting as a substitute for the other *gastaldia* for the past seventeen years. The Procuratia de Supra then sold the office on 13 March 1691 to Sebastiano Foresti, who was allowed to buy it on instal-

---

59^r, and Fascicolo 5; Busta 70, Processo 154, Fascicolo 3, fo. 143^v; Registro 153, fos. 43^v–44^r. On the regulations governing State posts in general see Ferro, *Dizionario del diritto comune e veneto*, iii. 70–80 (art. 'Cariche').

ments while he was concurrently paying back the instalments outstanding from the purchase from Ricci! This bizarre situation acted to Foresti's acute financial disadvantage, and the procurators had to make *ad hominem* arrangements to ensure that natural justice was done.

On 28 July 1702 Giovanni Alemanni bought the *gastaldia* for 4,011 ducats 23 *grossi* in anticipation (*in aspettiva*). This meant that he was putting down a first option on its purchase when, on Ricci's death, it would become vacant. On 22 April 1703 Nicolò Olmo bought the office from Foresti. On 5 September of that year, however, he was appointed *nodaro all'Arsenale* (notary for matters concerning the famous shipyard, the Arsenal) and found it difficult—or so he said—to combine the two posts. On 13 December 1704 the procurators agreed to allow the office to be exercised by a substitute, the very Giovanni Alemanni who had purchased it *in aspettiva*. On 12 May Olmo and Alemanni jointly petitioned the procurators for permission to pass on the office to Martino Alemanni, who was Giovanni's son and now Nicolò Olmo's son-in-law; the *gastaldia* was to be in lieu of a dowry. The procurators gave their assent, and Marino Alemanni served until 27 April 1721, when he sold the *gastaldia* to Giovanni Pietro Corner.[9] The procurators agreed to the transfer provided that Corner could find someone to deposit the customary 400 ducats as his surety—such pledges (*piegarie*) were essential in an age when the lack of conventions concerning extradition allowed a defaulter to escape to a neighbouring state almost with impunity. Corner failed to find a guarantor and on 7 June 1721 backed out. Into his shoes stepped Giovanni Marco Triva, who was able to raise an even larger surety of 5000 ducats. Triva's stewardship was marked by financial irregularities that the procurators were still trying to sort out many years later. At some stage he sold the *gastaldia* to Nicolò Manin, who as a noble was naturally ineligible to occupy it himself, though he could perhaps profit from dealing in it.

Pietro Antonio Vinaccesi's letter notifying the procurators of his purchase and requesting ratification gives us some information about his life. He writes of having been employed for over 10 years as an accountant familiar with double-entry book-keeping and the workings of the state bank. His guarantor is a local merchant, Giovanni Domenico Mosca. It is interesting that in accepting him, the procurators make no reference to his late father, even though one of them, Marin II Zorzi, was a close neighbour and the brother of his landlord.

The four years that Pietro Antonio spent in the service of the Procuratia de Supra seem to have been uneventful. In April 1727

---

[9] According to Tassini ('Notizie storiche', i. 34), Martino Alemanni was in 1730 the *guardian grande* of the Scuola di San Marco, one of the great Venetian confraternities called *scuole grandi*. In *I-Vmc*, Ms. Gradenigo 83, 'Cittadini veneziani'), i. fo. 28^r, we read that in the 1740s (the date is given as '174. . .') Alemanni died in the prison of San Marco, to which he had been sent for civil debt.

Marc'Antonio Ricci finally died, and the *gastaldia* reverted to the State. Vinaccesi was able, however, to serve out the rest of the year (*more veneto*) until the end of February 1728. Sadly, Giovanni Alemanni, the purchaser *in aspettiva*, was no longer alive to enjoy the fruits of his speculation. The next *gastaldo* was Bortolo Vuittieri, appointed on 29 March 1728. He may not have neeeded to buy the post, as exactly one month later the Senate decided, at the request of the procurators themselves, to make both *gastaldie* of the Procuratia de Supra purely elective in future.

After these four years as an administrator, Pietro Antonio seems to have taken up (or returned on a full-time basis to?) the traditional family occupation: that of *mercante*. At some point between 1719 and 1728 he entered a second marriage that was to prove both more fertile and more lucrative than the first. His new wife was Margarita Albergoni (or Albrigoni), who came from a prominent citizen family that had acquired the status of *cittadini originari* in 1704.[10] Margarita brought with her a superb dowry that included residential and commercial property in Venice, and large landholdings mostly in the neighbourhood of Padua that included a *casa dominicale* (landowner's house) in Villa delle Fratte, together with numerous cottages rented out to farm-workers.[11] This dowry was Margarita's portion of an accumulated family trust that had begun with the will of Nicolò Dolce in 1394 and continued with subsequent bequests from Giovanni Antonio Leffio (1604), Giovanni Antonio Faustini (1663), Margarita Armellini (1680), and the bride's father Francesco Albergoni (1728).[12] The real estate inherited by Pietro Antonio from his own family seems to have been nil, judging from the return he completed for the Venetian property census of 1740.[13] He did, however, own part of a large house on the Fondamenta della Misericordia in the *contrada* of San Marcilian, for which he paid an annual *livello* of 25 ducats to the church of the same name. At some point before 1740 Margarita died, and Pietro Antonio became the administrator of her property on behalf of their children, who numbered at least five.[14]

In 1741 Pietro Antonio embarked on a third, totally disastrous, marriage that was to wreck his own career and bequeath to his heirs an uphill, though eventually successful, struggle to recover the family property. The marriage and the legal wrangles accompanying its dissolution are related minutely in two documents. The first is the 164-page official printed

[10] Tassini, 'Notizie storiche', i. 24.

[11] *I-Vas*, Dieci Savi alle Redecime, Busta 324, Estimo del 1740, condizione della città, San Polo, no. 261.

[12] *I-Vas*, Giudici di Petizion, Busta 484/149, Inventario dal 1788 al 1789, no. 23, Sant'Agostino, inventory of Pietro Vinaccesi dated 26 Aug. 1789 (day of death).

[13] *I-Vas*, Dieci Savi alle Redecime, Busta 324, Estimo del 1740, condizione della città, San Polo, no. 260.

[14] See App. A.6 (nos. 87–91) for details of Pietro Antonio's children.

account of the case (supplemented by some loose manuscript documents) preserved in the archives of the Inquisitori di Stato;[15] the second is a report sent to the patriarch of Venice from the office of the abbot of Guastalla (who was the senior churchman in that city), following an investigation into the validity of the marriage.[16] It would be out of place here to relate the affair in detail, despite its intrinsic fascination, but a brief account can shed an interesting light on the life of the Venetian middle class in the mid-eighteenth century.

In the middle of 1741 Pietro Antonio had some business in Guastalla, a little duchy, adjoining that of Mantua, which remained, precariously, under the rule of the Gonzaga family. There he met the *marchesa* Giovanna Miseroni, widow of Gotthard Miseroni, a general in imperial service. Giovanna's previous home appears to have been Parma, then under occupation by imperial troops. Using the duchess's secretary as an intermediary, Pietro Antonio sought Giovanna's hand in marriage. In letters written to her from Venice he tried to convince her of his status as a count (improbable, but not impossible) and of the sincerity of his affections. After they had agreed to marry, the place in which the ceremony should be conducted presented a problem. Giovanna preferred to arrive in Venice, a city where she would be a stranger, already married, but as neither she nor the bridegroom had permanent residence in Guastalla, therefore no parish priest who knew either of them, one of them had to apply to the abbot of Guastalla for a special licence. Giovanna tried this but was refused, since she did not have the necessary *documenti di stato libero* confirming that neither was already married or otherwise debarred from marrying. Eventually, the ceremony was performed on 10 August in a highly improvised manner. Pietro Antonio travelled to Parma and was reunited with Giovanna in a house belonging to the Viotti brothers, old acquaintances of the bride. The priest who married them was a Dominican, Joseph Sellerigg, a chaplain to the Traun regiment stationed in Parma. On 12 August, after a fleeting visit to Guastalla in order to collect the rest of Giovanna's property, the pair transported themselves, and the property constituting the dowry, to Venice by boat. Subsequently, Pietro Antonio withdrew, acting on Giovanna's behalf, about 5,000 florins from her bank accounts in the Hapsburg lands.

The trouble began almost immediately, when Pietro Antonio refused to sign the inventory itemizing and valuing the property and money brought into the marriage by his wife. As we saw earlier, a wife's dowry was legally recoverable in certain circumstances, so it was essential to assess its

---

[15] See Ch. 1, n. 4.

[16] Venice, Archivio storico della Curia Patriarcale, Actorum, Filza 27. I am grateful to Gastone Vio for obtaining a photocopy of this document on my behalf.

value at the outset. The couple soon became estranged and within two years had separated. Giovanna moved out into other accommodation. It appears that at that time Pietro Antonio was absent from Venice, perhaps on business, and this fact gave Giovanna the opportunity to institute proceedings that would formalize their separation. On 8 August 1743 the Giudici dell'Esaminador, the competent legal authority, ordered the taking of an inventory of the contents of the house, which would subsequently be removed to a neutral place pending apportionment. This long list contains three items of musical interest: a harpsichord ('caocimbalo'), a spinet, and a trumpet.

While this was happening, Giovanni found witnesses to affirm that although they could not vouch for the accuracy of every item listed in her inventory or the exact sum of money belonging to her that her husband had drawn out, the claim appeared genuine. On 19 August Giovanni obtained the agreement of the authorities to have Pietro Antonio's account in the public savings bank (the Banco Giro) frozen. On 26 August we learn of the first counter-move on the husband's part. He made a certain Angelo Sticcotti guardian of his children. This man is listed as a tutor ('tien scuola') in the census of 1745 for the assessment of a special tax to pay for Venice's new public street lighting and as a clerk (*scrittural*) in the similar census of 1750.[17] His address is given in both documents as the Fondamenta della Misericordia: this refers to Pietro Antonio's former house, which he was by then occupying. It seems likely that Sticcotti was a business associate, perhaps an employee, of Pietro Antonio. The purpose of the guardianship was obviously to safeguard for the children the property that had come to them through their mother.

On 27 August the Giudici di Procurator, the magistrates to whom the case had been referred, had all the property of Pietro Antonio's house valued. Four lists were prepared. The first, valued at 1,898 ducats 5 *grossi*, comprised the goods that Giovanna claimed to have brought with her. The second, valued at 1,698 ducats 5 *grossi*, assessed her husband's property; to the instruments listed earlier is added a psaltery, an instrument very fashionable in the early eighteenth century. The third list was of Pietro Antonio's paintings, which were probably inherited in the main from his father. Since its contents are of special interest, both for what they tell us about Benedetto's connoisseurship and for the information they contain of interest to art historians, the list is transcribed as Appendix B.31. Surprisingly, in view of the presence among the paintings of works identified by the valuer (a local painter, Domenico Clucerino) as being by such great masters as Brueghel, Titian, and Tiepolo, their total

[17] *I-Vas*, Provveditori alle Pompe: Busta 14, Elenchi degli abitanti dei sestieri di . . . S. Polo, 1745; Busta 15, Elenchi . . . S. Polo, 1750.

value was assessed at only 191 ducats. A fourth list valued the jewellery at 1,295 ducats.

On 30 August Giovanna was instructed by the authorities, at Sticcotti's request, to return all goods she had removed from the house. The same day, the Giudici di Procurator awarded her the sum of 4,832 ducats 10 *grossi* (the total of the four lists minus the valuers' fees and other expenses), provided that there were no claims from other creditors. Then on 4 September they ordered the abbess of the convent of San Bernardo di Murano, where Pietro Antonio's daughter Angela was being educated, to yield up certain property that her father had sent there. However, although a witness was later to claim that Pietro Antonio, when leaving Venice, had indeed instructed him to take some valuable pieces of silverware to the convent, the sisters denied all knowledge of it.

On 4 September a lawyer representing Sticcotti obtained a stay of execution. The main grounds for the appeal were that Giovanna was being allowed to take property from Pietro Antonio to a greater value than the money (from the bank withdrawals) that he owed her. Giovanna's lawyer counter-attacked by demanding on 27 September to see the books of Pietro Antonio's business. To prevent either party from confusing the situation hopelessly by removing property in an unsupervised fashion from the house, the Giudici dell'Esaminador were sent there once more in order to check against the inventories what was missing and afterwards to seal all entrances. On 27 September the magistrates decided that until the end of her action to recover her dowry Giovanna should receive from Sticcotti 400 ducats per annum, plus an extra 100 ducats towards her legal expenses.

Meanwhile, Pietro Antonio had returned to Venice. He decided to conduct his own defence (leaving the lawyer, however, to represent his children and Sticcotti). The authorities now finally ordered the goods to be removed from his house to a neutral place, and the case was transferred to a higher court, that of the Consiglio dei Quaranta Civil Vecchia. In his preliminary statement on 17 February 1744 Pietro Antonio argued that he had been treated badly and exposed unfairly to public ridicule; Giovanna countered via her lawyer by describing how she had been left penniless through denial of her dowry. Pietro Antonio then had a small success: on 24 February the authorities revoked the sequestration of his money in the Banco Giro, which had been contrary to law, since he was not bankrupt. Resuming his case on 20 March, Pietro Antonio stated his willingness to pay Giovanna 5,000 ducats, the cash portion of her dowry, but disputed the inventory of her property, since, he claimed, several items listed in it had been purchased by him. He referred also to property listed in the first inventory (August 1743) but missing from the second (October 1743), obviously because Giovanna had removed it in the intervening period.

In her reply, Giovanna claimed that the cash portion of the dowry was greater than her husband allowed and denied that she had included any property of his in the list of her own property, challenging him to prove otherwise. On 12 May the magistrates ordered Pietro Antonio to pay over the agreed annual allowance and contribution towards Giovanna's legal expenses. Sensing, perhaps, that his cause was ultimately lost, Pietro Antonio on 23 May formally made over to Sticcotti, as guardian of his children, the dowry he had received from Margarita. It is interesting to see that the items entered under this head comprise not only the possessions on the *terraferma* but a good deal of the property in the house in San Marcilian, including all the paintings (which almost certainly did not come originally from Margarita!).

Pietro Antonio stalled over paying Giovanna the 500 ducats as instructed and on 7 June was fined another 500 ducats for non-compliance. Then on 9 September the court learned from the patriarch of Venice that the marriage was null and void 'ex defectu proprii parochi': the ceremony had been conducted neither by a parish priest nor by any other authorized person. On 15 October Giovanna married a Count Paolo Sormani, who had no doubt been her secret backer all along.

On 28 November the court delivered its verdict, awarding Giovanna half the value of the property in most of the categories. The total net value of the dowry was assessed as 5,967 ducats 4 *grossi*. Pietro Antonio appealed, finding irregularities in the calculation that unfairly favoured Giovanna; she, for her part, made allegations against him. To and fro the argument continued until, not before time, the lawyers representing both sides came to an agreement on 16 May 1745, whereby Pietro Antonio was to pay Giovanna a final, round sum of 2,000 ducats.

Rather than comply, the ex-husband chose to leave Venice. He made for Ferrara, taking some jewellery with him, and was followed there by Giovanna, who had him arrested. Some of the money owed was seized, but 898 ducats remained. Pietro Antonio fled once again, this time to Rome. On 26 December 1748 he was recognized in Venice, despite wearing a carnival mask, and was arrested again and imprisoned. On 27 August 1749 Giovanna magnanimously withdrew her claim for the outstanding money, clearing the way for Pietro Antonio's release on 6 September that year. We hear no more of him, and he presumably rejoined his family.

It is impossible to assess the rights and wrongs of this sorry affair with any certainty. One is left with the impression that both parties were at fault and that if Pietro Antonio behaved like an 'adventurer' at the beginning, Giovanna certainly played the part of an 'adventuress' later on.

Remarkably, in view of all the earlier acrimony, Giovanna seems later to have been a willing partner in the efforts of Pietro Antonio's children to recover their forfeited property. The fate of the *beni immobili*, at least, can be traced through the lists of acquisitions and disposals maintained by the Republic from the completion of the 1740 property census until 1797.[18] In 1740 Pietro Antonio, as administrator of his children's funds, had been assessed for a *decima* of 13 ducats 18 *grossi*; that is to say, the net income from rents and agricultural produce was 10 times that sum. On 9 June 1744 his house (free of a *decima*, since it was owner-occupied) was made over to Sticcotti. Then on 4 August the property was divided between the Vinaccesi children and Giovanna, now the *marchesa* Sormani; the latter's share of the *decima* was 9 ducats 13 *grossi*—considerably more than half. On 12 September 1757 the house in the Fondamenta della Misericordia was sold to Count Ferdinando Maldura and his brothers; these were probably members of the same family as the Paduan nobles of that name to whom, in 1740, Margarita's estate was paying an annual *livello* of 22 ducats. The implication is that the sale was made to pay off debts.

But as early as 28 September 1753 there is evidence of co-operation between Giovanna and the Vinaccesis, for on that day she acquired property from Margarita Albergoni's brother Giovanni Antonio and another Albergoni, Bortolo Maria, which was immediately transferred to Angela and Pietro Vinaccesi. This was probably a rationalization of landholdings in anticipation of the eventual reversion of their intended inheritance to Margarita's descendants. On 30 December 1786, less than three years before Pietro's death, that event occurred. It may well have been a disposition of Giovanna's will that it should happen, for this is the last transaction recorded under her name. The result was that in the inventory of Pietro's property made in 1789 the *beni immobili* were much as they had been in 1740.

Of the later Venetian Vinaccesis, only one further figure deserves comment. This was Francesco Maria (90), a younger brother of Pietro. He was a priest, and his small claim to fame is that he was the author of a published collection of panegyrics in praise of the Blessed Giovanni Marinoni delivered at the church of the Theatines (Teatini) in Venice on 4–6 September 1763.[19]

During the eighteenth century the Vinaccesis continued to exist—but little more—in Brescia. Near the beginning of the century parish records mention an Angelo (97) and a Gaetano (98) Vinaccesi, but their occupations are unknown. They were most likely descendants of the composer

[18] *I-Vas*: Dieci Savi sopra le decime in Rialto, Busta 1526, Libro trasporto Fia 1740, opening 495; Registro 1528, Quaderno trasporto Fia E (nos. 760–1000), openings 455, 954, and 985; Registro 1529, Quaderno trasporto Fia E (nos. 1001–1239), openings 1015, 1113, 1128, and 1161.

[19] Francesco Maria Vinaccesi, *Panegirici recitati da tre celebri oratori . . . adonate del Beato Giovanni Marinoni . . . in occasione del triduo solenizzato nella chiesa de RR. PP. Teatini li 4, 5, 6 settembre 1763 . . .* (Venice, 1763). An example is preserved in *I-Vnm*, Misc. 4185[2–3].

Benedetto's cousin Vinaccese (42), for they include a Faustino, a name that appears earlier only in his branch of the family, while, conversely, not including any of the names traditional in the 'legitimate' branch (Lodovico, Francesco, Bernardino, Benedetto, etc.). Significantly, no property census after 1687 mentions them, which implies that they descended rapidly in the economic and social scale.

The final Vinaccesi to be considered is something of an enigma, inasmuch as he can be linked to neither the Brescian nor the Venetian branch of the family, though he probably belonged to one or the other. He is the comic actor Giovanni Vinaccesi, of whom we learn through a petition to the heads of the Council of Ten submitted by his fellow actors on 25 February 1786.[20] Apparently, the impresario of the Teatro Sant'Angelo, where the troupe was playing, had refused, contrary to custom, to pay Vinaccesi his full nightly fee of five *lire* during a period when he was indisposed. This actor is probably the same man as a certain Antonio (full name Giovanni Antonio?) Vinaccesi, likewise taking the role of Pantalone, who performed in Pistoia in carnival 1780.[21]

So, with an incongruous Pantalone our family history concludes. Perhaps, though, it is not inappropriate that of all the *commedia dell'arte* characters Giovanni Vinaccesi could have portrayed, it should be this figure of a solid bourgeois, for that, indeed, was the nature of his family, at least in happier days.

---

[20] *I-Vas*, Inquisitori di Stato, Busta 914, Casini di giuoco e conversazioni, teatri, 1742–1792, Fascicolo 'Teatro S. Angelo'.

[21] Alberto Chiappelli, *Storia del teatro in Pistoia dalle origini alla fine del secolo XVIII* (Florence, 1913), 151.

6

The Sonatas

SINCE the whole of Vinaccesi's known music for instruments, discounting instrumental numbers in vocal works, comes from his early Brescian period, it is logical to seek his musical roots in his native city. Care must be taken, however, not to view the Brescian musical tradition as something necessarily distinctive or self-contained. In Italy, during the early modern age, literature and the arts were among the most genuinely 'pan-Italian' of enterprises, the very cement that held national consciousness together. The free circulation of musicians (especially singers), the immunity of musical notes to censorship, the unifying force of the Church and its more or less standardized ritual, the sensitivity to fashion: all these factors worked in favour of a common musical language and practice. Where differences between cities or regions are apparent, they can usually be accounted for by social and economic factors that expanded or limited opportunities for the cultivation of certain genres without altering the general consciousness of musicians and their public.

Brescia's strong tradition of metal-working is reflected in the famous dynasty of organ-builders, the Antegnati family, which enjoyed a pre-eminence in this art throughout Italy from the mid-fifteenth to the mid-seventeenth century. Violin-makers, too, flourished in Brescia, especially in the early period before the rise of Cremona. Among the most famous names are those of Gasparo da Salò (1540–1609), Giovanni Paolo Maggini (*c*.1581–*c*.1632), and Giovanni Battista Rogeri (*fl*.1670–1705).

These two instrument-manufacturing traditions were reflected very unequally in Brescian musical life. Composers for organ, all of whom were naturally practising organists, were abundant and could find satisfactory employment at the Duomo and Brescia's many other churches. Only the most proficient and ambitious were tempted to move to larger centres. Emigrants among these organists included Massimiliano Neri (*c*.1615–1666) and Carlo Francesco Pollarolo (*c*.1653–1723). Paris Francesco Alghisi (1666–1733), mentioned in Chapter 2, worked briefly in Poland before returning to Brescia. Francesco Turini (*c*.1589–1656), who was born in Prague, is an example of a famous immigrant organist, serving at the Duomo from 1616 until his death.

Because of the lack of a court in Brescia, accomplished string players tended to settle elsewhere. The outstanding example is Biagio Marini (*c*.1587–1663), who was born into a respected citizen family. In 1615 Marini joined the *cappella* of San Marco in Venice and thereafter travelled widely, spending long periods north of the Alps, in the Netherlands and Germany. He returned to Brescia intermittently, but more, it seems, for domestic than for professional reasons. Marini's sonatas, especially those of his Op. 1 (1617), Op. 8 (1629), and Op. 22 (1655), are among the most inventive and imaginative of their time, but one fails to find any direct echo of them in the music of his Brescian contemporaries and successors.

In so far as there is a local Brescian tradition of music for strings preceding, and contemporary with, Vinaccesi, this music is utilitarian, non-innovative, and largely the work of organist-composers schooled in vocal polyphony. It is idiomatic only in the negative sense of avoiding the unpractical, not in the positive one of exploring technical possibilities. In 1673, during a period when he was organist at the Duomo, Carlo Francesco Pollarolo's father Orazio produced a collection of dance-movements for two violins and bass (*Suonate da camera a tre*, Op. 1), which he dedicated to Paolo Martinengo, a local nobleman; the publisher was the Bolognese firm of Giacomo Monti. These unpretentious and frankly rather dull pieces—which, since they are among the compositions most likely to have been known by Vinaccesi, must be regarded as possible influences on him—conform absolutely to the above description. Two movements, the Giga prima and the Giga quarta, are inscribed to 'Don Camillo Alessio violinista celeberrimo'. To speak of so obscure a musician as 'very famous' illustrates, perhaps, the limited horizons of Brescian musical life. A much more polished result is achieved in Paris Francesco Alghisi's Op. 1, a set of *Sonate da camera a tre* (Modena, 1693), but this collection is so closely modelled on Corelli's Op. 2 that it can hardly be taken as representative of a local tradition and in fact reinforces the point made earlier about the common musical language employed throughout Italy.

Perhaps the most significant composers among the Brescian string-players who remained in their native city were the two Tagliettis, Giulio (violin) and Luigi (cello), each of whom issued several collections of sonatas and concertos around and after 1700.[1] Both joined the orchestra of Santa Maria della Pace in 1695, just around the time when Vinaccesi was

---

[1] Although Taglietti (in local dialect, 'Taietti') is the name of an established Brescian citizen family, neither Giulio nor his probable relative Luigi Taglietti are mentioned in census returns from the 17th cent., which leads one to wonder whether they were victims of downward social mobility. *New Grove* gives the date of death of Giulio as 1715 and that of Luigi as 1718; both dates are much too early, for the first man made appearances at Santa Maria della Pace up to at least 1728, while the second 'vivait encor en 1750' according to Paul-Louis Roualle de Boisgelou, 'Table biographique des auteurs et compositeurs de musique dont les ouvrages sont à la Bibliothèque Nationale' (*F-Pn*, Vm.[8] 22). Since Boisgelou was born as early as 1734, he may easily have had an informant who knew Luigi Taglietti personally.

supplying compositions to that church. It is unlikely, however, that our composer became acquainted with their music in time to apply what he learned from it to his own instrumental compositions, unless his lost Op. 4 holds some surprises.

As the account-books of the Chiesa della Pace suggest, a large part of the instrumental music played in Brescia, both in private homes and in churches, must have been taken, directly or via manuscript copies, from collections published in the major centres of Venice, Bologna, and Rome. In this way the repertory of the courts of Modena and Mantua, the great churches of Rome and Venice, and the *accademie* of Bologna and Ferrara, could filter down to provincial musicians and keep them in touch with the latest developments. If a limitation existed, it was not in obtaining this music but in performing it with adequate resources. So although Brescia was bound to be a place where musical fashions were followed rather than set, there is no evidence that public taste lagged very significantly behind that of metropolitan centres or that whatever conservatism could be said to be present took on an identifiably local colouring.

Nothing in either the Brescian musical tradition or that of the *sonata da camera* quite prepares us for the startling novelty of Vinaccesi's first opus.[2] As listed in the second volume of Sartori's *Bibliografia della musica strumentale italiana*, the works appear innocuous enough, progressing from a Sonata I to a Sonata VI. It is only when their individual movements are identified (Sartori does this only when the movements do not form larger structures such as sonatas) that their extraordinary character emerges. In the outline below the movements of each sonata are shown. The italicized movements are those in the subsidiary key of each work; in the second column this key follows the principal key after a diagonal stroke. Upper and lower case represent the major and minor mode respectively.

I   C/a   1. Preludio 2. Allemanda 3. Sua variatione 4. *Corrente* 5. *Balletto* 6. *Giga* 7. *Sarabanda* 8. Taiheg 9. Menuet 10. Pira 11. Gavotta 12. Chiusa

II   d/F   1. Preludio 2. Allemanda 3. Corrente 4. Sua variatione 5. Balletto 6. *Giga* 7. *Sarabanda* 8. *Menuet* 9. Pira 10. Aria 11. Gavotta 12. Chiusa

III e/b   1. Preludio 2. Brando 3. Corrente 4. Balletto 5. *Arcicorrente* 6. *Giga francese* 7. *Sarabanda* 8. Pira 9. Menuet 10. Gavotta 11. Chiusa

---

[2] Much of the present discussion of Vinaccesi's Op. 1 is anticipated in my article 'The Taiheg, the Pira and Other Curiosities of Benedetto Vinaccesi's *Suonate da camera a tre*, Op. 1', *Music and Letters*, 75 (1994). I have tried, however, to expand certain parts of the discussion that are treated in a condensed manner in the article and, conversely, to summarize others that have been argued adequately there.

IV F/B♭ 1. Preludio 2. Allemanda 3. Balletto francese 4. *Corrente*
          5. *Balletto* 6. *Giga* 7. *Sarabanda* 8. Brando 9. Menuet
          10. Borea 11. Chiusa
V   g/c   1. Preludio 2. Allemanda 3. Corrente francese 4. *Balletto*
          5. *Menuet* 6. *Pira* 7. *Borea* 8. Arcicorrente 9. Aria 10. Menuet
          11. Chiusa
VI A/D   1. Preludio 2. Allemanda 3. Balletto francese 4. *Corrente*
          5. *Balletto* 6. *Giga* 7. *Menuet* 8. Pira 9. Taiheg 10. Menuet
          11. Gavotta 12. Chiusa

To include in such a collection even one instrumental work with as many as eleven or twelve movements is quite foreign to the practice of Italian composers in the seventeenth century. A search in Sartori's *Bibliografia* reveals isolated cases of cycles containing eight movements (Tomaso Motta's *Armonia capricciosa di suonate musicali da camera*, Op. 1, 1681), occasionally also seven or six. But to have a dozen as a matter of course in every work is a real innovation.

From where did Vinaccesi get the idea? He cannot have found it in his native Italian tradition—at least, this tradition as it is at present known to us, principally from the published repertory—since in 1687 composers were, as we shall shortly see, only just becoming acquainted with the notion of grouping dance-movements into fixed, organized cycles. If we are reminded of anything, it is the French *livre* for harpsichord (also organ and lute) represented by such masters as Chambonnières, Lebègue, and Louis Couperin, in which the work consists of a long string of short movements in the same *ton*, some of which may be *doubles* of earlier movements (finding a counterpart in the two 'variatione' movements in Vinaccesi's set) or further examples of the same dance (as in Vinaccesi's 'second' ballettos and minuets). French suites for viol from the same period offer similar characteristics.

It is a fact that in the period immediately preceding the appearance of Corelli's chamber sonatas (his Op. 2 came out in 1685, Op. 4 in 1694) French influence in northern Italian courts was at its height. A good example is Modena, whose duke, Alfonso IV d'Este, had married Mazarin's niece Laura Martinozzi in 1665. This French influence is very evident in the music of the composers associated with the Modenese court, who included Giovanni Battista Vitali (1632–16) and Giovanni Maria Bononcini (1642–78). Not infrequently, this tribute is overt, the dance-movements being described as 'alla francese' or simply 'francese'.

The collection by the otherwise unknown Motta just mentioned could have served Vinaccesi as an inspiration, if perhaps not a direct model.[3] It

---

[3] An example of Motta's Op. 1 is preserved in *I-Bc*, BB 25. It is noticeable that in this collection the rhythmic style of such dances as the corrente and gavotta closely resembles the French prototypes rather than their Italian derivatives, which suggests that Motta was near to the 'point of transmission'

was published in Milan and dedicated to Tomás Enriquez y Cabrera, the province's Spanish governor. The works are notated in two-stave score and, in the absence of any contrary indication, can be understood as intended for violin and bass. At the head of the 31 movements, acting as an introduction to the whole set rather than to any individual cycle of movements within it, stands a Preludio, which must be among the very first examples of its type in the Italian repertory. One would assume that this movement-species was taken over by the Italians from the *prélude* of French harpsichord and lute music. Most of the following pieces stand alone or belong to a conventional group of movements (the groups can be identified by the common key and, sometimes, common thematic characteristics of adjacent pieces), but nos. 10–17 inclusive form a suite-like assembly of eight movements in G minor, presenting the sequence Balletto–Borea–Galiarda–Canario–Corrente–Minué–Sarabanda–Borea. The duplication of the Borea (bourrée) and the prominence of the lighter, newer dances introduced to European society by the Parisian court ballet and opera of the 1660s and 1670s (bourrée, minuet, canarie) are noteworthy.

The French concept of *ton* allowed for the use alongside each other of dual major and minor versions of keys with a given tonic. A characteristic arrangement of the two modes was to have a minor enclave within an overall major framework, or vice versa.[4] The three or four movements in a related key (variously relative major/minor, dominant, and subdominant) that Vinaccesi situates in the middle of his sonatas can be viewed as an adaptation of this convention to native conditions. Since Italian musicians at this time treated the major and minor keys on the same tonic as only distantly related, a substitute 'alternative' key had to be found; not surprisingly, Vinaccesi opts for the same keys that he—and other Italian composers of his time—would be likely to use for tonal variety within other kinds of multi-movement structure such as the church sonata or the cantata. Apart from their common tonal identity, the movements forming the central core of each sonata have no special bond with each other: in thematic terms, they are well integrated into the cycle as a whole. The purpose of the change of key is simply to provide tonal variety—desirable for its own sake in works lasting well over ten minutes—and perhaps also to create two points of articulation in an otherwise rather featureless succession of movements of similar length. Since no other Italian composer during the whole of the baroque period wrote chamber sonatas of comparable length (as measured by the number of movements), the conditions

of French dance-music from France to Italy. Although the quality of its music is uneven, this collection would repay detailed investigation.

[4] An enclave of this kind is formed by the *Seconde Sarabande* and the *Vénitienne* in A major sandwiched among the pieces in A minor making up Rameau's first book of *Pièces de clavecin* (1706).

giving rise to the employment, for several consecutive movements, of a second key centre never arose again. In this respect alone Vinaccesi's sonatas constitute a unique experiment.

Thus far, we have taken somewhat for granted what we understand by a 'chamber sonata'. A clearer perception of what this concept entailed during the seventeenth century will confirm Vinaccesi's originality still more strongly.

Musicology has dealt unkindly with the baroque chamber sonata, indeed with baroque dance-forms in general. Too often, this genre has been treated as the poor relation of the so-called church sonata, an inferior derivative replacing strenuous fugues by facile binary-form structures, instrumental virtuosity by the undemanding patter of dance-rhythms. The distortion affects not only questions of value but also the perception of historical development. From reading standard accounts of the early sonata such as those by William S. Newman and Willi Apel, one gains little idea of the completely different process by which the 'church' and 'chamber' varieties of sonata achieved their classic definition in the works of Corelli before converging or undergoing various forms of hybridization in the hands of his successors.[5]

The salient point to grasp is that in the beginning, at the start of the seventeenth century, the term 'sonata' (literally, 'piece for playing') was applied only to single movements, not to cycles containing several movements. Such single movements could be abstract in nature (in which case 'sonata' was almost the only possible term to apply if the movement was neither a 'canzona' nor a 'toccata') or, equally well, dances (in which case 'sonata' was merely a more general description).

Over the course of several decades the same term came to denote a composition in several movements. Judging by the appearance of Corelli's sonatas, in which both types of sonata usually contain between three and five movements, the process would seem to have been parallel and uniform. But this similarity masks a total dissimilarity in the evolution of each genre towards the same point. To use a metaphor drawn from nuclear physics: the church sonata became a multi-movement genre through fission, the chamber sonata through fusion.

Crucial to this discussion is the definition of what we mean by a 'movement'. This definition is more elusive than one might imagine. One cannot simply say that a new movement begins after a double-bar, a fermata, a change of tempo, a change of metre, or a change of key-centre. Each of these features contributes to a sense of demarcation between two move-

[5] William S. Newman, *The Sonata in the Baroque Era* (Chapel Hill, NC, 1959); Willi Apel, *Italian Violin Music of the Seventeenth Century* (Bloomington, Ind., 1990). The topic has, however, been addressed very fully in John Daverio, 'Formal Design and Terminology in the pre-Corellian "Sonata" and Related Instrumental Forms in the Printed Sources', Ph.D. diss. (Boston University, 1983).

ments, but none establishes it conclusively unless (and this scarcely happens outside programme music) the composer chooses to preface each movement by an individual name or number. So gradual and imperceptible was the emergence of the modern concept of a 'movement' that the point at which the sonata in one movement but several contrasted sections (as represented, say, by Monteverdi's *Sonata sopra Sancta Maria* in the Vespers of 1610) evolved into a sonata in several more or less homogeneous movements cannot be determined, even within the work of a single composer, without a high degree of arbitrariness. Apel has identified Maurizio Cazzati's *Canzoni a tre*, Op. 2 (1642), and Massimiliano Neri's *Sonate e canzone*, Op. 1 (1644), as the first published works to show a clear division into discrete movements.[6] But these collections are at best signposts, not landmarks. Even in Corelli's church sonatas (Op. 1, 1681, and Op. 3, 1685) there exist several slow portions whose status as separate movements or as opening or closing sections within a larger movement is uncertain. A work as late as the third Brandenburg Concerto of J. S. Bach has a 'middle' (two Adagio chords occupying a single bar) whose nature remains controversial. Is it an addendum to the first movement? A preface to the last movement? An embryonic slow movement requiring elaboration? To be sure, the seventeenth century was probably unconcerned about what was, or was not, a 'movement': all breaks in the course of a work were short; players had not yet developed the habit of retuning between movements; and audiences coughed as necessity, not custom, demanded.

All the qualifications introduced above do not mean, of course, that we should deny the basic fact that by the time of Corelli the church sonata was a work in several movements, even though it usually bears the stigmata of its single-movement origin (for example, in the close thematic relationships that often exist between quick movements, a throwback to the time when an opening section could be repeated in a different metre). The point is, rather, that the process was much less complete than is commonly imagined.

With the chamber sonata, the problem is quite different. Even when two or more dance-movements are thematically related—one movement may even be a simple rhythmic paraphrase of the other, after the fashion of the Renaissance *Tanz* and *Nachtanz*—their separate identity is not in doubt. What needs to be established, rather, is the point at which separate dances (or 'sonatas') join up to form a new kind of sonata comprising several of them at once.

This, too, was the result of a gradual process and is made more difficult for us to investigate by the fact that right up to the time of Corelli the

---

[6] *Italian Violin Music*, 9.

existence of these multi-movement entities is implicit rather than explicit—suggested by the juxtaposition (sometimes, the mere presence within the same collection) of thematically cognate movements in the same key rather than by the use of titles unambiguously separating off one work from the next.

Four preliminary stages in the evolution towards this state can be identified. The stages overlap very considerably in time and are consecutive in a logical rather than a simple chronological sense, even though they do certainly have the appearance of a line of historical progression. The first stage is represented by collections of dances in which, in so far as the sequence of movements is orderly, each dance-type forms a separate cluster. A very clear example of this approach is G. B. Vitali's set of *Correnti e balletti da camera*, Op. 1 (1666), which consists of twelve assorted balletti followed by twelve assorted correnti. The thought immediately arises whether each balletto can be teamed up with a corresponding corrente to make a composite work. As Ex. 1 shows, the attempt begins promisingly, for the first and second balletto and corrente, in D minor and C minor respectively, fit together very well not only tonally but also thematically. Unfortunately, the process then breaks down. Only the fourth balletto and fifth corrente, in C major, and the twelfth balletto and eleventh corrente, in B flat major, can be formed into a similar partnership; the rest of the dances resist pairing altogether. One has to conclude that the formation of such suites was at best facultative and occasional. Certainly, the presence, on widely separated pages, of movements meant to be played in sequence is an improbable situation to imagine.

Ex. 1. G. B. Vitali, Op. 1 nos. 1 and 2, movement openings

a
Balletto I

b
Corrente I

c
Balletto II

d
Corrente II

The second stage accords full recognition to the idea of a suite by placing in consecutive order whatever movements are intended to belong to it.

This system is followed by the eight pieces in G minor in Motta's Op. 1. The only rule of thumb to guide the performer is that the suite continues for as long as the key remains the same but no longer. As the similarly organized suites in Rameau's *livres de clavecin* show, this is a perfectly workable convention provided that unity of key (or *ton*) is maintained. Motta's collection illustrates the (for us) confusing variety of approach possible at the time, for while the eight-movement suite in G minor is partnered by similar groups in A minor (six movements, including the opening Preludio) and D major (three movements), the remaining fourteen movements all form simple pairs or remain singletons.

In the third stage the boundaries of each suite are made a little clearer by beginning each with a numbered movement of identical type. Pirro Albergati's *Balletti, correnti, sarabande e gighe a violino e violone con il secondo violino a beneplacito*, Op. 1 (1682), opens all its suites except the last two with a balletto, starting with Balletto I and ending with Balletto VII. This practice of making the later members of a group of dances subsidiary to the opening dance, whose title may then be used to connote the suite as a whole (rather as the term *ouverture* stands not merely for the opening movement of an orchestral suite but for the complete cycle of movements), goes back to the earliest times. It is implicit in cases where, for example, an allemanda is followed by 'sua corrente'.

Once the fixed opening movement of each suite has been numbered, the composer has to decide whether all the other movements should be numbered similarly, according to their respective type. Albergati, in his Op. 1, is among those who choose to number all the movements. But this consistent procedure gives rise to some curiously inconsistent results, since the make-up of each suite is not identical. Thus we have a suite in which Balletto V is followed by Giga IV and Sarabanda IV. One way round the problem was to make the composition of each suite completely uniform. This is the case in Giovanni Battista Bassani's *Balletti, correnti, gighe e sarabande a violino e violone . . . con il secondo violino a beneplacito*, Op. 1 (1677), which never deviates from the structure balletto–corrente–giga–sarabanda. But clarity has been achieved at a heavy price, which is the total standardization of structure.

It was Corelli himself who freed the suite (or, as we may now call it, the chamber sonata) from this unnecessary strait-jacket.[7] He identified each work by a name (Sonata I, etc.) that was different from the names used for individual movements. By this simplest of means, he enabled a sonata to contain one movement or several (the last sonata of Op. 2 in fact

[7] The hypothesis has been advanced that Corelli derived the idea of a multi-movement chamber sonata from Georg Muffat (and, via him, the German tradition in general). If true, this would be a startling reversal of the normal direction of influence. See John Daverio, 'In Search of the Sonata da Camera, before Corelli', *Acta musicologica*, 57 (1984), 195-214.

consists of a single long movement, a chaconne) and to vary the key of internal movements without restriction. In general, however, Corelli likes to pattern the chamber sonata fairly closely on the church sonata, compensating for the lack of any truly slow dance-types (the Italian sarabanda was at the time a quick dance) by using an abstract slow movement as an introductory prelude and occasionally inserting another at a later point. It is typical of Corelli's 'classicizing' approach that in his trio sonatas he should restrict himself to a very small selection of dance-types. Discounting the special case of the ciacona, we have only the allemanda, corrente, sarabanda, giga, and gavotta. The last-named dance is the sole representative of the non-traditional dances introduced via the ballet, a group that also includes the borea and the minuet, both of which were certainly popular in Italy by the 1680s. Because of Corelli's dominant influence, the Italian chamber sonata never came to cultivate the wide range of dance-types that we encounter, for instance, in the German keyboard suite. The narrowness of its repertory of dances had another consequence. In order to prevent repetitiveness within a collection that might contain as many as twelve examples of a single dance, the possible stylizations of each type (according to tempo, metrical and rhythmic prescription, melodic character, texture, and form) became increasingly diverse. This process tended to dissolve the identity of each dance so that virtually any slow or moderately paced movement in common time could be called an allemanda, any movement in compound time or dotted rhythm a giga. In the later violin sonatas of Vivaldi, which take this process to its ultimate point, the names of the dances finally become mere labels of convenience, a camouflage for an essentially abstract approach.

Seen in this perspective, Vinaccesi's Op. 1 represents 'the way not taken'. Together with Carlo Andrea Mazzolini's *Sonate per camera a tre*, Op. 1, also of 1687, it is the first known published collection of trio sonatas to imitate Corelli's Op. 2 by using the term 'sonata' with reference to an integrated cycle of several movements. To that extent, it looks ahead. But at the same time it is retrospective in its attempt to be all-encompassing: to complement the expected allemanda, corrente, sarabanda, and giga by, on one hand, the obsolescent brando and, on the other, the newly fashionable gavotta, borea, and minuet. Vinaccesi even finds space for 'novelty' movements—the taiheg and pira. In this important respect, his chamber sonatas have the appearance more of exotic transplants from the tradition of French *pièces* than of straightforward imitations of the Corellian, or any other Italian, model. If we knew more about court life at Castiglione delle Stiviere, we might gain some insight into the reason for this marked French orientation.

In Corelli's Op. 2, as in the informal groups of dances in earlier collections, certain more or less fixed principles appear to govern the order in which movements appear. This order probably reflects ballroom practice of the time. When present, the allemanda or balletto always appear in first place, followed by the corrente, the sarabanda, and the giga or gavotta. The arrangement also enshrines a general feature of the organization of musical works in the baroque (and early classical) period, which is that the longer, weightier movements precede the shorter, lighter ones. Later, as the dance-titles lost their intimate connection with practice on the dance-floor, Italian chamber sonatas often departed from the traditional system of ordering. Already in Corelli's Op. 4 (1694), two sonatas, nos. 1 and 11, place the allemanda after the corrente.

To a large extent, Vinaccesi's six sonatas follow a common plan. The underlying scheme is a sequence of nine movements: preludio–allemanda–corrente–balletta–giga–sarabanda–menuet–pira–chiusa. This allows two or three extra movements to be inserted at any point to make up the total of eleven or twelve. In addition, a few simple substitutions are made. Thus the Brando in Sonata III replaces the usual allemanda. In every collection of six or twelve works of the same kind for the identical combination of instruments a baroque composer has to weigh up the comparative advantages of uniformity and diversity: too much regularity, and the works lose their individuality; too little regularity, and the set loses its cohesiveness. Our composer steers a skilful course between these two opposite hazards.

It is appropriate to begin our discussion of the sonatas with a review of the different dance-types and their interpretation by Vinaccesi. Even after thirty years, the best general account in musicological literature of baroque dances as they appear in Italian chamber music of the mid-seventeenth century remains William Klenz's standard work on Giovanni Maria Bononcini, which draws heavily on knowledge gleaned from dancing primers of the period.[8] This source of information is gratefully acknowledged. However, some of the dances represented in Vinaccesi's set are late arrivals on the scene that Bononcini did not know, or at any rate did not cultivate; here other sources of information must suffice.

The allemanda, a dance of some antiquity, belongs to the category defined by Klenz as 'processional company dances' of 'group-linear' character.[9] In other words, it is a formal dance for the entire company entailing movement in straight lines (rather than rotation). Klenz describes it as a social stylization of a slow march that expresses the hierarchy of the members of the company prior to their entry into the more egalitarian world of the couple dances. Vinaccesi's five examples express between them the wide variety of tempo that an allemanda can accommodate, ranging from the 'largo' of that in Sonata I to the 'presto' movement in

---

[8] *Giovanni Maria Bononcini of Modena* (Durham, NC, [2]/1962).   [9] Ibid. 99.

Sonata VI. Only two (in Sonatas I and V) feature the semiquaver upbeat that is so much a hallmark of the dance. In all five the texture is kept fairly simple: such contrapuntal interplay as there is tends to occur between first violin and bass, leaving the second violin to its own devices. The absence of any conspicuous imitative patterns, canonic or fugal, is noteworthy, since the allemanda is one of only two dances (the other is the giga) in which imitative openings to the two sections are almost common enough to rank as a topos (cf. Corelli, Op. 2 nos. 5 and 7). Vinaccesi's intention here was probably to reduce the relative importance of the allemanda in view of the great length of the cycles, since in chamber sonatas of conventional dimensions this dance often carries a weight equivalent to that of the first allegro in a church sonata. The example in Sonata IV has the unusual performance direction 'allegro ma soave'. The suggestion that gaiety and suavity are normally to be regarded as antithetical reminds us that the usual mode of performing baroque dance-music for strings is light and springy. Before leaving the allemandas, we should note the 'variatione' that follows the example in Sonata I. This is a very straightforward type of variation that simply breaks down longer notes into a group of shorter notes (semiquavers), so producing a more even rhythmic flow. In the Italian baroque tradition such movements are very much rarer—at least, in a notated form open to scrutiny—than in French music of the same time; in that perspective, it is perhaps a shame that Vinaccesi's application of variation technique is here so modest and decorous.

The balletto, likewise a dance in common time, also belongs to the 'group-linear' category. Its specific function in the ballroom, according to Klenz, was to accompany the formal stylization of honours prior to the start of the couple dances.[10] Unlike the allemanda, it could contain 'elements of pantomime' (Klenz's phrase), expressed in music by little whimsical touches. Vinaccesi's seven examples (Sonatas IV and VI contain *balletti francesi* in addition to the balletto proper) bear this description out perfectly. In the first two sonatas, the humour derives from an exaggerated use of syncopation; in the fourth sonata, from cheeky fanfare-like motives tossed between the violins;[11] in the fifth sonata, from the contrapuntal opposition of dotted rhythms (dotted quaver plus semiquaver) and running semiquavers; in the sixth sonata, from long series of individually trilled crotchets. Most original of all is the use of the *tremolo* in Sonata III. Vinaccesi heads the movement 'Lireggiato ma presto'; *lireggiare* means 'to slur', and the fact that most of the marked slurs appear over four qua-

[10] *Giovanni Maria Bononcini of Modena* (Durham, NC, [2]/1962), 93.
[11] These quickfire exchanges find a close counterpart in the Balletto from the ninth of Albinoni's *Balletti a quattro* (*c*.1695), illustrated in Talbot, *Tomaso Albinoni: The Venetian Composer and his World* (Oxford, 1990), 113.

vers of the same pitch points to the *portato* effect usually conveyed in the seventeenth century by the term *tremolo*. The first section of this movement is shown as Ex. 2.

Ex. 2. Op. 1 no. 3, Balletto

The significance of the word 'francese' in the two additional ballettos (occurring as third movements in Sonatas IV and VI) is not easy to explain. In Italian music of the middle and late Baroque, the description is most commonly encountered in movements whose pervasive dotted rhythms recall French *inégalité* at its most extreme. This stylistic feature is clearly present in the Giga francese found in Sonata III of the present set. In these ballettos, however, dotted rhythms have no special prominence, for the movements outwardly resemble smoothly flowing correnti of the conventional Italian type. Since both are in triple time rather than the usual common time, one is tempted to hazard a guess that this metrical peculiarity is the defining characteristic of the appellation 'French'. Whatever the true explanation, this case shows how difficult it is to distinguish dance-types on the basis of musical criteria alone without a detailed knowledge of ballroom practice in the relevant place at the relevant time.

The aria is a less formal equivalent of the balletto designed, in Klenz's words, for 'improvised honours' not requiring a high degree of stylization.[12] Its name can easily mislead, for this is not an instrumental derivative of the vocal aria but an autonomous dance-form sharing the general characteristics of other dances. This is as evident from the movements called 'air' or 'aria' in J. S. Bach's suites and partitas for keyboard as from the examples in Vinaccesi's second and fifth sonatas. As befits the lack of solemnity required of this dance, Vinaccesi's two arias are jauntily tuneful.

As 'the most popular couple dance of the day',[13] the corrente could hardly be omitted from any of Vinaccesi's sonatas. The composer treats it as a dreamily reflective rather than vigorous dance, and this quality is suggested by the direction 'affettuoso' heading every corrente except the one in Sonata V. Whether the movement is notated in 3/4, 3/2, or 6/4 (treated exactly like two bars in 3/4), the traditional rhythmic character of the Italian corrente is carefully preserved. In essence, this consists of varying the position of the subsidiary metrical accent (which is often reinforced by a harmonic change) between the second and third beats in the bar. The formula minim–crotchet–crotchet–minim (in 3/2 metre the note-values are doubled) is used in pre-cadential position to produce the characteristic *pas de courante*. The example in Sonata III is a 'Corrente francese'. Nothing remotely identifiable as a 'French' quality is evident from the rhythmic structure of this movement. The one thing setting it apart from the rest is its 'allegro' direction. Perhaps, then, this is a reference merely to the speed or mood of the dance, which in the ballroom might well have given rise to slightly different steps. The variation of the corrente in the second sonata is a straightforward *double* similar in nature to the variation of the allemanda in the preceding work.

Sonatas III and V contain a separate movement described as an 'arci-corrente'. I have been able to find no mention of this type in musicological literature, contemporary or modern. Outwardly, the two examples resemble ordinary correnti. That in Sonata III, notated in 3/2 metre, is marked 'grave'; that in Sonata V, in 6/4, is another 'affettuoso' movement. Perhaps we should infer from the 'grave' direction that the distinguishing characteristic of an 'arch'-*corrente* is its slow tempo, but this conclusion must remain, at best, tentative.

The first four sonatas have a sarabanda. In Italy this dance, in triple metre, retained its original fast tempo throughout the seventeenth century and beyond, in contrast to the French sarabande, which slowed down and eventually acquired a reflective character. All four of Vinaccesi's examples are marked 'presto' or 'prestissimo'. The most distinctive rhythmic feature

---

[12] *Giovanni Maria Bononcini*, 99.   [13] Ibid. 94.

of the Italian sarabanda is its predilection for feminine cadences in which the tonic chord arrives on the third beat of the bar. A simple, incisive style with a change of chord on nearly every beat is the norm, but Vinaccesi varies this stereotype effectively in the second sonata, whose sarabanda contains some magnificent long sweeps of slurred quavers, and in the fourth sonata, where flashes of semiquavers add zest to the rhythm.

By origin, the giga, like its ancestor, the English or Irish jig, was a solo dance. It required rollicking athletic movement of a kind that could easily be made grotesque or obscene. Examples of the dance in Italian music often draw attention to these aspects by indulging in exceptionally large melodic leaps suggestive of clowning. The increased propensity of Italian violin music, from Corelli's time onwards, to alter register abruptly by 'skipping' intermediate strings, or by descending to an open string from a high position on the next string up, naturally aided this form of expression. In comparison with Corelli's—still more, Vivaldi's—examples, Vinaccesi's five gighe (Sonata V lacks one) seem rather subdued, entirely eschewing compound melodic intervals. They clearly betray the fact that he himself was not a violinist. However, their fairly high level of contrapuntal interest lends them vitality of a different kind. The examples in the fourth and fifth sonatas have the imitative section-openings common, though not *de rigueur*, in this movement-type.

It remains to describe, among the dances making up the more traditional group, the two examples of the *brando*. Descended from the French *branles*, the Italian *brando* was a composite dance comprising a string of three, four, or more contrasted sections played without interruption. An example from Bononcini's Op. 1 transcribed by Klenz begins with what French writers call a 'branle simple', a binary-form structure in cut time (¢), continues with a 'branle gai', a single repeated section in 3/4 metre, and ends with a similarly constructed 'branle à mener',[14] Vinaccesi, whose *brandi* are among the last to appear in an Italian published collection, adopts a more integrated approach. In Sonata III the Brando has the appearance of two juxtaposed binary-form movements, both marked 'allegro' and in common time. He knits the two structures together by making the opening of the 'first' movement return to round off the 'second'. In Sonata V the repeated sections are reduced to three. Because of the greater length of the *brandi* in comparison with the other movements, they allow Vinaccesi exceptional scope to develop his musical ideas and are particularly welcome on that account.

Most numerous among the 'newer' dances are the minuets. Every sonata has at least one, and the last two works find room for a couple. At the bottom of the list of contents at the end of the Violino Primo and

[14] Ibid. suppl., pp. 75-8.

Cembalo volumes (lack of space prevented its appearance in the Violino
Secondo and Violoncello books) the composer appended a brief note that
makes special mention of these movements:

Gracious Reader,

Do not be surprised if you find minuets scattered among these chamber sonatas,
this having been done solely to gratify lovers of dancing. If they [the sonatas]
please you, I will make special efforts to let you enjoy my second opus, which
will be in the church style and different in character[.] Love me, and farewell.
[transcribed as Appendix B.32]

The puzzling thing is that the minuets in this collection are far from
being its least expected or most 'exotic' movements. So rapidly and
enthusiastically had the dance been taken up in Italy that by 1687 it was
hardly a novelty. Tomaso Motta includes it in his Op. 1 (1681), and it
appears also in G. B. Vitali's Op. 2 (1685) and Torelli's Op. 2 (1686).
Perhaps Vinaccesi merely wished to suggest that, unlike the other movements, his minuets are genuinely 'da ballo'—for dancing to. This would
accord with their very simple, symmetrical construction. All eight examples contain precisely eight bars in each repeated section, whereas we
know from contemporary collections that more complex schemes were
equally possible.[15]

The four gavottas in the collection exemplify the specifically Italian
variant of this dance in one of its earliest manifestations. In Motta's Op. 1
and in Vitali's Op. 12 (the whole of which is explicitly 'in stile francese')
the French prototype, characterized by a beginning on the second beat in
cut time, is reproduced without significant alteration. However, Corelli
and later Italian composers cultivate a new type of gavotta that begins on
the main beat of the bar. This change can sometimes appear more visual
than aural, in that the stress is transferred from the first to the second
beat; in other words, the barline rather than the accent is displaced. Not
every case is so simple, however, and the fact that not a few gavottas of
the new type reach their final cadential chord on the first beat of the bar
(equivalent, in terms of our previous argument, to ending a French
gavotte on the second beat and holding the chord over) shows that sometimes the metre has to be taken at face value. Vinaccesi's examples feature
the rigid, march-like rhythms familiar from Corelli and his imitators such
as Albinoni and Vivaldi.

The borea is hard to distinguish from the gavotta on the basis of its
appearance on the page. However, Vinaccesi marks both his examples
'prestissimo', maintains dotted rhythms throughout, and provides semi-

---

[15] Both the Motta and Vitali collections mentioned include minuets in which the two sections are 8
and 16 bars long respectively.

quaver upbeats to each section. The first two features are encountered in some, but not all, of his gavottas; the third is absent and so can be taken as the essential distinguishing characteristic.

The title 'Taiheg' appearing before movements in Sonatas I and VI provokes disbelief. Is this some bizarre printer's error or perhaps an exotic Turkish dance left behind from the siege of Vienna? The probable explanation is much simpler. The word appears to be Brescian dialect for 'taglio vecchio', translatable as 'old cut' ('cut' here in the sense of style). From the *Vocabolario bresciano-italiano* of G. B. Melchiori we learn that 'tai' is the local contraction of 'taglio', while Italian 'vecchio' is shortened to 'veg', sometimes losing also its initial consonant to become 'eg' (of which 'heg' is an obvious possible variant, given that in Italian the letter H is silent).[16] Sadly, etymological enlightenment brings us no closer to establishing what kind of dance is indicated—if, indeed, the two movements are genuine dances and not simply character pieces after the fashion of Couperin's *Les Vieux Seigneurs*. Both are in common time and marked 'presto', but no other common element of significance is discernible. The Taiheg of the sixth sonata is perhaps the most boisterous piece in the whole collection; Ex. 3 shows the beginning of its second section.

Ex. 3. Op. 1 no. 6, Taiheg

[16] Giovan-Battista Melchiori, *Vocabolario bresciano-italiano* (Brescia, 1817), ii. 277 and 310; iii. 13.

The significance of the title 'Pira', used to describe a type of movement present in all the sonatas except the fourth, remains mysterious. In both standard Italian and north Italian dialects a *pira* is simply a pyre such as a funeral pyre. There is no possibility that the word is a misprint for *piva* (an Italian form of bagpipe and the type of pastorale played on it), for it appears twenty times in the same form—and in any case, none of the examples features a drone bass. All five piras are in a genuinely slow tempo ('grave' or 'adagio'), those in the first three sonatas being marked 'affettuoso' in addition. They are attractive movements with a touch of wistful *gravitas* and some welcome contrapuntal activity. The first section of the Pira of Sonata V, illustrated as Ex. 4, will convey the flavour.

Ex. 4. Op. 1 no. 5, Pira

We come last to the abstract framing movements, the preludio and the *chiusa* (literally, 'close'). If the preludes are of obviously Corellian inspiration, the *chiuse* look back to the mid-baroque church sonata, where slow concluding sections or movements are quite usual (in Corelli's sonatas they survive only in vestigial form as 'adagio' markings introduced at or just before a final cadence). A good example occurs in the sonata on 'Fuggi, dolente core' from Biagio Marini's Op. 22 (1655), and others can be found in the sonatas of G. B. Vitali—and, indeed, of Henry Purcell, whose sonatas are heavily indebted to the same tradition. But to include an abstract concluding movement in a chamber sonata with several movements is an absolute novelty. It is a shame that no later composer, apparently, took up this idea, for a return to the style of the opening can create a particularly satisfying ending. Vinaccesi reinforces the impression that the final movement is a resumption of the opening movement after an interruption by making five of the *chiuse* begin 'outside' the key of the work, to which they return in time for the final cadence. The exception, that of Sonata V, deviates from the expected path in a different way: it opens with the tonic chord, G minor, but ends, with a half-close, on a major chord of D. Here Vinaccesi is perhaps trying to show the depth of his erudition by reviving the Phrygian mode.

The musical language of the preludes and conclusions certainly does have something recherché about it. Vinaccesi includes a stiff canon *per arsin et thesin* (with displaced accents in the imitating voice) in the Preludio of Sonata I, and chromaticism appears both more often and with more pungent effect than in the dances. A few of the movements feature shifting metres. The most striking among them is the Preludio of Sonata II, reproduced complete as Ex. 5. Note how the composer 'cancels' the change from common time to 6/4 metre not by reintroducing the normal symbol for common time but by reversing the 'proportional' change with a 4/6 time-signature, a very studied touch. At the same time, his debt to Corelli emerges elsewhere in such features as 'walking' basses in quavers underneath chains of suspensions and the use of the older composer's favourite opening gambit of a short, enquiring phrase that is immediately repeated in a different key.

Ex. 5. Op. 1 no. 2, Preludio

(*continued*)

Ex. 5. (*continued*)

Bar 14 of Ex. 5 illustrates a type of harmonic licence that Vinaccesi, even in his maturest works, likes to take. The first *a″* of violin 1 obviously belongs with the *c″* of violin 2 and the first *A* of the bass but arrives one crotchet later, leaving the *g″* to create friction against the other parts. It would be possible to classify this effect as an upward-resolving suspension, but one encounters many cases where the dissonant note is quitted by leap, which invalidates this explanation. It is perhaps best to speak simply of a 'harmonic dislocation', whose purpose is more to give an attractive rhythmic shape to a part than to set up harmonic tension *per se*. The second half of the preceding bar, however, admits of no easy explanation. The clash of first *d″*, then *f#″*, against the *e″* of violin 2 is obviously an intended effect, as the figuring of the bass shows, but it can be described only as a simultaneous combination of 5–3 and 4–2 chords over the note *c*—possibly pleasing, but certainly wildly unorthodox.

Ex. 5 also offers a good introduction to Vinaccesi's treatment of the violins. The G string is generally avoided, and the player rarely has to venture beyond the first position (the absolute upper limit, as in Corelli's trio sonatas, is *d‴*). Vinaccesi's writing is remarkable for its lack of angularity, its emphasis on stepwise motion. Where there is a clash of interest between harmonic fulness and smoothness of line, our composer nearly always opts for the second. The first note of bar 10, for instance, would certainly have become *e′* in Corelli's music, in order to complete the triad, but Vinaccesi prefers the melodically more elegant *a′*. His tolerance of bare fifths, seen in the very first chord (and also on the last beat of bar 5 in Ex. 4), is unusual. No doubt, he expected the harpsichordist to supply the missing third.

That separate harpsichord and cello players are needed for these sonatas is a twofold innovation. In the first place, it was traditional to accompany dance music for strings with an undifferentiated bass part that could be performed either by a keyboard instrument or a melody instrument such as the bass violin (*violone piccolo*). For either of these a lute could be substituted. Musicologists have long agonized over whether the description of a part as 'Violone o Cembalo' in seventeenth-century sources should be taken at face value, so that either the stringed instrument or the keyboard instrument—but not both simultaneously—should be used.[17] The debate is far from concluded, since it can also be argued that 'Violone o Cembalo' denotes a minimum rather than an ideal requirement or else that the description means simply that the notes are apt for either instrument without distinction. The 'literalist' view is probably more often correct than not, since there are very few instances where separate parts for a keyboard and a melody instrument (identical except for the presence of bass figures in the first) were published, and one cannot imagine that it was routine practice either for an extra bass part to be copied out by hand (in which case many more examples would have survived) or for the bass violinist or lutenist to read over the harpsichordist's shoulder.[18] So, simply by having two bass parts with divergent musical texts, Vinaccesi was breaking new ground (though the usage that he was introducing had existed for a long time in the domain of the church sonata).

The introduction of the cello to dance-music was no less of a breakthrough. A small version of the bass violin ('violone') with covered strings, the cello had been introduced by Bolognese musicians not long before the middle of the seventeenth century.[19] A 'violoncino', which must be a similar instrument, appeared in a set of sonatas by Giovanni Battista Fontana as early as 1641, and from the 1660s onwards the replacement of the bass violin by the smaller instrument slowly gathered pace in church sonatas. The superior sound-quality and greater agility of the cello encouraged composers to make its part semi-independent, exploiting in particular its ability to execute wide leaps and swift running passages or to make effective forays into the tenor register. In places where the cello and harpsichord (or organ) do not proceed in unison, the stringed instrument may have variants of register (most often, in a higher octave) or play 'divisions'. Alternatively, the cello may have the bass line in its fully elaborated form, leaving the keyboard instrument to present a simplified version. The most radical option—to allow the cello to become an independent 'tenor' part—is reserved for special moments; composers of trio sonatas had no wish, in the normal course of events, to depart from simple three-part writing.

[17] A good exposition of the 'literalist' case is made by Tharald Borgir in *The Performance of the Basso Continuo in Seventeenth-Century Italian Music* (Ann Arbor, Mich., 1987), 51-9.

[18] On the rare occasions when separate *violone* and keyboard parts were printed for dance-music (one of them is Orazio Pollarolo's Op. 1, mentioned earlier), the musical text was normally the same, apart from the addition of bass figures to the latter.

[19] On the emergence of the cello see Stephen Bonta, 'From Violone to Violoncello: A Question of Strings?', *Journal of the American Instrument Society*, 3 (1977), 64-99.

Before 1687 the cello is not found in dance-music or in chamber sonatas containing dances. The original Roman edition of Corelli's Op. 2 still prescribes for the bass the traditional 'Violone o Cimbalo'. Vinaccesi's innovation never took strong root in the realm of the chamber sonata, which by and large remained faithful to the old principle of an undifferentiated bass. The most noteworthy collection to follow his lead was Albinoni's set of *Balletti a tre*, Op. 3 (1701). In a few decades the issue became academic, since the chamber sonata merged completely into the stream of the former church sonata.

Vinaccesi's treatment of the cello is fairly conventional, employing all the devices mentioned in the penultimate paragraph. There remains, however, a certain capriciousness, suggestive of inexperience, in the relationship of the cembalo and violoncello parts. In some places, the keyboard instrument has to perform exactly the same semiquaver passages as its partner, where simplification would seem desirable; elsewhere, the variants of the cello are trivial or not carried through consistently. The emergence of a totally independent cello part is rare but always telling. Perhaps the supreme moment for the cello occurs in the middle of the second section of the Balletto in the fifth sonata, shown as Ex. 6. The rich texture that results recalls the world of the organist—one could imagine the *Pfundnoten* of the harpsichord bass being thundered out on organ pedals.

Ex. 6. Op. 1 no. 5, Balletto

Ex. 6 reveals Vinaccesi's attachment to elaborate counterpoint, which is given little rein in this collection outside a few of the abstract movements. In fact, he experiences his greatest difficulty as a composer—paradoxically—in situations where counterpoint is suspended and his task is merely to insert a 'filling' part for second violin between the first violin and the bass. These inner voices, which remind one a little of the second violin parts in trios written by Nicola Matteis the elder a little earlier (*Ayrs*, 1685), have a tendency to be too individual in shape, too unsystematized. Here and there, Vinaccesi lapses, through the conduct of the second violin part, into solecisms such as consecutive octaves or fifths (although the sympathetic reader will recognize a certain proportion of these apparent errors as printing mistakes). It is instructive to compare the present trios with Albinoni's *Balletti a tre*, which are homophonic and treble-dominated to a comparable extent. Albinoni knows exactly what to do with his subsidiary upper part: when it does not imitate (or sometimes, indeed, anticipate) the first violin, it is content to remain severely functional—filling out the harmony and texture and aiding the rhythmic impetus but drawing no attention to itself while it does so. Schooled in ecclesiastical polyphony, our composer still had something to learn about writing a part whose chief merit lay precisely in its lack of individuality.

Some instances of humour in Vinaccesi's balletto movements were mentioned earlier. By far the most extravagant of them is a rhythmic effect occurring in the balletto of Sonata IV (Ex. 7). In a three-bar passage running from the third beat of bar 22 to the second beat of bar 25 the second violin and bass descend by step sequentially at the rate of one scale-degree every two beats. However, the first violin executes simultaneously a falling sequence of similar type that is repeated only every three beats. The result is that the upper part falls behind the lower two parts at a steady rate, slowly widening the interval of separation. At the same time, one hears the cross-rhythm. To be honest, the effect is quite crude and the counterpoint not impeccable. But the joke works, and Vinaccesi must at least be given credit for originality.

All the dance-movements except the two *brandi* are in binary form. Students of musical form have tended to neglect the finer analytical points of this type of construction despite its dominance over all other instrumental forms in the late baroque period and its great historical importance as the ancestor of sonata form. To state that a binary-form movement consists of two repeated sections is only the starting-point of an investigation that ought also to pay attention to the relative lengths of those sections, the thematic correspondences between them, and the nature and placing of modulations. These three aspects are subject to great variation in different periods, in the hands of different composers, and in different

Ex. 7. Op. 1 no. 4, Balletto

species of dance. Composers reveal a lot about their composing methods by their choices among the several possibilities.

Like all other Italian composers of his time, Vinaccesi distinguishes carefully between binary-form movements that are in principle symmetrical, each section being genuinely a 'half', and ones that are weighted in favour of the second section, thus asymmetrical. Unless a movement is very concise and has a highly regular phrase-structure, it is hard—indeed, it takes a Bach—to achieve perfect symmetry with total naturalness. A certain deviation from pure symmetry is tolerated: in the first sonata the Allemanda (and its variation), the Corrente, the Giga, and the Menuet are literally symmetrical, while the Pira has a second section longer by one bar (6 : 7) and the Balletto and Taiheg have second sections shorter by one bar (8 : 7 and 10 : 9 respectively). Even with the benefit of this tolerance, composers often have to resort to special 'tricks' in order to achieve the desired balance. The simplest of these is to elaborate, through figures based on repeated notes or broken chords, the final chord of a section. This device is much used by composers when they find that the section otherwise ends a whole bar or half-bar too early. Vinaccesi introduces such flourishes very sparingly (a good example comes at the end of the Taiheg in the last sonata); indeed, there are many cases where the performers themselves would be well advised to 'run on the spot' with improvised elaboration in order to animate some of the semibreves at the end of sections in common time (a metre that often functions, in baroque music, as if it were 2/4 with every other barline suppressed). Another 'device of prolongation', which Vinaccesi this time uses freely, is that of the *petite reprise*. This entails the repetition, echo fashion, of a concluding phrase. The danger with using the *petite reprise* for this purpose is that the gain in length is not matched by an enrichment of the musical substance. In one or two instances in the present sonatas, the artificiality of the device becomes all too apparent.

Other movements, including most of the correnti and sarabandas, are clearly asymmetrical (the extreme case is the Balletto francese of the second sonata, where the ratio between the sections is 4 : 15). In an obvious sense, asymmetry, which by definition is more elastic than symmetry, is less constraining for the composer, since it allows him, in the second section, to extend and repeat material, and even to digress, without penalty. Vinaccesi takes advantage of this freedom to introduce many happy ideas and to multiply the number of thematic back-references to the first section.

One must be careful how one uses the terms 'theme' and 'thematic' when discussing music of this kind. In binary-form movements from this period a theme is rarely an entity with both a fixed beginning and a fixed ending, like a fugue subject. It is likely to be either an opening that sooner or later veers away from its earlier course or a conclusion into which many different openings may debouch; very occasionally, it is a piece of connective tissue inserted into the middle of a musical sentence. In the seventeenth century composers tend to view the structure of a binary-form movement holistically, paying careful attention to the flow of the melodic line but making little attempt to organize the individual melodic components into patterns. Vinaccesi belongs to the first generation of Italian composers to articulate, still haphazardly and often in a very approximate way, the subgroupings of notes that represent embryonically what are later to become, after much expansion, the principal divisions of sonata form.

In the longer movements it is more normal than not for the openings of the two sections to be matched in some way. Sometimes the second section opens with a simple transposition of the initial idea, as occurs in the Giga of the fourth sonata, but a degree of modification is more usual. With distinctly less frequency, the respective endings are matched; sometimes, only the cadence is reproduced. Reprises of the initial idea midway through the second section—the genesis of the sonata-form recapitulation—occur infrequently, and predominantly in asymmetrical movements, since this device requires extra space in which to operate. In

comparison with his contemporaries, Vinaccesi is neither noticeably progressive nor noticeably conservative in the manner and frequency with
which he brings back themes.

Where he does evince strong progessive tendencies, however, is in his
treatment of modulation both in its own right and in relation to the main
structural division of binary form, the central double barline. The modulation scheme of a baroque (or classical) movement can be likened to an
electrical circuit. One starts from a given point (the tonic), makes one or
more excursions, and finally closes the circuit by returning to the point of
departure. Except for some very short movements, in which modulation
would be otiose, all the pieces under discussion make one principal modulation followed, where space allows, by one or two supplementary modulations to closely related keys.[20] The principal variable in this scheme is the
point at which the cadence establishing the principal modulation is
reached. In binary-form movements of the late Baroque, such as the
sonatas of Domenico Scarlatti or the allemandes and courantes of Bach,
the principal modulation invariably occurs just before the double-bar. But
in their counterparts from the Renaissance and the early Baroque it is
more usual to end the first section in the tonic (either with a full close or
with a half-close), deferring the principal modulation until the start of the
second section. The mid-Baroque is a period during which the later
arrangement gradually replaces the earlier. The change proceeds unevenly:
composers do not necessarily progress in a straight line within their own
œuvre—and in any case personal choices often go against the general
trend. In a table presented elsewhere, I have compared the incidence, at
the end of the first section, of full closes in the tonic, half-closes in the
tonic, and closes in another key (generally the dominant or the relative
major key) in binary-form movements found in 24 collections of instrumental music published in Italy between 1666 (G. B. Vitali, Op. 1) and
1695 (G. Taglietti, Op. 1).[21] Among the fifteen composers represented,
Vinaccesi is one of only two (the other is the Bergamask composer
Giovanni Battista Brevi) who never end the first section with a full close
in the tonic. Even Corelli, in his Op. 2, is conservative to the extent of
having 19 full closes in the tonic, 19 half-closes in the tonic, and 62
cadences in other keys.

Vinaccesi is quite enterprising, too, in his choice of key for the principal modulation. In major keys the dominant is for most composers the
automatic choice, but our composer on occasion substitutes the mediant
(minor)—wisely, in view of the great need for variety when the movements are so numerous. Where minor keys are concerned, composers

[20] By a 'closely related' key I mean one whose tonic chord is a diatonic chord within the home key.
For every key, major or minor, there are precisely five other keys related in this way.
[21] 'The Taiheg, the Pira and Other Curiosities', table 2.

often follow fixed habits. Albinoni, for instance, virtually never addresses the first section to a key other than the dominant (minor), while Benedetto Marcello employs the relative major almost exclusively. Vinaccesi adopts the two solutions with equal frequency, once more setting a high premium on variety.

Were one to champion these sonatas on the grounds of one particular feature, it would have to be the extraordinarily sophisticated way in which the 11 or 12 separate movements forming each work are integrated motivically. One is no doubt talking of a result achieved intuitively rather than methodically, but in that perspective the achievement is perhaps even more remarkable. Thematic integration achieved through the 'translation' of a given portion of musical material into a different metre, perhaps with light paraphrasing, is a commonplace of seventeenth-century music. In its most thorough-going form it is encountered in the variation suites of Schein and Froberger at the beginning and in the middle of the seventeenth century, but even at the end of the century—for example, in the sonatas of Corelli—one finds many instances of movements within the same work that move 'in parallel': they may begin with similar ideas, follow exactly the same scheme of modulation, feature the same chromatic chords at equivalent points. Naturally, Vinaccesi does not eschew transformations of this simple variety. But he goes further than that: by isolating short musical motives and using them in a multitude of permutations to saturate an entire composition, he attains unity of a more pervasive and interesting kind—one, moreover, that is little in evidence in the music of his own time, although it has been common at certain times both before and since.

Each sonata works intensively with a group of between two and four elementary motives. None of them is especially distinctive in its own right: virtually all could appear, at least in passing, in any baroque work. What matters is not what the motives are in themselves but how often and how prominently they occur. All, naturally, are susceptible to the usual sorts of transformation, which include transposition, change of mode, inversion, retrograde statement, expansion through the intercalation of extra notes, and contraction through the omission of notes. The motives I have identified (there may well be more) can be tabulated as follows. For ease of comparison, all have been brought within the same pair of octaves (*C–B* and *c–b* in the Helmholtz system of pitch-identification).

Sonata I   *e–a–g; g–f–e–d–c; G–c–d–e; e–f–f♯–g–g♯–a*
Sonata II   *d–e–f; b♭–g♯; b♭–c♯; a–g–g–f–f–e*
Sonata III *g–f♯–e–d♯; e–d♯–e*
Sonata IV *a–f–e; e–f–d–e; (F)–B♭–c–d; f–e♭–d*
Sonata V   *d–e♭–d–c–b♭; d–e–f♯–g; f–e♭–e♭–d*
Sonata VI *b–e–a–d♯–g♯; d–A–d–f♯; (a–g♯)–a–e–f♯–e*

This is not the place to conduct a detailed analysis of motivic development in these works. It will help, however, to give examples of the use of
a motive in one particular sonata. The work selected for this purpose is
Sonata V in G minor. In the following diagram its 11 movements are
listed, and against each a musical fragment is placed. These fragments
record one instance (chosen from many) of the appearance, in the given
movement, of the first of the three motives pervading Sonata V
(*d–eb–d–c–bb*). In some cases, the motive appears two or even three times
in the course of the fragment. Bar-numbers are shown.

Motivic Recurrence in Op.1 no.5

On its merits, Vinaccesi's Op. 1 ought to have been influential. Everything indicates, however, that it was not. Like so many other publications by provincial composers riding on the crest of the Corellian wave, it was soon forgotten. One feature in particular militated against its being taken as a model. At the end of the seventeenth century music, literature, and the visual arts all entered a 'classical' phase (to use this term in its more universal sense) characterized by a preference for larger—but fewer—units.[22] The mosaic-like aggregations of small units gave way to streamlined, rationally organized forms in which the parts were strictly subordinate to the whole. In this new climate a sonata with three or four substantial movements was preferable to one with twelve miniature movements. The triad Corelli–Vivaldi–Tartini symbolizes the intensification of this process during the eighteenth century. Ultimately, Vinaccesi's Op. 1 is an individual synthesis of both backward-looking and forward-looking elements. We do not have to consider its historical position in order to appreciate its musical value, but we need to understand why its impact was so slight.

The set of church sonatas promised in the note to the reader at the end of Op. 1 duly appeared as Op. 2 in 1692. Since only its continuo part (Organo) has survived, only a limited number of deductions about it can usefully be made. There are twelve sonatas, covering between them all the major keys between B flat major and A major, and all the minor keys between C minor and B minor. Without exception, they follow the typical Corellian plan of four movements, generally in the tempo sequence slow–fast–slow–fast. One opening movement is quick, however, and two others offer a kaleidoscopic succesion of slow and fast tempos. All the movements are through-composed, many of the fast ones being fugal. The complex and diverse figuring of the bass (which in Italian baroque music tends to reflect dissonances and chromatic alterations already present in the obbligato parts rather than extra elements to be supplied by the accompanist) suggests that their language was as least as rich as that of Op. 1.

Without recovering the rest of this collection or the lost Op. 4, we cannot say whether, with the benefit of greater experience, Vinaccesi fulfilled the promise shown in Op. 1. That collection alone, however, marks him out as one of the most interesting Italian composers of instrumental music of his generation—and one of the few to learn from Corelli without slavishly imitating him.

---

[22] For these observations I am indebted to an essay by David Burrows: 'Style in Culture: Vivaldi, Zeno and Ricci', *Journal of Interdisciplinary History*, 4 (1973-4), 1-23.

7

The Cantatas

Since none of Vinaccesi's serenatas has survived, his non-operatic secular vocal music is represented today only by cantatas for solo voice and continuo, of which eight are extant. No doubt, these constitute a mere fraction of the number he composed in the course of his career, but they are enough to show his mastery of the genre and considerable individuality within it.

Were one to judge the relative popularity, in Italy, of the late-baroque cantata and sonata from published sources alone, the latter would seem consistently to have enjoyed a much greater vogue. However, the position is totally reversed if one turns to manuscript sources. The reasons for this contrast are complex and numerous, but some factors deserve mention.

First, the cantata for solo voice and continuo (which we will call, for the sake of simplicity, the 'solo cantata', although this term fails to specify the nature of the accompaniment) was a genre cultivated especially at courts. These were institutions that had ready access to professional copyists, in whose hands the transmission of cantatas—at least, within Italy— largely rested.

Second, the solo cantata, by virtue of the poetry to which it was set, was the cultural property exclusively of educated society; it was not for the church or the theatre, let alone the tavern. This set a natural limit on its circulation and so diminished the economic advantage of publication.

Third, the need for very careful co-ordination, in performance, between the voice and its accompaniment caused the music of solo cantatas nearly always to be notated in the form of a score on two staves.[1] The process of printing music from movable type, which in Italy was not superseded on a mass scale by that of engraving until the very end of the eighteenth century, coped relatively badly with this layout, its problems aggravated by the underlaid words.[2] In this respect, the advantage that manuscripts could offer over printed examples could be both aesthetic and practical.

---

[1] The many singers who accompanied themselves at the harpsichord naturally had no choice but to use a score.

[2] The 'solo' sonata for violin and continuo offers an interesting parallel. For reasons similar to those applying to the solo cantata, violin sonatas were usually notated in score. It is striking how much less strongly, both absolutely and relatively, this genre is represented in Italian typeset edns. of the late 17th and early 18th cents. than in contemporary engraved edns. produced in Holland, England, and later France. Indeed, some of the Italian edns. of violin sonatas constitute rare instances,

Lastly, it often happened that a cantata had to be transposed or other-wise modified to suit a voice of different character. Only manuscript transmission offered this degree of flexibility.

In view of all these negative factors, it is perhaps surprising that collec-tions of cantatas published in Italy were not even fewer. However, the disadvantages could be outweighed by the prestige gained from submitting one's music to wide public scrutiny and the usefulness of a publication in cementing the relationship between an artist and his patron (who would have a special stake in the enterprise in those cases, perhaps quite fre-quent, where he was also the anonymous author of the poetic texts). *Il consiglio degl'amanti*, Vinaccesi's published set of cantatas hurriedly dedi-cated in 1688 to Ferdinando de' Medici, had an obvious 'political' func-tion quite separate from its artistic intentions.

Because of its small scale, a solo cantata was normally copied out together with other, similar works rather than singly. The resulting groups rarely form themselves into the predictable sixes and twelves beloved of printers, for the simple reason that unless a published collec-tion was in prospect, composers (and, one imagines, also their poets) liked to conceive cantatas individually and put them into circulation immedi-ately rather than hold them back until they could form part of some large opus. It was therefore the responsiblity of users to order and group them as they saw fit. Many manuscript collections of cantatas must have been assembled as much by chance as by design: one copied simply what was available for copying at the time. Sometimes, however, a rationale for par-ticular groups can be discerned. One finds groups of cantatas written for a single voice-type and possibly sharing other technical characteristics; these will often have been compiled originally for the use of a single singer.[3] Elsewhere, there exist groups of cantatas by a single composer, probably copied out for some admirer or patron.[4] Less often, one encounters groups whose unifying element is the poet.[5] Where the voice-types,

for that country, of the use of the engraving process in music publishing, and by that very fact bear witness to the inadequacies, for this particular purpose, of printing from type.

[3] The 18 cantatas by Albinoni forming the MS Berlin, Staatsbibliothek Preussischer Kulturbesitz (hereafter *D-B*), Mus. ms. 447, are all for soprano. Since this composer, on the evidence of other sources, wrote cantatas almost as frequently for alto as for soprano, it appears that the Berlin copyist has deliberately screened out the first type, a policy that would make sense if these cantatas were des-tined for a specific singer.

[4] As one would expect, the composers whose cantatas appear most often in collections containing their works alone are also the most productive and celebrated masters working in this genre; Alessandro Scarlatti and Benedetto Marcello are the foremost examples contemporary with Vinaccesi. Nevertheless, large MS collections of cantatas by composers of the second rank can also be found. Besides the MS of Albinoni cantatas mentioned in the previous note, one may cite the 22 cantatas by the minor Venetian composer Diogenio Bigaglia preserved in Paris, Bibliothèque du Conservatoire (hereafter *F-Pc*), D.1111.

[5] The British Library possesses, under the shelfmark Add. Mss. 34056–7, two volumes together containing 40 solo cantatas (and one sacred dialogue) by various composers that are all settings of

composers, and poets are diverse, the common element can sometimes be the institution—court, salon, or *accademia*—for which the works were originally composed or the copyist to whom they were entrusted at some stage in their transmission. Naturally, these categories often overlap.

A similar diversity characterizes the manner in which the separate cantatas are collated. Sometimes, each work occupies its own quire (generally, for solo cantatas, a single bifolio), which means that when the time for binding arrives there is no restriction on the number of works included or the sequence in which they are ordered. Where cantatas are bibliographically independent in this way, no inferences about the chronology of the copying (still less, that of the composition) can be drawn from the order in which the works appear. In other cases, the music is written in larger quires that can each accommodate several cantatas in whole or part. Here it is normal to begin a new cantata immediately after another ends, irrespective of the pattern of quiring. Usually, this means that within each bloc of continuous notation the order of the works reflects the sequence of copying, which may provide some clue to provenance, chronology, or the manuscript's relationship to other sources. One must always be aware, however, that the process of binding and rebinding, to which many manuscripts containing cantatas have been subjected, has often resulted in changes affecting the order of the quires and, most significantly, in the juxtaposition of wholly unrelated works and groups. A much rarer but very interesting kind of manuscript is the album, a bound volume into which works are entered one after the other until the pages are filled. Here, the chronology of copying is usually self-evident, and the integrity of the collection virtually certain.

The three manuscripts containing cantatas by Vinaccesi can offer some useful contextual evidence in the light of the factors mentioned in the last two paragraphs. The table below gives the textual incipit of each work, followed by the library (identified by *RISM* sigla), the shelfmark, and the folio numbers occupied. Each work is preserved only in the one source mentioned.

Both cantatas in the Bibliothèque Nationale, Paris (*F-Pn*), are for bass: the five in the Staatsbibliothek Preussischer Kulturbesitz, Berlin (*D-B*), are for soprano with the exception of the cantata *Filli, un solo tuo sguardo*, which is for alto. The last cantata, which belongs to the section of the library of the Paris Conservatoire (*F-Pc*) today housed in the Bibliothèque Nationale, is also for soprano.

The Bibliothèque Nationale cantatas appear in the third of a set of five

poetry by Antonio Ottoboni performed in Rome at the court of his son Pietro during 1709–10. See Michael Talbot and Colin Timms, 'Music and the Poetry of Antonio Ottoboni (1646–1721)', in Nino Pirrotta and Agostino Ziino (eds.), *Händel e gli Scarlatti a Roma: Atti del Convegno internazionale di studi (Roma 12–14 giugno 1985)* (Florence, 1987), 367–438: 389–392.

Textual incipit	Location
Là nelle verdi spiagge[a]	*F–Pn*, Vm.[7] 30 III, fos. 10^r–17^v
Quanto [in source: quando] mi vien da ridere[b]	*F–Pn*, Vm.[7] 30 III, fos. 25^v–30^r
Su la sponda d'un rio	*D–B*, Mus. ms. 22370/10, pp. 1–6
Dal tuono il lampo aspetta[c]	*D–B*, Mus. ms. 22370/10, pp. 6–12
Or [in source: hor] fia mai vero, o lontananza infida	*D–B*, Mus. ms. 22370/10, pp. 13–19
Ingratissima Clori	*D–B*, Mus. ms. 22370/10, pp. 19–24
Filli, un solo tuo sguardo	*D–B*, Mus. ms. 22370/10, pp. 25–8
Belve, se mai provaste	*F–Pc*, Rés. 1451, fos. 94^v–101^v

[a] With the separate title *In lontananza della sua donna*.
[b] With the separate title *Il disinganno de gli amanti*.
[c] With the separate title *Amor pericoloso*, which does not appear in the cantata MS but is present in its literary concordance, *I-Vmc*, Ms. Correr 466, pp. 425–6.

volumes mostly containing cantatas and arias by Italian composers active in the second half of the seventeenth century. The oldest composer represented is Giacomo Carissimi (1605–74); the youngest, Giovanni Bononcini (1670–1747). No regional bias is discernible. Each volume carries on its spine the generic title 'ARIA' followed by the respective volume number ('TOM. 1' etc.). The library stamp is that of the Bibliothèque Impériale, indicating that the set of volumes was not acquired until Napoleonic times; perhaps it is one of the many items in the library confiscated from the aristocracy during and after the Revolution.

All the music is written in the same experienced and stylish hand, which must have been French, since the instruction to turn the page is always written as 'tournez'. Some errors in the underlaid Italian texts— e.g. the substitution of 'Quando' (when) for 'Quanto' (how much) in the opening line of the second Vinaccesi cantata listed—also betray the foreigner. The material contained in the five volumes can be broken down into a number of discrete bibliographical sub-units identifiable from, among other things, the pattern of collation, the original quiring numbers, and the position of void pages (which normally come at the end of a sub-unit). These sub-units do not necessarily respect the boundaries that were established when the folios were later divided between separate volumes. In fact, the one containing the two cantatas by Vinaccesi straddles the second and third volumes; it comprises the last eleven quires (each of four folios and numbered consecutively from 1 to 11) of the second volume (Vm.[7] 30 II, fos. 75–118) and the first thirteen quires (numbered 12–24) of the third volume (Vm.[7] 30 III, fos. 1–52). These ninety-six folios contain two cantatas by Bassani (probably Giovanni Battista, *c*.1657–1716), three by Legrenzi, three by Francesco Petrobelli (died 1695, *maestro di cappella* at Padua cathedral), and the two by Vinaccesi, as well as two independent arias by Bassani, three by Legrenzi, and two by Alessandro Scarlatti. These seventeen compositions follow a seemingly arbitrary order, as if the French collector were dipping into more than one copytext as the mood took him. However, this is mere speculation: what is clear is that the repertory transmitted by these folios—in fact, by the set of volumes as a whole—must date from the last decade or two of the seventeenth century. This would place the Vinaccesi cantatas in the composer's 'pre-Venetian' period, a belief supported, as we shall see, by stylistic evidence.

The choice of bass voice is interesting, for Italian cantatas of this period share, even accentuate, the cultural preference for high voices manifested in opera. Most solo cantatas are for soprano; a somewhat smaller number are for alto. Cantatas for tenor with plain continuo accompaniment are almost non-existent; one assumes—in the absence of evidence to the contrary—that tenors were in the habit of performing cantatas for soprano with their vocal part transposed down an octave. A similar procedure for basses (i.e. the downward transposition of cantatas for alto) was unsatisfactory on stylistic grounds, given the special melodic character of bass parts (to be discussed later): hence the need, small but real, for solo cantatas written specifically for basses. Many singers of such works must have been active mainly outside the operatic circuit, in the service of churches rather than courts.

The thought occurs whether *Quanto mi vien da ridere* might not have been included in Vinaccesi's collection *Il consiglio degl'amanti*, which certainly belongs to the right phase of his life. One would suppose the collection, from its title, to contain a series of humorously didactic pieces following the convention of the *lezione amorosa* ('lesson in love')—a description that fits this cantata perfectly. Its possession of a title distinct from its textual incipit (*Il disinganno de gli amanti*) also favours this theory, since the more formal nature of a published work would have encouraged the presence of one. However, the choice of the bass voice for a published cantata would be highly unusual. Moreover, the second cantata, *Là nelle verdi spiagge* (*In lontananza della sua donna*), which on every other relevant count is so similar to *Quanto mi vien da ridere* that it must have originated as a companion piece, can by no stretch of the imagination be classed as a *lezione amorosa*: it is only the familiar plaint of a lovelorn Arcadian shepherd. The evidence for linking either cantata with *Il consiglio degl'amanti* is therefore rather unconvincing.

One might also speculate on a possible connection between these bass cantatas by Vinaccesi and two similar pieces by Petrobelli, *O voi ch'andate altieri* and *Venghi il canchero ad Amore*, found in the same group of seventeen compositions (none of the remaining works is for bass). It could well be that the French collector took all four bass cantatas from the same earlier source; the common political allegiance and relative geographical proximity of Brescia and Padua might be significant here. Nevertheless, a degree of caution is once again advisable. The singer for whom the two composers wrote was almost certainly not the same; whereas in both works Vinaccesi takes his vocal part only up to *c′*, Petrobelli ascends to *e′*. The difference is too consistent to be entirely coincidental.

The five cantatas in Berlin originate from the collection of Georg Österreich (1664–1735), which contained both secular and sacred vocal works in great quantity.[6] Whereas most of the sacred works can be linked to Österreich's employment at Gottorf as *Kapellmeister* to Duke Christian Albrecht of Schleswig-Holstein between 1689 and 1702, the Italian secular works are thought to have been copied after his subsequent move first to Braunschweig and later to Wolfenbüttel, where his daughter Sophie Amalia was active as a singer. Österreich finally sold the bulk of his collection, over 1,800 items, to his ex-pupil Heinrich Bokemeyer; the subsequent owners were Bokemeyer's son-in-law Johann Christian Winter, Johann Nikolaus Forkel, the Königliches Institut für Kirchenmusik, Berlin, and the Preussische Staatsbibliothek in the same city, whose holdings (including the Österreich-Bokemeyer collection) were divided after World War II between the Deutsche Staatsbibliothek in East Berlin and the Staatsbibliothek Preussischer Kulturbesitz in West Berlin.

The catalogue of the collection by Harald Kümmerling contains bibliographical information of great interest.[7] Mus. ms. 22370/10, the volume containing the five Vinaccesi cantatas, is written in an unidentified hand— probably German, to judge from the presence of an explanatory 'e' (rather than 'mi') clarifying the pitch of one unclearly written note—on paper with a distinctive, though fragmentary, watermark that appears to show the lower half of a pair of crossed keys.[8] Only one other work in the whole collection exhibits the same combination of hand and watermark: the cantata *Per un volto di gigli e di rose* bearing the name of Albinoni.[9] In other manuscripts, however, this work is elsewhere attributed variously to Alessandro Scarlatti and Francesco Pistocchi, so its authorship remains

[6] On Österreich and his collection see Kerala Snyder's article 'Österreich, Georg', in *New Grove*, xiv. 8–9.

[7] Harald Kümmerling, *Katalog der Sammlung Bokemeyer* (Kassel, 1970).

[8] Ibid. 146 (items 1608–12). Kümmerling has mistranscribed the abbreviation 'K.r' (for 'Kavalier', Vinaccesi's title) as 'Ru', obviously believing these letters to be part of the composer's given name.

[9] Mus. ms. 30136/5 (item 1178). Kümmerling classifies the hand in question as '2c'. While I have been able to verify personally that Mus. ms. 22370/10 and 30136/5 are the work of the same copyist, neither corresponds in appearance to the sample of this hand reproduced by Kümmerling (*Katalog*, 177). The present argument is unaffected, since no other MS attributed to hand 2c shares the watermark (Kümmerling's no. 478, reproduced ibid. 423).

highly uncertain and can give no help in regard to chronology or provenance.[10]

Because the cantatas in Mus. ms. 22370/10 are written as a continuous
bloc, it is quite likely that they existed already as a set of five (or more?)
works at the time when Österreich's copyist gained access to them. One
cantata, *Dal tuono il lampo aspetta*, has words by a known poet: Antonio
Ottoboni.[11] Since Vinaccesi is unlikely to have come into contact with
Ottoboni before settling in Venice in 1698, that year can be regarded as a
terminus post quem. The literary text of this cantata is included in a volume
of Ottoboni's *Trattenimenti poetici* (a set of manuscripts preserved in the
Museo Civico Correr) that contains no poems written prior to his banish-
ment from Venice in 1712.[12] It is therefore reasonable to infer that *Dal
tuono il lampo aspetta*—and by extension, the whole group of five cantatas—was composed between 1698 and 1712; the manuscript itself probably dates, as we saw, from no earlier than 1702. The style of the cantatas
is consistent, which suggests that they were all written around the same
time. One would guess that they belong to the earlier part of this time-
frame, since their musical language, though certainly more advanced than
that of the two cantatas for bass, remains conservative in some respects.

The cantata in the Paris Conservatoire collection is from the same
period or perhaps slightly later. It is the last work in a volume of 102
pages, all notated in the same hand on the same type of paper. The volume divides into four subunits, identifiable by the one or more blank
pages with which their last quire ends. It is not clear to what extent the
separate groups of works found in each were taken from different sources.
The first six quires (pp. 1–24) contain three anonymous cantatas with
French words (the second known to be by Jean-Baptiste Morin).[13] The
next seven (pp. 25–52) have three more French cantatas—one by Fiocco,
one by Morin, and one anonymous (but again by Morin).[14] They are followed by a single quire (pp. 53–8) containing another Morin cantata.[15]
The final eleven quires (pp. 59–102) are occupied entirely by solo cantatas
for soprano with Italian texts: five by Giovanni Battista Stuck, one by
Franceso Mancini, and Vinaccesi's *Belve, se mai provaste*. Our composer's
association here with a Florentine and a Neapolitan composer is perhaps a

[10] See Talbot, *Tomaso Albinoni*, 117–18.

[11] *I-Vmc*, Ms. Correr 466, 425–6. See Talbot and Timms, 'Music and the Poetry of Antonio
Ottoboni', 412.

[12] Ibid. 376.

[13] The Morin work is *L'Incertitude*, published in the composer's second book of cantatas (1707).
The first work, *L'Infidélité*, is attributed to a composer named 'Manani' in David Tunley, *The
Eighteenth-Century French Cantata* (London, 1974), 228. This appears to be a misreading of 'Mancini',
which, as a later addition in a hand different from the copyist's, carries no authority in any case.

[14] The anonymous cantata is *La Rose*, another work included in Morin's second book.

[15] This is *L'Esloignement*, an alternative title for *L'Absence*, another cantata published in Morin's
second book. See Tunley, *Eighteenth-Century French Cantata*, 71 n.

little unexpected, but one must remember that the Italian solo cantata was a genre that travelled as freely as the language to whose words it was set, the singers who performed it, and the nobility and gentry who cultivated it; in other words, the Venetian, Florentine, and Neapolitan cantata flowed into a common pool, making it impossible to speak easily of local 'schools' or regional areas of cultivation.

Stuck's movements provide a clue to dating. This celebrated cellist, born *c.*1680, came to Paris, where he settled permanently, in 1705. Since no cantatas by him with Italian words are known besides the present five (those he wrote in his adopted home all use the local language), it is probably safe to assume that he composed them while still resident in Italy. The earliest music by Stuck on which a date can be set is his adaptation of Albinoni's opera *Rodrigo in Algeri* (Naples, December 1702). A likely time-frame for the composition of the Italian cantatas is therefore 1700–5. A similar dating would certainly appear to fit Vinaccesi's cantata, which is just a little more expansive than the Berlin cantatas (a general expansion in the dimensions of arias, the reason for which we will explain later, is characteristic of the solo cantata in the first years of the eighteenth century). From what has been said, the date of copying of the volume as a whole cannot be earlier than 1705, and from the fact that three of the cantatas by Morin contained in it were published in 1707 in that composer's second book one would guess that this year marks a *terminus ad quem*.

It is quite likely, in fact, that the volume originated in the circle of musicians around Philippe, duke of Orleans (1674–1723), the leading advocate of Italian music among the French nobility during the first decade of the eighteenth century. Both Stuck and Morin, pioneers of the French cantata, were *ordinaires de la musique* in the duke's service around this time, and it may be that Fiocco—probably Pietro Antonio Fiocco (*c.*1650–1714), founding father of the famous dynasty of musicians—was also associated with the circle, for it seems no coincidence that he, Morin, and Stuck all wrote cantatas, perhaps competitively, on the same *Philomèle* text;[16] two of these (those by Fiocco and Morin) are contained in our source. If this inference is correct, Vinaccesi's piece could have been one of a small number of Italian cantatas that exerted a seminal influence on the nascent French cantata.

It is always fitting to begin a discussion of baroque cantatas with an examination of their literary texts, not merely because, in a simple chronological sense, the words came first in the vast majority of settings, but

---

[16] Fiocco's possible role in the transmission of the cantata from Italy to France seems to have been overlooked. Tunley's study does not mention his name, and his setting of *Philomèle* is listed as an anonymous composition ('del Fiocco' obviously having been understood as part of the title!) in Gene E. Vollen, *The French Cantata: A Survey and Thematic Catalog* (Ann Arbor, Mich., 1982), 144–5.

even more because in doing so they prescribed the agenda for the composer to a degree that few song-writing traditions, before or since, have wished, or been able, to match. Notwithstanding the fact that, as poetry, cantata texts stood on average much lower in the artistic scale of values than their settings did as music, the social superiority of the poet, usually a noble amateur, ensured that the composer, a hired professional, respected the integrity and artistic completeness of the literary text, which, as we saw in the case of Ottoboni, could be deemed worthy of preservation merely as a poem. The basic task of the baroque composer was not to use the literary text as malleable raw material for a different (i.e. essentially musical) kind of artistic experience; rather, it was to 'clothe' the words in suitable notes. To be sure, the music had to be well fitting; but in the final analysis, its validity, no less than that of the poem, depended principally on its adequacy measured by the rules of its own art. A baroque cantata is a mutually convenient alliance, not a genuine synthesis, of words and music.

The development of the cantata, from its origins in the continuo madrigal and aria of the early Baroque, can be seen as the result of a continuing process of 'negotiation' between four interested parties: poets, composers, singers, and audiences.[17] By the closing decades of the seventeenth century a large degree of consensus between the parties had been achieved. A poet could send a new text to a composer he had never met in the certain knowledge that his collaborator would know at a glance exactly how to treat each stanza. In turn, the singer could trust the composer to give him exactly the right amount of florid, and of declamatory, writing, while the audience knew in advance what kind of work in respect of style, form, and even (usually) duration to expect. These conditions were conducive to mass-production of a highly standardized article; but mass-production was exactly what was needed if the cantata was to fulfil its social function as the staple fare of weekly *conversazioni*.

These observations should not be taken to mean that one cantata is as good (or bad) as the next. What they do mean, however, is that the composer has to show his skill, imagination, and sensitivity by the manner in which a familiar plan is executed rather than through his invention of a new plan. Exactly the same is true for the poet.

At the end of the seventeenth century the subject-matter and imagery of cantata verse became dominated as never before by Arcadian conventions, which transported the listener into a make-believe world that, in the case of the Roman Arcadia and its colonies, spilled over into the organiza-

---

[17] One is tempted to include among the 'interested parties' also the instrumentalists who performed in cantatas. It is noticeable how composers who were also cellists—Stuck, Caldara, and Giovanni Bononcini among them—rarely missed an occasion to give the continuo part idiomatic figures showing off their instrument.

tional life of the institutions where the poetry was cultivated. This narrowing of the poetic vision was described by the critic Giuseppe Baretti in terms that exaggerate only slightly:

The madness of pastoral became now universal Every body who had the least knack for poetry, was metamorphosed into a shepherd, and fell directly upon composing rustic sonnets, eclogues, ydylliums, and bucolics. Nothing was heard from the foot of the Alps to the farthermost end of Calabria but descriptions of purling streams rolling gently along flowery meadows situated by the sides of verdant hills shaded by spreading trees, among whose leafy branches the sad Progne with her melancholy sister Philomela warbled their chaste loves, or murmured their doleful lamentations.[18]

The prolixity of Baretti's second sentence, which imitates with satirical intent a property of the very subject it is describing, is easily outdone by the opening stanza of Vinaccesi's *Là nelle verdi spiagge*, a single sentence marching unimpeded over eighteen lines:

Là nelle verdi spiagge	There, on the green slopes,
dove rustica mano	where a rustic hand
dall'abete e dal faggio	on supports of fir and beech
alla gravida vite	used to take from the laden vine,
con barbarie usitate	with a customary barbarity
ma di giusta natura ambita legge	sanctioned, however, by a just law of nature,
toglieva i dolci parti,	the sweet fruits,
cui dall'aura gelata	in a spot protected from the chilly breeze
delle rigide figlie di Latona	of Latona's icy daughters
ver l'Iperboree parti	coming from the Hyperborean regions
del più calido sole in faccia al raggio	by a solitary rock
difende orfana rupe	facing the hottest rays of the sun,
Mirtillo che dolente	Mirtillo, who, lamenting
della cara Amarilli	for his dear Amarilli,
soffrir più non potea la lontananza	could no longer bear the separation,
al mormorio del pianto	to the murmur of the tears
che dagl'occhi versò	that poured from his eyes
un dì così cantò.	one day sang these words.

Anyone half familiar with the genre will recognize in this passage all the salient features of late-seventeenth-century cantata verse: the saturation of its vocabulary by a small number of favourite words and locutions (e.g. 'spiaggia', 'aura', 'dolente', 'caro', 'pianto'); its ostentatiously Latinate syntax (seen, for instance, in the suppression of the indefinite article before 'rustica mano' in the second line); the almost mandatory references to classical mythology.

---

[18] Joseph [Giuseppe] Baretti, *An Account of the Manners and Customs of Italy, with Observations on the Mistakes of some Travellers, with Regard to that Country* (London, 2/1769), i. 251.

With few exceptions, then, the dramatis personae are the nymphs and shepherds of Arcadia, that mythical wooded valley of the Peloponnese. Vinaccesi's eight cantatas present three very common types of 'scenario'. Three works treat the subject of a shepherd's separation (*lontananza*) from his beloved: *Là nelle verdi spiagge*, *Or fia mai vero, o lontananza infida*, and *Su la sponda d'un rio*. *Filli, un solo tuo sguardo* and *Belve, se mai provaste* are a shepherd's protestations of an evidently unrequited love. In *Ingratissima Clori* we find a related theme, for here the eponymous nymph is chided for her unresponsiveness.

All six poems are dominated by the idea of reproach—whether against fate, the god of love, or the beloved herself. The dominant mood is therefore that described by Eugen Schmitz, the pioneering researcher into the baroque cantata, as 'elegiac [and] painfully passionate'.[19] Nevertheless, in the interests of a more varied expression, which will give the composer scope for livelier and more cheerful emotions, all the poems contain passages in which the protagonist imagines a happier state of being (in *Ingratissima Clori* this consists merely of deserting the ingrate in favour of a certain Fillide!).

The remaining two cantatas, *Quanto mi vien da ridere* and *Dal tuono il lampo aspetta*, are both examples of a variety already mentioned, the *lezione amorosa*. Here the subject is neither Arcadian nor contemporary: it is simply atemporal. In the first work the poet reflects on the follies of male lovers and the wiles of women; in the second he convinces himself that, for all its perils, being a lover is recommendable. Fortunately, the didacticism never becomes too heavy.

Although all these works are to some extent 'dramatic' in the loose modern sense of possessing vivid, sometimes even violent, imagery, the terminology of the time preferred to reserve this description for poetic creations in which two or more characters engage in dialogue in the manner of a theatrical piece. For Johann Mattheson, writing in 1739, cantatas were 'historical' works on account of their narrative element; for Johann Adolph Scheibe (1745), they were 'epic' in nature; only later on in the eighteenth century, when it had become more common to cast a cantata in the form of a monologue by an identifiable character (Telemann's *Ino* is one such work) and omit all external narration, did solo cantatas become readily classifiable as 'dramatic' compositions, as occurs in a treatise on poetry intended for musical setting by Christian Gottfried Krause (1753).[20]

For the purposes of analysis today, which naturally does not have to

[19] Eugen Schmitz, *Geschichte der weltlichen Solokantate* (Leipzig, 1914), 150. Schmitz's phrase 'elegischer, schmerzlich leidschaftlicher Ausdruck' refers to Albinoni's arias but is applicable to a large part of the cantata repertory around 1700.

[20] The categorization of the cantata by baroque theorists and their concept of the dramatic in relation to it are explored in Colin Timms, 'The Dramatic in Vivaldi's Cantatas', in Lorenzo Bianconi and Giovanni Morelli (eds.), *Antonio Vivaldi: Teatro musicale, cultura e società* (Florence, 1982), 97–129.

remain imprisoned in the categories current when the works were written, four types of presentation—we will call them 'voices'—can be identified in the Italian solo cantata cultivated by Vinaccesi and his contemporaries. The first is the 'lyric' voice, where the poet addresses the reader as himself. The second is the 'narrative' voice, where he sets a scene or describes an event. The third is the 'quoting' voice, where he presents in direct speech the words of a character introduced in the narration. The fourth is the 'dramatic' voice (in Krause's sense), where he pretends to be a historical or invented character.

The texts of Vinaccesi's cantatas show an interesting variety in their option for one or more of these voices. The two *lezioni amorose* are, as one would expect, in the lyric voice. *Ingratissima Clori, Filli, un solo tuo sguardo*, and *Belve, se mai provaste* all adopt the dramatic voice—in the last work the poet even introduces himself by name as 'Eurillo'. This leaves three cantatas in which the narrative and quoting voices are mixed. In each case the formula is different. *Là nelle verdi spiagge* frames the poem with recitative stanzas in the narrative voice, while both of its arias and also the recitative separating them are framed in direct speech. In *Su la sponda d'un rio* each of the three arias quoting the words of Alcindo addressed to Clori is preceded by a scene-setting recitative. *Or fia mai vero, o lontananza infida* starts out and continues almost to the end as if it were a 'dramatic' cantata; only in a final recitative stanza does the poet adopt the narrative voice, suggesting that the speaker of the previous lines was not the poet himself but only a 'tortured soul' (*anima affannata*) observed by him.

One might imagine that in those cantatas where the poetic voice changes, the composer would find some means of reflecting those changes in music, perhaps by varying the intensity of expression. Surprisingly and perhaps regrettably, this does not seem to be the case in Vinaccesi's cantatas or, indeed, in most of those of his contemporaries. Nor do the 'dramatic' cantatas appear any more vivid, in their poetic imagery or musical word-painting, than the 'lyric' ones. One is bound to conclude that the poetic voice or combination of voices employed in a cantata text was seen as a purely formal choice without any important implications for the composer.

In the mid-seventeenth century cantata texts often comprised a great number of stanzas. By the last decade of the century, however, their typical number had been reduced to between three and seven, including two or three aria stanzas. This move towards standardization and rationalization, which was accompanied by a compensatory expansion in the musical dimensions of the arias, was part of a general mutation in 'cultural style' that began to manifest itself just before 1700.[21] The new principles

---

[21] See Ch. 6, n. 22.

consolidated themselves in the solo cantata during the first half of the eighteenth century, when a two-aria scheme began to be favoured over a three-aria one and both the number and the length of the recitative stanzas tended to shrink.

Between them, Vinaccesi's cantatas exhibit five of the most common patterns of alternating recitative and aria found around 1700. In the diagram below, 'R' stands for a recitative stanza, 'A' for an aria stanza.

R A R A R A	*Su la sponda d'un rio*
R A R A R A	*Filli, un solo tuo sguardo*
R A R A R A	*Belve, se mai provaste*
A R A R A	*Dal tuono il lampo aspetta*
R A R A R	*Là nelle verdi spiagge*
R A R A R	*Or fia mai vero, o lontananza infida*
R A R A	*Ingratissima Clori*
A R A	*Quanto mi vien da ridere*

Recitative stanzas are invariably written in *versi sciolti*: lines, mostly unrhymed, of variously seven and eleven syllables. The shifting metre and pattern of accentuation provide the flexibility needed to give recitative its spontaneous, *parlando* character. The last line is virtually always rhymed with either the penultimate or the antepenultimate line. Because of the generally swift, syllabic manner in which recitative verse is delivered, such rhymes, unlike most rhymes in poetry set to music, are clearly audible to the listener and are thefore able to serve as markers announcing the end of the stanza. For their part, composers like to signal the end of a recitative stanza by changing to a more elaborate treatment: repeating words or phrases, inserting brief melismatic passages, enlivening the bass: in short, adopting an *arioso* style. Where a still greater degree of elaboration is required—this applies particularly to recitative stanzas concluding a work—the composer can introduce a *cavata*, a separate section in which the words of the last line or pair of lines are treated intensively, often with imitative play between the voice and the bass.[22]

Aria verse is more fully rhymed and in general favours 'short' metres of between three and six syllables, although *ottonari*, eight-syllable lines, are also popular on account of their easy compatibility with a symmetrical phrase-structure. Whereas recitative verse is dominated by *piano* line-endings (a stressed syllable followed by an unstressed one), aria verse shows greater favour to *sdrucciolo* (stressed–unstressed–unstressed) and *tronco* (stressed) endings; the latter are especially appropriate for cadence-points where the composer wishes to end a phrase with a long note placed

---

[22] The origin and nature of the *cavata* are discussed in Colin Timms, 'The Cavata at the Time of Vivaldi', in Antonio Fanna and Giovanni Morelli (eds.), *Nuovi studi vivaldiani: Edizione e cronologia critica dell'opera* (Florence, 1988), 451–77.

on a strong beat. As well as arias in a fixed metre one finds polymetric examples. As a rule of thumb, the stronger the poet's reliance on rhyme as an organizing principle, the greater his licence to vary the metre; conversely, the higher the incidence of unrhymed lines, the greater the need for metrical regularity.

For most of the seventeenth century, arias, in cantatas and operas alike, were often cast in several stanzas and set as strophic songs. Strophic construction was well-nigh obsolete by Vinaccesi's time. However, the division of aria stanzas into two semistrophes, the first of which was repeated after the second, had become almost mandatory. It was not incumbent on the composer to make the repeated 'A' section identical in every respect with the first statement, and until almost the end of the century reprises were commonly written out *in extenso*, a practice that encouraged the composer to introduce minor (or even major) deviations from the original statement. However, the growing average length of arias and perhaps also the desire of singers to take on single-handedly the responsibility, via improvised embellishment, for varying the 'A' material on its reprise encouraged composers to finish their notation of arias with the double-bar after the B section, to which they could append an instruction such as 'Da capo' or 'Dal segno'. This usage became general well before the turn of the century.

Any valid appraisal of Vinaccesi's cantatas has, in principle, to distinguish carefully between those features characteristic of him as an individual composer and those—the majority—shared with the whole generation of Italian composers to which he belonged. In the present state of knowledge, this is something of a counsel of perfection. While many excellent studies of cantatas by individual composers have been produced in recent times, there is a distinct lack of works of synthesis longer than an encyclopedia article.[23] This means, unfortunately, that the norms against which Vinaccesi's cantatas are measured have the status of impressions rather than of established facts. Yet it is only by making an attempt, however tentative, to locate Vinaccesi within a larger framework that we can take the measure of his skill and originality.

It is appropriate to consider his settings of recitative separately from his arias, since the two genera (as conceived around 1700) are so contrasted in nature that a composer has to bring into play quite different techniques.

One striking way in which recitative differs from aria is in the much greater complexity of its tonal circuit.[24] With only rare exceptions, tonally closed forms, in which the key of the opening is also that of the ending,

---

[23] *New Grove* lists no fewer than six academic dissertations on the chamber cantatas of Alessandro Scarlatti alone. The problem lies less in the vol. of research undertaken than in the lack of subsequent co-ordination of its findings.

[24] See the discussion of Vinaccesi's treatment of tonality in Ch. 6, 152.

limit their field of modulation to the group of closely related keys. An aria in C major may visit G major, F major, A minor, E minor, and D minor, but is unlikely to venture further afield. Moreover, not only the choice of keys but also the order in which they are visited is largely governed by convention.

In recitative, however, tonal closure is the exception rather than the rule. For reasons both practical (to bridge the gap between tonally closed movements in distantly related keys) and expressive (to mirror the sense of the words), no limit is set on the choice of keys visited or their order. The tight circuit has become a meandering path. Two special new techniques of modulation are employed to enable the composer to traverse rapidly and efficiently the much greater tonal distances that now become available. Not by coincidence, they are the same techniques that were widely used in sonata-form movements in the later eighteenth century (though tonally closed, such movements have an expanded field of modulation equivalent to that previously enjoyed, with few exceptions, only by recitative). The first technique may be termed 'sequential modulation': a single type of modulation (e.g. from C major to D major) is replicated exactly to make a progression of three or more keys (e.g. C major–D major–E major–F♯ major). This differs from the more normal form of modulation through several keys by keeping the modality, major or minor, constant, thus preventing the semitonal adjustments that would produce instead a progression such as C major–D minor–E minor–F major, which keeps the music anchored to the area around the original key. The second technique is to switch between the major and minor keys sharing a tonic note (and, equally vitally, a dominant chord). Any such substitution of mode moves the tonality at a stroke three degrees forward or back along the circle of fifths.

When we examine Vinaccesi's recitatives, we find that surprisingly little use is made of these techniques. The composer is mostly content to remain within the same tonal area that he would explore in a more structured movement. The reason is no doubt partly sheer conservatism, but Vinaccesi also seems motivated positively by a concern for the continuity of the work; he wishes the music to flow easily from recitative to aria and back again. A clear symptom of this concern for integration is the fact that his recitatives end as often as not in the key of the succeeding aria. When the key is the same, the listener perceives no disjunction between the final chord of the recitative and the first chord of the aria (a hiatus that some later composers, including Vivaldi, will deliberately exploit for its affective significance);[25] rather, the aria is experienced as a lyrical pro-

---

[25] The tonal relationship between adjacent arias and recitatives is closely examined in an introductory essay by Paul Everett and the present author to a forthcoming facsimile edn. of two Vivaldi serenatas in the series *Drammaturgia musicale veneta*.

longation of the recitative. On the other hand, Vinaccesi relishes a mild degree of tonal disjunction between the opening of a recitative and a preceding aria. This has the effect of turning the recitatives even more firmly into introductions to the arias following them rather than sequels to those preceding them. Except where an aria begins a cantata or a recitative ends it (such movements have perforce to stand alone), the music proceeds as a series of recitative–aria pairs.

The opening recitative of *Belve, se mai provaste*, shown as Ex. 8, typifies Vinaccesi's handling of recitative at its most assured. The first three bars offer a version of a favourite opening formula in which the initial tonic chord is followed by a dissonance over a tonic pedal that constitutes, or leads to, a dominant seventh chord resolving into tonic harmony again.[26] This leisurely, tonally closed progression is especially well suited to the start of an opening recitative, since it enables the listener to take stock of the key to which the music will return at the end of the work and also has the virtue of drawing him gently rather than abruptly into the musical discourse. In bar 4 Vinaccesi introduces a G major chord (a powerful effect because of the abrupt change from B flat to B natural and the initial unprepared seventh in the voice) that one initially interprets as the dominant chord of C minor; however, by a process of ellipsis he substitutes in bar 6 a diminished triad on C sharp (chord VII in D minor) for the expected minor triad on C natural. Retrospectively, therefore, the G major chord has to be interpreted as a subdominant chord (with major third) in D minor. This kind of implied ellipsis, which entails the short-circuiting of our expectations rather than the removal of an actual harmonic link, is very common in Vinaccesi's recitatives. Here the device helps to raise tension as we enter more deeply into the world of Eurillo's sufferings and, impassioned, the voice sweeps up to *f″*. In bars 7–10 the bass intensifies the doleful atmosphere by introducing the traditional *lamento* progression, a chromaticized tetrachord descending from tonic to dominant (*d–A*). The avoidance of a simple perfect cadence through stepwise movement in the bass is deftly contrived in bar 10. In bars 12–16 Vinaccesi adopts the *arioso* manner with which, as we saw, he likes to end his recitatives. Its most striking features are an extravagant vocal melisma in bars 13–14 and a poignantly expressive augmented fifth at the junction of bars 15 and 16. This closing section is underpinned by a bass that opens with the *lamento* formula in its diatonic version: G (equivalent to *g*), *f*, *e♭*, *d*. This progression balances the earlier appearance of the *lamento* formula in D minor in a subtle and effective way.

Vinaccesi applies word-painting in a highly selective manner. By the late seventeenth century composers had largely given up the intention of

---

[26] The progression is, of course, a topos of late-baroque music—one used especially often by J. S. Bach to begin the preludes of his '48'.

The Cantatas

Ex. 8. *Belve, se mai provaste*, opening recitative

faithfully reflecting the imagery of the text word by word, phrase by phrase, since, when taken to an extreme, this process can result in too episodic a form of construction and stultify the process of composition by demanding too automatic a response from the music. This selectivity means that in bar 3 'gli estremi affanni' (the ultimate torments) go entirely unregistered, as do the 'mesti accenti' (sad accents) in bars 11–12. But, as we saw, the bass depicts the 'agonie d'un cuore' (agonies of a heart) in bars 7–8, while the soprano is permitted to 'sprigionar' (release, pour out) its sorrows ornately in bars 12–16. The result is a precisely calculated density of word-painting that avoids all hint of studiedness. In other circumstances, our composer might well have chosen to highlight 'mesti accenti'; but to have done so would have meant restoring the balance by foregoing word-painting somewhere else in the recitative.

A similar feeling for a just balance informs the style of word-setting. As the poetic text of Ex. 8 (see below) shows, several phrases flow uninterrupted over line-breaks, and the composer has an important choice to make: does he enable the listener always to perceive line-breaks clearly by inserting rests and thus translate the visual appearance of the poem into aural terms; or does he take his cue from the sense of the words alone, responding to *enjambement* with an unbroken flow of notes? In practice, neither course is followed consistently to the exclusion of the other. Overall, the bias is certainly towards the first (quasi-visual) approach, in which not only line-breaks but also caesuras within the lines are clearly marked. At moments of high tension, however, the composer may sometimes allow himself to be swept along by the poet's *enjambement*, a sudden liberation that is all the more effective for being exceptional. In Ex. 8 such a moment occurs in bar 8, where 'Fatto' follows 'cuore' without a break. Here the continuity of the vocal line helps to draw attention to the slowly moving *lamento* figure in the bass.

Belve, se mai provaste	Animals, if ever you experienced
d'un amoroso cor gl'estremi affanni,	the ultimate torments of a loving heart,
queste querule voci	these doleful sounds
ch'interrotte sentite uscir dal petto	that you hear coming without respite
dell'infelice Eurillo	from the breast of luckless Eurillo
son l'agonie d'un cuore	are the agonies of a heart
fatto scherzo di pene a un cieco	whose pains give sport to a blind love.
amore.	
A la bella Amarilli in mesti accenti	Hear him divulge his sorrows
a sprigionar sentite i suoi lamenti.	to fair Amarilli in sad accents.

One initially surprising aspect of Vinaccesi's word-setting in recitatives is his willingness to place the unstressed syllables that open many lines in a metrically accented position. In example 8 this situation applies to lines 2, 3, 6, and 7. In fact, the same oddity is found in the recitative of several Italian composers of his time.[27] The underlying reason is probably a desire to draw attention to the line-divisions of the poetry; it is significant that the first syllable after a caesura, to which this consideration does not apply, is always set by Vinaccesi as unaccented when appropriate.

[27] I have commented on it in *Tomaso Albinoni*, 133–4. The reason given there for the apparent misaccentuation (the composer's overriding predilection for a dactylic rhythmic group consisting of a quaver and two semiquavers) now convinces me less than the one offered here.

To a large extent, the musical punctuation, in the form of cadences, is closely matched to the implied verbal punctuation.[28] The only perfect cadence in Ex. 8 to have both chords (V and I) in root position is the concluding one; the next most important break, in bar 10, is represented by an 'inverted' perfect cadence (one in which the tonic chord appears in first inversion). The cadences in bars 3, 6–7, 11–12, and 14–15 are of various weaker kinds, corresponding to the points of division between clauses or phrases. However, it is important to recognize that Vinaccesi and his contemporaries do not observe a 'grammar' of recitative cadences as precise and unvaried as that suggested by the examples in Johann Joseph Fux's *Gradus ad Parnassum*.[29] For instance, the distinctive cadential formula (a type of half-close) equated by Fux with a question mark, though indeed used by Vinaccesi in this context many times, is by no means restricted to it.

Between them, the eight cantatas include three cavatas. *Là nelle verdi spiagge* appends cavatas to its second and third recitatives; the other occurs at the end of *Or fia mai vero, o lontananza infida*. They are rather brief, as cavatas go, and although all feature imitation between voice and bass, none offers fugal treatment or double counterpoint in the manner of Albinoni or Caldara. The most interesting is the one in *Or fia mai vero, o lontananza infida*, quoted as Ex. 9. Its most impressive quality is the inventiveness of its plan of modulation. The last aria having ended in B minor, the task of the final recitative and cavata is to steer the music back to F sharp minor, the key in which the cantata opened.

The movement starts dramatically with a plunge into C sharp minor, introduced via its dominant chord. By the beginning of bar 6, where the recitative proper ends, F sharp minor has—apparently—been regained. But Vinaccesi unexpectedly sidesteps the cadential implication of the dominant chord and begins the cavata in D major. From there he returns to F sharp minor in a circuitous but purposeful way. To re-establish a tonic successfully when moving to it, as Vinaccesi is doing here, from the 'flat' side requires perfect control of pacing.

For all their many felicities, Vinaccesi's recitatives inevitably offer only limited scope for personal expression. It is to the arias, rather, that we must look for signs of originality. These are thoughtfully varied in style, in accordance with the diverse *affetti* suggested by the poetic texts. However, the contrasts between the two or three arias appearing in the same cantata are less great in the two works for bass than in their

[28] 'Implied', because few underlaid texts in MSS of the time are punctuated fully. Moreover, one must always take account of differences between older and modern conventions (for instance, in careful older usage a comma is automatically inserted before conjunctions, even though no pause is implied).
[29] Johann Joseph Fux, *Gradus ad Parnassum* (Vienna, 1725), 277–8.

Ex. 9. *Or fia mai vero, o lontananza infida*, final recitative and cavata companions. In the former, both arias are cast in the same key. This was unavoidable in *Quanto mi vien da ridere*, with its simple A–R–A plan, but not in *Là nelle verdi spiagge*, whose second aria, had the composer so wished, could have provided tonal contrast. The uniformity, tonal and metrical, of the arias in the two bass cantatas is one of the stylistic features that set these works apart from the rest and suggest an earlier date. Elsewhere, Vinaccesi sees to it that the keys, metres, tempi, and characteristic rhythms of the arias are duplicated as little as possible within each cantata.

Only one aria is not in 'ABA' form: 'Se t'arrivo un dì, mia vita', the second aria of *Or fia mai vero, o lontananza infida*. Even that aria is ternary insofar as the ritornello of the 'A' section comes back after the 'B' section to round off the movement. However, the cantatas present two quite different versions of *da capo* form. The first occurs in the cantatas for bass, the second in the remaining works. Each version belongs to a distinct chronological phase in the development of the Italian baroque aria. The earlier type is associated with the generation of composers active around 1660–80 (Legrenzi, Stradella, and Sartorio are representative figures), while the later type comes to replace it during the last two decades of the seventeenth century in the cantatas and operas of such composers as Albinoni and Giovanni Bononcini. Like Alessandro Scarlatti, Vinaccesi belongs to an intermediate generation that grew up with the first, more primitive, form but switched to the second later on. His cantatas are testimony to an important historical evolution that has received all too little mention in scholarly literature.[30]

Numerous instances of *da capo* form can be found in the music of the early Baroque. The composer's setting of an opening line or pair of lines that often has the character of a *sentenza*, or moralistic observation, is used as a refrain. It returns at the end of the aria, and in longer movements or sections may also be restated at intermediate points. Ellen Rosand has coined the very appropriate term 'da capo refrain aria' to denote this type.[31] The fundamental point is that the 'meat' of the aria, including all its modulation, is concentrated in the 'B' section, while the 'A' section, attractive and memorable though it may be, is subordinate in structural terms.

[30] The earlier formal model is encountered in the cantata *Prendea con man di latte*, RV 753, attributed in its single source to Vivaldi. Since this composer elsewhere uniformly adheres to the later model, the anomaly has justifiably been used as an argument against his authorship. See Colin Timms, '*Prendea con man di latte*: A Vivaldi Spuriosity?', *Informazioni e studi vivaldiani*, 6 (1985), 64–73. Timms implies, but does not develop, the proposition that the more concise form is the earlier. In fact, other unusual features of RV 753—the tonal closure of the two recitatives, the turn to *arioso* at their conclusion, the choice of the home key for both arias—echo Vinaccesi's usage in the two cantatas for bass. One is not suggesting that Vinaccesi should replace Vivaldi as the presumed author, but merely that *Prendea con man di latte* represents the solo cantata at a very similar stage of development.

[31] Ellen Rosand, *Opera in Seventeenth-Century Venice: The Creation of a Genre* (Berkeley, 1991), 299–304.

The second stage in this process occurs when, through expansion (aided by liberal word and phrase repetition) and the adoption of a more articulated internal structure, the 'A' section achieves parity of length and weight with the 'B' section. This is illustrated by 'Mi promette una dolce speranza', the second aria of Vinaccesi's *Là nelle verdi spiagge*, whose 'A' section is quoted as Ex. 10. The section constitutes a single musical period, punctuated by a half-close in bar 5. If one discounts the twofold repetition of the words of the third line, the text is presented only once. In this instance the concluding cadence is in the tonic, D minor, which gives the composer the opportunity to make the written-out reprise literal (though he appends a three-bar ritornello to strengthen the feeling of finality). In some other cases, the 'A' section leads to another key on its first statement, which compels a modification of the reprise. The 'B' section of the same aria, which begins in B flat major and modulates via F major to A minor, is almost exactly equal in length (seven bars as compared with six and a half) and sets its text in similar manner. In the first aria from the same cantata, 'Quando mai, luci adorate', Vinaccesi has a tonally closed 'B' section, a feature that almost creates the impression that two self-contained miniature movements (the 'A' and 'B' sections) are alternating with one another.

Ex. 10. *Là nelle verdi spiagge*, second aria

The next evolutionary stage—the final one to concern us—is very familiar from the later cantatas and operas of Alessandro Scarlatti and the works of such composers as Handel and Vivaldi. Here the 'A' section contains two vocal periods, each of which presents the text, with the usual repetitions, in full. The first section cadences in a new key; the second returns to the tonic, where it closes (the point of return varies but is usually close to the start of the second period). The effect of this more complex structuring of the 'A' section, which is now routinely at least twice as long as the 'B' section, is to shift the whole emphasis of the movement towards it. Indeed, in the hands of lesser composers of the early and mid eighteenth century, the 'B' section all too often seems perfunctory, as if its only reason for existence were to provide a brief interval before the return of the 'A' section. In most respects, the aria form benefits from having three vocal periods (two in the 'A' section, one in the 'B') instead of only two, since the composer has so much more scope for invention. On the other hand, the simpler form blends into the surrounding recitative more easily and can have, at its best, an appealingly epigrammic quality.

It is this more advanced form that occurs in the Berlin cantatas and also in *Belve, se mai provaste*. The only vestige of the previous stage is the appearance here and there (but actually in all three arias of *Su la sponda d'un rio!*) of tonally closed 'B' sections, which are uncharacteristic of the mature form. Within the general scheme as described, however, Vinaccesi's treatment of detail is very varied.

Concerning the thematic relationship between the openings of the three vocal sections, no uniform procedure obtains. One is reminded of the same fluidity of treatment in the binary-form movements of Vinaccesi's sonatas. On one hand, there are straightforward requotations, transposed or otherwise, that provide unity at a thematic level; on the other, oblique or partial references that contribute, at most, to what one may term motivic unity. There is no suggestion here of an established norm to be followed (or overridden).

Certain arias, generally light and strongly rhythmic in character, prescribe repetition of the first vocal section. This is a feature encountered very often in cantata arias around 1700; it recalls the binary-form aria of the early and mid Baroque but may, in fact, have stronger links to instrumental dance music of the time.

A clear majority of the arias in the group of six under discussion employ what Hugo Riemann called the *Devise*—a motto with which the singer makes his entry. This motto is then cut short by an instrumental passage usually long enough to be called a ritornello that introduces the first vocal period proper. The *Devise* had its heyday in the years immediately preceding and following 1700. If Alessandro Scarlatti was not its inventor (such 'inventions' are notoriously hard to establish), he must, at least, have played an important part in its dissemination, given the popularity and wide circulation of his cantatas.

Such mottoes are of two main types. The first can be described as a preview or false start, since the same phrase is used to open the first vocal period. The second, usually very short, is more neutral in character, giving the singer an opportunity to impress his audience with the aid of improvised embellishment. An illustration of the first type will be seen later in example 13 (note, however, that in this instance the phrase opening the first vocal period starts slightly differently). The second type is represented in its most extreme form by bar 11 of the aria 'Cerca, cerca novo piacer' ending *Ingratissima Clori*, whose opening is shown as Ex. 11. As if to draw attention to the self-contained nature of this motto, Vinaccesi notates it in a bar of common time that stands out very graphically from the surrounding '3' (i.e. 3/8) metre. This is pure 'eye-music', however: he could have obtained exactly the same effect by retaining the original metre but placing fermatas over the notes in that bar.

Ex. 11. *Ingratissima Clori*, second aria

In his aria ritornellos our composer repeatedly gives evidence of his fine natural musicianship. More often than not, arias begin with a ritornello for continuo, although this is *de rigueur* only when the movement in question opens the cantata and the singer is thus given the problem of finding his or her first note.[32] Even if there is no introductory ritornello, one may

---

[32] Very unusually, *Quanto mi vien da ridere* opens with an aria that has no initial ritornello, even though voice and accompaniment begin together. There is no suggestion from text or music that a preceding recitative has been lost; nor does the cantata appear to be the *seconda parte* of a composite work. It would seem, therefore, that the singer has to be given his first note in advance.

be provided for the 'A' section on its repeat. This may be either a
straightforward introduction in the same key or a lead-back from the 'B'
section. The presence of a ritornello statement at the end of the 'A' section is even more usual, though its nature varies. While it most often
functions as an epilogue to what it follows, it can also act as a modulating
link to the 'B' section (as in the aria from *Belve, se mai provaste* from
which Ex. 12 is taken) or even as a separate introduction to the 'B' section
itself (as in Ex. 13, taken from the same work). Ritornellos forming a
transition between the 'A' and 'B' sections (or vice-versa) are not a standard feature of *da capo* movements from this period, and the instances we
find in these cantatas (and, later, in his motets) bear witness to Vinaccesi's
unusual degree of concern (by the standards of his time) for musical continuity.

Ex. 12. *Belve, se mai provaste*, third aria

Other points at which ritornello statements may be found are the junction of the first two vocal periods and the gap between the *Devise* and the
first period. In these cases it is perhaps exaggerated to speak of a 'ritornello', since the instrumental passage is usually very short—sometimes a
mere half-bar. What is important, however, is that the motivic substance
of all introductory, concluding, and linking passages preserves a common
character throughout the aria and in doing so contributes significantly to
the movement's unity.

   As regards the relationship between the ritornello and the vocal line,
one can distinguish between two basic approaches. The first is to model
the ritornello on the vocal melody, making only whatever modifications
are required by its function as a bass line. This approach is clearly evident
in Ex. 12 (but note how in bar 3 Vinaccesi takes welcome advantage of

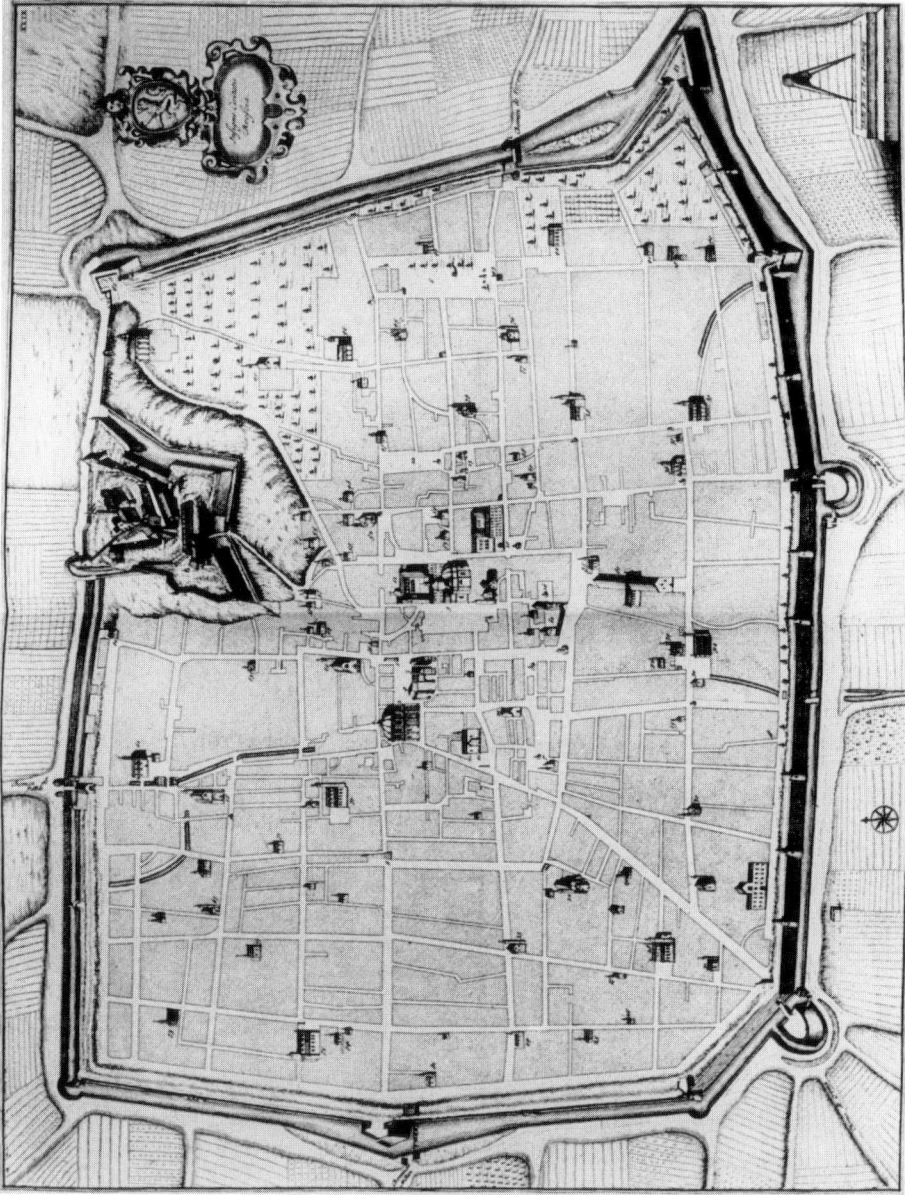

1. Map of Brescia c. 1700 reproduced in J. Blaeu, *Novum Italiae Theatrum* (1724) (*The Liverpool University Library*)

2. Façade of the church of the Ospedaletto as engraved *c.*1700
by Luca Carlevaris

3. Autograph receipt in which Vinaccesi acknowledges payment for acting as organist at San Nicolò di Lido on Ascension Day 1707
(*Archivio di Stato, Venice*)

Adi 20 Decembre 1719 Venetia

4. Vinaccesi's will, dated 20 December 1719 (*Archivio di Stato, Venice*)

5. Page 11 from the Violino Primo part of Vinaccesi's *Suonate da camera a tre*, Op. 1, ([Ms.] Mus. Sch. E. 554a) containing two movements of Sonata I (*The Bodleian Library, University of Oxford*)

6. Opening of Vinaccesi's motet *Alme Jesu, sponse care* (*Venice, Conservatorio di Musica 'Benedetto Marcello'*)

7. Opening of Vinaccesi's setting of the Compline psalm *Cum invocarem* (*Biblioteca Nazionale Marciana, Venice*)

8. Opening of Act I of Vinaccesi's pastoral opera *Chi è causa del suo mal pianga sé stesso* (*Bibliothèque Nationale, Paris*)

the greater agility that an instrument possesses). Alternatively, the composer can opt for complete motivic independence. This allows the figuration of the ritornello, and of the fragments of it used in the accompaniment of the voice, to acquire an idiomatic instrumental character. In making this choice, the composer loses the opportunity for imitative play between the two parts (as occurs at the start of Ex. 14) but gains an element of contrast that can also be used to generate powerful contrapuntal tension, albeit of a different kind. This type of relationship is seen in extreme form in Ex. 13. It is naturally also possible for ritornellos to be 'semi-independent' (i.e. of mixed character), as illustrated by Exx. 11 and 15.[33]

Whatever kind of ritornello Vinaccesi chooses to have, he shows an extraordinary ability to make it relevant for its context and always precisely the right length. The specimens seen in Exx. 11 and 13 are evidence enough of his eloquence, which never lapses into garrulity, while the ritornello ending Ex. 15 demonstrates his gift for unostentatiously condensing the essence of a whole movement into a handful of notes. Moreover, his experience as an organist ensures that all his ritornellos can be harmonized by the continuo player in an obvious and natural-sounding manner (this point is made because many composers, particularly ones who were singers or string players, wrote cantata ritornellos with an 'upper-part' character that makes them very awkward to harmonize).

The importance of the ritornello obviously increases if it is used as a ground bass appearing throughout the movement. In the eight cantatas under discussion two arias are of this type: 'Armati, o mia speranza', first aria of *Or fia mai vero, o lontananza infida*, and 'Che pena è il vivere', first aria of *Belve, se mai provaste*. The latter is perhaps the most impressive single movement in Vinaccesi's surviving cantatas and is quoted entire as Ex. 13.

It will be useful to begin discussion of this movement by outlining its form in tabular fashion. The numbers in the first column refer to statements of the ostinato theme. In its basic version this is three and a half bars long, but the insertion of rests between statements as well as modifications of the theme (e.g. in statement 6, where its final phrase is repeated) allow its effective length to increase by up to one and a half bars. Statements 5 and 9 are fragmentary, employing material from the theme in modulating sequences.

It is always interesting to examine, in this kind of movement, the extent to which the vocal line adheres to, or contradicts, the phrase-structure and

---

[33] The thematic relationship of aria ritornellos to the vocal line and its accompaniment is considered in greater detail in Michael Talbot, 'The Function and Character of the Instrumental Ritornello in the Solo Cantatas of Tomaso Albinoni (1671–1751)', *Quaderni della Civica Scuola di Musica*, 19–20 (1990), 77–90: 87–8.

Ex. 13. *Belve, se mai provaste*, second aria

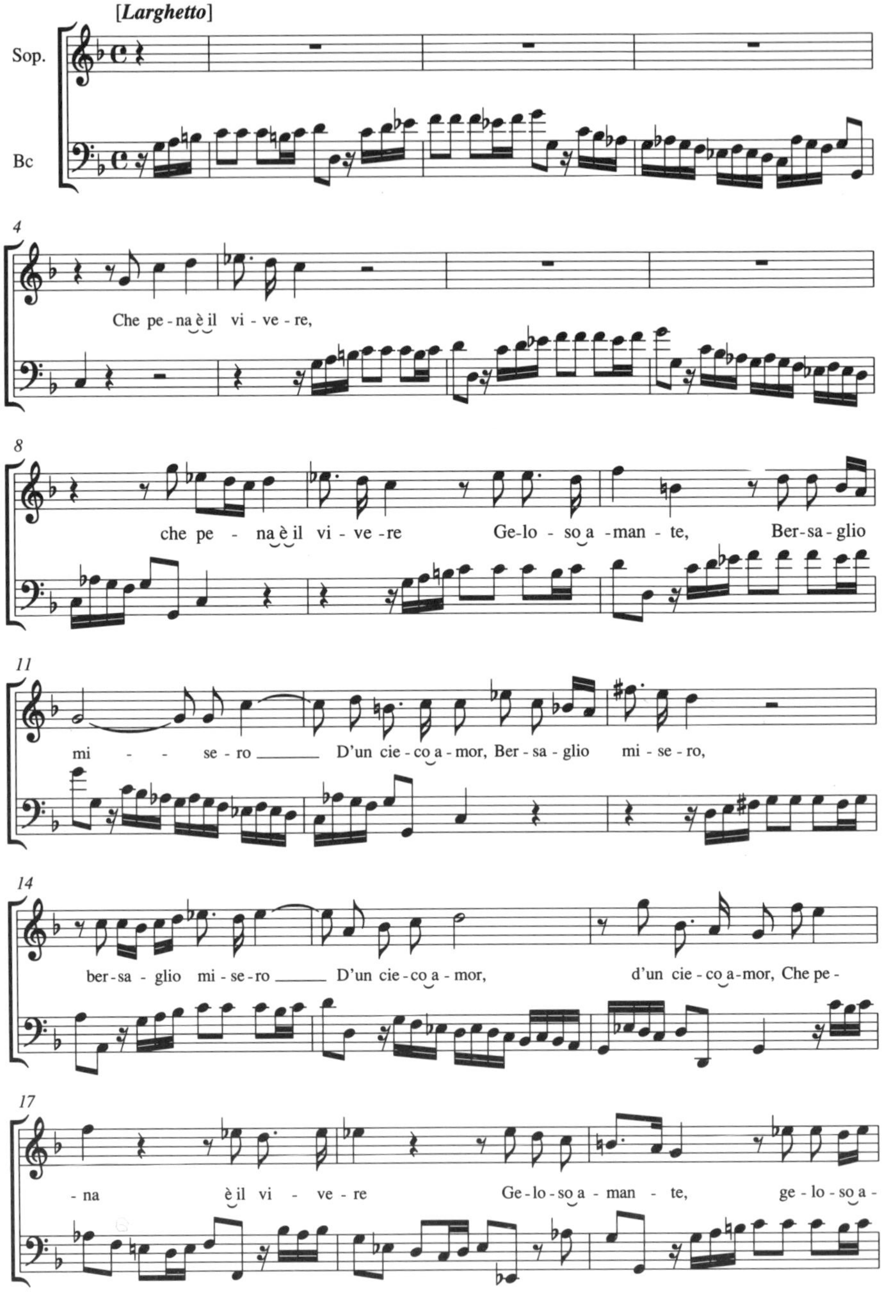

20
- man - te, Ber - sa - glio mi - se - ro d'un cie - co a - mor, d'un cie - co a - mor,
23
d'un cie - co a - mor, d'un cie - co a - mor.
26
Che gio - va il pian - ge - re? Non è ba -
29
- stan - te Un mar di la - gri - me A un tan - to ar - dor, a un tan - to ar - dor, Non è ba -
32
- stan - te Un mar di la - gri - me A un tan - to ar -
35
- dor, Non è ba - stan - te Un mar di la - gri - me A un tan - to ar -

(continued)

Da capo [from bar 6]

Statement	Bars	Section	Period	Keys
1	1–4	A	ritornello	c
2	5–8	A	*Devise* and ritornello	c
3	9–12	A	1st vocal period	c
4	13–16	A	1st vocal period (cont.)	g
5	17–18	A	2nd vocal period	f–E♭–c
6	19–23	A	2nd vocal period (cont.)	c
7	24–27	B	ritornello	E♭
8	28–31	B	3rd vocal period	E♭
9	32–24	B	3rd vocal period (cont.)	c–g
10	35–39	B	3rd vocal period (cont.)	g
11–	40–	A	*da capo* (from statement 2)	c

cadential implications of the bass. The Italian masters of the mid-Baroque—Cavalli, Cesti, and Stradella among them—seem to consider it a point of honour to make the vocal phrases frequently overlap those of the bass and, on occasion, to frustrate obvious cadences and introduce unexpected ones in their place.

This technique is still very much alive in Scarlatti's cantatas. In the late Baroque, however, more attention tends to be paid to the niceties of vocal ornamentation than to structural subtlety; as a result, the repetitions of a ground bass can become just a peg on which to hang a series of simple variations. Albinoni's cantatas (e.g. Op. 4, published in 1702) typify this new approach.

In this matter, Vinaccesi definitely inclines to the old school. Although there are many points in this movement where voice and bass phrase and cadence similarly, there is enough contrast to banish easy predictability. The counterpoint has an attractive grittiness that emphasizes the separateness of the two parts (consider, for instance, the last beat of bar 10 or the first half of bar 15).

Perhaps the most authentically Vinaccesian touch is the sudden flourish in demisemiquavers with which the unaccompanied voice, in bars 38–9, extends the final cadence of the 'B' section to take the music back to C minor for the *da capo*. Thrilling in its effect and totally unexpected, this melisma—one more demonstration of the composer's concern for musical continuity—has counterparts in several other movements (e.g. the opening recitative of the same cantata transcribed as Ex. 8) and may unquestionably be regarded as a stylistic fingerprint.

The performance of the bass part in these cantatas deserves comment. There is evidence that in the years around 1700 it was sometimes the practice to use for it only a melody instrument (cello or lute)—in which case interior harmonies had to be drastically reduced if not forgone altogether; alternatively, a keyboard instrument alone could suffice, this being the obvious solution for a self-accompanied performance. To use harpsichord and cello together strikes one, on empirical grounds, as having the best of both worlds, and so it certainly appeared to C. P. E. Bach in 1753. But there is rarely any overwhelming internal evidence in the bass part of a solo cantata that any particular instrument, or combination of instruments, should be employed.[34] It is true, in Vinaccesi's case, that the style of figuration and especially the exploitation of wide intervals, as in Ex. 11, tend to suggest 'the sound of horsehair on gut', but there are hardly any instances where a performance on harpsichord or spinet alone would be ineffective.

One cantata, however, contains an aria in which the bass divides, for certain passages, into a more active upper part, presumably intended for cello, and a less active lower part, presumably for the keyboard instrument. This is *Dal tuono il lampo aspetta* (*Amor pericoloso*). Ex. 14 illustrates one such passage (the main part of the second vocal period) from the aria in question, 'Di quel mal che ti sovrasta'. The richer texture and contrapuntal interest arising from this inner part make a good effect, and one wishes that Vinaccesi had used a divided bass part more often. This aria proves that in at least one instance he required both a keyboard and a stringed instrument, but one should of course remain wary of generalizing for the eight cantatas as a whole.

Vinaccesi's treatment of the bass voice in the two early cantatas tackles very successfully the particular difficulty—which is at the same time a stimulus to the composer's imagination—of writing for it. From the days of Renaissance polyphony up till the present century the morphology of bass parts, which receive the lion's share of the angular movement in fourths and fifths required at cadences, has always been distinctive. However, the advent of monodic writing at the beginning of the Baroque posed a serious dilemma. If the vocal bass was consistently to be kept above the instrumental bass, becoming in effect an alto part transposed down an octave, this traditional character would be lost, and problems of textural balance and variety could arise from the closeness of the two

---

[34] This question is discussed more fully in Talbot, *Tomaso Albinoni*, 123.

Ex. 14. *Dal tuono il lampo aspetta*, second aria

parts. On the other hand, merely to double the instrumental bass part would be dull and show a lack of enterprise. The preferred solution by baroque composers of bass cantatas was to alternate freely the two modalities of performance, adding to them a third, intermediate option: that of elaborating the instrumental bass in the manner already discussed in Chapter 6 in connection with the cello part in Vinaccesi's trio sonatas. Ex. 10 illustrates this flexible technique perfectly. In bars 1–2 the vocal part is fully independent, but from bar 3 onwards it shadows the instrumental bass. In the sequence employing semiquavers (bars 3–4) the voice becomes, as it were, two parts in one: the higher notes belong to a 'tenor', the lower to a 'bass'. This kind of feigned dialogue works for a bass as for no other type of voice, arising naturally from its dual persona.

The bass voice also possessed a distinctive ethos, sanctified and reinforced by baroque operatic practice, which liked to cast basses as comic servants, old men, or cruel tyrants. In keeping with these associations, an unmistakably jocular vein informs *Quanto mi vien da ridere*. This is already present in the lumbering imitations with which it opens but emerges most clearly in its final aria, 'Ite pur lungi da me', whose freely varied reprise of the 'A' section concludes with a kind of coda (bars 19–22), where striding octaves on one hand conform to the normal principles of word-paint-ing—the concept 'lungi' (far) openly invites the use of wide intervals—but on the other provide just a hint of the grotesquerie proper to a *basso buffo*. This subtle and original ending, which, with its *piano* repetition, leaves a slightly bitter-sweet taste after so much bluff humour, is shown in Ex. 15.

Ex. 15. *Quanto mi vien da ridere*, second aria

In the final analysis, it is in such details rather than in the broad con-ception that Vinaccesi's cantatas display their quality. As was explained earlier, there were clear limits to the amount of latitude enjoyed by an Italian composer working in this genre. It is no surprise that the com-posers who proved most inventive in the overall design of cantatas (one thinks above all of Benedetto Marcello) either wrote their own literary texts or, because of their high social standing, were able to deal with poets as equals. What can confidently be claimed, nevertheless, is that *Belve, se mai provaste* is a small masterpiece that one would unquestionably include in a latter-day equivalent of Riemann's anthology *Ausgewählte Kammer-Kantaten der Zeit um 1700*, while each of the seven others has sufficient merit to deserve an occasional performance. Because of its distinctly supe-rior poetic text, *Dal tuono il lampo aspetta* holds a special interest, while the scarcity value of the two cantatas for bass needs no emphasizing.

8

The Oratorios

DURING the 1690s Vinaccesi, with four oratorios of which we have record, was bidding to become an important contributor to the genre. This activity was apparently not sustained after his move to Venice, unless we count the one or possibly more Christmas pastorals he wrote for the Ospedaletto as the equivalent of oratorios. It is noteworthy that none of the extant four works was sponsored by an oratory or other religious institution: as we learned in Chapter 2, two (*Gioseffo che interpreta i sogni* and *Susanna*) were written for the Este court at Modena, one (*Il cuor nello scrigno*) for a Cremonese academy, and one (*Li diecimila martiri crocefissi*) for a Brescian nobleman. In Venice the tradition of performing oratorios at places other than the four *ospedali grandi* and the Philippine (Oratorian) church of Santa Maria della Consolazione (or 'della Fava') was not strong—only 56 of the 573 compositions listed in the Arnolds' survey of Venetian oratorios were presented independently of these five institutions—and we may therefore surmise that behind Vinaccesi's seeming loss of interest lay a simple lack of opportunity.[1]

The literary and musical sources of the four oratorios are listed below.

Gioseffo che interpreta i sogni (performed Modena, 1692)
> libretto (Soliani, Modena, 1692): Modena, Biblioteca Estense, LXX.I.18.
> music: lost.

Susanna (performed Modena, 1694)
> libretto (printer's Ms.): Modena, Archivio di Stato, Archivio per materie, Spettacoli pubblici, Busta 1.
> libretto (Soliani, Modena, 1694): Modena, Biblioteca Estense, LXX.I.23(3).
> music: Modena, Biblioteca Estense, Mus. F. 1230 (non-autograph score).

Il cuor nello scrigno (performed Cremona, 1696)
> libretto (Ghisolfi, Milan, 1696): Washington, Library of Congress, ML 48.M.2.G.
> music: lost.

---

[1] Statistics taken from the list of Venetian oratorios for the period 1662–1797 in Arnold and Arnold, *The Oratorio in Venice*, 77–103.

Li diecimila martiri crocefissi (performed Brescia, 1698)
libretto (Rizzardi, Brescia, 1698): Milan, Biblioteca Nazionale Braidense, Rac. dramm. 5477/7.
music: lost.

The fact that the published librettos survive, in each case, in only one known example shows how precarious the survival even of the mere knowledge of the existence of a work of this kind can be. It is more than likely that similar works have simply disappeared from the record without trace. The music has fared even worse, for, as the list shows, the only extant score is that of *Susanna*.

While a purely librettological discussion would treat all four works equally, this would be out of place in the present book, with its focus on the music. The rest of this chapter will therefore be given over to an examination of *Susanna*, though occasional points of comparison will be made with the other three works as revealed through their libretti. Fortunately, *Susanna* is a masterpiece deserving the closest attention. It is the one composition by Vinaccesi (discounting the motets) to have attracted critical attention in modern times. The Arnolds devote an approving paragraph to it (their scarcely exaggerated description of it as an 'opera in all but name' can certainly be taken, in the light of their general viewpoint, as a commendation!).[2] In his book on Modenese oratorio Victor Crowther chooses *Susanna* as the subject of the last of ten case-studies, comparing it closely with Stradella's somewhat earlier *La Susanna* (1681, revived 1692), the subject of another critical essay. Although Crowther awards the palm, in the final analysis, to Stradella, he appreciates the many virtues of Vinaccesi's oratorio, drawing particular attention to the virtuosity of its vocal writing and the demonstration of contrapuntal skill in its ensembles.[3]

Vinaccesi's *Susanna* is a perfect specimen of the kind of 'quasi-operatic' oratorio that came into vogue all over Italy in the closing years of the seventeenth century. While preserving certain independent features (some of which are, however, shared by the contemporary serenata genre), this type of oratorio aims to reproduce operatic style and conventions as far as these are consistent with its ostensibly didactic purpose and the decorum

---

[2] Ibid. 18.

[3] Victor Crowther, *The Oratorio in Modena* (Oxford, 1992). I am grateful to Dr Crowther for allowing me to consult portions of his book in typescript prior to its publication. As the present book was going to press, I was made aware, through the kindness of Olga Termini, of an even more recent study of Vinaccesi's *Susanna*. This is Angela Romagnoli, 'La componente strumentale ne "La Susanna" di Benedetto Vinaccesi', in Rosa Cafiero and Maria Teresa Rosa Barezzani (eds.), *Liuteria e musica strumentale a Brescia tra Cinque e Seicento* (Brescia, 1992), 333–53. Much of this article is concerned—understandably enough, in view of his obscurity—with generalities about Vinaccesi, but the part devoted specifically to *Susanna* in fact says disappointingly little beyond the obvious about his use and treatment of instruments, though one is grateful for the well-chosen and copious music examples.

appropriate to a sacred subject. An important advocate of this new
approach was Cardinal Ottoboni's *maestro di casa*, Archangelo Spagna,
who in 1706 published, in two volumes, his collected oratorio texts.[4]
Spagna introduces the first volume with a *Discorso intorno a gl'oratorii*,
which is a combination of preface and treatise. The *Discorso* reveals him to
have been, over the previous half-century, a prime mover in the change
from the original type of oratorio, represented in the vernacular tradition
(*oratorio volgare*) by such composers as Luigi Rossi and Alessandro
Stradella and in the Latin tradition (*oratorio latino*) by Giacomo Carissimi,
to that adopted by Vinaccesi's librettist in *Susanna* (but not, however, in
the other three oratorios).[5]

The innovations centre around the elimination from the *dramatis personae* of a narrator (most often called *testo* in vernacular oratorios) and the
reduction or suppression of the role of the chorus. In the early days of
mature oratorio the recounting of the biblical or other story by a singer
(usually a tenor) external to both the direct speech of the other characters
and the moralistic commentary of the chorus preserved a direct link back
to the sacred sources even when, as normally occurred, the story was
paraphrased and embellished. Spagna admits that for some librettists the
presence of a narrator represented more than a technical device: it came to
symbolize the very distinction between the secular (opera) and the sacred
(oratorio). (He observes, however, that the defenders of the *testo* had an
ulterior motive—to retain the validity and currency of their previously
written libretti in the face of the growing popularity of the new-style
texts.) As inherent drawbacks to the use of a separate narrator Spagna
mentions the excessive preponderance of recitative over aria ('pochissime
arie e molti recitativi') and the likely overshadowing of all the other roles
(to illustrate this point, he introduces the punning metaphor of 'una gran
testa in picciol corpo' in reference to the *testo*). For him, therefore, the
narrator represents both an untidy anomaly and a distraction from the
drama proper.

Spagna claims the credit for having written the libretto for the first
testo-less oratorio (*Debora*) in 1656. That he was moved still to plead the
case in 1706 shows how tenacious the practice of having a narrator was. In
fact, in his enthusiasm for what he calls a 'perfetto melodramma spiri-

[4] *Oratorii overo melodrammi sacri* (2 vols., Rome, 1706). The *Discorso* is reprinted, with minor cuts,
in Domenico Alaleona, *Studi su la storia dell'oratorio musicale in Italia* (Turin, 1908), 382–91.
[5] Because of the difficulty of finding satisfactory criteria for distinguishing the oratorio from similar
older genres, in particular the *dialogo sacro*, it is impossible to find a universally agreed 'starting-point'
for it. What is certain, however, is that by the 1640s several composers were writing works known by
title or from contemporary reference as 'oratorio', and that the general characteristics of the genre had
by then become established. The best detailed introduction to 17th-cent. oratorio remains Howard E.
Smither, *A History of the Oratorio, i. The Oratorio in the Baroque Era: Italy, Vienna, Paris* (Chapel
Hill, NC, 1977).

tuale' Spagna disregards the frequent usefulness of the narrator as a device for preserving decorum and bridging temporal or spatial hiatuses in the story. As it happens, the *Susanna* of Bottalino and Vinaccesi is a drama enacted entirely among humans and, moreover, in a single place (Joakim's house in Babylon) within the space of one solar day (from one noon to the next). No problems of propriety, continuity, or dramatic unity therefore arise if the *testo* is dispensed with. But in a story featuring divine intervention or unfolding, like that of Joseph, over a long period in several places, the value of a narrator is obvious. Apostolo Zeno refers with evident feeling to the main point of contention in the preface to the collected edition of his *Poesie sacre drammatiche* (Venice, 1735), where he wonders how earlier oratorio librettists could have sunk so low as to place in the mouths of divine persons 'certain profane expressions, certain low comparisons, and even musical arias'.[6]

Spagna's views on the chorus (*coro*) are less partisan. To appreciate them one must be aware that few choruses in seventeenth-century Italian oratorio include singers additional to the principals (in this respect, the Latin oratorios of Carissimi are rather exceptional): the *coro* is merely the ensemble, complete or partial, of the singers taking individual parts. Such an ensemble may represent either the community of the faithful to whom the oratorio is addressed (this applies, for instance, to the traditional finale, or so-called *madrigale*, that sums up the moral lesson) or a homogeneous group participating in the story itself. In both cases, the singer is allowed to step outside his or her normal dramatic role and momentarily become an anonymous voice among other voices. Spagna gives two revealing reasons why concluding *cori* are (in 1706) falling into disuse. The first is that members of the audience have a habit of leaving prematurely, deeming that the 'action' has already finished, and the noise that this causes ruins the musical effect. The second is that not all composers possess the skill in counterpoint needed for writing such ensembles, which tempts many to leave them out and finish the work with 'a lively air that sends everyone away feeling satisfied'. He adds an interesting observation concerning the effect of this omission on the choice of voices for the individual roles. When a *madrigale* is included, composers naturally want to have it sung by a balanced group of singers. This means that in an oratorio for four voices the distribution is likely to be: soprano, alto, tenor, bass. Spagna hints that he finds this requirement unfortunate because it gives low voices parity with the high voices preferred by audiences (he

[6] Quoted in Guido Pasquetti, *L'oratorio musicale in Italia* (Florence, [2]/1914), 409–10. Together with his fellow reformers, Zeno strove to 'purify' oratorio in a similar manner to opera, observing the Aristotelian unities more strictly and paying greater attention to decorum. His ideal was a sacred drama that—in the imagination, if not in reality—was capable of being staged.

states that without sopranos 'any cantata remains insipid'). Omitting *cori* thus gives the composer a greater measure of flexibility in casting.

In Spagna's terms Vinaccesi's *Susanna* is a little conservative. It retains the traditional nucleus of four voice-types (though this was rather inevitable, seeing that the two Elders could hardly be sung by high voices!), while nodding in the direction of Spagna's recommendation by making the additional, fifth voice a second soprano. Bottalino limits the appearance of the *coro* to a final *madrigale* of six lines.[7] However, Vinaccesi somewhat subverts the thinking behind this parsimony by drawing out the *madrigale* to the greatest length it will bear and treating the audience (whether about to depart or not!) to a feast of imitative counterpoint and rich sonorities. Still, his work presents a clear contrast to Stradella's *La Susanna*, which not only ends each separate part with a *madrigale* but also inserts choruses at various points to amplify the message of the *testo*.

In most other respects *Susanna* conforms in its general outline to Spagna's prescriptions. The length of its text, 451 lines, approximates to the 500 lines stated by him to be the norm (contemporary practice suggests that 500 lines should be regarded more as a maximum than an average length). It is cast in the usual two parts. The reason for this division, apart from the obvious one of giving the audience some relief after up to an hour of continuous music, was to allow a sermon to be preached, if the oratorio was being given under religious auspices, or for refreshments to be served, if the locale was secular. Bottalino provides, in addition, a short *introduzione* that describes the subject of the oratorio and sets the scene. For convenience, this is placed in the mouth of the character Daniel (Daniele), who as a prophet and as the hero of the story has, so to speak, the authority to act as a substitute *testo*. Spagna would have been disappointed, however, by one feature of the libretto: its recitatives are written, absolutely conventionally, in unrhymed *versi sciolti*—whereas he himself was a strong champion of rhyme in all circumstances.

Since he is principally concerned with the literary history of the genre and some of its technical aspects, Spagna has little to say about its socioreligious purpose and dramaturgy. Yet these are ingredients vital to our understanding of its distinctive nature. In an Italian baroque oratorio the functions of education, edification, and entertainment are reconciled and, where possible, blended. On the first two functions Lorenzo Bianconi has written very aptly: 'The oratorio . . . acted as both vehicle and filter for the controlled divulgation and popularization of the Scriptures in a way

---

[7] Rather unusually, the score of *Susanna* includes in its *madrigale* not only the final chorus but also the setting of the five lines of recitative for Daniel that precede it. As used here, the term *madrigale* must refer not to a specific type of musical setting but to the special function of the text at this point, which is to deliver a final moral after the 'drama' proper has concluded.

that was undoubtedly more attractive—and innocuous—than anything offered by direct reading of the original sacred texts (whose perusal was not to be abandoned to the initiative of private individuals).'[8] While the Counter-Reformation had given the Catholic Church greater zeal to promote religious knowledge among the laity, it had also confirmed the Church's view of itself as the sole authoritative interpreter of sacred writings. For this reason, the fidelity with which a particular biblical story or life of a saint was recounted was regarded as less important than the correctness of the moral lesson drawn from it: a paraphrase or gloss was actually more suitable for the purpose than a straightforward retelling. Hence the great tolerance shown towards fictional embellishments. This degree of licence enabled librettists to make their creations more original, even in the case of a well-worn subject such as the Nativity (Spagna justifies digressions from the source by remarking that without them an oratorio remains a mere history, not a poetic drama).

The same freedom served equally the cause of entertainment. Modern commentators have perhaps tended to draw over-neat conclusions from the fact that during Lent, when theatres were closed, oratorios filled the void—since to act as a substitute for opera does not of itself mean becoming exactly the same thing. But there is no doubt that a drift towards operatic style and practice occurred at many levels. The love of vocal display for its own sake informs oratorio hardly less than opera—perhaps unsurprisingly, when the singers were the same persons. All the favourite dramatic situations found in opera (heroines languishing in prison, heroes invoking divine aid, villains threatening diabolical tortures) occur also in oratorio and prompt the composer to give musical expression to the very same *affetti*. Even amorous passion has a legitimate place in the sacred genre, provided that the original story offers the slightest pretext for introducing it. Oratorios on the subject of Susanna naturally give the librettist a heaven-sent opportunity to write what musicologists have termed an *oratorio erotico*.[9] It is true that the lust of the two Elders has consequences very different from, say, Nero's passion for Poppea (in Monteverdi's opera), but the extreme disparity of reward has no effect on the full-bloodedness of the subject's treatment on the part of either poet or musician. Indeed, the fact that Susanna's nakedness and the Elders' lust are recorded in Holy Scripture gives the librettist licence to be voyeuristic (Victor Crowther's term) to an unusual degree.

The assimilation between oratorio and opera should not be regarded as an entirely one-way process. There is a sense in which the reform of

---

[8] *Music in the Seventeenth Century* (Cambridge, 1987), 126.

[9] Smither, *Oratorio in the Baroque Era*, i. 302–3. It must be emphasized that the *oratorio erotico* was not a subgenre recognized in the 17th cent.; it is merely a convenient category invented in modern times.

late-baroque opera culminating after 1720 in the dramas of Metastasio includes an attempt to reclaim an ethical purpose that is the exact counterpart, expressed in secular terms, of that of oratorio. But this is looking some way into the future and has little relevance for the period of *Susanna*.

One particular feature of the texts of Italian baroque oratorios may surprise and disconcert the modern reader. This is the heavy infusion of pastoral imagery coupled with references to classical history and mythology. In a way, these elements are not unexpected, for the cumulative effect of the Renaissance, the growth of Humanism, and the vogue for pastoralism that reached its acme in the Arcadian Academy had made references to 'bei lumi', the 'fonte d'Elicone', or the 'Cieco Nume' (Cupid) central to the poetic language. Rather than oppose the pagan Ancient World, the Church incorporated it. Just as the Old Testament prefigured the New Testament, the gods and heroes of classical Greece and Rome could be viewed as analogues of Christian angels (or devils) and martyrs. In doctrinal terms, both classical and Jewish traditions were naturally subservient to the Christian one and had no independent value, but in poetic terms the relationship was non-hierarchical. In this spirit of tolerant eclecticism the pagan classical tradition was allowed to infiltrate not merely the sacred (oratorio) but even the paraliturgical (motet). If the poet's mind belonged to the Bible and to the canon of patristic writings, his imagination remained with Homer, Virgil, and Ovid. Naturally, librettists sought out and exploited the many points of convergence between the three traditions, which, after all, shared a Mediterranean locale. The vineyards of En Gedi are not unlike those of Sicily, and the shepherds who pursued nymphs in Arcadia are cousins to those who adored the Christ-Child.[10]

This is the background against which to judge such lines in *Susanna* as the Second Elder's description of the approach of Daniel:

Ma quale a noi s'avanza	But look how,
furioso e baccante	furious and like a Bacchante,
Daniele il Profeta;	Daniel the Prophet rushes towards us;

In strict logic, neither the inventor of the biblical story nor the Elder himself could have been familiar with the frenzied devotees of Dionysus, and Bottalino could hardly have been unaware of this fact. The point is that, for him, as for most of his contemporaries, the historical incongruity of such a simile was completely outweighed by its poetic felicity. The figure of the Bacchante is simply an evocative image to be extracted as needed from the melting-pot of images, not an argument to be dissected.

[10] Not by coincidence did the Roman Arcadia choose as its *nume tutelare* the infant Jesus and as its motto a set of pan-pipes, for the image of the simple but virtuous shepherd that links them is—albeit fortuitously—one of the most potent common elements in the Classical and Christian traditions.

The mind that could introduce Scythian arrows, ancient Satyrs, and palms of victory into a celebration of an Old Testament heroine (as Bottalino does in the introductory section of his oratorio) was the same mind that tolerated the appearance, on the operatic stage, of Roman generals wearing elegant gloves.

The biblical story of Susanna is a gift to the oratorio genre: simple, cogent, and full of human interest and dramatic incident. Within the Christian canon it exists as an apocryphal addition to the book of Daniel. In its original Hebrew version, which has not survived, its function seems to have been to serve as a parable showing the need to cross-examine witnesses carefully before accepting their testimony, but in the popular imagination this 'lesson' has always taken second place to a celebration of Susanna's innocence and fidelity to her husband. The association of the story with the prophet Daniel is problematic, not being found in the earliest versions. It achieved something close to its present form in the Septuagint, the pre-Christian translation into Greek of the Old Testament. The version found in the Vulgate and later Bibles is based, however, on an elaboration of the story by Theodotion, a second-century editor of the Septuagint. There is some variation among Bibles in the positioning of the story within the book of Daniel, but the Vulgate version, with sixty-five verses, presents it as chapter 13.[11]

The story of Susanna has always been excluded from the Jewish canon, perhaps because of the discreditable light in which it places the two Elders (or Judges), but, partly for that very reason, proved attractive to Christian theologians, who liked to interpret the figure of Susanna as a symbol of the Church, her husband Joakim as a prefiguration of Christ (to whom the Church is, of course, metaphorically wedded), and the Elders as symbols of the Jewish and pagan traditions respectively. The malicious calumnies of the Elders could therefore be equated with slanders against Christianity by her enemies. In the ritual of the Catholic Church the chapter is the Old Testament reading for Mass on the Vigil of the fourth Sunday in Lent, and it is highly likely that Vinaccesi's oratorio was performed in 1694 on, or close to, that day (27 March).

As recounted in the Old Testament, the story is set in Babylon during the period of exile. Susanna is the wife of Joakim, a wealthy man whose home serves as a courthouse for the Jewish community and whose walled garden is, during the morning, a favourite place of resort for his co-religionists. Susanna, famed for her beauty and piety, likes to appear in the garden at noon, when visitors customarily leave. Two elderly judges, corrupted by Babylonian ways, independently conceive a passion for her. For

[11] For my account of the biblical source and its significance I am indebted chiefly to Robert Henry Charles, *The Apocrypha and Pseudepigrapha of the Old Testament in English with Introductions and Critical and Explanatory Notes to the Several Books* (Oxford, 1913), 638–51.

a while they suppress their secret desires, but eventually each discovers the other's intentions, and the two old men join forces in a conspiracy against Susanna's virtue. They hide in the garden when other visitors depart, lying in wait for her. She arrives and, having instructed her servants to close the gates into the garden from the outside, takes a bath. The Elders then reveal themselves, to their victim's horror, and make their indecent proposal. To render Susanna more compliant, they threaten to denounce her as an adulteress (with a man unknown, who escaped before being apprehended) if she does not submit. In a famous pair of verses (vv. 22–3), often treated, in paraphrase, as a 'punch-line', the heroine confronts her dilemma: if she consents, she commits a mortal sin; if she refuses, she incurs the death penalty. She opts for virtue and cries out to her servants. The Elders also call them (in order to suggest that the initiative is theirs, not hers) and carry out their threat.

The next morning, Joakim's house is the scene of his wife's trial. The two Elders, acting by turns as accusers, witnesses, and judges, convince the people that they caught Susanna in the act of adultery. The accused, who has been made to appear before the multitude in an unclothed state in order to make the charge seem more plausible, is unable to defend herself except by affirming her innocence before God. The mandatory sentence of death by stoning is pronounced.[12] God then prompts the young Daniel, whose reputation as a prophet already commands respect among the people, to protest against the irregularity of the trial.[13] He is given leave to cross-examine the Elders separately. Each is asked under which tree the adultery took place. One identifies the mastick, the other the holm. This inconsistency exposes the falsity of their accusation, and it is the turn of the Judges to receive the death penalty. Susanna is reunited with her joyful family.

The general shape of Bottalino's libretto is determined by two important choices. The first is the absence of a *testo*. This means that the characters take turns in describing, in the course of dialogue or through a soliloquy, the successive scenes and events of the story. The second is to allot a major role to Susanna's husband Joakim (Gioacchino). Joakim plays no active part in the biblical account and hence has no guaranteed place in an oratorio libretto—Giovanni Battista Giardini's text for Stradella's *La Susanna*, which includes a *testo*, dispenses with him altogether. Bottalino skilfully contrives to make Gioacchino an important participant in, and commentator on, the story, so that his role grows into that of the *primo*

---

[12] The particular significance of the penalty of death by stoning was that since it was impossible to establish which single stone struck the fatal blow, none of the participating individuals would have to take the moral responsibility for throwing it.

[13] Jewish law, as later codified in the Mishnah, laid down that between the passing and the carrying out of a death sentence the court should appeal for new evidence that would show the defendant's innocence.

uomo, the 'opposite lead' to Susanna. Moreover, Gioacchino expresses a wider range of emotions than any other character, not excluding the heroine herself. When he greets her in the garden, prior to hearing the allegations of the Elders, he is the concerned spouse; after swallowing their tale, he becomes a wronged and vengeful husband; during the trial he experiences involuntary feelings of pity; these turn into stirrings of hope as Daniel questions the evidence; finally, when the perjury is proved, he becomes suitably contrite and soon returns to his former conjugal bliss. The contrasted emotions expressed in Gioacchino's five aria texts constitute, for the composer, an irresistible invitation to explore a wide range of *affetti* within the framework of a single character (and thus singer).

The obvious place to make the break between the two parts of the oratorio is at the close of the first day, after the Elders' denunciation of Susanna to her servants but before the trial proper. However, both Giardini and Bottalino modify the biblical account in such a way as to include elements of the trial at the end of the first part. In a way, this is a pity, for there would have been distinct dramatic potential in leaving the heroine in uncertainty of her fate (and the wisdom of her decision) until the formal hearing. The two librettists were perhaps motivated by a concern not to make the trial sequence (i.e. the initial hearing and condemnation followed by Daniel's retrial) overlong. Giardini's restructuring is the more cautious: the Judges conduct a preliminary hearing and on the strength of it have Susanna thrown into prison, where she spends the night (this gives him the opportunity to open the second part with a lament by the incarcerated heroine, a topos of the opera of that time). The trial does indeed occur on the following day but is very condensed. More boldly, Bottalino closes the first part with a full-scale trial on the spot before Joakim, requiring nothing more than a simple public endorsement of the sentence in the second part.

After the *introduzione*, which ends with a witty remark about how the two Elders feel a 'double' heat—that of summer and that of love ('E sentian doppio ardore, | Quel di fervida estate e quel d'amore')—Bottalino moves straight to a dialogue between them as they lie in wait. He thus decides, unlike Giardini, to make no reference to the psychologically very convincing biblical description of how the Elders conduct an inner struggle against their lust until, by chance, they discover each other's feelings and allow the common purpose to override their inhibitions. Their description of Susanna's disrobing prior to stepping into the bath is marked by a lubricity in which librettist and audience are willy-nilly complicit ('Già si spoglia la gonna: | O vaghe, o care membra, in cui discerno | Le bellezze dell'Alba'). When Susanna first speaks (to herself, naturally), she praises water for its purity, emblematic of her fidelity. Here Bottalino introduces the popular device of an echo. As no separate singer is

available for the echoed words, which perforce have to issue from the
mouth of Susanna herself, the Second Elder (Secondo Vecchio) has, in
defiance of dramatic plausibility, to take the step of forewarning the audi-
ence of the echo before it first appears ('e par che seco | Vaga del suo
cantar ragioni un eco')!

Many echoes in seventeenth-century music merely have the force of
piano repeats and may not even be 'scripted' by the author of the text.
Such are the well-known examples, sung by two voices, of the Daughter's
words 'ululate', 'lachrimate', and 'resonate' in Giacomo Carissimi's *Jephte*.
However, there also existed, as an inheritance from the Renaissance, a tradition of 'significant' echoes. This significance can be of two kinds. First,
by echoing not the complete word but only its latter portion, the poet can
create a new word that acts as a commentary on, or revelation of the hidden sense of, the original one. Second, by forming a sequence out of the
echoed words in the manner of an acrostic, the poet can form an entire
subtext. One of the best-known examples of these devices used in combination occurs in Scene 5 of Emilio de' Cavalieri's *Rappresentatione di
anima e di corpo*, where Anima has the following lines:

Ama il mondan piacer l'uomo saggio o fugge?	*Fugge.*
Che cosa è l'uom che 'l cerca e cerca in vano?	*vano.*
Chi dà la morte al cor con dispiacere?	*piacere.*
Come la vita ottien chi vita brama?	*ama.*
Ama del mondo le bellezze o Dio?	*Dio.*
Dunque morrà ch'il piacer brama: è vero?	*vero.*

Here the echoes supply the Divine answer to the soul-searching: 'fugge
vano piacere: ama Dio vero' (Shun vain pleasure: love [the] true God).[14]

In similar fashion Bottalino forms the sequence 'Angue coperto insidia
l'onore' ([a] hidden snake lies in ambush for [my] honour) from the scattered words 'sangue/langue', 'coperto', 'insidia', and 'l'onore'. As Susanna
hears each echoed word she puzzles over its meaning, and Bottalino spins
out with great dramatic irony her naïve and unsuccessful attempts to deci-
pher the message as it unfolds. She realizes, at least, that the threatened
honour is her own and in the true style of an operatic heroine proclaims
her constancy just before the Elders emerge.

The ensuing dialogue is nothing if not operatic. It is full of cut and
thrust, of one proposition 'capping' another. When Susanna asserts that
honour is the highest form of beauty ('È bellezza l'onore'), she receives
the rhyming riposte from the Second Elder that physical love is sanc-
tioned by custom ('È costume l'amore'). There is a frankly playful dimen-

---

[14] An even more striking exploitation of the echo motif occurs in the anonymous text of Carlo
Grossi's Christmas motet *Currite, pastores*, published in his Op. 8 (1676). Here each echo gives birth
to a new keyword that is included in the next line.

sion to the discourse; the words of the duet sung by the Elders could be those of comic servants in an opera.

VECCHIO 1	Se fredda polvere	If you have no desire
	non brami d'essere,	to become cold ashes,
	t'hai da risolvere	you must resolve
	a dir di sì.	to say yes.
VECCHIO 2	O ch'hai da frangere	How you must soften
	quel cor durissimo,	your hard heart,
	o ch'hai da piangere	How you must weep
	in questo dì.	on this day.

Bottalino chooses to allow Susanna to express her famous dilemma in the form of an aria. Here the beautiful antithesis of the biblical words ('si enim hoc egero, mors mihi est; si autem non egero, non effugiam manus vestras') is neatly paraphrased in the two semistrophes of a *da capo* structure.

S'io resisto, eterno scorno	If I resist, a harsh fate
mi minaccia iniqua sorte:	promises me eternal shame:
S'io consento, in questo giorno	If I consent, on this day
compro all'alma eterna morte.	my soul will earn eternal death.

After the servants have been summoned, it is in fact Gioacchino who arrives on the scene. His opening words, sung as an aria, invite Susanna to explain her distress. The dramatic irony of this unanticipated oasis of calm is a happy stroke. However, the Elders' account rapidly convinces Susanna's husband, whose next aria is one of rage that invokes the Furies of classical mythology. He himself is the first to pronounce the death sentence on her. The first part closes with a protestation of innocence and a renewed pledge of fidelity by Susanna. There is more than a whiff of that masochism on the part of a wrongfully accused wife which would soon reach its apogee in Zeno's *Griselda*.

The second part opens with the Elders, supported by the people, clamouring for Susanna's death. Susanna remains courageously defiant in the certainty of her innocence. Bottalino has to be careful how he phrases her view of her own fate. Since the Jews of the Old Testament had—or were held by Christian doctrine to have—no belief in an afterlife for ordinary humans, Susanna cannot look forward to a glorious future in Heaven and, perhaps more movingly as a result, accepts death at face value. Gioacchino's involuntary admiration of his wife's fortitude causes him to look back at their married life in painful remembrance. This is another well-conceived invention that adds a fresh colour to the palette of emotions. Daniel's stormy entry, his vituperation of the Judges, and his cross-examination of them largely do justice to the biblical original. Bottalino exercises his poetic licence by turning the two trees into an oak and a pine

(Giardini, incidentally, made them a myrtle and a cedar). Several interesting extra details are added. Daniel mentions the impropriety of performing more than one role in the judicial process (which the Elders excuse by saying that it is permitted under Babylonian law). Bottalino also makes Daniel order the court to cover Susanna's nudity, a good deed not found in the biblical account but very evocative in dramatic and symbolic terms.

One addition, however, is an unfortunate indiscretion. The Vulgate has Susanna instructing her maids to close the garden gates (her words are: 'ostia pomarii claudite'). In classical Latin 'claudere' has the sense not of locking—an anachronism, in fact—but merely of shutting. In Italian, however, the cognate verb carries the added implication of locking, which is how Bottalino interprets it. Hence Daniel is able to ask the First Elder, before proceeding to the question about the tree, how Susanna's alleged partner was able to escape from the garden from the inside (to which no satisfactory answer is made). This extra question is a miscalculation not only because it destroys the symmetry of the two interrogations but also because the practical impossibility of the man's escape is an even stronger argument against his existence than the misnaming of the tree, and so ought to render further questioning superfluous.

As the cross-examination proceeds, Joakim and Susanna raise their spirits. His exercise completed, Daniel condemns the Elders to death. Their appeal for clemency is rejected, since they deserve to be paid back in the same coin. It remains for Gioacchino and Susanna to restore their former relationship—Bottalino gives the reunited couple an idyllic duet of reconciliation—and for Gioacchino, Daniele, and the full ensemble to spell out the moral.

We may legitimately argue about the poetic, dramatic, and, indeed, theological merits of Bottalino's libretto. Much depends on how willing we are to set aside ingrained notions of 'timeless' values and step inside the very circumscribed but nevertheless impressively cogent intellectual and aesthetic world of his period. It cannot be denied, however, that it provides a highly efficient vehicle for a composer to display his gifts within a context that mirrors the contemporary opera remarkably closely. At the very least, we have to admire the sheer variety of incident and expression found in it.

Although the twenty-one closed numbers (arias and ensembles) of Bottalino's libretto make virtually no autonomous contribution to the dramatic development, being conceived as lyrical expansions of thoughts already uttered in the preceding recitative, their siting and density obviously influence the structure and pacing of the drama. A simple chart of these numbers will convey some interesting information.

From the numbers of arias allotted to each role one obtains an accurate picture of the hierarchy of the singers (which then becomes the hierarchy

Character	Introduction	Part I			Part II					Madrigale
Susanna		4, 5	7	10	12		16	18	20⎫	21 ⎫
Gioacchino			8, 9			13	15	17	20⎭	21 ⎪
Daniele	1, 2					14			19	21 ⎬
Vecchi I e II		3	6		11					21 ⎭

of the dramatis personae in fact if not in theory). With seven and five arias respectively, plus a duet for both, Susanna and Gioacchino are indisputably the *prima donna* and *primo uomo*. The complementary lower tier is occupied by Daniele, with four arias (two in the *introduzione*), and the two Elders, with three. In the opera of the time it is normal also to have a bottom tier for 'bit parts', whose singers have few or no arias, but the more economical casting of *Susanna*—in this respect, typical of oratorio—rules that out.[15] All three numbers for the Elders are conceived by the librettist as duets or double arias; that is, the singers have metrically identical texts and express similar sentiments. Clearly, Bottalino has no interest (any more than the Bible has) in differentiating the character or temperament of his villains, who are in every way equivalent. He nevertheless offers the composer an interesting choice: the numbers can be set either as contrapuntal duets in which the two texts are presented simultaneously or as *arie a due* in which they are heard successively.

Whereas the general organizing principle is that of the systematic rotation of closed numbers between the characters, Bottalino is not averse on occasion to giving a singer two arias in succession. This is entirely typical of librettos written immediately prior to the reforms of Zeno and his colleagues, which were eventually to lead, in the hands of Metastasio, to a type of drama in which the principle of constant rotation was a significant element of structural planning.[16] It is noticeable, however, that the two consecutive arias for Daniele, Susanna, and Gioacchino are all well contrasted in poetic terms, inviting the composer to reinforce the differentiation by musical means.

Rather unusually for the time, there are no differences, except for minor variations of orthography, between the underlaid text in Vinaccesi's score and either the manuscript or the published version of the libretto. The probable explanation for this perfect agreement is that the manuscript libretto, which was intended to serve as the printer's copy, was

[15] The fact that Bottalino did not envisage, and Vinaccesi does not provide, a separate singer for the echoes in Susanna's first aria is an illustration of this economy. *Gioseffo che interpreta i sogni* and *Li diecimila martiri crocefissi* likewise place their singers in two tiers rather than three.

[16] Consecutive arias for a single character are equally numerous in Antonio Marchi's opera libretto *Zenobia, regina de' Palmireni* whose setting by Albinoni was performed in Venice earlier in the same year, 1694. It would be interesting to know whether they were regarded by contemporaries as a device with a purpose or simply as a consequence of tolerance.

derived directly from the underlaid text. This is consistent with the hypothesis, put forward in Chapter 2, that it was Vinaccesi, not Bottalino, who approached the Modenese court. The tell-tale sign that the manuscript libretto was not copied from a purely literary source is that in a great number of instances eleven-syllable lines consisting of a 'major' hemistich of seven syllables followed by a 'minor' hemistich of four (or five with opening synaloepha) were initially mistaken for *settenari*. Such mistakes would be impossible if the manuscript was copied from a pre-existing libretto and highly improbable if it was an original draft of the poet. As every modern editor of cantatas knows, however, this is precisely the kind of slip that is liable to be made when one transcribes from an underlaid text that does not show line-divisions. In a few cases one notices that words originally transcribed literally from the score have been subsequently amended editorially by the writer of the manuscript libretto. For instance, the word 'umanità' on fo. 47^v of the score has been given a more elegant, Latinate form by the late addition of an initial H. That the manuscript libretto in question was used as printer's copy is shown by its indications for division into pages, which correspond exactly to those of the printed text, and by the censors' marks of approval at the end.

We do not know whether, at the time of writing the oratorio, Vinaccesi was in a position to anticipate the choice of particular singers. It may well be that by opting for the common formation SSATB he simply trusted to the ability and willingness of the court to find the required voices. The assigning of the alto part to Susanna was an inspired decision, for this is a character whose persona, as defined both by her conduct in the story and by the *affetti* of her arias, is simple and modest: more passive victim than dynamic protagonist. The mellow tone and relative 'unshowiness' traditionally associated with the alto register, whether sung by a male or female voice, suit this role to perfection. The imperious Daniele and the volatile Gioacchino, on the other hand, are both natural candidates for the soprano voice. As for the Elders, it was a foregone conclusion that they should be the lowest two voices. There are no great differences in the level of ability required for the successful performance of the five voices. All have testing melismas to sing at various points, although the lion's share of the coloratura writing falls, fairly predictably, to the two sopranos.

The accompaniment to the oratorio is orchestral. In late-seventeenth-century terms this means, first, that one or more inner parts for viola are present, and, second, that certainly the outer parts and ideally all the parts should be doubled. Orchestras formed on these principles seem to have taken root in Rome during the 1660s or 1670s and gradually spread throughout the peninsula, replacing the older standard accompaniment of two violins and continuo (which is still used, incidentally, in Stradella's

La Susanna). Roman orchestras with two violin parts (often increased to four through the division into *concertino* and *concerto grosso* sections) tended to have one rather than two viola parts, as can be observed in the concertos of Corelli. Until the second decade of the next century, however, the rest of Italy generally preferred to have two viola parts, carrying on the tradition of five-part texture inherited from Renaissance polyphony and transmitted by the sonatas and dance-music of the seventeenth century.

Vinaccesi chooses to have two viola parts, both notated in the alto clef (other composers often used the tenor clef for the lower instrument). As one would expect from an Italian composer at this time, these are primarily 'filler' parts that have brief moments of glory where the writing is imitative but in most places serve merely to fill out the texture and reinforce the rhythm.

The Sinfonia in E minor standing at the head of the introduction to the oratorio is the most extended and by far the most impressive piece of purely instrumental writing by Vinaccesi to have survived. It comprises five connected sections, well contrasted in tempo and texture. Its continuity is aided by the fact that all the sections except the last end with a half-close in the home key that 'launches' the one that follows. The first section ('Allegro', 4/4, six repeated bars) is stormy, employing repeated notes (*note raddoppiate*) simultaneously in all parts after completing a set of canonic entries. The second section ('Grave ma spiccato', 4/4, eleven bars) opens with a series of detached crotchet chords whose strange chromatic alterations create an air of nervous expectancy (see Ex. 16); halfway through, the first violin interposes three descending scales in hemidemisemiquavers between pairs of chords. The oddity of this occurrence already hints at some special significance. The 'Grave' gives way to a 'Presto', a *moto perpetuo* in semiquavers for the first violin with an accompaniment of crotchet chords interspersed with crotchet rests. This section is extraordinarily reminiscent of the 'Presto' episodes that some early composers of concertos, including Torelli and Albinoni, liked to insert into central slow movements. But whereas the semiquaver figurations favoured by those composers tend to be based on chordal shapes, Vinaccesi's motion is here predominantly linear, featuring rushing scales similar to those heard in the previous section. After 15 bars the 'Presto' continues as a 'stretto' fugue (i.e. a fugue in which the subject and answer are already in close imitation on their initial appearance) on a subject of a somewhat learned cast.

Sixteen bars later the fugue debouches into a gentle concluding section ('Largo', 3/4, nine bars), which doubles as the ritornello to Daniele's aria 'Frange l'onde al mar turbato'. The neat linkage between the Sinfonia and the first aria is noteworthy enough; even more remarkable is the calculated

way in which the Sinfonia anticipates, through the prominence it accords
to rapid figures based on the scale, the melisma with which Daniele will
later highlight the word 'frange'. The metaphor is that of the rock-like
constancy of Susanna's innocence 'breaking' and thereby dissipating the
waves of a raging sea. It is emblematic of what one could call the
unofficial, dramatic moral of the oratorio (the official, biblical one being
the dire consequences of bearing false witness). By prefiguring the shatter-
ing of the waves—arguably, the opening section represents the turbulence

Ex. 16. *Susanna*, Sinfonia, extract

of the sea itself, a conventional metaphor for the vicissitudes of existence—Vinaccesi has linked the Sinfonia not only to Daniele's aria but
also, by extension, to the oratorio as a whole.

Ex. 17. *Susanna*, end of Sinfonia and start of 'Frange l'onde al mar turbato'

This high degree of 'thematic' integration (in both senses of the term!)
is very unusual for a pre-1700 sinfonia. In opera and oratorio alike, sinfonias around 1700 were usually utilitarian pieces that were sometimes borrowed from the sonata literature and were often recycled from work to
work. Not until Mattheson in 1739, followed by Quantz in 1752 and
Algarotti in 1755, proposed that the overture should attempt to sum up
the plot or the emotional climate of a drama did composers begin
consciously and systematically to apply this principle, which achieved

normative status only in the period after Gluck.[17] Vinaccesi's early espousal of it is a natural outcome of his strong feeling for congruity and continuity.

The nineteen solo arias in *Susanna* divide, according to their instrumentation, into three types. Most common are the continuo arias, which account for twelve. A further five, headed 'con istrumenti', are accompanied by the full string band. The last two omit the orchestra but include obbligato instruments. These proportions are absolutely typical for the age, balancing the desire for variety against the convenience of tried and tested formulas.

The continuo arias themselves can be subdivided into three categories. The first comprises a pair without orchestral ritornellos. These are identical in conception to arias in solo cantatas, using the continuo itself to supply the ritornellos. The majority, eight, employ orchestral ritornellos variously before, after, and during the aria proper. Two further examples mix the use of orchestral and continuo ritornellos.

It is interesting to observe how flexibly Vinaccesi uses these 'detached' ritornellos. The most obvious procedure would have been always to introduce them either twice (before and after the aria) or four times (before and after each statement of the A section). The first scheme (rABAr) occurs on precisely two occasions, the second (rArBrAr) on three. In all the remaining arias belonging to this category asymmetrical designs of some kind (rABrAr, rArBA, etc.) are preferred. The ritornello often exists in more than one form within the same movement—for example, when it ends with a half-close on its first appearance, introducing the voice, but subsequently exchanges this for a full close.

The relationship between the ritornello and the aria proper is illustrated in Ex. 17. Essentially, the function of the former is to encapsulate in miniature the essence of the movement. The ritornello is rarely content merely to anticipate, or to restate, the opening of the vocal line. Instead, the composer seeks to develop the material in some way. Rather unexpectedly, Vinaccesi chooses to develop more through lyrical expansion than through imitative treatment of significant motives. In this respect, he differs sharply from Alessandro Scarlatti, who in oratorios of the same period (e.g. *Agar ed Ismaele*, *Davidis pugna et victoria*) likes to style such ritornellos as elaborate *fugati*. It may well be that in the vocal movements of this oratorio Vinaccesi bridled his contrapuntal instincts deliberately, having gauged—accurately or otherwise—the taste of the Modenese court.

---

[17] Johann Mattheson, *Der vollkommene Capellmeister* (Hamburg, 1739), 234; Johann Joachim Quantz, *On Playing the Flute*, trans. and ed. Edward R. Reilly (London, 1976), 316; Francesco Algarotti, *Saggio sopra l'opera in musica* (Livorno, [2]/1763), 30. The overtures to Handel's *Belshazzar* (1745) and Rameau's *Zoroastre* (1749) are early instances of the new approach. Stradella's *La Susanna* (1681) and Albinoni's *Zenobia, regina de' Palmireni* (1694) exemplify the old practice of co-opting existing sonatas as sinfonias to dramatic works.

The instrumentally accompanied arias represent the way of the future, in the sense that by the end of the first decade of the eighteenth century the continuo aria, with or without detached ritornellos, was on the wane in dramatic music (it is still prominent, however, in the *Engelberta* (1709) of Albinoni and Gasparini). One must not exaggerate the difference between the continuo arias and the instrumentally accompanied ones. True, the ritornello is 'integral' in the latter, but not neccesarily longer or more frequent in its appearances. During much of the vocal periods the voice is supported by the continuo alone. The main function of the instruments outside the ritornellos is to dialogue with the voice, with which they exchange brief phrases in *concertato* fashion.

In general, instrumental and vocal material are not differentiated thematically. The instruments do not introduce motives of their own as a background to the voice (this device belongs, rather, to the eighteenth century), and when they join forces with the singer at climactic points they retain their contrapuntal independence as far as practicable. In short, they function to a large extent as abstract 'voices' different in timbre from the singer but very similar in expressive effect.

To illustrate Vinaccesi's *concertato* style at its most vigorous, we shall quote, as Ex. 18, a passage from Gioacchino's magnificent aria 'Empie Furie che m'agitate', in which the angry husband rounds on his supposedly errant wife. The extract begins at the first vocal entry in the second vocal period of the 'A' section.

The 'redoubling' of their cruelty by the Furies is expressed here not by *note raddoppiate* as one might have expected but on one hand by breaking down crotchets into triplet quavers and on the other by incessantly repeating short phrases in *concertato* fashion. In the 'B' section Vinaccesi highlights the word 'flagellate' by having the soprano sustain its penultimate syllable on a high monotone; this deliberately punishing treatment recalls Bach's treatment of 'der Würger' (the Throttler, or Satan!) in his cantata *Christ lag in Todesbanden*, BWV 4. The last line of text in this aria reads 'questo seno che pace non ha' (this breast that enjoys no peace). With typically baroque insouciance Vinaccesi fastens on to an individual word ('pace') that is at odds with the general sense of the phrase to which it belongs, and makes it raw material for word-painting; the tempo slows down from 'Presto e spiritoso' to 'Adagio', and the metre changes to 3/4.

The two arias with obbligato instruments are naturally of special interest. The first is Susanna's 'Caro, amato, diletto mio sposo', the closing number of the first part, in which the heroine insists on her innocence while proclaiming *malgré tout* her undying love for Gioacchino. Here Vinaccesi introduces a solo violin, whose sweet tone projects a suitable atmosphere. The violin part is attractively intricate and in places thoroughly idiomatic, with triple-stopped chords, although the constraints

Ex. 18. *Susanna*, 'Empie Furie che m'agitate'

inherent in the *concertato* style make the instrument more an *alter ego* of the singer than an independent commentator.

The other aria in this category is Susanna's last solo number, 'Vedervi a piangere', her tender expression of forgiveness towards Gioacchino for his doubts about her fidelity. The obbligato instruments are two solo cellos, which play much of the time as a 'team' in parallel thirds and sixths, though they also engage in imitation with each other as well as with the voice. The second cello frequently doubles the continuo bass an octave higher. The sonority and texture resulting from this practice are unusual, even disconcerting, for modern ears, particularly when the obbligato instrument steps in and out of its doubling 'mode' with such freedom, but they are typical for the seventeenth century. Ex. 19 quotes the entire 'B' section. It will be noticed that the music is at one point three degrees further 'sharp' around the circle of fifths than the key of the movement (i.e. in B minor as compared with D minor). This is, for Vinaccesi, an unusually wide tonal ambit. Another aria, Gioacchino's 'Rimembranze penose', ventures exactly as far (to A minor from F sharp minor) in a 'flatward' direction. These two examples show that although wide-ranging modulation may not be a characteristic feature of Vinaccesi's style, it belongs securely to his repertory of devices.

With the exception of one example employing binary form, all the arias are constructed on the *da capo* principle. Typically for a work dating from this transitional period, whereas a good number contain two vocal periods within the 'A' section, many still have only one.

In conformity with his apparent desire, mentioned earlier, to ration contrapuntal complexity severely, Vinaccesi spurns the option provided by Bottalino to set the three numbers for the Elders as duets. Instead, he treats them as 'double' arias. In each case, Vecchio 1 (tenor) leads off with his own aria, which is then repeated in a heavily paraphrased version by Vecchio 2 (bass). In one instance Vecchio 1 repeats his aria to produce a tripartite arrangement. To create his paraphrases, Vinaccesi exploits very skilfully the traditional practice of a bass voice, mentioned in Chapter 7, to oscillate between doubling the bass in plain or elaborated form and singing an independent upper part. However, some of the variations between the two versions have nothing to do with technical questions but result from the lure of word-painting. The openings of the paired arias 'La beltà cui l'alma adora' and 'L'aureo crin che m'incatena', in which the Elders mimic the commonplace utterances of lovers with a comic ponderousness, give an idea of the nature of the paraphrasing (see Ex. 20).

As in his cantatas, Vinaccesi resorts to word-painting very selectively. No aria contains more than three examples of overt word-painting, and most have no more than one. The devices used for *Tonmalerei* range from the banal to the abstruse. In the second category we can place the ties and

Ex. 19. *Susanna*, 'Vedervi a piangere'

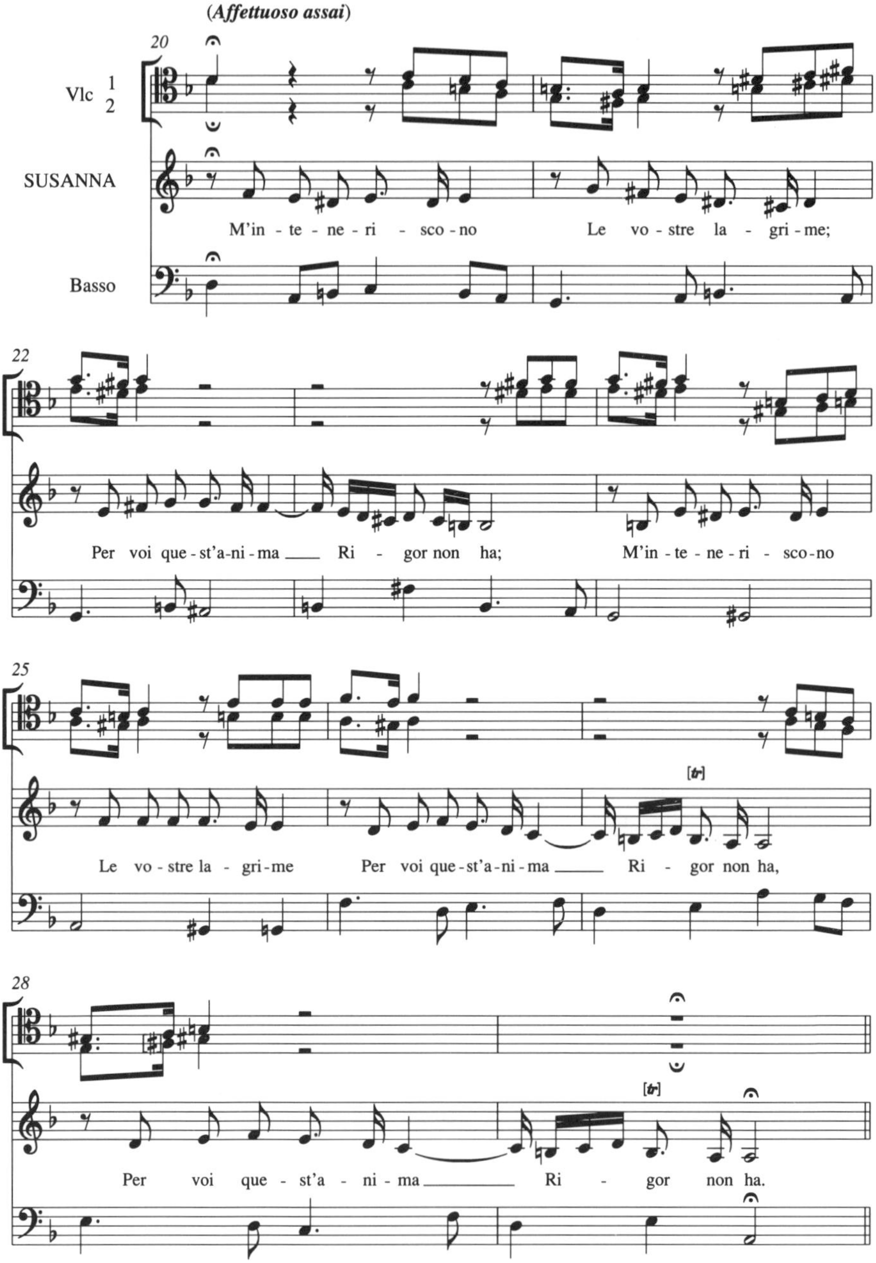

Da capo

Ex. 20. *Susanna*, *a* 'La beltà cui l'alma adora', *b* 'l'aureo crin che m'incatena'

ornamental resolutions to suspensions in Daniele's second aria, 'A chi oblia l'eterna luce', which suggest, in the venerable tradition of 'eye-music', the chains ('catene') that can ensnare the unwary in illicit love, and also the chromatic meanderings in Susanna's 'Caro, amato, diletto mio sposo' expressing the idea of deceit ('inganno').

Some technical features familiar from the cantatas reappear here. Two arias follow the final cadence of the 'B' section with a melismatic flourish similar to the one in the first aria of *Belve, se mai provaste*. Another aria, Daniele's 'La cieca umanità', employs an elaborate ground-bass structure resembling that in the cantata movement just mentioned. Several arias have a lilt and a rhythmic uniformity suggestive of the dance—the ritornello to the second 'double aria' of the Elders is even titled 'Menuè'. This feature is very characteristic of north Italian (as opposed to Neapolitan) opera of the time and seems more than a little beholden to French music, which exhibits the same trait even more strongly.

The absence of duets for the Elders throws into stronger relief the charming duet of reconciliation between Gioacchino and Susanna. Nothing need be said about this movement here, except that in style, form, and technique it closely resembles the duets in Vinaccesi's motets to be discussed in Chapter 10.

It remains to examine the concluding chorus. Its elaborate structure, contained within fifty-three bars, grows out of a mere six lines of verse:

Di sì tragica scena	You, who have heard the outcome
tu, che il successo ascolti,	of this tragic scene,
sappi che il giusto Dio	should know that a just God
sotto un monte di sassi i rei coprio,	covered the culprits under a heap of stones
perché veder ricusa	because he will allow no one
chi pecca amando e l'innocenza accusa.	to love illicitly and accuse the innocent.

The chorus falls into six sections as shown in the table below:

Lines	Bars	Scoring	Observations
1–2	1–5	voices and instruments	A block-chordal introduction capturing the listener's attention. It ends with a half-close in E minor.
3–4	6–19	voices alone	A *fugato* ending with densely packed *stretto* entries. It leads to another half-close in E minor.
5	20–21	voices and instruments	A block-chordal punctuating passage that cadences in G major.
6	22–34	voices only	The first section of a fugue on two subjects. It ends with a full close in B minor.
	35–42	instruments only	The same fugue continued. The section leads to another cadence in G major.
	43–53	voices and instruments	The third and final section of the fugue. The instruments enter after five bars. At the final climax, the dense counterpoint admits remarkably little doubling between voices and instruments.

Everything about this chorus is carefully planned and meticulously executed: scoring, texture, tonality, and proportions. It is as if the composer were saying to his courtly audience, 'See what I can do if you only let me'. In the final fugue Vinaccesi allows himself a subtle piece of musical punning in the Monteverdian tradition. The first syllable of the word 'pecca' (literally, 'sins') is set to the second note of the principal subject. When harmonizing this note, Vinaccesi normally makes it the seventh of the chord. But there is a significant irregularity: the seventh is unprepared. (Even though the note that becomes this seventh is sometimes present in the preceding chord, it always occurs in another part—not in the one in which it should in theory appear as a preparation.) The licentious seventh causes a definite *frisson*—as if to suggest that sinning can be, at the time, very exciting. Ex. 21 joins the music at the beginning of the fugue.

Note that this chorus returns to the key of the Sinfonia, E minor. It would be anachronistic to claim that overall tonal closure is either significant or to be expected in large-scale music of this period, particularly when a break occurs in the middle. Nevertheless, in so far as any key possesses a particular colouring that affects the composer's choice of notes and the listener's perception of them, the tonal identity of the first and last movements can be used to a create a common aura that is somehow representative of the work as a whole. In the present case, the shared key links the 'unofficial' theme of the drama (Susanna's rock standing firm against the waves of adversity) with the 'official' one (the punishment of perjurers) and in so doing integrates the work, at least at a symbolical level. Although E minor makes other appearances between these two points, one would perhaps go too far in viewing it as a 'nodal' tonality with a broader architectural significance.

Less need be said about the recitative, which conforms very closely in style to that found in the cantatas. At times it can seem a little dry and unadventurous, especially in passages of dialogue, though it is not wholly devoid of moments of real inspiration; for instance, the bars for Susanna immediately preceding the second double aria for the Elders express brilliantly, in their abrupt slithering down from D minor to C minor, the heroine's helpless desperation.

The tonal organization of the recitatives follows the familiar principles, though now applied on a more expansive scale. Of the 19 passages of recitative, 11 end in the key of the following closed number, 5 in its mediant or submediant key (in the 'opposite' mode), 2 in its dominant or subdominant (in the same mode), and only 1 in a less closely related key. Conversely, 9 begin in the mediant or submediant key of the preceding number, 9 in its dominant or subdominant, 1 in a less closely related key, and none at all in the same key. These statistics show with startling clarity that Vinaccesi regards each new recitative as a 'fresh start' that leads smoothly to the tonal area of the next aria or ensemble.

Many recitatives end with a few bars in *arioso* style. Those in the recitatives preceding 'A chi oblia l'eterna luce' (Daniele) and

'Perdonatemi' (Gioacchino) are especially interesting, since they prefigure the musical content of those arias, each offering a preview of the walking bass employed there.

Having dealt with several aspects of this oratorio in isolation, we must now finally address the central question: how well does Vinaccesi knit the parts together to make a convincing drama in musical, as distinct from poetic, terms? Much depends on what one expects from a seventeenth-century work, for not all the criteria that one customarily applies to more recent musical dramas may be relevant.

Take, for instance, the question of 'character development'. In an oper-

Ex. 21. *Susanna*, final ensemble

atic work from the time of Mozart onwards we expect the music to reveal progressively changing aspects, some perhaps previously only latent, of the personality of a participant in the drama. This view of drama presupposes that 'people change'. The baroque approach is rather different. It imagines that every person possesses an 'essential' personality, or ethos, rooted for the most part in class, caste, or heredity. The ethos becomes modified at times by transient passions manifesting themselves as pathos. But an important ideological function of baroque drama is to show how, in the fullness of time and with the support of higher powers, ethos prevails over pathos: people revert to their natural state. In an important sense, therefore, the concept of character development is inimical to the older notion, favoured by baroque drama, that true essences are inherited or God-given, not acquired. What one does find, however, is that persons are colonized, as it were, by a succession of contrasted feelings. These feelings are themselves 'essences' that merely require a person in which to lodge. In a sense, the drama resembles a game of cards: the players (the dramatis personae) are dealt a hand by fate. The hands contain cards that may appear favourable or unfavourable, and the players make their reactions felt accordingly. The ultimate outcome, however, depends on their innate aptitude and the overall distribution of the cards (which is unknown to them), not on skills learnt in the course of playing the hand.

Even so, if we reinterpret 'character development' as 'the successive states of mind that inhabit a given character', we are still left with a dynamic element that can provoke either sympathy or repugnance and is ultimately not so very different in practical terms. In *Susanna* Vinaccesi, anticipated in this by Bottalino, skilfully counterposes one volatile personality, Gioacchino, to four stable ones. In a sense, Gioacchino, not

Susanna, is the real protagonist of the drama, for his fate is to go full circle through a succession of emotions (love–hate–pity–hope–love), while her feelings remain rock-solid. Vinaccesi compensates for the one-dimensional characterization of Susanna, Daniele, and the two Elders by making each an amalgam of potentially contradictory qualities. Susanna's heroism is the obverse of her naïveté—an accidental product of her simple honesty. Daniele is, quite literally, on the side of the Angels, but his vehemence and self-righteous inflexibility give him a remote, almost inhuman, quality (easily captured in the brilliant blandness of his music) that differentiates him very sharply from the other soprano, Gioacchino. The Elders are indeed menacing and unscrupulous but at the same time have a bumbling inefficiency that music, even more than words, is able to bring out. They are not hardened criminals but recently corrupted men, and their inexperience at villainy emerges at every turn. Fear of exposure, not malice for its own sake, moves them to accuse Susanna and thereby raise the stakes. By treating the Elders as *bassi buffi*, Vinaccesi, far from trivializing them, points to their fundamental ordinariness; this banality remains a part of them even as they rush towards the abyss. One might have wished that first Bottalino and then Vinaccesi had attempted to differentiate the characters of the Elders.[18] But there are certainly compensatory advantages in not so doing, for the interchangeability of the two characters is itself a comic element and justifies the routine of giving them double arias, an attractive musical feature that would lose its dramatic justification if the two Elders had differing personalities.

Having established that Vinaccesi has the imagination and resourcefulness to produce a series of well-contrasted and characterized arias, one may ask a further, perhaps more provocative, question: does he organize this long string of relatively short movements into larger units so as to shape climaxes and enable dramatic currents to flow through several numbers in a row?

In a way, the question is unfair and historically inapposite. With regard to drama, the composer is the junior partner, the librettist the senior. As the seventeenth century understood it, the primary task of the musician was to clothe the words in suitable notes. The text was not raw material to be hammered into shape but a finished product to be shown off to its best advantage. Of course, this oversimplifies the position a little, for merely by coming second (in a chronological sense), music had the opportunity to create 'added value'. The point is, however, that this 'added value' was not a factor that composers consciously strove to create

---

[18] In his text for Stradella's *La Susanna*, Giardini begins as if he wishes to keep the personalities of the two Elders separate, for one is troubled by his conscience, while the other is almost light-hearted. But once their purpose becomes common, so too do their characters, which blend into one in Stradella's contrapuntal duets for them.

autonomously but rather an incidental by-product of the skill and efficiency with which they performed their allotted task.

Vinaccesi would therefore not have wished to upstage Bottalino by ramming home too forcefully points that were already made with sufficient force in the libretto, still less to make quite separate points or to use music as a separate agent of dramatic irony. But he would certainly have considered it proper to highlight by discreet musical means passages of text or dramatic situations that stood out from the rest. One can see evidence of this attitude in the instrumentation of the arias. The five arias 'con istrumenti', which tend for obvious reasons to be longer and richer in content than those with continuo alone, are all situated at a dramatic crux. Susanna's 'Onde placide', with its echo, is her dimly apprehended presentiment of disaster just before it strikes; Gioacchino's 'Che chiedi, mia vita' signals his entry into the drama—an entry made all the more significant by his non-participation in the biblical story; his next aria, 'Empie Furie che m'agitate', marks the furthest limit of his estrangement from Susanna; the Elders' 'Caderà, caderà quell'ingrata' portrays their overweening arrogance at the height of their power; Daniele's 'Scenda nel popolo' is a Divine decree uttered through a human mouth. The two arias with obbligato instruments, in contrast, are both associated with poignant moments of reflection by the heroine. By means of this delicate *chiaroscuro*, Vinaccesi is able in some measure to match the ebb and flow of dramatic excitement. He does not, however, join movements into longer sequences; one is still very conscious that the aria and its preceding recitative are the separate building blocks out of which the whole edifice is formed (unlike in French baroque opera, where individual numbers are often grouped into movement-complexes that create an intermediate tier of construction).

In all respects, *Susanna* is a work of the highest quality that fully deserves performance today. If Vinaccesi does not quite have the contrapuntal facility of Stradella, the flair for lyrical expansion of Colonna, or the dramatic sensibility of Alessandro Scarlatti, he certainly displays a thoughtful inventiveness and capacity for originality that confer a touch of distinction on this score. One can only regret that his other oratorios have not survived.

9

The Operas

THE three known Vinaccesi operas fall within the period 1697–1703 and by so doing appear to straddle the Brescia-Venice divide in his career. This impression is misleading, however, for whereas the earliest, *Chi è causa del suo mal pianga sé stesso*, was composed for performance on private premises (probably in the Ottoboni palace in Rome), the other two were written for the public stage. Vinaccesi's involvement with public opera was therefore exclusively a product of his early years of residence in Venice. As we saw in Chapter 2, he soon became disenchanted with it, and his security in his posts at San Marco and the Ospedaletto allowed him to bow out of writing operas for the public stage with no apparent detriment to his reputation. After all, the three musicians with whom he competed in 1704 for the post of organist at San Marco—Andrea Paulati, Marco Martini, and Alvise Tavelli—exposed themselves even less to the Venetian stage: each contributed precisely one opera. Besides, the musical techniques that Vinaccesi had learnt in the sphere of opera could continue to be applied in serenatas such as *Sfoghi di giubilo* (1704), and in that sense his renunciation of the dramatic genre was not total.

The literary and musical sources of the three works are as follows:

Chi è causa del suo mal pianga sé stesso (probably performed Rome, 1697)
  libretto: lost (possibly never published separately).
  score: Paris, Bibliothèque Nationale, Vm.⁴ 13.
L'innocenza giustificata (Venice, San Salvatore, carnival 1699)
  libretto (Nicolini, Venice, 1699): Venice, Biblioteca Nazionale Marciana, and many other locations.
  score: lost. A 'short' score of the aria 'Non ti credo mai più' is preserved in London, British Library, Harley Ms. 1272, fos. 73ᵛ–74ʳ.
Gli amanti generosi (Venice, Sant'Angelo, carnival 1703)
  libretto (Rossetti, Venice, 1703): Venice, Biblioteca Nazionale Marciana, and many other locations.
  score: lost.

One should not be surprised that no score of either of the Venetian operas is extant. It was a normal condition of the composer's contract with the theatre management that he should hand over his score permanently to the latter (who might choose to revive it on a later occasion).

The pressure of time was often so great that a composer would not have been able make a separate copy of the work for himself, even if he had wished to.[1] However, once the copyists working for the theatre had finished preparing the parts for the performance, it was customary to allow them to retain the score for a fixed period of time, so that they could prepare scores or extracts for private customers. A few customers requested complete scores, but the vast majority made do with collections of individual arias ('loose airs', as the English called them).

There were two ways in which to copy out an aria. The first was to notate it in all its parts, complete with instrumental ritornellos. From the point of view of a scrupulous musician, this was the only proper way, but it naturally cost more than the alternative way, which was to copy out only the voice and the bass, since copyists charged according to the amount of paper consumed.[2] 'Short' scores (based on the parts used by singers in rehearsal) could in fact be more convenient than full versions since they provided all the essential material for a domestic performance, which was unlikely to include a string ensemble.

A thorough trawl for 'loose airs' of an Italian baroque opera would in theory entail matching the textual incipits of the arias in the librettos of all its known productions against those of the underlaid texts in the tens of thousands of such arias preserved in publicly accessible collections, many of which are anonymous (one would guess from the inscriptions for these arias that many souvenir-hunters cared more about the identity of the singer or the theatre than that of the composer). Regrettably, the practical conditions that would enable such a search to be conducted systematically do not yet exist. So the fact that I have so far found only one separate aria traceable back to one of these Venetian operas should not be taken as a final statement of the position.

'Non ti credo mai più', existing in the form of a 'short' score for soprano and bass, is the penultimate of seventy-four Italian arias and cantatas contained in Harley Ms. 1272. The latter part of the manuscript is in the hand of Humphrey Wanley (died 1726), a British collector of whom little is known.[3] Although the aria is not attributed to any composer, Vinaccesi's authorship seems assured. In the first place, the only opera librettos in which the text has been found are those for the productions of *L'innocenza giustificata* in Venice (1699), Genoa (1699), Mantua

---

[1] The urgency was sometimes so great that composers had to send each act of an opera to be copied as soon as it was finished. This is probably one reason why several baroque operas exist today only in incomplete form, one or more acts having become detached from the rest and subsequently lost.

[2] One observes a contrast between the careful use of paper in composers' autographs and its more generous use in manuscripts produced by professional copyists. Both approaches were rational in economic terms.

[3] A. Hyatt King, *Some British Collectors of Music* (Cambridge, 1963), 90, 148.

(1700), and Crema (1701), all of which have it sung by the heroine, Giuditta, in Act III Scene 5.[4] As explained in Chapter 3, the music for all these productions was by Vinaccesi. However, it cannot be excluded a priori that the aria text was borrowed for use in another opera, so the evidence of the librettos is not absolutely conclusive.

What clinches the attribution is the musical style. The vocal line has a rhythmic variety, especially in its melismatic details, very typical of Vinaccesi. The 'B' section presents another very characteristic feature: its thematic substance, though motivically related to that of the 'A' section, is largely independent. From his Op. 1 sonatas to his late motets, Vinaccesi shows a disinclination, unusual for his time, to open new sections with transposed versions of earlier material, generally preferring to employ new themes that are linked obliquely rather than directly with their predecessors.

Ex. 22 gives the openings of the 'A' and 'B' sections of this aria. The accompaniment must have have been 'con istrumenti', since the B section includes three short passages where the voice is interrupted by the instru-

Ex. 22. *L'innocenza giustificata*, 'Non ti credo mai più',

[4] In the Crema libretto, the opening line becomes modified to 'Non vi credo mai più'.

mental bass, whose non-melodic character indicates beyond doubt the presence of upper parts.

Before we pass to an examination of *Chi è causa del suo mal pianga sé stesso*, it will not be out of place to insert an excursus discussing briefly the text of *L'innocenza giustificata* and the qualities of its author, Francesco Silvani, since both hold points of special interest.

Active, as we saw, between 1682 and 1716, Silvani began his career among Venetian librettists of the 'old' (i.e. pre-reform) school such as Aurelio Aureli and Matteo Noris and ended it as a follower of the reform movement led by Zeno, Girolamo Frigimelica Roberti, and Domenico David. He was not a prime mover in the drive to eliminate perceived abuses (such as the coexistence of serious and comic within the same work and the violation of the dramatic unities) but went along with the dominant current. La Borde opined that his work improved 'à mesure qu'il avance vers le dix-huitième siècle' (which is really another way of saying, 'the more he espoused reform principles') and rated highly his dramatic judgement and ability to construct a plot, while conceding that he had less 'fire' than some of his contemporaries.[5] Literary connoisseurs of his own time had little good to say about him. A particularly vitriolic opponent was the satirical poet Bartolomeo Dotti (1651–1713), who happened to be a distant relative of the composer Vinaccesi, since his mother Ottavia was Fortunato Vinaccesi's sister. In his long satire entitled 'Il carnovale', which must have been penned around the 1690s, he mentions six librettists: Fulgenzio Maria Gualazzi, Domenico David, Matteo Noris, Girolamo Frigimelica Roberti, Giovanni Appolonio Appoloni, and Silvani. Frigimelica Roberti and David are reproached only very lightly for their high ideals; Gualazzi is criticized for his Latinate verse, Noris for the extravagance of his ideas; Appoloni and Silvani, however, are likened to Midas on account of their asinine judgements ('Certi Mida italiani | Dan giudizii all'asinesca | Fra gli Appoloni e i Silvani').[6]

Dotti also attacked Silvani in a sonnet entitled 'Del Dotti contro il Silvani'.[7] In it the latter's literary career is represented as a kind of Rake's Progress. The librettist begins with tragic operas that make the stage 'tremble' and the orchestra 'weep'; he then turns to the pastoral genre (Dotti plays wittily on the 'sylvan' connection of his subject's surname); his descent continues, as he embraces the world of comedy; finally, Dotti imagines a fourth period, in which Silvani sets up as a travelling showman (*ciarlatano*).

---

[5] *Essai sur la musique ancienne et moderne*, iii. 293.

[6] *Satire del Cavalier Dotti* (Geneva, 1757), 92–105.

[7] *I-Vmc*, Ms. Cicogna 1283, 'Sonetti del K[avalie]r Bortalamio Dotti et enigmatici', opening 60 (Sonetto 112). The title of the vol. plays on the double significance of the word 'Dotti': as a surname and as an adjective meaning 'learned' (hence complementary to 'enigmatici').

Benedetto Marcello, too, did not spare Silvani, satirizing his preference for titles that stated, sometimes in oxymoronic form, the moral of the opera rather than the names of its principal characters.[8] Marcello's first example of such a title, *L'ingratitudine generosa*, is in fact a portmanteau version of two actual titles of Silvani operas: *L'ingratitudine gastigata* and *La pace generosa*.

Because of his great practical sense of the theatre and understanding of the musical requirements of an opera, Silvani easily rode out such attacks. Librettos were commissioned from him by the foremost Venetian opera-houses (including the fashionable San Giovanni Grisostomo), set by many of the leading composers (Marc'Antonio Ziani, Francesco Gasparini, Tomaso Albinoni, Antonio Lotti, Carlo Francesco Pollarolo, *et al.*), and frequently re-used for new settings or revivals all over Italy and beyond. The Mantuan court showed its appreciation in 1699 by appointing him as its official poet. *L'innocenza giustificata*, with thirty-three known productions under various titles and settings by at least nine composers, is testimony enough to Silvani's popularity among impresarios and the opera-going public until long after his presumed death (see Appendix C.4). This opera even received a 'face-lift' in a version that turns up first in Fano in 1731; here, the locale is changed from the Holy Roman Empire in the early Middle Ages to the ancient Persian capital of Persepolis, and all the characters are renamed accordingly.[9] In 1744 a collected edition of Silvani's dramatic works began to appear, but in the event only four out of seven projected volumes were published.[10]

There remains in Silvani's librettos a certain whimsical tone that belongs to the pre-reform period. In *Il tradimento tradito*, an opera on a pastoral subject dedicated to the Danish king Frederik IV on the occasion of his unofficial state visit to Venice in the winter of 1708–9, one character, Erifile, steps outside the action in Act III Scene 11 to deliver to the audience a librettist's view of his audience.

Fui a l'opera ier sera.	I went to the opera last night.
Volea dire ognun la sua.	Everyone wanted to voice an opinion.
Un diceva, 'Bene, bene';	One person said, 'Good, good';
Dicea l'altro, 'Male, male';	Another said, 'Bad, bad';
Qualchedun, 'Così, così'.	Someone else, 'So, so'.

[8] *Il teatro alla moda*, ed. Andrea d'Angeli (Milan, 1956), 9.

[9] In the process of its refurbishment for new productions *L'innocenza giustificata* underwent the usual 'drift' away from the original text, as cuts, transpositions, additions, and substitutions had their cumulative effect. So much of the later versions is new that Reinhard Strohm concluded that the text of Vivaldi's *Feraspe* (1739) had nothing in common with Silvani's original drama (*Italienische Opernarien des frühen Settecento* (Cologne, 1976), ii. 256). However, Vivaldi's opera preserves even among its closed numbers a residue of the 1699 text, since Feraspe's aria 'Troppo bella è la mia colpa' (Act I Scene 8) is an only slightly altered version of Lotario's 'Troppo bella è quella colpa' (Act II Scene 2). Naturally, its connections with intermediate versions of the drama are stronger.

[10] *Opere drammatiche del Signor abate Francesco Silvani* (4 vols., Venice, 1744).

'O che musica, o che libro!'	'O what music, what a libretto!'
'Egli è buono, e ben l'intendo.'	'This is good: I can understand it.'
'Io l'esamino e lo cribro.'	'I'm studying it carefully.'
'È cattivo e nol comprendo.'	'This is bad: I don't get it.'
Quel che poi parlava peggio	The person who passed the severest opinion
uno egli era che non sa	was someone quite ignorant of the
l'a.b.c. nel fa sol la.	first principles of music.
Così andavan di carriera	So they went on
sin che l'opera finì.	until the opera was over.

It is significant that in this light-hearted dig Silvani does not defend his separate interest as a dramatic poet but takes up the cudgels on behalf of his musician colleague as well—something one could never imagine Zeno doing. Silvani is above all a man of the theatre, with an arguable lack of decorum and poetic finesse (as contemporaries understood these terms) but a strong feeling for action on stage. *L'innocenza giustificata* contains one splendidly vital scene towards the end of the first act (Scene 14) in which the chief characters, from two opposing camps, sit down together to a banquet, supposedly of reconciliation. A studied insult triggers off an armed brawl, and the unexpected alignment of the characters provides fresh impetus to the forward movement of the drama. To make sense of the following extract, one should be aware that:

Lotario (Lothair), son of Louis the Pious, is the emperor;
Adalgiso, his son, is secretly in love with Edvige (q.v.);
Giuditta is Lotario's stepmother;
Gildippe, her daughter, is being wooed by Berardo (q.v.);
Edvige, her other daughter, reciprocates Adalgiso's love;
Berardo, Giuditta's champion, is in love with a reluctant Gildippe;
Asprando, a follower of Giuditta, is a secret adherent of Lotario;
Carlo, Giuditta's infant son (a non-singing part), has been left territories
    by his late father, Louis the Pious; these Lotario hopes to keep for
    himself by having Carlo declared illegitimate or otherwise eliminated.

LOT/GIU	Meschi il riso il suo sereno al seren di sì bel dì,	May laughter add its brightness to the brightness of so fair a day.
ADA/EDV	Mai di gioia un giorno sì pieno	Never was such a joy-filled day
EDV/BER	l'alba lucida non aprì.	opened by the radiant dawn.
	[Siedono a mensa e siegue il ballo di cavalieri spagnuoli e francesi.]	*[They sit down at table, and there follows a ballet of Spanish and French knights.]*
LOT	Spumi Bromio ne' vetri!	May Bromius foam in our glasses![11]
GIU	E beva Augusto!	And let Augustus drink!

[11] Bromius, a beetle that feeds on the vine, was popularly known as 'il fremente' (the frother) and used as a synonym for Dionysus.

ADA	[*ad Edvige*] Bevo il mio foco in voi, luci serene.	[*to Edvige*] I drink of my love for you, bright eyes.
EDV	[*a parte*] Mi tormentano il cuor barbare pene.	[*aside*] Fierce pains wrack my heart.
GIL	Ebra son io di lucido contento.	I am drunk with pure happiness.
ASP	[*a parte*] Vola al fine l'impresa;	[*aside*] The enterprise hastens to its conclusion;
	sia propizia fortuna al gran cimento.	may fortune favour me in this great test.

[*Berardo porge la coppia a Lotario.*] [*Berardo proffers the goblet to Lotario.*]

LOT	Fellon, sul ciglio augusto l'orrendo volto ancor mi rechi?	Villain, are you still showing your horrible face before Augustus?
EDV/GIL	[*a parte*] O Dei!	[*aside*] Oh Gods!
BER	Cesare, è troppo indegno	Caesar, the name with which you insult me
	de le mie fasce e di mia fede il nome	is too unworthy of my lineage and my fealty;
	con cui m'oltraggi; io nacqui principe e tale io vissi.	I was born a prince, and thus have I lived.
LOT	Tu de' talami augusti profanator sagrilego . . .	You sacriligeous defiler of the Augustan bed . . .
ADA	[*a parte*] Che sento?	[*aside*] What do I hear?
LOT	Del mio gran genitor ingiuria e scorno,	Shamer and disgracer of my great father,
	per cui non empie ancora forse gli Elisi suoi l'ombra innocente. . .	on account of whom his innocent shade has perhaps not yet been admitted to Elysium. . .
BER	Berardo è cavalier	Berardo is a knight
GIU	e Augusto mente.	and Augustus is a liar.
LOT	A me?	Me?
GIU	Sì.	Yes.
BER	La mentita	The denial of an offended prince
	difenderà se d'uopo sia la spada d'un principe oltraggiato.	will be upheld, if need be, by the sword.
LOT	Amici, olà!	To my aid, friends!

And the battle proceeds, with physical blows joined to the verbal brickbats. Adalgiso unexpectedly intervenes to ensure the safety of Giuditta and her children, while Asprando, in a parallel (but covert) act of disloyalty, allows Lotario to escape. The most original aspect of this passage is having the entire company seated—at least, initially—at table. This provides a novel context for the familiar sequence of insult and combat. Silvani shows himself also to be an adept fashioner of dramatic dialogue, varying the length of each character's utterances in a way that approximates the spontaneous, irregular character of real speech.

Although Vinaccesi's music for *L'innocenza giustificata* is largely lost, its text remains to provide strong grounds for a revaluation of a poet who, perhaps because he was more a practitioner than a theorist, has been unjustly neglected in modern studies of Italian baroque opera.

Like most of the leading dramatic poets contemporary with him, Silvani made contributions to the operatic subgenre that we have referred to earlier as the 'pastoral' and which, in its literary guise, appears in the baroque period under a variety of generic descriptions such as *dramma pastorale*, *favola pastorale*, and *tragicommedia pastorale*.[12] Vinaccesi's *Chi è causa del suo mal pianga sé stesso* is almost a textbook example of pastoral drama of the purest kind as it was conceived at the end of the seventeenth century. A highly attractive work in its own right, it invites one to consider more general aspects, musical and dramaturgical, of pastoralism in opera.

Unlike tragedy and comedy, pastoral drama has no place within an Aristotelian frame of reference—for the good reason that it is an invention of the Moderns, not the Ancients. In deference to the theorists it was sometimes placed in an intermediate, 'tragicomic' category, principally because its characters, simple shepherds and shepherdesses or nymphs, were low-born (hence 'comic') but their sentiments and utterances were high-flown (hence 'tragic'). As Ellen Harris has accurately observed, tragedy in its pure Aristotelian form is—and was at the time recognized as—foreign to the baroque operatic tradition, for which reason she uses the term 'tragicomic' to describe baroque *opera seria* as a whole.[13] In this respect a distinction is possible, however, between ordinary 'heroic' opera and pastoral opera. The first is generally 'tragic' with a measured admixture of 'comic' elements for light relief, while the second is a consistent synthesis of the two elements.

The roots of pastoral drama are found in the pastoral poetry of the Ancients: principally, the *Idylls* of Theocritus and the *Eclogues* of Virgil. These set the parameters of the tradition in respect of the types of person represented, the poetic themes, the types of locale, and the overall tone— by turns light-hearted and elegiac. The Italian Renaissance revived the genre, one of whose classic works is Jacopo Sannazaro's *L'Arcadia* (1504). In the sixteenth century the first true pastoral dramas appeared: Giambattista Giraldi's *L'Egle* (1545), Agostino de' Beccari's *Il sacrificio* (1554), Torquato Tasso's *Aminta* (1574), and Battista Guarini's *Il pastor*

---

[12] The Christmas pastoral is best regarded not as a subspecies of the ordinary pastoral but as a parallel sacred genre related to it rather as the oratorio was related to the serenata or to opera.

[13] *Handel and the Pastoral Tradition* (London, 1980), 1.

fido (1590).[14] All these works were produced within the ambit of the Este court at Ferrara. Spoken pastoral drama established a species of plot that was later taken over without modification by pastoral opera. In the words of Harris: 'Its action represents a wooing or courtship, the lover's seeking, and winning or losing, of his beloved'.[15] Its dramatis personae are described by the same writer as 'normally non-specific and nondescript'.[16] Here, the adjectives are perhaps unfortunate. A Daphnis and a Phyllis are identifiable as separate individuals and may have strongly marked personalities. What is nevertheless true is that the names are generally arbitrary and interchangeable.

The spirit of pastoralism soon came to fertilize works that were not in themselves pastoral. Harris identifies two important categories in which this influence is manifest.[17] The first is the pastoral episode in a work of epic character, exemplified by the amours of Angelica and Medoro in Ludovico Ariosto's *Orlando furioso* and the sojourn of Erminia among the shepherds in Tasso's *Gerusalemme liberata*. The second is the 'pastoralized' myth, often drawing on such tales from Ovid's *Metamorphoses* as those of Orpheus and Eurydice, Apollo and Daphne, and Acis and Galatea.

When opera was born, near the end of the sixteenth century, it was natural that pastoral or pastoralized themes should be the ones preferred. In the first place, having a pastoral subject circumvented a perceived problem of verisimilitude. For a Roman emperor, *recitar cantando* was obviously unrealistic, but for a Daphne or a Eurydice, idealized figures from a lost golden age, it was possible to imagine song as a normal medium of communication. For another thing, the grace and lightness proper to the pastoral tradition mirrored the self-image of the courts that were opera's first sponsors. All through the baroque period, irrespective of the fluctuating fashionability of pastoral opera in public opera houses, operas in a straight line of descent from Peri's *Dafne* and Monteverdi's *L'Orfeo* continued to be performed at Italian and some foreign courts.[18]

Public opera was born in Venice in 1637. In its early years pastoral subjects were very popular, but, as Harris has observed, there was a distinct 'dip' in its fortunes approximately between 1650 and 1670, at least as far as Venice, Italy's operatic 'capital', was concerned.[19] One can well understand how an appreciation of the ethos and ambience of pastoral opera may have come less naturally to the heterogeneous audiences attending public opera in the metropolitan centres than to the select few invited to

---

[14] The dates given here are those of the first publication of the definitive version. Renaissance pastorals, like epics, were often many years in the making.

[15] *Handel and the Pastoral Tradition*, 2.   [16] Ibid. 4.   [17] Ibid. 3–5.

[18] Harris does not emphasize enough the continuity of pastoral opera in a courtly setting. Most of the mid-17th-cent. operas concerned are lost, but their existence can be ascertained from surviving librettos and libretto registers.

[19] Harris, *Handel and the Pastoral Tradition*, 30.

functions at court. The revival, in Italy, of pastoral opera, which reached its high point at the very end of the century, seems to have occurred first in Rome, initiated by the circle around ex-Queen Christina of Sweden and continued by the Arcadian Academy after her death. Cardinal Ottoboni, at whose court Vinaccesi's opera was almost certainly first performed, was himself, as a librettist, a contributor to the pastoral subgenre.[20] In Venice the *Accademia animosa*, founded in 1691 and reconstituted as a 'colony' of the Roman Arcadia in 1698, cultivated the genre enthusiastically. Among its members, Apostolo Zeno and Girolamo Frigimelica Roberti were prominent exponents.[21]

From her examination of two early operas written in Rome, near the beginning of his career, by Alessandro Scarlatti—*Gli equivoci nel sembiante* (1679: performed in the Teatro Cesi Bernini) and *Gli equivoci in amore o vero La Rosaura* (1690: performed in Ottoboni's palace, the Cancelleria)—Harris has produced an admirably clear characterization of pastoral opera as it was conceived at the end of the seventeenth century. One qualification is needed, however. The description, as Harris clearly recognizes, refers not to pastoral opera *tout court* but to examples performed under private auspices and thus with smaller resources than those available to public opera houses. Pastoral opera given in public theatres tended to be on a scale similar to that of opera generally.[22]

The revitalized operatic pastoral was rarely conceived in its renaissance form but was a diminutive version of the heroic and mythological operas performed concurrently in the public operatic houses. The number of scenes in these pastorals was reduced, often to half that in an heroic opera. There were usually no more than four or five characters—two couples and a confidant. The musical style was simplified and concise. A strict avoidance of contrast of any type became the stylistic ideal.[23]

In every respect, Vinaccesi's pastoral conforms to this description. Its three acts contain 7, 9, and 9 scenes respectively, as compared with up to 15–20 per act in standard opera. Actually, counting the number of scenes is a rather rough and ready way of assessing length, since the criterion for the move to a new scene is the purely mechanical one of a change, through an arrival or a departure, to the characters on stage. Scenes can

[20] Ottoboni's librettos for pastorals included *Amore eroico tra i pastori* and *Adonia*, both highly regarded by the first historian of the Arcadians, Giovan Mario Crescimbeni.

[21] Zeno's first three published dramas were pastorals: *Gl'inganni felici* (Venice, Sant'Angelo, autumn 1695, with music by C. F. Pollarolo); *Il Tirsi* (Venice, San Salvatore, autumn 1696, with music by Attilio Ariosti, Antonio Lotti, and Antonio Caldara); *Narciso* (Ansbach, court theatre, March 1697, with music by Francesco Pistocchi). Pollarolo also set Frigimelica Roberti's pastoral *Il pastor d'Anfriso* (Venice, San Giovanni Grisostomo, carnival 1695).

[22] This statement is borne out by the average number of pages in pastoral and non-pastoral librettos respectively, which shows no significant difference.

[23] Harris, *Handel and the Pastoral Tradition*, 38.

therefore be either very short or very long. A better measure—if one is not to go to the trouble of counting lines—is the number of 'closed' movements, both arias and ensembles. For Vinaccesi's pastoral these can be charted as follows:

Character	Act I			Act II				Act III		
Eurilla	1 3 6, 7			17		21		23⎱	26	31⎱
Tirsi	2 4, 5	10	12⎱	15		20	23⎰ 24	28	⎰32⎱
Selvaggio	8, 9 11		14	18, 19				29⎱30,31⎰	
Filli	12⎰ 13	16		22		25	27	29⎰	32⎰

With thirty-two closed numbers divided almost equally between the acts, *Chi è causa del suo mal pianga sé stesso* has about two-thirds as many as an average contemporary 'heroic' opera given in a Venetian theatre.[24] It calls for only four characters—two shepherds (Selvaggio and Tirsi) and two shepherdesses (Eurilla and Filli). Within each pair of roles, the first singer is a soprano, the second an alto. Symmetry is thus programmed into the work from the outset. It will be noted from the chart how equally the closed numbers are distributed among the singers, who occupy a single 'tier': all four participate in two or three numbers *a due* and have seven or eight solo arias—except for Filli, whose arias total only five (but once she makes her first appearance, at the start of the second act, she receives, in partial compensation, more arias than any of her companions).

Vinaccesi strives for brevity not only by limiting the number of arias and ensembles (and, *pro rata*, the length of the connecting recitatives) but also by selecting options, with regard to form, that are conducive to that aim. For instance, only 5 of the 31 movements in *da capo* form have two distinct vocal periods, each presenting the complete text, in the 'A' section; the remainder follow the older, more compact system of having a single vocal period with a central point of articulation. Only a minority (12) of the solo arias employ the *Devise*—generally such a prominent feature around 1700. The use of detached orchestral ritornellos is severely cut back: of the continuo-accompanied arias, numbering 23, 4 dispense with an orchestral ritornello altogether, 6 place it before the movement (rABA), and 9 place it after the movement (ABAr).[25] In only 3 of the

[24] The number of arias and other closed numbers specified in the librettos (by various poets) of the seven operas by Albinoni given in Venice from 1694 to 1698 is as follows: *Zenobia, regina de' Palmireni*: 53; *Il prodigio dell'innocenza*: 55; *Zenone, imperator d'Oriente*: 45; *Il Tigrane, re d'Armenia*: 52; *Primislao, primo re di Boemia*: 52; *L'ingratitudine gastigata*: 38; *Radamisto*: 45—an average of 48.5. This figure declines significantly over the next decade: five Albinoni operas from the period 1700–3 yield an average of 43.4 closed numbers; five from the period 1705–9 average only 38.2. What seems to have happened is that poets began to take account of the greater length of individual arias arising from the adoption of the expanded form with two separate statements of the text in the 'A' section.

[25] These statistics omit Tirsi's aria in Act I Scene 3, 'Torna, torna', which has two stanzas, separated by an orchestral ritornello. This single ritornello thus serves as both an introduction and a conclusion.

continuo-accompanied arias is the orchestral ritornello heard more than once. The high incidence of continuo-accompanied arias, as compared with those accompanied by the full ensemble (4) or by an obbligato instrument (1), is in itself a factor making for conciseness, since the *concertato* interplay of voice and instruments in a movement 'con istrumenti' tends to draw out its length.

Harris's description 'simplified and concise' is not inappropriate for the style of Vinaccesi's pastoral. One observes his liking for an uncomplicated, often quadratic, phrase-structure which almost anticipates that of the Venetian comic intermezzo in its early phase as represented by Gasparini and Albinoni a decade later. *Fortspinnung* and melismatic writing do, of course, occur, but their use is on the discreet side.

The 'strict avoidance of contrast' to which Harris refers is applicable if one interprets that phrase in a precise way. There is plenty of contrast of a purely musical kind in relation to elements such as key, tempo, rhythm, and melodic design. What is more limited, however, is the range of *affetti*. This is perhaps only to be expected in a drama treating only of love—and that in a fairly light-hearted way. One does not feel that anything vital is missed through the absence of arias expressing valour or vindictiveness; indeed, the narrowness of the emotional compass contributes positively to the work's unity.

Within the admittedly narrow conventions of its genre, the libretto (which, as we saw in Chapter 3, was probably written by G. B. Neri) exhibits literary finesse and not a little ingenuity of construction. The plot can be summarized as follows:

(I, 1) The scene is Mount Ida. Eurilla is collecting flowers (lilies and roses) in her basket in order to make garlands. She comments that roses, like love, have thorns, and declares that she wants no ties ('non vo' catene'). An unknown voice, from the distance, echoes her words without the negative ('vo' catene'). Realizing that this is not a true echo, Eurilla concludes that it is some deranged fool. The culprit, Tirsi, arrives and declares his love. She reproves him: he is already Filli's lover. He replies that courting Filli is hopeless: if Eurilla returns his love, he will give her up. To Tirsi's surprise, Eurilla reacts positively and invites him to sit next to her. She asks him whether he would first like a cuddle or a kiss. He opts for the kiss and describes how he would like it. He gives her his cheek, and she slaps it hard, running off. (I, 2) Confused and indignant, Tirsi resolves to return to Filli. (I, 3) Opportunely, Filli now arrives. She reproaches him for deserting her. He replies disingenuously that absence makes the heart grow fonder. She remarks that one of his cheeks is red (it is coloured like a rose unlike the other, which has the colour of a lily). Tirsi explains his blush by saying that he happened upon Eurilla, who was weaving flowers into a garland. She fled out of modesty, but then a bee stung him. Filli invites him to go to her animal pen, where her heifer's milk will cool him down. Tirsi declines, saying that he first has to go to the hut where his friend Selvaggio is awaiting him impatiently. Filli asks whether this is the handsome shepherd of whom Tirsi has spoken to her before. He confirms this and pledges his fidelity to Filli as he departs. (I, 4) Eurilla returns to collect her basket. Filli advises her to take her wreaths elsewhere since whoever touches them gets stung by a bee. Eurilla asks whether this has happened to Filli, who explains that the victim was Tirsi. Eurilla then invites Filli to see this bee, which she is holding in her hand. She opens her hand to reveal . . . nothing. The hand itself is the bee! Eurilla explains that Tirsi made a pass at her. Filli is indignant at his treachery. Eurilla tells Filli to join her in forsaking love, since men are disloyal by nature. Filli admits that she is not quite yet willing to take this step. (I, 5) Her friend having departed, she reflects that if Tirsi is unfaithful to her, she is not obliged to remain faithful to him. (I, 6) Filli herself having left, Tirsi enters with Selvaggio, who is lamenting his lost love. Tirsi asks him how this can be, since he refuses to become a lover. Selvaggio relates how fifteen years earlier his father Titiro rescued a child, Orinda, from a wild boar. In gratitude, her father Montano gave Orinda's hand in marriage to Selvaggio. Then suddenly she went missing, and he has searched in vain for her ever since. Tirsi asks how he will recognize her after so many years. Selvaggio replies that Orinda has three large scars, in the place where the boar attacked her, under her right shoulder. Tirsi remarks that his friend will have to divide his affections between many nymphs in order to search for these signs. Selvaggio confesses that he is hard to please in love: he dislikes the idea of fidelity and relishes rebuffs. Tirsi says that he knows of a nymph who is just right for him; Selvaggio expresses eagerness to meet her. (I, 7) In a soliloquy Selvaggio confesses that not knowing whether he is still a husband makes him unable to form attachments and causes him to treat love lightly.

(II, 1) Arriving from opposite directions, Tirsi and Filli confront each other. Tirsi vows fidelity; Filli disbelieves him. She declares that she no longer loves him and cites the episode of the 'bee'. Tirsi refuses to own up. Filli tells him to seek solace with Eurilla instead. (II, 2) Selvaggio, hearing the quarrel, arrives. Filli is immediately struck by his good looks. Tirsi asks Selvaggio to intercede for him. Meanwhile, Filli, *sotto voce*, continues with her expressions of adoration for Selvaggio. Selvaggio's pleas for Tirsi fall on deaf ears: Filli declares that she no longer loves Tirsi and sends him packing. (II, 3) Turning to Selvaggio, she asks him not to speak to her any more of Tirsi and says that her companion Eurilla, just now arriving, will explain. Eurilla is surprised at Filli's total repudiation of her former lover. Filli betrays obliquely that her real reason for giving up Tirsi is that she has found a greater love. Filli then leaves.

(II, 4) Eurilla explains to Selvaggio that Filli is in love with him. Selvaggio replies that he cannot love Filli. Eurilla presses him for a reason, suspecting an old love. Selvaggio replies that loyalty to his friend Tirsi is one factor; the other is that he loves her, Eurilla. She replies that she cannot love him in return. It is now Selvaggio's turn to press for a reason, similarly suspecting a prior attachment. Eurilla explains that loyalty to her friend Filli is one reason—but she would prefer in any case to stay unattached. She leaves. (II, 5) Selvaggio reflects on the unrequitedness of three loves: his (for Eurilla), Tirsi's (for Filli) and Filli's (for him). (II, 6) Tirsi rejoins him. Selvaggio reports that Filli remains obdurate but informs his friend that he loves Eurilla and (not strictly accurately) that she returns his love. He reflects that since Tirsi no longer loves Eurilla, it is morally permissible for him now to do so. Tirsi is glumly resentful: Selvaggio now has a love, while he has none. Before leaving, Selvaggio tries to raise Tirsi's spirits by observing that women (i.e. Filli) are changeable in their moods. (II, 7) Tirsi observes acidly that people who are happy themselves find it all too easy to give advice to the miserable. (II, 8) Filli and Eurilla now hold a conference. Filli asks Eurilla why she has been the one on whom Selvaggio's choice has fallen. Eurilla replies that it is simply out of loyalty to Tirsi that he is forgoing Filli. She reassures her friend that it is likewise out of loyalty to her she is rebuffing Selvaggio's advances. Filli comments that this loyalty to a friend is admirable in Eurilla but regrettable in Selvaggio. She reports the mysterious words of the oracle of Apollo that she has heard: 'Una non deve amar ché l'altra è moglie' (One woman must not love since the other woman is a wife). Eurilla says that the ban on love obviously refers to her (Eurilla). She tells Filli to carve the oracle's words on the bark of an elm and to ask Selvaggio for an explanation. (II, 9) Filli duly inscribes the riddle on the tree.

(III, 1) Eurilla and Tirsi meet. She reiterates her refusal to love. Tirsi counters that she has nevertheless encouraged, at different times, both him and Selvaggio. He reproaches her for ingratitude since it was he, Tirsi, who gave her succour when she arrived alone in Ida. She retorts that she owes him for this service only filial, not sexual, love. He continues to press his suit. She then tells him that she will put his fidelity to the test: he must inform Selvaggio that he has 'made over' his love for Filli to him. If he does this, she will no longer be jealous. Tirsi leaves to perform his task. (III, 2) Filli arrives. Eurilla explains her stratagem: for her friend's sake, she is trying to release Selvaggio from his bond of loyalty to Tirsi, though she herself has ultimately no intention of loving Tirsi or anyone else. (III, 3) Selvaggio, joining them, pays court to the shepherdesses, likening them to the goddesses between whom Paris (also on Mount Ida) judged. Eurilla asks to be excluded from the contest,

explaining that a divine decree forbids her to be a lover. Filli invites
Selvaggio to inspect the oracle's words. He too interprets them as an
interdict relating to Eurilla—as well as a confirmation of Tirsi's impending marriage to Filli. Selvaggio declares that he must leave and bewail his
lost love. Filli and Eurilla beg him to explain who this lost love is, and
Selvaggio repeats the story related earlier to Tirsi. He once again
identifies his wife as Orinda, a name unfamiliar to the two shepherdesses.
Eurilla spots Tirsi approaching and goes to join him. (III, 4) Selvaggio
tells Filli that he will consent to be her lover if Tirsi first gives her up.
(III, 5) Tirsi arrives. He asks Selvaggio how the women are feeling.
Selvaggio replies that despite everything they remain persuadable. Even
before Tirsi is able to carry out his promise by telling his friend that he
has renounced Filli, Selvaggio falls in with Eurilla's plan by proposing to
cede her to Tirsi and to take Filli in her place. He is nevertheless unsure
whether this is really Heaven's wish and refers Tirsi to the words written
on the elm. Like the others, Tirsi interprets their meaning to be that
Eurilla may not love Selvaggio since his bride is destined to be Filli.
Selvaggio confirms the exchange but, on further reflection, wonders
whether Filli will accept it. Tirsi reassures him and then leaves. (III, 6)
Filli arrives and immediately assures Selvaggio of her love, which he reciprocates. (III, 7) Eurilla rushes in, highly agitated, and collapses.
Selvaggio and Filli rush to her aid. They see a wild beast fleeing. Eurilla
is unhurt, but her cloak is torn. Selvaggio sends Filli to fetch water to
revive her. (III, 8) Examining Eurilla, he discovers the three scars. He
laments that he has just given her up to Tirsi. (III, 9) Filli arrives with
water, followed by Tirsi. She revives Eurilla, while he reports that the
beast is dead. Selvaggio then informs Eurilla that she is Orinda and asks
Filli to release him. She consents but expresses regret that by doing so
she loses her own love. Seeing his opportunity, Tirsi offers to become
Filli's lover again. She, however, reproaches him for having given her up
without protest to Selvaggio and points out that the oracle has forbidden
her to love. Tirsi laments the fact that by loving two women, he has lost
both; Filli tells him that he has paid the price of his infidelity and has
only himself to blame: 'Chi è causa del suo mal pianga sé stesso'.

The moral of the story is clear: fidelity (on the part of Selvaggio and
Eurilla) is rewarded, infidelity (on that of Tirsi) punished. However, there
are some interesting nuances. Eurilla's fidelity to her lost husband is
unconditional, albeit concealed even from Filli: she will not even play at
love on her own account, though she is willing to lead Tirsi on (in III, 1)
for Filli's sake. In contrast, Selvaggio's loyalty to his lost wife is an involuntary inhibition rather than a moral principle; he tries to love deeply but
finds that he cannot. (Had Selvaggio shared Eurilla's total rejection of
love, there would have been no drama, since Tirsi and Filli would have

fallen into each other's arms for want of competition!) Tirsi is fickle by nature; it is his opportunism rather than the changeability of his affections that is really culpable. Filli's character is more complex; one wonders whether she would not have abandoned Tirsi for Selvaggio even without provocation, and there is also an unpleasantly vindictive side to her. The fineness with which the moral distinctions are drawn makes the outcome seem a little extreme. However, one has to approach the final resolution, like the drama itself, in the spirit of a game where fate and justice are not perfectly aligned.

All drama has to prevent a premature resolution of the issues with which it deals. This problem is especially acute in a work with only four characters that observes the Aristotelian unities of time, place, and action. The librettist of *Chi è causa del suo mal pianga sé stesso* shows great resourcefulness in his invention of delaying mechanisms. Chief among these is the aversion towards emotional commitment on the part of Eurilla and Selvaggio, which frustrates the attempts of Tirsi and Filli to find alternative lovers. However, no single mechanism can be employed indefinitely without provoking tedium, and the librettist eventually has to find alternative mechanisms. In the second act, at the point where Selvaggio is at risk of succumbing to Filli's advances, and Eurilla to those of Tirsi, ties of friendship are used to block further progress. Later, the misinterpretation of the oracle's words nullifies those acts of solidarity and renews the prospect of binding Selvaggio to Filli, Tirsi to Eurilla. It is left to the final *dénouement*, set in motion by a second wild boar, to reverse the polarities for the last time.

A discussion of the music of this pastoral can conveniently begin with a brief description of the source, already mentioned briefly in Chapter 4. The score in Paris is handsomely bound in brown leather. The paper is in upright folio format (in itself, evidence of non-Italian provenance, for the Italians preferred quarto format) and measures 375 by 255 mm. The spine records the work's title (PASTORAL / DEL SIGR / VINANCCE [*sic*]) and original shelfmark (Vm.738).[26] The stamp of the Bibliothèque Royale is visible on the title-page, which means that the volume was acquired prior to the French Revolution, although it was not part of Sébastien de Brossard's donation. The title-page (fo.1ʳ) reads: Chi è causa del suo / mal pianga se stesso. / Pastorale / Musica del Sig:ᵒʳ Kʳ Benedetto Vinaccesi. After the Sinfonia, on fo.3ʳ, the characters and their respective voices are listed; Act I begins on fo. 3ᵛ.

In general, the score is neatly, almost calligraphically, written out. However, in addition to the many mistakes in the underlaid text already referred to in Chapter 4, the musical notation is littered with errors both

[26] On the verso of the free endpaper inside the front cover the old shelfmark is given, however, as Vm. 788. It is not known whether this, or Vm. 738 as on the spine, is correct.

trivial (such as missing accidentals) and more serious. Fortunately, there are not many instances where the composer's intention is unclear.

Our first observations concern the recitative. It is possible to make a general distinction, in Italian music of this time, between recitative performed from memory (principally in operas) and that performed reading from a part (in cantatas and motets—usually, too, in serenatas and oratorios). The first is necessarily formula-bound, conceived for problem-free rehearsal and rapid delivery on stage. The second has the opportunity (which it does not always take) to be more inventive in vocal terms and more leisurely in pace. For this reason, *arioso* excursions are common in cantatas, rarer in operas. One must also remember that in opera the singer could use gesture and movement to make his utterances expressive, a possibility denied to the other genres.

If, on first reading or hearing, the recitative in Vinaccesi's pastoral appears dry and repetitive, the missing factor of acting should be borne in mind. In fact, this music is not at all inexpressive, but the vehicle for its expression is less the voice than the accompaniment. The very pace of the singing allows the listener to perceive the chordal progressions and the patterns they form all the more clearly. A simple exposition of a pleasant or emotional neutral thought is usually accompanied by static harmony and stable tonality; an abrupt turn of thought or a contradiction can be mirrored by an unexpected chord-progression or by chromatic harmony. The opening recitative of the pastoral, shown in Ex. 23, is a good illustration. Eurilla's first two lines, presented in bars 1–3 over a tonic pedal in F major, reflect on the pleasures and pains of love. The next two, delivered in bars 4–6, develop the thought further and, by modulating to the dominant, C major, satisfyingly balance the opening phrase. The third phrase, acting as the consequent of the first two combined, occupies bars 6 (second half) to 13 (first half) and completes Eurilla's eight-line monologue. It begins tranquilly enough, with a C major triad outlined by the singer (on the line 'O quanto dolce, o quanto'), but a bar later, just before she reflects on the darker side of love, the bass moves up a semitone to $c\sharp$ making 'anguished' diminished sevenths with the voice and moving to a cadence in D minor. The dimished seventh and the cadence are immediately balanced, in bar 12, by a similar progression in G minor, before the voice marks the end of the passage (the words 'non vo' catene') with a strong cadence in G minor. In this way the musical period balances a pair of bright keys (F major and C major) against a pair of sombre ones (D minor and G minor).

Tirsi then introduces his feigned echo ('Vo' catene'), which is a variant of Eurilla's cadential phrase without its accompaniment. This device has no deeper purpose here than to contrast, in a wittily emblematic manner, Eurilla's flight from love and Tirsi's pursuit of it. When Eurilla responds

Ex. 23. *Chi è causa del suo mal pianga sé stesso*, opening recitative

to the interruption, the composer underlines her surprise by leading off with the first inversion of the dominant chord of E minor. This is a striking, elliptical progression that follows on from the previous chord of G minor as if this had first been altered to a major chord. After Tirsi's second echo, Eurilla's anger at being contradicted is matched by a sudden lurch of the harmony towards A minor. Tirsi cannot resist abandoning his echo-game in favour of a straightforward riposte to Eurilla, thus giving the game away, but not before the two singers have concluded the period in flamboyant style, *a due*.

Five of the closed movements, an unexpectedly high number, involve a pair of characters (there are no ensembles for three or four singers). One, the final number, is merely a *da capo* aria in two stanzas; Tirsi sings the first stanza, Filli the second. Two are genuine duets in the style of Vinaccesi's motets. Of these, the more impressive is the one in Act III Scene 6 in which Filli and Selvaggio celebrate their impending union just before Eurilla, pursued by a boar, makes her dramatic entrance. The penultimate closed number in the last act is an aria shared between Eurilla (who takes the 'A' section) and Selvaggio (with the 'B' section).

It seems that the librettist intended a similar arrangement for the opening number of Act III, in which a semistrophe for Filli, where she vehemently resists Tirsi's advances, is followed by one for her complaining suitor. Since the two semistrophes are not equal in length (Filli has two lines, Tirsi three), it is unlikely that they were meant to be delivered simultaneously. Vinaccesi, however, sees the dramatic possibility of juxtaposing the characters contrapuntally. After the expected 'A' section for Filli alone, Tirsi begins the 'B' section, but two bars later he is joined by Filli, who repeats her original text, drawing on her earlier musical material. The contest is unequal, for Filli's intrusion is so violent that Tirsi has difficulty getting through his lines. With a neat modification to her opening phrase that steers the music back from E minor to B minor, Filli then repeats the 'A' section.

Vinaccesi contrasts the two characters admirably in this movement, transcribed complete as Ex. 24. Filli's section is marked 'allegro', while Tirsi's slows down to 'adagio'. Whereas her manner is confident and imperious, employing many wide intervals, his is hesitant and craven (note the appearance of the mock-pathetic 'Neapolitan' second, F natural). One is reminded strongly of the style of the comic intermezzo. Indeed, the closing duet of Albinoni's *Pimpinone* (1708) contrasts its two characters in exactly the same way.[27]

Another aria in which Vinaccesi handles the text in an imaginative manner probably not foreseen by the librettist is Filli's 'È pur poco a

---

[27] Albinoni's *Pimpinone* can be consulted in an edn. by the present author (A-R Editions, Madison, Wisc., 1983).

tanto foco' (II, 3), in which the shepherdess gives expression to her new-found infatuation with Selvaggio. The aria stanza is followed by a single line of recitative, as she instructs Eurilla to tell Tirsi that she no longer loves him.

È pur poco a tanto foco	One heart alone, o dear eyes,
un sol cor, o luci care.	is not enough for such great passion.
A portare il vostro ardore	To support my ardour for you
io cent'anime nel core	I could wish for
in sen mi bramo.	a hundred souls in my heart.
Così a Tirsi dica, ma più non l'amo.	Tell this to Tirsi, but I no longer love him.

The single line of recitative prevents this from being a conventional 'exit' aria in which the singer, to the applause of the audience, sweeps off from the stage. It was perhaps in order to ensure that the final line would be heard clearly without a forced separation from the aria caused by the applause, that Vinaccesi decided to build it into the aria itself, where it forms the last part of the 'B' section. This snatch of simple recitative is made all the more effective by the fact that the aria is one of the few to be instrumentally accompanied; the contrast, therefore, is not only of style but also of scoring.

Another notable aria is the first one for Selvaggio (I, 6). Like many such first arias, it has the task of defining the ethos of the character who sings it. To illustrate the private and obsessive nature of Selvaggio's thoughts—his incessant grieving for Orinda—Vinaccesi casts it as a continuo aria without any instrumental ritornello but with an ostinato bass. The general character of the movement, in which the composer tries as usual to keep the phrase-structure of the vocal part as independent of the bass as possible, is familiar from the other ground-bass movements we have discussed; an attractive new touch, however, is the inversion of the bass pattern in the 'B' section.

As in *Susanna*, one aria of an especially 'pathetic' nature features an obbligato violin. This is Tirsi's 'Abbandonato, | È forza piangere' (II, 7), his reaction against Selvaggio's attempt to raise his spirits. Within the usual limitations of the *concertato* style, which forces the instrument and the voice into a common musical mould, Vinaccesi gives the violin a thoroughly idiomatic part that enhances the poignancy of the movement considerably. The closing part of the 'A' section, in which voice and violin unite in counterpoint for the first time, illustrates one attractive feature of Vinaccesi's polyphonic writing: his willingness to employ non-standard melodic progressions at cadences. As bars 30–2 of Ex. 25 show, each upper voice makes its own way to the cadential note. In his late motets this independence of part-writing will become even more marked.

French influence is, if anything, stronger than in *Susanna*. This would certainly fit the presumed circumstances of performance at the Ottoboni court, since the cardinal was a noted francophile and later became Protector of the Affairs of France at the Holy See. No fewer than three movements are in gavotte rhythm, and the detached ritornello preceding Eurilla's aria 'Sì, prepara i dolci affetti' (III, 3) is actually labelled 'Menuet'. The 'A' and 'B' sections of this aria are each styled as minuets (the first is the expected paraphrase of the ritornello), thus producing the familiar combination of a minuet and trio.

The most conspicuous homage to the French style occurs in the opening Sinfonia, which synthesizes, on a miniature scale, elements of the French and Italian styles in a most original way. Wholly Italian is the finale, a vivacious binary-form movement in 3/8 metre. The preceding two movements, however, follow the outline of a French overture. The first is marked 'concitato e adagio' and features the dotted rhythms and *tirades* of its model. This is followed by a Presto that opens with a set of fugal entries, moving in a straight line down from the first violins to the bass, just as in the second section of a typical *ouverture*. Remarkably, neither movement of the pair is tonally closed: the first begins in A minor and ends in C major; the second begins in C major and ends in E minor. The expected tonal closure is effected only when the third movement begins in A minor.

The orchestra employed in the sinfonia and the rest of the opera follows the contemporary Roman layout of two violin parts, one viola part, and bass (the refinement of a division into *concertino* and *concerto grosso* is not adopted, however). Vinaccesi's writing for the string ensemble is fluent and idiomatic, with inner parts that are sometimes surprisingly

Ex. 24. *Chi è causa del suo mal pianga sé stesso*, 'Gelo dissi e torno a dire'

7
EURILLA
Adagio
no, non, no a-mar, non a - me - rò. Ge-lo
TIRSI
Do-vrò dun-que, Id-dio, sof - fri-re Tan-te pe-ne,
10
Allegro
dis - si, e tor - no a di - re Non, no a - mar, non a - mar, no, no, no,
tan - ti af - fan - ni
13
Adagio
Allegro
no. Ge - lo dis - si, ge-lo dis - si, e tor - no a di - re Non, no a-
Io mo - ri - rò.
16
EURILLA
- mar, non a - me - rò, no, no, no, no, non, no a - mar, non a - me - rò, non, no a-
19
- mar, non a - me-rò.

Ex. 25 *Chi è causa del suo mal pianga sé stesso*, 'Abbandonato | È forza piangere'

complex. The first bars of the three movements of the Sinfonia, shown in Ex. 26, give an accurate impression.

It is difficult to evaluate the quality of this pastoral in relation to *Susanna* without bringing into play a whole set of preconceptions that belong to our own age, not Vinaccesi's. Whereas *Susanna* is connected with our experience through its adherence to a familiar biblical story and consequently to what may be termed universal values, everything about *Chi è causa del suo mal pianga sé stesso* challenges our established preferences. Where we would like to have low male voices included, we have only high voices. Where we would like to see vocal terzets and quartets, we have only duets. Where we would like to hear the full sound of an

Ex. 26. *Chi è causa del suo mal pianga sé stesso*, Sinfonia, section openings orchestra, we have only continuo. Where we would like to experience extremes of emotion, we have only the ups and downs of civilized courtship. To appreciate the pastoral adequately, one needs to enter fully into the world that gave it birth, accepting its values as one would the rules of a game. Once this is done, its consistently high quality and cunning artistry become immediately apparent. Like *Susanna*, albeit on a more intimate scale, it is a masterpiece fully deserving revival.

Our survey of the pastoral is not complete without a brief look at the subsequent vicissitudes of its libretto. During the annual fair of Reggio Emilia, which lasted from 29 April until the end of May, the first performance was given in 1698 of a *favola pastorale* entitled *L'enigma disciolto* (The Riddle Resolved), for which the music was composed by C. F. Pollarolo. Its libretto is an expanded and largely rewritten version, for the public stage, of *Chi è cause del suo mal pianga sé stesso*. Instead of twenty-five scenes there are now twenty-nine, and the number of arias has risen *pro rata*. An additional character, Satiro, has been introduced. This is a *parte buffa* inspired, perhaps, by Filli's lines (II, 1) 'Se più penso ad amarti, abbia il mio volto | Del Satiro più nero | Di questi boschi l'orrida sembianza'. Whenever the Satyr enters, the elegant conversation ceases and pure buffoonery reigns. An extra riddle, relating to the well that provides the water with which Eurilla–Orinda is revived, is worked into the plot. Most surprisingly, the ending is altered so that Filli, instead of punishing Tirsi with rejection, gladly accepts him. It is improbable that audiences in public theatres insisted on a totally 'happy' ending, since in Vincenzo Cassani's pastoral drama *L'incostanza schernita*, set by Albinoni for the Teatro San Samuele in 1727 and frequently revived, the protagonist, aptly named Filandro, pays exactly the same price as the original Tirsi for the same mistake. A more likely explanation is that, with the Satyr now providing most of the villainy and reaping a just reward for it (he ends up insane and the target of a bird's aerial bombardment), Tirsi's shortcomings seem comparatively venial.

L'enigma disciolto, under a variety of titles (others were *Gli amici rivali*, *La fede nell'incostanza*, *Amor indovino*, and *Le vicende amorose*), enjoyed great popularity in northern Italy for almost four decades. It was given no fewer than three times (1705, 1715, 1726) in Venice alone. Many of the productions—including, probably, the first—were organized by the impresario Giovanni Orsatto, immortalized by the satirical references to 'L'orso' (the bear) in Marcello's *Il teatro alla moda*. Pollarolo's original music lasted for some while before being replaced, in whole or part, by that of a series of other composers: Floriano Arresti, Antonio Bononcini, Baldassarre Galuppi, Antonio Tonelli, Allegro Allegri, and Gaetano Schiassi. Appendix C.8 lists the twenty-three known productions.

10

The Sacred Vocal Music

BOTH quantitatively and qualitatively, sacred vocal music forms the heart of Vinaccesi's *œuvre*, including both his maturest and artistically most ambitious compositions. As a fluent contrapuntist, he was drawn naturally to a type of composition that allowed him to engage in polyphonic writing, and as an organist, reared on church music, he was thoroughly at home with its liturgical and stylistic requirements. It would probably be no exaggeration to say that from his last years in Brescia onwards, all his essays in other musical domains were strictly 'occasional'.

The extant works that may safely be regarded as authentic are the following:

Messa concertata a 8 in A minor. For eight voices (SATB × 2), oboe, trumpet, strings (violin, two violas, all × 2), and organ. Non-autograph parts (incomplete): Rome, Biblioteca Corsiniana, Accademia Nazionale dei Lincei e Corsiniana, Mus. V. 6.

Compieta a 8. For eight voices (SATB × 2), two violins, and bass. Non-autograph score comprising psalms *Cum invocarem* (B flat major), *In te Domine speravi* (A major), *Qui habitat in adjutorio* (F major), and *Ecce nunc benedicite* (A minor), and the canticle *Nunc dimittis* (E minor): Venice, Biblioteca Nazionale Marciana, Cod. it. IV–1538 (= 11655).

Mottetti a due e tre voci (Venice, G. Sala, 1714). *RISM* V1576. Four parts labelled *Canto*, *Alto*, *Tenore*, and *Organo*. Contains 14 motets, variously for two and three voices with organ. Individual works are listed in Appendix C.9.[1] Extant examples: Aosta, Archivio della Chiesa Collegiata di Sant'Orso (*Canto* and *Organo* only); Bologna, Civico Museo Bibliografico Musicale; Paris, Bibliothèque Nationale; Rome, Biblioteca Apostolica Vaticana (*Organo* only); Venice, Biblioteca di San Marco (currently at the Fondazione Levi); Vienna, Gesellschaft der Musikfreunde; Wiesentheid, Bibliothek der Grafen von Schönborn-Wiesentheid. Manuscript score (non-autograph copy) in Bologna, Civico Museo Bibliografico Musicale, KK 306. Other manuscripts, mostly of individual movements or movement sections from single motets, are listed in Appendix C.10.

---

[1] The textual incipit of each movement and the musical incipits of the first movements are found in Zobeley, *Musikalien der Grafen von Schönborn-Wiesentheid*, i. 125–6.

Motet fragments (single arias or sections therefrom): *Caelestis horti* (ATB), *Stellarum fulgores* (ATB), *Videte, filiae Sion* (ATB, Tenor missing), *Adeste canentes* (SSB), *O Maria, si me amas* (SAB). Aria sections in non-autograph parts: Padua, Biblioteca Antoniana, B.II.618/1–2, 619, and 620/1–2 respectively. *Mensa dulcis et iucunda* (complete aria, TTB). Non autograph score: Venice, Biblioteca Nazionale Marciana, Cod. it. IV–1073 (= 10845).

Alme Jesu, sponse care. Motet for alto and continuo. Non-autograph score: Venice, Conservatorio di Musica 'Benedetto Marcello', Fondo Esposti, Busta 66 n. 212.

Astra campi, belli flores. Motet for alto, 2 violins, viola, and bass. Non-autograph score: Berlin, Staatsbibliothek Preussischer Kulturbesitz, Mus. ms. 30095.

These twenty-two works, together with the listed fragments, constitute all the sacred vocal music by Vinaccesi—a mere fraction of his total output—that is currently known to survive. Two other works have been attributed to him in the past. The first is a *Beatus vir* for four voices and orchestra preserved in the library of the Fondazione Levi, Venice.[2] The manuscript parts containing it bear no composer's name, and the music is clearly in the style of the late eighteenth century. The work is nevertheless attributed to Vinaccesi in a fairly recent description of the holdings of this library.[3] The second composition is a nativity motet for soprano or tenor, two violins, and bass, *Angelici chori*, preserved in the Staatsbibliothek Preussischer Kulturbesitz, Berlin.[4] Like *Astra campi, belli flores* and five of the cantatas discussed in Chapter 7, it comes from the Österreich-Bokemeyer collection. It was originally superscribed with the name of Bassani (Giovanni Battista?), but a later owner has added 'B: Vinacesi' in red crayon under the first name. The style of the music shows no features especially characteristic of our composer, and it is safest to regard its attribution to him as capricious.

Two other ostensibly sacred works by Vinaccesi, both lost, are listed in the inventory of music once possessed by the church of St. Francis Serafin in Prague. This church belonged to the military order of the Kreuzherren (Ordo Crucerigorum cum Rubea Stella), who cultivated a rich musical life there during the eighteenth century. The inventory records under Vinaccesi's name a 'cantata de omni sancto' for alto, *Huc festini*, and another 'cantata' for alto, *Licet irae*, which is listed among the

[2] Shelfmark CF.B.57. See Franco Rossi, *La Fondazione Levi di Venezia: Catalogo del fondo musicale* (Venice, 1986), pp. 20, 310.

[3] Siro Cisilino, *Stampi e manoscritti preziosi e rari della Biblioteca del Palazzo Giustinian Lolin a San Vidal* (Venice, 1966), pp. 34–5.

[4] Shelfmark Mus. ms. 1162, fos. 31ʳ–34ʳ.

offertories.[5] It is uncertain whether such works were complete motets, single arias extracted from motets, or *contrafacta* of operatic arias.

Apart from the published motets, composed expressly for San Marco, none of the other works gives any direct hint of its original destination, still less of its date of composition. A certain conservatism of style observable in some of the motet fragments in Padua suggests that this music may predate Vinaccesi's arrival in Venice, but one imagines that the bulk of the works were written in Venice during the first fifteen years of the eighteenth century. The scoring can sometimes offer a clue to the destination, but more often, alas, in a negative than a positive sense. The singers at San Marco comprised sopranos, altos, tenors, and basses capable, in each section, of taking both choral and solo parts. The eight-voice settings of the Mass and Compline would have been highly suitable for the ducal *cappella*. However, they would have served equally well for the solemn celebration, with male voices, of a major feast in some other Venetian church—either one with a *cappella* of its own such as the Frari or one that had to recruit its musicians externally. Even a similar occasion in some other city within the Venetian sphere of influence is not unthinkable. When we consider the Ospedaletto, with its all-female singers, the position is very different. Whereas both the Pietà and the Mendicanti routinely employed *figlie di coro* as tenors and basses (the latter probably transposing their part up an octave as need arose), and the Pietà, as we know from Vivaldi's music, occasionally produced tenor and bass soloists, the Ospedaletto and the Incurabili used only soprano and alto voices in solo and choral roles.[6] As a substitute for SATB scoring, the last two *ospedali* developed a peculiar kind of SSAA scoring in which the second alto part doubled the instrumental bass one or even two octaves higher.[7] Hence neither the Mass nor the Compline setting can have been composed for the Ospedaletto, although a solo motet for high voice with instruments such as *Astra campi, belli flores* would have been absolutely typical of its repertory. *Alme Jesu, sponse care* is an interesting and rather puzzling case. Virtually all the works in the Fondo Esposti at the Venice Conservatorio belong to the old repertory of the Pietà, and it is hard to imagine how this institution could have acquired a work written for the

[5] Jiří Fukač, 'Křižovnický hudební inventář', diss. (University of Brno, 1959), ii. 51, 61.

[6] Had male singers been present in the *cori* of the *ospedali*, as writers until recently suggested, the scandal would have been enormous. For that reason alone the possibility can be discounted. It remains to be established, however, whether the female basses at the Pietà and the Mendicanti sang their parts as far as possible at written pitch or routinely transposed them up an octave.

[7] The sacred vocal works by Porpora preserved in dated autograph MSS in the British Library include several written for the Ospedaletto and the Incurabili that feature this unusual SSAA scoring. It must be to the singers of the second alto part in these two *ospedali* that Charles Burney refers when he writes, in *The Present State of Music in France and Italy* ((London, 1771), p. 142): 'In these hospitals many of the girls sing in the counter tenor as low as A and G, which enables them always to keep below the *soprano* and *mezzo soprano*, to which they sing the base.'

Ospedaletto or, alternatively, how Vinaccesi, an outsider working at a rival institution, could have been asked to provide it with a new composition. A possible explanation is that this simple, intimate work was intended for the private recreation of one of the *figlie di coro*, being commissioned by a governor who was acting as her 'protector'.[8] In other words, it was not necessarily a repertory piece.

The full title of the Mass, appearing on fo. 7 of the vocal bass part of the first *coro* ('Basso primo'), runs:

Messa à Otto voci / Concertata con Stromenti e pol / servire sol li due primi violini / e due violette e in loco della Tromba / e del Obue puol sonare il Secondo / violino con Rinforzo del Terzo coro / Con il primo, e del quarto con il Secon/do, con il suo Basso Continuo per il / Secondo Choro, e Partitura per chi batte, / Parte num.° sedici due bassi continui et / una partitura e stromenti numero / Quattordici [deleted and replaced by 'Tredici'].

The name of the composer is not given here but heads each of the three sections (Kyrie, Gloria, Credo) in the organ part. The first and second vocal choirs each have reinforcing choirs (described respectively as 'third' and 'fourth' choirs). That this is not part of the original conception but a later addition is shown by the work's title, which specifies eight rather than 16 voices, and by the fact that the surviving parts for the extra choirs are written in a different hand from the rest. The parts for the third choir contain exactly the same music as the first choir in those movements for the full ensemble in which they participate, and similarly with the fourth and second choirs. The reason for creating the extra *cori* rather than simply writing 'tutti' in the original parts and their duplicates was doubtless that the singers were to be dispersed in four groups located in different parts of the church, following the contemporary vogue for polychordal performance.

The title goes on to speak of a complement of sixteen vocal parts and thirteen vocal ones. Unfortunately, only eleven vocal parts and six instrumental parts (three of these containing music for the Credo only) survive. One part, the second violin of the second choir, is a duplicate. The table below lists the full set of parts. Missing parts are enclosed in square brackets.

With so many parts lost, one might despair of gaining even a general impression of this massive work. Indeed, there is little that can be usefully said about the composition as a whole except that each of its component

---

[8] The complaints of Francesco Corner in 1718 that his colleagues on the governing board were interfering with his duties as *deputato sopra le figlie* show that at the Ospedaletto, as at the other *ospedali*, individual governors were apt to take a special interest in chosen *figlie di coro*. Another MS in the Fondo Esposti (Busta 127, no number) contains figured basses by Vinaccesi and Pollarolo, but it has proved impossible to tell to what type of composition these basses belong (if, indeed, they are not conceived purely as exercises). I am grateful to Paul Everett for informing me of this fragmentary source.

Coro I	Canto	Alto	[Tenore]	Basso	
Coro III	Canto	[Alto]	Tenore	[Basso]	
Coro I	[Violino]	[Violetta alto]	Violetta tenore	[Basso]^a	Organo^b
Coro I (?)	[Tromba]				
Coro I (?)	[Oboè]				
Coro II	[Canto]	Alto	Tenore	Basso	
Coro IV	[Canto]	Alto	Tenore	Basso	
Coro II	Violino	Violetta alto^c	Violetta tenore^c	[Basso]^a	[Organo]^b

^{a} No separate parts for bass stringed instruments survive, but they were probably present if the instrumental parts originally totalled 13.
^{b} These are presumably the 'due bassi continui' listed in the title.
^{c} These parts, together with a duplicate part for the second violin of the second *coro*, contain only the music of the Credo.

sections is divided into a number of movements differentiated by key, metre, tempo, and scoring, and that solo voices and instruments are employed copiously (hence the description 'concertata'). By a fortunate chance, however, there are two movements that can be reconstructed almost in their entirety: the two fugues ending the Kyrie and Credo sections respectively. Both are headed 'à capella'. In baroque terminology, as we saw, this means that any instruments present cease to be independent and attach themselves to a vocal part in an appropriate register. Thus the violin part of the second *coro* contains all the notes of the lost soprano (*canto*) part. The 'Et vitam venturi' fugue ending the Credo is complete in its essentials—except, conceivably, for a phrase on the violin of the first *coro* bridging the transition, in bars 11–12, between the separate expositions of the two subjects, which seems uncharacteristically thin.

This impressive fugue is fashioned in a highly methodical manner, as shown in the tabular analysis below.

Bars 1–12. Exposition of Subject 1 by Coro I.

Order of entries	T1	A1	S1	B1
Bar:	1	3	6	8
Key:	a	d	a	d

Bars 13–20. Exposition of Subject 2 by Coro II.

Order of entries:	S2	A2	T2	B2
Bar:	13	14	16	18
Key	a	d	a	d

Bars 21–5. Episode (bars 21–3 by Coro II, bars 24–5 by Coro I).
Bars 26–35. Simultaneous presentation of the two subjects (the two choirs exchange subjects but have entries in the same order as before).

Order of entries: Subj. 1	T2	A2	S2	B2
Order of entries: Subj. 2	S1	A1	T1	B1
Bar:	26	28	31	33
Key:	a	d	a	d

Bars 36–9. Stretto on first bar and a half of Subject 1.

Order of entries:	S1	T1	A1
Bar:	36	38	39
Key:	a	a	d

continued as:

Bars 40–4. Coda leading to final cadence in a.

This is a double fugue in the classic mould, introducing its two subjects in separate expositions and then combining them contrapuntally. Such fugues are much less common in the Italian tradition than in the German, which tends to value structural complexity more highly. Vinaccesi judges the relative proportions of the individual sections excellently. Although each voice enters just once in each of the three main sections (discounting the *stretto*), there is enough variety of spacing between successive entries to prevent an over-mechanical effect.

In three respects, the fugue is ultra-conservative. First, each voice presents each subject in only one key (and therefore only one register), preserving in an exceptionally strict form the old modal concept of *ambitus*. Second, the entries are confined to the tonic and one other key. This oscillation back and forth between only two tonal centres is quite common in fugues of the late seventeenth century (Buxtehude and Albinoni provide many examples) but is rarely insisted on so rigorously as here. Third, and most surprising, the second tonal centre (i.e. that of the fugal answer) is the subdominant, not the dominant. The home key, A minor, does not stand in the centre of its tonal universe, but at the periphery, since other cadences in minor keys occur only in D minor and G minor, never in E minor.[9] This, too, is a modal trait, albeit one coexisting with 'modern' tonal harmony.

Vinaccesi confronts head on the problem of writing for an exceptionally large number of contrapuntal voices, in this case as many as ten. Because of the high risk of committing solecisms (as well as overloading the texture), baroque composers commonly resort to a number of simple expedients to facilitate their task. The first is to rest several of the voices at any one time, so reducing the number of real parts. Antiphonal technique is here a useful device: two or more choirs can alternate with no, or only minimal, overlap. Undeniably, this can be a facile way of composing if used to excess, for it simply evades, rather than solves, the problem. The second technique is to use wherever possible chord progressions between triads whose roots are a third apart (thus with two notes in common) or,

[9] A comparable example of a 'peripheral' tonic is found in the setting of the fourth chorale verse in J. S. Bach's cantata *Christ lag in Todesbanden*, BWV 4. Here the home key, E minor, is located at the 'flat' extremity; the other minor keys visited are B and F sharp.

failing that, a fifth apart (with one note in common). This maximizes the opportunity to have 'binding notes' present in the same part in both chords (every good contrapuntist knows that oblique motion—where one part stays put—is virtually proof against solecisms). A third way is to 'double up' parts. Until the last few decades of the baroque period, composers tend to treat parts either as wholly independent of each other or as wholly dependent (i.e. identical). Exceptions are made for accompanying string parts, which are allowed to drift in and out of doubling the voices at the unison or the octave, and, naturally, for the continuo. It is rare, however, for two vocal parts to come together casually, unless special emphasis is required (as we shall see later in Ex. 29).

Barring these three kinds of solution (which can, of course, be combined in the same movement), the composer has to get round his problems of part-writing by taking various small licences. Consecutive fifths and octaves are avoided, as usual, when produced by similar motion but are now tolerated in contrary motion. The overlapping ('leapfrogging') of two parts moving in the same direction is allowed, and angularities of line that would be bizarre in writing for only four or five parts become almost the norm in voices not bearing a theme. In Ex. 27, which takes the fugue from the second half of the central episode up to the end of the 'combined' exposition, we see Vinaccesi introducing numerous minor irregularities of this kind once the number of active voices has passed the critical point, with the two entries in bar 30. It is characteristic of him not to seek easy solutions that would dilute the contrapuntal strength, but rather to revel in the kaleidoscopic interplay of the parts at the price of a little incorrectness that is hardly, if at all, perceptible to the listener. The music has a splendid panache, enhanced by some sudden florid excursions (e.g. in the tenor part of the first choir in bar 33).

The other *a cappella* fugue, the main part of the second Kyrie eleison, is another highly 'constructed' piece. Here there are also two subjects, but this time both are heard together right from the outset, each choir taking one subject. A set of middle entries allows the choirs to exchange subjects and reverse the sequence of keys (a, e, a, e becoming e, a, e, a). For the climax of the movement Vinaccesi produces a four-part *stretto* of one subject, accompanied by fragments of the other subject. The coda opens on a massive pedal-point.

The five compositions making up Vinaccesi's Compline setting have a similar style and scoring, except that the accompanying instruments are limited to two semi-obbligato violins and continuo. Lacking the glamour, in the modern perception, of Mass and Vespers, music for Compline has been little studied. Yet it held great importance in the seventeenth and early eighteenth centuries, as references in *Pallade veneta* to solemn celebrations of the service attest. It has rightly been pointed out that since its

Ex. 27. *Messa concertata a 8*, 'Et vitam venturi' (words omitted)

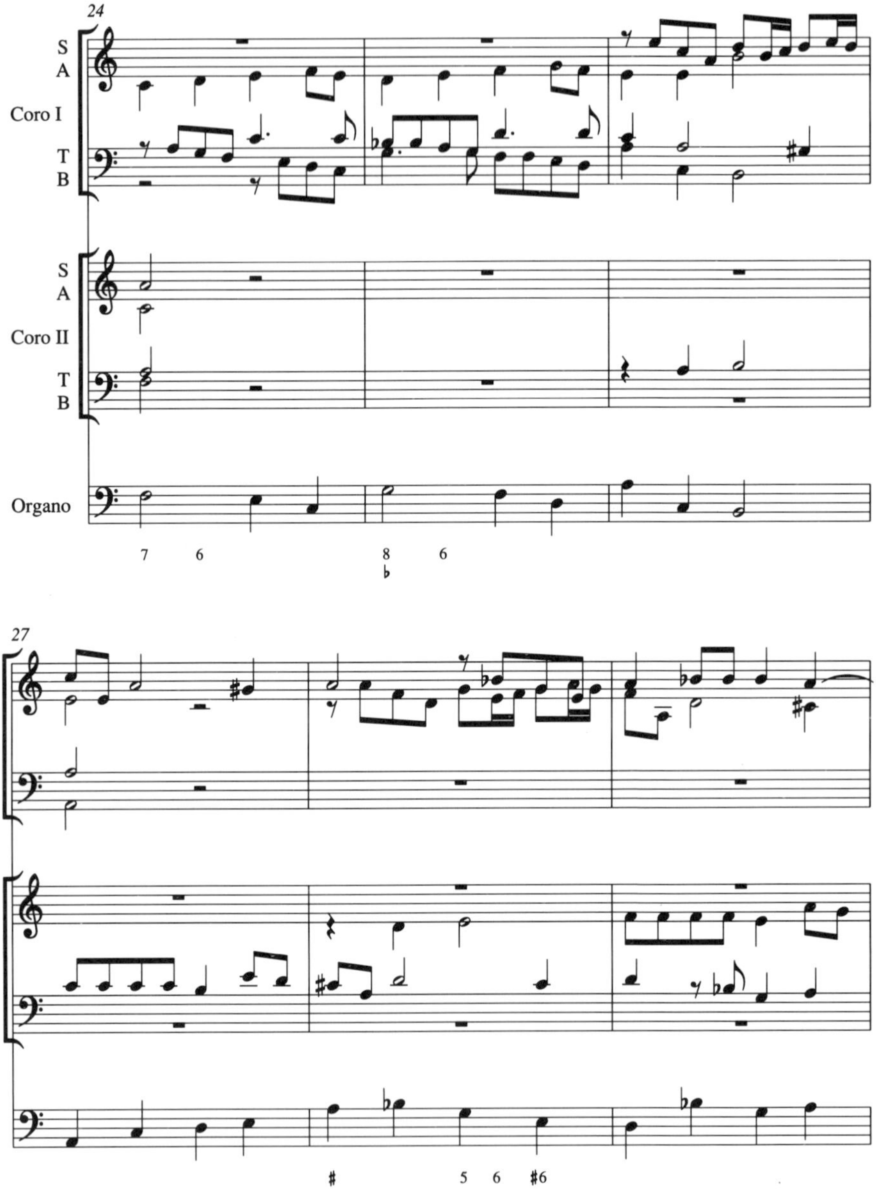

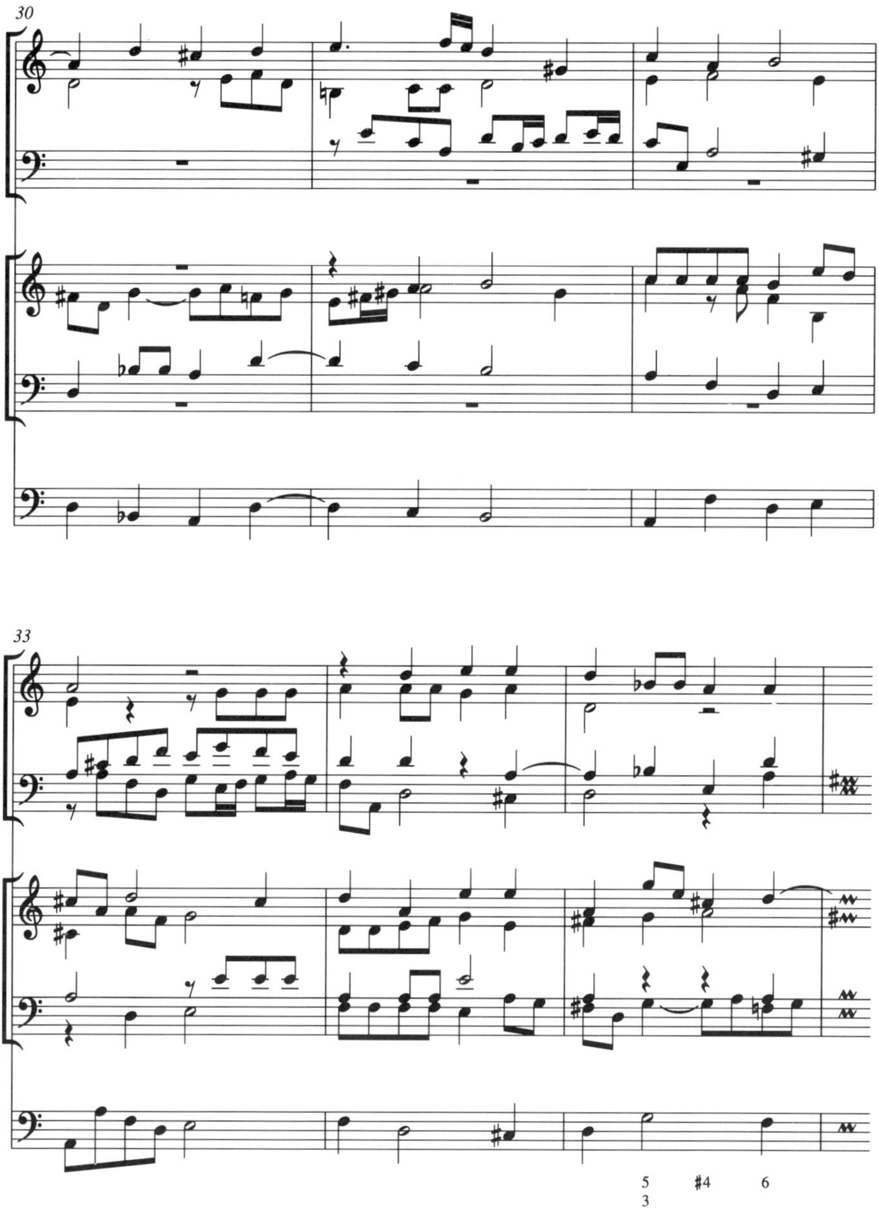
30
33
5
3
♯4
6

liturgy was simple and virtually unchanging from day to day, Compline was actually much better suited than Vespers to providing a framework for a 'sacred concert'.[10] The four psalms and the canticle that make up Vinaccesi's cycle of movements constituted the heart of the service, although many other portions, such as the hymn, the blessing, the confession, and the short responsory, were often set to music.[11]

If perhaps not actually written for San Marco, Vinaccesi's *Compieta a 8* is certainly in the style of the basilica. It makes an interesting comparison with an anonymous *De profundis a 8* for double SATB choir and continuo in the library of the Paris Conservatoire.[12] This work in the *stile antico*, dated 12 July 1700 (thus possibly an autograph), has been attributed by later hands first to Monferrato and subsequently to Partenio. A rather dull piece, the *De profundis* captures the responsorial style of psalmody by employing strict antiphony between the choirs, which usually take a semi-verse in turn. Climaxes are achieved when required by momentarily uniting the choirs.

Vinaccesi employs this technique in a more sophisticated and varied manner. The splendidly exuberant opening of his *In te Domine speravi*, shows as Ex. 28, demonstrates his consummate musicianship. The opening period (bars 1–5, overlapping into bar 6) begins with a snatch of unison canon, continued with imitation at the lower fifth. In the second half of bar 5 the choirs come together, synchronizing their words for the first time, in preparation for the cadence. The second period introduces the antiphonal style. To the words 'Inclina ad me aurem tuam', sung block-chordally by the second choir, the first choir responds with 'accelera ut eruas me', and so the pattern proceeds. The phrases to which the successive semiverses are set are made to overlap, which produces a tauter structure and a richer texture. Vinaccesi's treatment of the violins is instructive. Their relationship to the voices is ever-changing, entailing both doubling (usually at the upper octave in order to keep the violins in their favourite register and add a touch of lustre) and the provision of extra counterpoints. The composer pays careful attention to the coherence of the instrumental component in its own right—it would still make good musical sense if one were to play the two violin parts with the continuo bass in the manner of a trio sonata.

Ex. 29, taken from the end of *Qui habitat in adjutorio* just before the Doxology, shows one of Vinaccesi's most brilliant special effects. To illustrate the idea of longevity expressed in the words 'Longitudine dierum replebo eum' (With long life will I satisfy him) he segregates the two

[10] Jerome Roche, 'Musica diversa di Compieta: Compline and its Music in Seventeenth-Century Italy', *Proceedings of the Royal Musical Association*, 109 (1982–3), 60–79.
[11] In a table on pp. 64–5 Roche lists the parts of the service included in 84 settings of Compline published in Italy between 1601 and 1699.   [12] Shelfmark Ms. 2150.

Ex. 28. *In te Domine speravi*

soprano parts from the rest of the ensemble and gives them a slowly moving unison line in the style of a *cantus firmus* (or, perhaps better, a hexachord fantasia). Meanwhile, the lively antiphonal imitation of the lower parts continues unimpeded. In bars 63–5 Vinaccesi has a very attractive slow hemiola: the sopranos proceed upwards in three stages ($b\flat'$–c''–d''), while the bass executes a triadic figure sequentially in only two (g–e–c, f–d–$B\flat$). This kind of rhythmic manipulation belongs to the same category as that illustrated in Chapter 6 by Ex. 7, though now executed at a much higher artistic level.

Both Ex. 28 and Ex. 29 make copious use of the contrapuntal licences mentioned earlier. The final cadence of Ex. 29 is a case in point. On the third beat of bar 68 the second violin and the tenor of the second choir both have a D, while the soprano of the first choir has a C sharp. Moreover, the tenor, to avoid moving in consecutive octaves with the second violin, 'resolves' its suspension by leaping down a fourth. In practice, however, there would be nothing to offend the ear. Even the soprano's C sharp would be heard less as a harmony note than as a kind of accented lower auxiliary note to the suspended D.

If the *Compieta a 8* is, both as a cycle and in terms of its individual movements, Vinaccesi's most imposing sacred vocal work to have

Ex. 29. *Qui habitat in adjutorio*

63
- di - - - ne di - - - -
et o - sten - dam il - li,
e - um: et o - sten - dam il - li sa - lu - ta - re,
- di - - - ne di - - - -
et o - sten - dam il - li, et o - sten - dam
et o - sten - dam il - li sa - lu - ta - re, et o - sten - dam il - li sa - lu -
66
- e - - rum il - li sa - lu - ta - re, sa - lu - ta - re me - um.
et o - sten - dam il - li sa - lu - ta - re me - - um.
et o - sten - dam il - li sa - lu - ta - re, sa - lu - ta - re me - - um.
- e - - rum sa - lu - ta - re, sa - lu - ta - re me - - um.
il - li,
- ta - re, sa - lu - ta - re, sa - lu - ta - re me - - um.

survived, it does not have the originality of vision and perfection of workmanship found in many of his motets. The 1714 collection is a synthesis of all that is best in his music in any genre, marrying counterpoint to virtuosity, tradition to innovation.

By 'motet' one means, in the context of Italian music around 1700, something quite precise. Nowadays, the term is applicable to virtually any setting of a sacred text other than one conventionally identified by its liturgical function (e.g. Mass) or the first line of its text (e.g. Stabat Mater, Magnificat). In baroque France its range of meaning was, if anything, even wider, embracing almost any kind of composition employing sacred words, whether intended for performance in a church or not. In Italy, however, the term was reserved for a setting of an extra-liturgical text intended either as a substitute for a sung part of the liturgy or as a musical interpolation comparable with the instrumental pieces that were customarily performed during solemn services. The text could be a compilation from Scripture, patristic writings, or parts of the liturgy itself, or it could be freely invented. In either case, the ostensible function of a motet was to supply a pious commentary on the part of the service into which it was inserted, though its purely musical attraction, particularly as a means of putting solo voices on display, cannot be gainsaid.

In the seventeenth century, when the spirit of the Counter-Reformation remained strong, the papacy took a largely negative attitude towards the introduction of motets, attempting to control the choice of their texts and restrict the points in the service where they could be heard. In a series of bulls Alexander VII (1657, 1665), Innocent XI (1678), and Innocent XII (1692) instructed churches within the diocese of Rome not to substitute non-liturgical for liturgical items and to confine additions, at prescribed points, to settings of previously vetted extracts from canonical writings.[13] The fact that the three later edicts merely reiterate the code of practice laid down in the first shows how difficult it must have been for a central authority to regulate the use of motets in the face of established practice and popular feeling. Other localities attempted to impose similar restrictions. In Venice the Provveditori di Comun, responsible for most of the Venetian *scuole* (lay confraternities), ruled in 1639 that non-liturgical sung items were to be limited during Mass to the Offertory, the Elevation, and the Agnus Dei, and during Vespers to the intervals between the psalms.[14]

The ecclesiastical authorities had more success in determining the location of motets within services than in influencing their character. Throughout the baroque period there was a steady drift from polyphonic

[13] All four papal bulls are reprinted in trans. in Robert F. Hayburn, *Papal Legislation on Sacred Music, 95 A.D. to 1977 A.D.* (Collegeville, Minn., 1979), 76–81.

[14] *I-Vas*, Provveditori di Comun, Busta 47, fo. 52.

to solo motets (this despite the Church's official dislike of solo singing, expressed in the papal bulls just mentioned) and from compiled to invented texts. Both processes entailed secularization inasmuch as the stylistic models to be followed could no longer be found within the tradition of sacred music and had perforce to be taken from the secular realm.

The assimilation of the motet to the operatic aesthetic is shown very clearly in the practice of San Marco at Christmas, when it was the custom of the ducal church to engage five *musici forastieri* to sing solo motets. Four were performed at Mass on Christmas Night—respectively after the Epistle, during the Offertory, during the Sanctus or the Elevation, and during the Agnus Dei—and one after the Epistle at Mass on Christmas Day.[15] The singers were all well-known virtuosi who had come to Venice to sing in opera during the carnival season. However, it was more normal at San Marco for only one or two motets to be performed during a single Mass or Vespers. The *ospedali* followed the same practice: in the minutebook of the governors of the Mendicanti we find a reference, dated 27 December 1749, to 'l'antica usanza, comune a tutti gli altri luoghi pii della città, di eseguire per ogni vespero due mottetti; lo stesso in occasione delle messe solenne' ('the old practice, common to all the charitable institutions of the city, of performing two motets at each Vespers and likewise at each solemn Mass').[16]

Whereas texts assembled from canonical writings remained normal for choral motets, most of which were cast in the through-composed, multi-sectional form traditionally employed for settings of prose, free poetic texts soon gained the ascendancy in solo motets. Their verse took over virtually without alteration the metres, rhyme-schemes, and imagery of their closest secular counterpart, the cantata. The alternation of recitative and aria stanzas was firmly established by the last quarter of the seventeenth century, and the division of aria stanzas into two semistrophes, in anticipation of a *da capo* setting, followed soon afterwards.[17] One important feature sets the motet apart from the cantata, however: the custom of ending the work with an extended 'Alleluja'. This simple word, each of whose four syllables can bear an accent or receive a melisma, offers the composer a chance to forget the constraints that normally apply in

---

[15] *I-Vas*, PdS, Registro 40, Libro di scontro 1708–1719, entries dated 28 Feb. 1708 [m.v.], 16 Mar. 1710, 14 Mar. 1711, 29 Dec. 1711, and 30 Dec. 1712. In 1711 a violinist, Francesco Veracini, replaced the customary singer at the Agnus Dei on Christmas Night. This substitution suggests that there was a considerable overlap of function between vocal and instrumental interpolations (i.e. between motets and sonatas) in Italian church music around 1700. In 1711, exceptionally, a second motet was sung on Christmas Day, at the Offertory.

[16] Transcribed in Scarpa, *Arte e musica all'Ospedaletto*, 188.

[17] G. B. Quaglia's 2 vols. of *Motetti sacri a voce sola* (respectively Bologna, 1668, and Bergamo, 1675) exemplify the new-style solo motet. Although *da capo* structure is not employed, a distinction between aria and recitative is clearly evident—some movements in the 2nd vol. are even given the title 'Aria'.

text-setting and enter the world, almost, of pure music. Nowhere do solo motets more justify their description as 'concertos for voice' (an expression first coined by Denis Arnold for Vivaldi's motets) than in these exultant closing movements or sections.

The poetic texts of such motets resemble those of cantatas in another respect: they are nearly all anonymous. As regards literary quality, they are at best workmanlike, at worst execrable. The traveller Pierre Jean Grosley exaggerated very little when he described them as 'un mauvais assemblage rimé de mots latins, où les barbarismes et les solécismes sont plus communs que le sens et la raison'.[18] The same writer believed that they were commonly the work of sacristans—persons of limited education occupying one of the lowest rungs in the ecclesiastical hierarchy—and even if this is an unfair generalization, we have no better information. As a sample of a typical text for a solo motet, we may quote that of Vinaccesi's *Astra campi, belli flores*.

Astra campi, belli flores,	Stars of the meadow, pretty flowers,
gemebunda, suspirando,	groaning and sighing,
amo, quaero, volo vos.	I love, seek, and desire you.
Dilectum meum quaesivi	I searched for my loved one
per vicos et plateas.	along streets and squares.
In simplicitate cordis mei circuivi	In the simplicity of my heart
civitatem, quaesivi	I crossed the city in search of him
illum e non inveni.	but did not find him.
Venti placidi, amati Zephyri,	Gentle winds, beloved Zephyrs,
inter lilia	you blow among the lilies
ventilate sed tacete.	but remain silent.
Ubi quiescit amor meus,	Whisper to me, o breezes,
bonus Deus,	where my love, my good God,
aurae tacite docete.	is resting.
Alleluja	Alleluja.

Atrocious dog-Latin this may be, but it serves its religious and musical purposes very adequately. The theme is simplicity itself: the soul's yearning for God, likened to the search for a lost lover. This is truly a motet 'per ogni tempo', appropriate to any occasion in the church year. The imagery, replete with the usual Arcadianisms, makes play with symbols common to the pagan and Christian traditions such as the lily, emblem of purity. The structure of two arias framing a brief recitative plus a final 'Alleluja' is exactly tailored to the requirements of both the singer and the occasion.

Although *Astra campi, belli flores* is the only motet for solo voice and

---

[18] *Nouveaux mémoires ou observations sur l'Italie et sur les Italiens par deux gentilshommes suédois* (Paris, 1764), ii. p. 53.

string accompaniment by Vinaccesi to have survived, he must have written, in the course of his career, a very large number of similar works, primarily for the Ospedaletto but perhaps also for other Venetian institutions. The manuscript originates from the Österreich-Bokemeyer collection but unlike the unreliably attributed *Angelici chori*, discussed earlier, is not copied in Österreich's own hand. The two arias, of which only the first is in *da capo* form, are attractive specimens of the 'aria con istrumenti', as already encountered in Vinaccesi's dramatic music. The 'Alleluja', however, follows different structural principles. There are four vocal sections, all accompanied only by bass; each is followed by a section for the string ensemble. To knit together the eight sections, all of which save two are complete musical periods in their own right, Vinaccesi employs the same 'motto' technique that one encounters in the pre-Vivaldian instrumental concerto.[19] Each new period begins with a transposition or paraphrase of the opening idea, continued differently each time. The form can be represented schematically as in the table below.

Period	Bars	Scoring	Tonality
1	1–11	voice	C modulating to G
2	12–21	strings	G modulating to a
3	22–30	voice	a modulating to d
4	31–38	strings	d modulating to C (half-close)
5	39–51	voice	C
6.1	52–55	strings	C
6.2	56–60	voice	C
7	61–66	strings	C

In all periods except the first and fifth the first chord overlaps with the cadential note of the previous period, preserving continuity. Ex. 30 gives the first two periods and the beginning of the third. It shows Vinaccesi in his best *bel canto* mood. Nevertheless, one finds the usual mild asperities: the *notes échappées* in bars 5, 6, and 16 (unison violins); the upwardly transposed resolution of a suspension in bar 12 (bass); the rhythmic dislocation in bar 22 (voice and bass). In each period the melodic line ends with an upward sweep, expressive of the joyful sentiment.

Alme Jesu, sponse care is virtually indistinguishable in style from the simple type of continuo cantata, even lacking the final 'Alleluja' that, as we saw, is a distinguishing mark of the motet. It consists merely of two rather bland *da capo* arias that enclose a short recitative. It would be interesting to know whether there existed, in late-baroque Italy, a tradition of

---

[19] 'Motto' form is employed in most of the fast movements of the concertos in Torelli's Op. 6 (1698) and Albinoni's Op. 2 (1700).

Ex. 30. *Astra campi, belli flores*, fourth movement

motets identical with the *cantata spirituale* except for the the choice of Latin in preference to the vernacular, or whether *Alme Jesu, sponse care* was an occasional composition belonging to no established subgenre.

Vinaccesi's remaining motets—the fourteen in the 1714 collection and six other pieces whose status as independent works or fragments of longer works is problematic—are all, as the composer writes in his preface to his publication, sacred duets and terzets.[20] That is, they are the equivalent, in the sacred sphere, of chamber duets and terzets such as Steffani and Handel composed, and they accordingly have free, madrigalian texts. This concept was very progressive within the tradition of the 'few-voiced' motet, which even in the first decades after 1700 more commonly retained the prose texts and multisectional structure (within the framework of a single movement) inherited from the Renaissance. Monferrato's Op. 18 (1681), Colonna's Op. 3 (1681), Caldara's Op. 4 (1715): all adopt the old approach. Even Biffi's manuscript collection of 18 motets for three voices, which was assembled, possibly as a valedictory act, near the end of his life, remains faithful to tradition, though in purely stylistic terms it is scarcely less modern than Vinaccesi's collection.[21] Like that of his colleague, Biffi's collection is expressly intended for performance at San Marco, which suggests that the basilica was, after all, rather conservative in its tastes. What our composer has done, in fact, is to marry the 'secular' form of the new-style solo motet to the polyphonic musical language of the old-style ensemble motet. The synthesis seems entirely original: unprecedented and indeed unrepeated.

Appendix C.9 lists the works in the 1714 collection. The ten three-voice compositions are all for soprano, alto, and bass, with organ accompaniment. To judge from Biffi's collection, a third of whose works are for exactly the same combination, this was a popular form of scoring at San Marco; Monferrato also employs it. The four works for only two voices are variously for soprano and alto (no. 11), soprano and bass (no. 14), and two sopranos (nos. 9 and 10); in the last case the part for the second soprano, termed 'Canto secondo', is contained in the volume normally for alto. With only two exceptions, the works are laid out in four movements following the plan Aria-Recitative-Aria-Alleluja.[22]

---

[20] Much of the material in the later part of this chapter is anticipated in the author's article 'The Marcian Motets of Benedetto Vinaccesi'.

[21] Biffi's collection is preserved in two separate MSS. One (Venice, Biblioteca di San Marco, B. 314) gives its title in Italian as 'Mottetti a tre sole voci e organo'; the other (Florence, Conservatorio di Musica 'Luigi Cherubini', B. 357) gives it in Latin as 'Cantica sacra duodeviginti tribus vocibus concinenda'. Both are dated 1731.

[22] The description 'recitative' refers in the first instance to the character of the verse, which is written, in imitation of Italian *versi sciolti*, in generally unrhymed lines of seven and eleven syllables. However, the type of musical setting employed by Vinaccesi for recitative stanzas is not limited to ordinary recitative sung by a single voice at a time but also includes 'ensemble' recitative, *arioso*, and cavata. Very often, more than one type of setting is employed during a single stanza.

An eighteenth-century manuscript score of the complete 1714 collection, perhaps prepared for purposes of study, exists in Bologna.[23] The second and fifth motets, copied into parts, survive in Aosta.[24] In each case, the manuscript can be shown, from the nature of the errors it contains, to be a copy derived from the printed parts rather than an earlier source for the work in question. The remaining contemporary sources, divided between Assisi (Sacro Convento di San Francesco) and Padua (Biblioteca Antoniana, the library of the Basilica del Santo), between them transmit portions of all except two of the motets, but in a curiously dismembered form. Details are given in Appendix C.10. All the fragments were copied by only two hands. Originally, they must have constituted a unified collection, but at some stage—perhaps in consequence of the circulation of music between Franciscan houses—the group of manuscripts was divided into two.[25] It seems that the two-voice settings went to Assisi, while the three-voice ones went to (or remained in?) Padua.[26]

The most common way in which material from the motets was used was by extracting a *da capo* aria and presenting its two sections ('A' and 'B') as ostensibly separate 'motets' forming a pair comparable with the sonata-pairs of Domenico Scarlatti. There is never any indication of a *da capo* reprise of the first 'motet' (i.e. the 'A' section), which is quite remarkable in view of the fact that not all the 'B' sections are tonally closed. In one case (no. 5) the arranger pairs two different arias from the same work; this is made possible by the fact that both arias are unitary in form and have no *da capo*. The Padua manuscript B.II.608 even manages to combine the 'A' section of no. 12 with the 'B' section of no. 1.

Other manuscripts form single 'motets' out of various combinations of aria sections, settings of recitative stanzas (not those, however, in which actual recitative occurs), and 'Alleluja' final movements taken from the

---

[23] *I-Bc*, KK 306.

[24] Biblioteca Capitolare, Cartella 5, fos. 95–103, and Cartella 7, fos. 35–6, respectively. The first MS contains five parts (the four of the printed edition plus an extra part for cello, doubling the *Organo*), while the second has only the soprano (*Canto*) part. It is possible that the copy-text of these MSS was the printed edn. today in the archive of the collegiate church of Sant'Orso, also in Aosta.

[25] Claudio Sartori comments on the exchange of musical MSS between Franciscan communities (a practice certainly shared by other religious orders) in the preface to his catalogue *Assisi: La Cappella della Basilica di S. Francesco, i: Catalogo del fondo musicale nella Biblioteca Comunale di Assisi* (Milan, 1962). Since the catalogue was published, the collection has moved back from the Biblioteca Comunale to its original home, the Convento di San Francesco. The presence of the autograph MS of Vivaldi's motet *Vos aurae per montes*, RV 634, in Assisi rather than in the archive of the Basilica del Santo, for whose patronal festival it was written, confirms the link between the Franciscans of Padua and Assisi.

[26] The first aria of the sixth motet, which is for three voices, is an apparent exception to this statement, since it is found in Assisi rather than Padua. The interesting and perhaps significant thing is, however, that the Assisi source lacks its bass part: by default the aria has become a movement *a due voci*.

same work. This procedure is used for nos. 2, 4, 6, and 12. In no. 4 the first of the paired movements is the 'A' section of the second aria, while the second is its opening aria (in unitary form). The puzzling reversal of the original sequence is explained by the fact that the opening aria begins with the word 'alleluja', anticipating the text and music of the 'Alleluja' proper that rounds off the work; in other words, the abridger is using this aria as a substitute 'Alleluja' finale. In one case (no. 2) three rather than two elements are joined together: a recitative with cavata, the 'A' section of the aria following it, and the final 'Alleluja'.

As we learned in Chapter 4, the Paduan 'motets' were discovered and evaluated before the printed originals, of which they are mere fractions, became widely known. The manuscript B.II.604 contains two modern scores and a set of parts (totalling, with duplicates, 48) for the 'B' sections of the second and the first motets from the 1714 collection respectively. A note on one score tells us that this new concoction, which must have been prepared from the manuscripts B.II.621 and B.II.608/2, was performed, presumably by the Cappella Antoniana, in 1913. B.II.621, as well as containing the original parts for the 'A' and 'B' sections of the second aria of no. 2, *Adorata stella maris*, holds a score and set of parts for the same music prepared by Giovanni Tebaldini. This edition was published in 1959, seven years after Tebaldini's death, under the title of *Si consurgis quasi aurora*, the first line of the aria.[27] It represents the first music by Vinaccesi to have appeared in print since 1714. Three years later there appeared a similar edition by Vittore Zaccaria of the opening aria of the thirteenth motet, *Ad amantis Christi mensam* (from B.II.614).[28]

Zaccaria's edition was a supplement to an article by him summarizing the state of knowledge about Vinaccesi in 1962.[29] Because he was aware that most of the so-called motets in Padua (he seems not to have known of those in Assisi) also occurred as constituent movements of the motets in the 1714 print, Zaccaria had to explain the relationship between the manuscript and published sources. Perversely, he assumed that the manuscript compositions were the original 'motets', each printed work forming, as it were, a 'suite' of five or six movements.[30] This thesis is absolutely unsustainable. Multi-movement motets were the norm, not the exception, when free poetic texts were employed. In any case, the literary texts of

[27] Suppl. (5 pp.) to *Musica sacra*,[2] 4 (1959). The edn., generously supplied with editorial marks of expression, includes a realization of the organ continuo. It is interesting to note that Tebaldini recognizes that the first 'motet' is to be repeated after the second in *da capo* fashion—a correct inference, but not one indicated by the source.

[28] Suppl. (7 pp.) to *Musica sacra*,[2] 7 (1962). Zaccaria's manner of editing is similar to Tebaldini's but more restrained with regard to suggestions for performance.

[29] 'Benedetto Vinaccesi (Brescia 1670c.–Venezia 1719): Profilo bio-bibliografico', *Musica sacra*,[2] 7 (1962), 12–15, 86–9, and 119–25.

[30] Ibid. 124.

the Paduan movements are manifestly incomplete, and those apparent movements (in reality, only sections) that lack tonal closure can never have been intended to stand on their own.

But one has then to explain why those for whom the copyists of the Padua and Assisi manuscripts wrote out this music wished to have extracts from the original compositions rather than the whole. Any answer must be tentative. It does seem, however, that the exceptional length and complexity of the printed motets were a deterrent to their dissemination. Few *cappelle* can have had the expertise of the singers of San Marco or the style of service that would accommodate an extra-liturgical piece lasting ten minutes or more. The Padua and Assisi manuscripts perhaps represent an attempt to 'domesticate' the motets, to save them for the active repertory of a provincial church by reducing them to a more familiar scale.

The Padua collection also contains five pieces, described individually as 'motteto', that are not found in the 1714 print. They are written in a distinct hand and come in the form of separate parts without a score (whereas the remainder always include both a score and parts). All are intended for feasts of the Blessed Virgin Mary. These movements are:

B.II.619/2	Videte, filiae Sion	[S], A, B, Organ[31]
B.II.620	Adeste canentes	S, S, B, Organ
	O Maria, si me amas	S, A, B, Organ
B.II.621	Caelestis horti	A, T, B, Organ
	Stellarum fulgores	A, T, B, Organ.

Unlike many of the other 'motets' in Padua these five appear complete enough to stand as whole movements (arias), although none employs the *da capo* convention. There is a suspicion, judging from their style, that they belong to a slightly earlier phase of Vinaccesi's career. *Caelestis horti*, for instance, has a strong Mixolydian flavour. The keynote is A, but the key signature has two sharps, and for its tonal excursions the music cadences in the subdominant, D, in preference to the dominant, E. By far the most impressive movement is *Adeste canentes*. It shows Vinaccesi's skill at handling contrast-motives. Each particle of text has its own characteristic motive, which the composer repeats, develops, and presents in counterpoint against other motives with superb inventiveness and flair. The ground plan of this movement is as shown in the table below.

The music gains much of its strength from effective dramatization. Lines 1–2 beseech the heavenly hosts to come ('Adeste canentes, | O chori superni'), while lines 3–4 bid the dragons of Hell fly away in dread ('Volate timentes, | Dracones Inferni'). Initially, Vinaccesi allots the former to the sopranos, whose high register and parallel thirds (varied with

---

[31] B.II.619/1 is 'Si consurgis quasi aurora', the 'A' section of the second aria of the second motet in the 1714 collection (also found, paired with its matching 'B' section, in B.II.621).

Period	Bars	Key	Voice(s)	Lines	Comments
1	1–9	A	S1	1–2	Exposition for one voice.
2	10–20	A	S1, S2	1–2	The same for two voices. S2 anticipates the cadence by entering in bar 8.
3	21–7	A–E	B	3–4	Exposition for one voice.
4	28–38	E	S1, S2	1–2	Slightly abridged repeat of period 2, with some voice-exchange.
5	39–45	E–A	B	3–4	Version of period 3 to fit the new tonal context.
6	46–62	A	S1, S2	1–2	Rapid dialoguing between SS and B.
			B	3–4	
7	63–71	A	S1, S2, B	1–2	Imitative elaboration by all voices.
8	72–84	A	S1, S2, B	3–4	Imitative elaboration by all voices.

intertwining imitations) readily conjure up a choir of angels. Conversely, the bass voice, with its inherent weakness for braggadocio, is the ideal mouthpiece for the infernal powers. Vinaccesi allows the movement to develop at a leisurely pace. The dramatic antithesis is first proposed in periods 1–3, is repeated in paraphrased form in periods 4–5, and finally comes to a head in period 6, where the fragmentation of melodic lines (now broken down into their constituent motives) suggests the cut-and-thrust of a skirmish at close quarters. It is left to periods 7 and 8 to supply an apotheosis: the heavenly hosts and the dragons of Hell are accorded the full contrapuntal treatment in turn . Nothing less than a complete transcription can show quite how cogent this movement is, but Ex. 31, comprising the third and eighth periods, will illustrate both Vinaccesi's skill at word-painting and his ability to plan ahead.

One further motet-fragment survives separately from the 1714 print. This is the *da capo* aria *Mensa dulcis et iucunda* in the Marciana.[32] Scored for two tenors and bass, a combination that became popular at San Marco in the nineteenth century with the decline and eventual demise of the castrato tradition, this movement is identical in general conception to the arias in the 1714 motets, although one detail—the provision of an organ ritornello in the dominant midway through the 'A' section—is individual.

Turning now to the 1714 collection itself, we may begin by considering the place of motets in services held in the ducal church. Information of a general kind is abundant, since successive *Ceremoniali* lay down quite precisely when motets are to be performed and what type of motet is required.[33] Some services call for 'mottetti a cappella'. These are old-style

[32] *I-Vnm*, Cod. it. IV–1073 (= 10845).
[33] Transcribed and discussed in Moore, *Vespers at St. Mark's*, i. 68–71 and 231–330 *passim*.

Ex. 31. *Adeste canentes,*

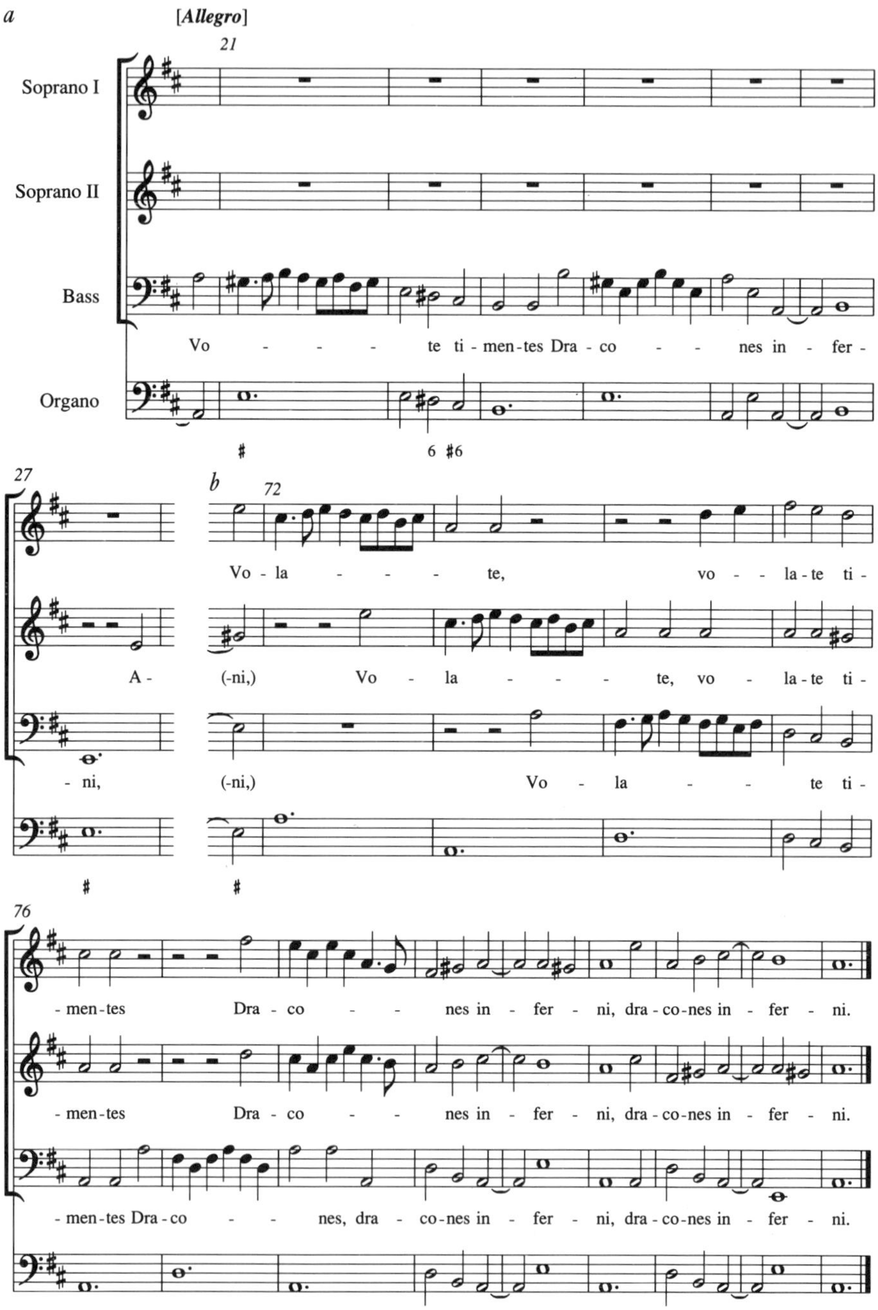

choral motets, performed with or without organ and perhaps sometimes with doubling strings. For obvious reasons, they were preferred on those occasions when the *cappella ducale* travelled with the doge to other Venetian churches. Most motets, however, are specified as 'in organo' (or 'nell'organo'). The 1761 edition of a *tavola* enumerating the duties of members of the *cappella* prescribes that at every Mass during which the *pala d'oro*, the gold altarpiece, is displayed (almost equivalent to saying: on every important festival) a 'mottetto a tre in organo' is to be sung.[34] As for Vespers, the *Ceremoniale magnum* of 1678 stipulates that when the *pala d'oro* is displayed and the doge is not present, the singers should perform 'un mottetto in organo a due voci, o come pare al loro Maestro'.[35]

The placing of the two or three singers needed for these motets, assuming that it was fixed by custom, is not easy to determine. James Moore is probably right to identify the *nicchie*, housing the portable organs, as the favoured sites.[36] In fact, a reference in the procurators' minutes not only reinforces this belief but also suggests that it was the *nicchia* on the North side of the church—the same side as the larger principal organ—from which the singers traditionally performed. On 23 July 1730 the procurators resolved to scrap the *organetto* 'ove cantano li Moteti' on account of its old age and general unserviceability.[37] Since the *organetto* on the South side had been rebuilt by Felice de Beni in late 1720, the other instrument must have been the one meant. The identification of the organ that accompanied the singers is equally problematic, for since the players of the *organetti* were required to attend only on especially important feasts, the principal organist on duty for the week must have been their normal accompanist. This raises the possibility that the organ used for these motets was not the portable instrument in the *nicchia* concerned but one of the main organs.

Despite the close connection of the fourteen motets with liturgical practice at San Marco, only one of them, *Inter cantica votiva*, is related by text to a specifically 'Marcian' occasion. The subject is St Mark, the patron saint of Venice, who was commemorated in four separate feasts at the basilica: the saint's day itself (25 April), the Translation of his Body (31 January), the Apparition of his Body (25 June), and the Dedication of the Church (8 October). We may note also that three of the motets have texts relating to the Blessed Sacrament. Although this was a common enough subject, San Marco laid special emphasis on feasts connected with it. The first three days of January constituted a triduum when the Blessed Sacrament was exposed, and the devotional theme returned on Corpus Domini and in the two feasts (the third Friday in March and 3 May) when the Most Precious Blood was displayed.

[34] *Vespers at St. Mark's*, 306.   [35] Ibid. 151.   [36] Ibid. 83.
[37] *I-Vas*, PdS, Registro 153, fo. 126^v.

What has been said earlier about the mutual assimilation of Christian, Jewish, and pagan imagery applies with especial force to the texts of these works. The 'Stella maris' (punning on the name of Mary) is sister to the 'astrum' that governs a person's fate. The 'turtur' grieving for a lost mate is the same as the 'columba' whose white colour is emblematic of purity. The 'Olympi regnans' is as much Jehovah as Jupiter. The favourite operatic motif of a storm at sea (evoked with words such as 'procella', 'nubes', and 'unda') now becomes a metaphor for moral uncertainty: the safe haven sought by the lost soul has become the Redeemer himself.

As usual, the poet has to a large extent 'programmed' the form of setting to be adopted, in each movement, by the composer. But Vinaccesi has in five cases boldly overridden the poet's prescription. In no. 8, *Turtur amans lamentatur*, the text for the third aria (as we will continue to call lyrical movements, even though most are set for the full complement of two or three voices), clearly identified as such by its metre, rhyme-scheme, and division into two balanced semistrophes, is set instead as an 'ensemble' recitative (first semistrophe) plus cavata (second semistrophe). The reason for the change was probably that, having already provided two arias, the composer felt that an alternative form of treatment was now needed for the sake of variety. In the second aria of no. 3, *Floret iam in horto caeli*, Vinaccesi has a fully written-out reprise of the 'A' section that differs considerably from its first statement, which ended with a cadence in the dominant. 'Vide quas purpurea gerunt', the second aria of no. 4, *Alleluja | Gaudeat orbis*, goes even further in the direction of varying the repeat of the 'A' section, since the reprise is completely reworked from the original motives. Both arias of no. 14, *Si nescis cor meum*, depart from the expected simple *da capo* form. The first reverts to an old model by assigning each semistrophe to the respective section of a binary-form movement. The second becomes a kind of *aria a due* reminiscent of the double arias for the Elders in *Susanna*. The soprano alone sings the first semistrophe, whose music, paraphrased and taken into the dominant key, is used by the bass for the second semistrophe. Finally, the two voices sing together in counterpoint, returning to the text of the first semistrophe. Vinaccesi was perhaps prompted to adopt this unusual but very satisfying scheme by the strong textual link between the semistrophes, both of which begin with the words 'Sat non fuit'.[38]

All the motets begin with an aria. Although motets beginning with recitative are not unknown, they are far less common, proportionately

[38] The form of tripartite organization that makes one instrument or voice present its material in the tonic, another repeat it in the dominant, and both together restate it in the tonic is not uncommon in the late baroque. It is found in the central movement of a concerto for trumpet and two oboes by Telemann, and Vivaldi employs it in the duet 'Qui per darci amabil pace' in *La Senna festeggiante*, RV 693. The naïvety of this form is often complemented by simplicity of musical material.

speaking, than cantatas opening in that way. The main reason for this is probably a desire for brevity, but another factor may be a wish to engage the attention—to ravish the senses—of the listener without preliminaries. Fortunately, the presence of an 'Alleluja', which confirms the original key, allows the composer to place the second aria in a different tonality—an opportunity for variety lacking in a cantata that adheres to the ARA scheme. Vinaccesi's second arias are generally in a closely related key; only that of no. 8 ventures further afield, being in the flattened mediant (G major as compared with E major). The poet has done his best to differentiate the mood of the arias, and the composer responds with contrasts of tempo, metre, and other elements.

Were one to sum up what lends distinction to these motets (leaving aside the originality of their form), one would mention three things in particular. The first is the breadth of their musical treatment—the same quality for which Handel and Bach are rightly prized. Seventeenth-century Italian music tends to be short-winded: it allows itself little room in which to develop its ideas. Vinaccesi's motets, however, breathe the air of the eighteenth century, limiting the number of significant motives but allowing each to unfold logically over a relatively long time-span. Their second special quality is the boldness of their part-writing. By occasionally admitting the inadmissible, the composer is enabled to introduce contrapuntal combinations of startling novelty and piquancy. But perhaps their most remarkable achievement is to maintain a strong lyrical impulse in every voice regardless of the complexity of the counterpoint.

Two musical examples will illustrate these points. The first, Ex. 32, shows the opening of the second aria of the first motet, *Inter cantica votiva*. Like many such arias, it launches itself with a fugal exposition, whose motives are then developed further, in association with new musical ideas, to end the section.[39] The long subject is bipartite, employing first conjunct, then disjunct, motion. Its answer enters, in bar 7, on an 'illicit' dissonance—a seventh over the bass that doubles the seventh already present in the soprano part. Two bars later the soprano pauses, keeping the texture open and helping to highlight the entry of the countersubject on the upbeat to bar 12. This countersubject, vigorously thrusting from side to side, is an effective representation in music of a lion (standing for St Mark and for Venice) spreading his wings. Once the bass has delivered the subject and countersubject, Vinaccesi strikes out towards the region of the related minor keys, eventually reaching a cadence in A minor in bar 34, halfway through the 'A' section. After bar 25 the counterpoint becomes denser and more intricate, almost Bachian in its use of contrary motion to generate tension.

---

[39] 'B' sections are constructed similarly to 'A' sections, except that they are generally less expansive. Several are tonally 'open', which almost inevitably makes their nature more discursive.

Ex. 33 shows the end of the 'A' section of the first aria of *Conversae in pias lacrimas*, no. 11. The extract begins with a familiar Corellian topos, the V–I melodic progression answered by VI–II, and appears to be about to continue with another—a 'leapfrogging' sequence in which suspensions, in alternate voices, are heard one note higher each time. But at the start of bar 20 Vinaccesi frustrates this expectation, and the sequence develops in an original fashion (though still in strict imitation), with extravagant flights in both voices. The 'A 'section is rounded off, in Vinaccesi's normal manner, with a brief organ ritornello that without repeating earlier material in literal form provides a satisfying conclusion. Although the manuscript parts for *Adorata stella maris* in Aosta include a cello part, it is uncertain whether the composer intended the bass of the organ part to be

Ex. 32. *Inter cantica votiva*, third movement

15
- dat, a - las su - as ex - pan-dat
le - o, ex - pan - - - - dat le-o,
hoc Re-ga-le Im-pe - ri-um A - las su - as ex - pan-dat le-o, ex-
5 6 6 7 ♮6 5 6
22
le - o, ex-pan - - - - -
a - las su - as ex - pan-dat le-o, ex-pan - - -
- pan - - - - - dat, ex - pan -
7 6 7 6 7 6 6 ♮4 #6 6 6 #6 6 #6
28
- - - - - - - - - - - - - - dat le - o,
- - - - - - - - - dat, ex - pan - - dat le - o,
- dat le - o, ex-pan - - - - dat le - o,
#

Ex. 33. *Conversae in pias lacrimas*, first movement

reinforced by a melody instrument as a matter of course; at any rate, there seems to be no pragmatic objection to employing organ alone.

The spirit of the eighteenth century informs the 'Alleluja' movements even more strongly. Here one can find virtuosic roulades, often organized into long sequences, that point to Vinaccesi's younger contemporary Vivaldi. The most taxing of them occurs in no. 10, *Amor care, o Jesu dilecte*, where the first soprano leads off with a stream of 38 semiquavers. Many of the 'Alleluja' movements adopt the 'motto' form mentioned earlier in connection with the solo motet.

In many ways, the most interesting movements are the through-composed ones that are settings of recitative verse. None of them is content purely to employ simple recitative. Half introduce 'ensemble' recitative (i.e. block-chordal, syllabic delivery of the lines by the full complement of voices), and all contain at least one cavata in imitative style following a section of recitative. The second movement of no. 8, *Turtur amans lamentatur*, ends each of its two sections of solo recitative with a few bars of *arioso*. Eight of the movements are rounded off by a ritornello.

It is impossible to convey briefly the full variety of treatment in these movements, but the second movement of no. 12, *Densae nubes solem velant*, is not untypical. This motet is one of the three intended for celebrations of the Blessed Sacrament, and the purpose of the second stanza is to comment on the mystery of the Host more directly than is appropriate in the aria stanzas. This is its text:

Hic deitas immensa	Here an immense deity
brevi stringitur giro.	is confined within a narrow compass.
Et quem non valent circumscribere caeli	And He whom the heavens cannot circumscribe

Ex. 34. *Densae nubes solem velant*, second movement

Ex. 34. *Cont.*

17
an - ge - lo - rum pa - nis,
hic pe - cto - ri - bus hu - ma - nis Ne - ctar cae - le - ste et an - ge - lo -
Pa - ra - tur hic pe -
5 4
20
Pa - ra - tur hic Ne - - ctar cae - le - ste et
- rum pa - nis, ne - - ctar cae - le - ste, cae - le - ste,
- cto - ri - bus hu - ma - nis Ne - ctar cae - le - ste et an - ge -
4 3 4 3 4 3 4 #3
23
an - ge - lo - rum pa - - nis,
Pa - ra - tur hic pe - cto - ri - bus hu - ma - nis Ne -
- lo - rum pa - - nis, Pa - ra - tur hic pe - cto - ri - bus hu -

26
Pa - ra - tur hic pe - cto - ri - bus hu - ma - nis Ne -
- ctar cae - le - ste et an - ge - lo - - rum pa - nis,
- ma - nis Ne - - ctar cae - le - ste et an - ge - lo - rum pa - nis,
2 #6 #4 6
29
- ctar cae - le - ste et an - ge - lo - rum pa - - nis, ne - ctar cae -
ne - ctar cae - le - ste et an - ge - lo - rum
ne - - ctar cae - le - ste et an - ge - lo - rum, et an - ge - lo - rum
#4 6 #6
32
- le - ste et an - ge - lo - rum, et an - ge - lo - - rum pa - nis,
pa - nis, ne - ctar cae - le - ste et an - ge - lo - rum, an - ge - lo - rum pa - nis,
pa - nis, ne - - ctar cae - le - ste et an - ge - lo - rum pa - nis,
5 6 2 #6

sfera capit angusta.	is held inside a small sphere.
Maestas vere augusta	Truly, an august majesty
latet sub umbra umili.	is concealed under a humble shade.
Hic datur servo vili	Here a common servant
pro cibo salutari aeterna vita.	receives eternal life as his wholesome food.
Paratur hic pectoribus humanis	Here heavenly nectar, the bread of angels,
nectar caeleste et angelorum panis.	is prepared for human nourishment.

The movement is articulated in five sections, each corresponding to a sentence occupying two lines. The first, an ensemble recitative, establishes the tonality of F sharp minor. Successive solo recitatives for soprano, bass, and alto take the music in turn to E major, B minor, and D major. The bulk of the movement, 24 bars, is given over to a fugal cavata. This is best regarded as a section based in D major but which eventually slips back to the starting key, F sharp minor, in a three-bar coda. Ex. 34 contains the whole of the cavata up to the coda.

Points to note are: the treatment of the subject's second note as an unprepared appoggiatura (bars 16, 19, 23, 24, and 27); the skilful use of the second part of the subject, appearing in close imitation, to form episodes (bars 20–2 and 28–32); the *stretto* of the subject (bars 23–6); the tolerance of bare fifths even in a three-part texture (bars 18, 20, 25, and 28); the frequent liberation of the bass from the organ line (especially in bars 27–8). The essence of Vinaccesi's style is distilled in these bars; were one to discover a similar passage in an unattributed composition, there would be more than enough evidence to support a strong claim for his authorship.

Giovanni Tebaldini did not exaggerate when, in 1895, he wrote that the compositions in this collection possessed 'a truly classical purity of line' ('una purezza di linee veramente classica') and that some of them were 'genuine, splendid masterworks' ('dei veri e splendidi capolavori').[40] More recently, this view has been echoed in the *New Grove* by Sven Hansell, who commends the quality of the works. It is high time that they were published in a modern edition and took their place alongside the duets of Steffani and Handel as the extremely fine specimens of baroque chamber music for voices that they are.

Vinaccesi probably intended to make these fourteen works his parting gesture to the musical world. One year earlier he had offered his resignation to the Ospedaletto; five years later he was dead. It was a chance encounter with them that led me to the conviction that their author was a composer of real talent whose present obscurity is undeserved.

[40] *L'archivio musicale della Cappella Antoniana di Padova*, 117.

11

Conclusion

ANY composer is likely to be both original and representative. The tension between these two properties is a prime subject for study by historians and critics. In the best composers they are finely balanced. A superabundance of originality suggests that a composer has wilfully renounced, or remained sadly ignorant of, the achievements of his predecessors and contemporaries. Conversely, if the representative quality predominates, his music risks appearing insipid and unmemorable.

By any reckoning, Vinaccesi achieves this balance. In every genre for which music by him is extant he absorbs and transmits a tradition. The chamber sonatas express his familiarity with the dance-types current in northern Italy, his Brescian musical inheritance, and the innovations of Corelli. The cantatas conform to the general pattern that we find in Alessandro Scarlatti and Giovanni Bononcini, remaining abreast of the developments that occurred at the end of the seventeenth century. The surviving oratorio and opera, too, remain in their essentials close to the norm for the time. The church music, more heterogeneous, has roots in the baroque polychoral tradition, the few-voiced *concertato*, and the respective practices of the Ospedaletto and San Marco.

Yet in each genre Vinaccesi's personal voice is unmistakable. He is without question an innovator, even though his innovations were not imitated, so far as we know, and therefore did not pass into the general musical language. This urge towards novelty is evident not only from such obvious features as the creation of chamber sonatas with as many as twelve movements or the combination of elements from the solo motet and the polyphonic motet, but also from the 'nuts and bolts' of the musical language itself, which is idiosyncratic in a systematic and convincing manner. At the same time, he is surprisingly conservative in some matters, notably in his handling of tonality and retention of modal characteristics. The combination in the same work of backward-looking and forward-looking elements is not the least part of his originality.

His biography, too, is partly representative, partly original. The milieu from which he came—cultivated but provincial—and his training as an organist are reproduced in countless composers of his time. The same is true of the type of post he held in both Brescia and Venice. His freelance activity, in particular his peripheral involvement with opera, is equally typical for a church musician. But there is an unusual contrast, almost a contradiction, between the immobility of his life, seemingly physical as well as occupational, once he had secured his position at San Marco, and the almost ostentatious enterprise shown in his music. Here is no Vivaldi seeking everywhere appointments and commissions, patrons and pupils.

The most fascinating and, for an Italian composer of his time, unexpected aspect of Vinaccesi's music is its conscious intellectual control. What composers of today call pre-compositional planning—the design of an overall formal scheme for a movement or work even before a note is written—seems to be only vaguely present in most of his Italian contemporaries, although one observes it in many northern composers such as Biber and Kuhnau, and later Bach and Zelenka. Corelli, Alessandro Scarlatti, Vivaldi, and Albinoni compose a movement rather as one would write a letter. They start at the beginning and carry on to the end, relying on tried and tested formulas that have become part and parcel of their musical imagination. There is an element of *bricolage* even in (perhaps one should say 'especially in') the most extended movements of Colonna and Stradella. Of course, one must not draw too hard and fast a distinction between 'planned' and 'spontaneous' ways of composing, for all is a matter of degree. Nevertheless, Vinaccesi has in this respect more in common with the German than the Italian tradition. It would indeed be interesting to find out whether this was an individual choice or the result of belonging to a submerged subculture awaiting discovery. One should not be deceived by collections such as G. B. Vitali's *Artificii musicali* into thinking that the Italians took readily to musical intellectuality, for much of the ingenuity they display resides in titles and verbal descriptions rather than in the patterns woven by the actual notes. In contrast, Vinaccesi's cunning is covert, unadvertised, and purely musical in nature.

A final question to be addressed is: do we really 'need' this music? Can we not admit Vinaccesi to the gallery of Interesting Historical Figures and leave it at that? After all, he does not really belong to the great musical chain of being that is perceived as extending from Monteverdi to Vivaldi and beyond.

On the issue of how to treat baroque composers of the second rank there are two sharply opposed views as well as many gradations in between. Some critics extend the notion of an essential canon of masterworks backwards from the Viennese Classics. According to this viewpoint at its most dogmatic, it is a higher priority to become acquainted with the minor works of Bach than with the major works of Telemann, because the first composer belongs to the 'Great Tradition', while the second does not. There are two objections to this position. The first is that although it is unlikely that the incidence in the human population of superior musical gifts varies from age to age, it is quite possible that the means for adequate musical expression can be more accessible in one period than in another. The expertise and musicality needed to write a good piano sonata in the nineteenth century may have overtaxed all but the select few, but who is to say that a flute sonata provided an equally great challenge to a composer of the early eighteenth century? Where the test is less severe and the insistence on originality less absolute, a *Kleinmeister* can happily rub shoulders with a *Grossmeister*.

The second objection is that imperfect market conditions in the baroque and earlier periods may have privileged certain composers and penalized others. Fame and influence (or their lack) were doubtless largely a reflection of musical accomplishment—but not wholly so, for the local nature of much musical production and consumption tended to reduce the competition between composers. Nor has the revival of early music from the second half of the nineteenth century onwards provided a level playing-field. Any secular work has enjoyed an advantage over any sacred work, any instrumental work over any vocal one (particularly when its words are in Latin or older Italian). Any piece performable by a violinist or singer and a pianist or by a string orchestra has had a head start over a trio sonata or a chamber duet. Nicholas Temperley was perhaps right to assert: 'Greatness depends in the last resort on the verdict of the people. It cannot be overridden by argument, or by the individual opinions of critics or scholars.'[1] But the corollary of this position is that greatness, being a social construct rather than an objective fact, is not fixed for all time: it is continuously being negotiated through performance, dissemination, and discussion. In that special sense, Marc-Antoine Charpentier is a composer who formerly was not 'great' but is now rapidly becoming so, while his contemporary and fellow countryman Lully obstinately refuses to acquire in the public mind the 'greatness' to which his historical position clearly entitles him.

The rival view is one that perceives musical value very broadly and seeks to maximize the number of composers brought to our attention through the revival of their works. Theodor Adorno was scornful about what he called the 'Kleinmeister-compulsion', identifying with merciless accuracy a type of music-lover drawn for preference towards the obscure or the curious in the spirit of a collector of rare butterflies. His *bon mot* 'They say Bach but they mean Telemann' wittily illustrates the modern phenomenon described by Laurence Dreyfus as 'a grand *nivellement* of value'.[2] In its extreme form this view is even less tenable than the exaltation of the narrow canon of masterworks, for it is absolutely perverse to regard something as intrinsically more valuable or interesting simply

[1] Contribution to 'The Limits of Authenticity: A Discussion', *Early Music*, 12 (1984), 20.
[2] 'Early Music defended against its Devotees: A Theory of Historical Performance in the Twentieth Century', *Musical Quarterly*, 69 (1983), 302.

because it is less well known. It is also inimical to the development of
musical discrimination.

In my view, the proper attitude to the revival of Vinaccesi's music is
one that avoids both extremes. Let the motets be published and the oratorio or the pastoral be given a performance. I firmly believe that they
would win favour and before long open the door to other compositions. If
they failed to ignite a spark, the attempt would still not have been entirely
in vain, since, as this study has tried to show, their historical interest and
their relevance to many areas of current musicological inquiry is very considerable. In the preface to his published motets Vinaccesi, perhaps conscious of his originality, quoted the observation of Tacitus that human
malignity causes familiar things to be esteemed more highly than novelties. It is my hope that the novelties described in the preceding pages will
enjoy better fortune.

Appendix A
Genealogy of the Vinaccesi Family

Each member of the Vinaccesi family included in the seven tables comprising this genealogy, wives excepted, has an appended number, which can be used to identify the person heading one table with the same person as he appears in a previous table. For example, the Primo (25) heading Appendix A.3 is the same man as the Primo (25) in the last line of Appendix A.2.

The names of wives appear in bold print under those of their husbands. The lines leading to legitimate children proceed from their mothers; those for illegitimate children lead from their fathers.

Only the first given name is supplied, except in cases where two given names normally appear in association (e.g. Francesco Maria (89) in A.6) or where the first name is normally suppressed in favour of the second (e.g. (Giovanni) Pietro (88) in the same table).

Where only one date is given, it is a date of birth. An asterisk means 'circa'. When the choice lies between two years, the later year, asterisked, appears.

A dotted line (in A.1 and A.7) indicates some uncertainty of relationship. A question mark denotes a person unknown.

A few family members whose relationship to the others is so unclear that to include them would be too risky have been omitted. They have, however, been mentioned in the text of the present book and can be found in the index.

A.1

The Vinaccesi family in Venice: *c*.1370–*c*.1525

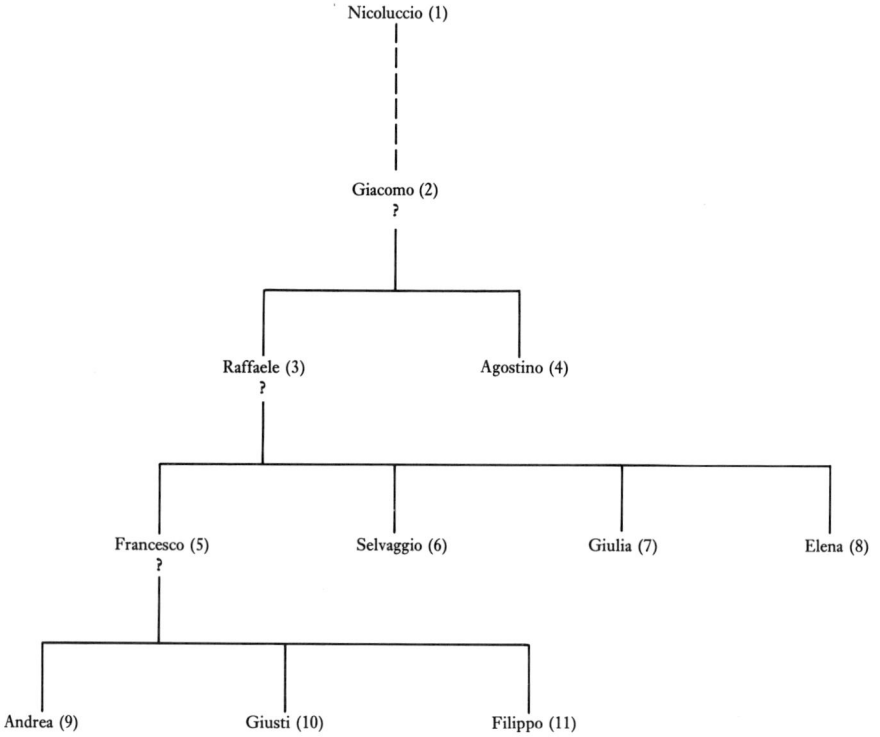

A.2

The Vinaccesi family in Brescia: *c.*1525–*c.*1575

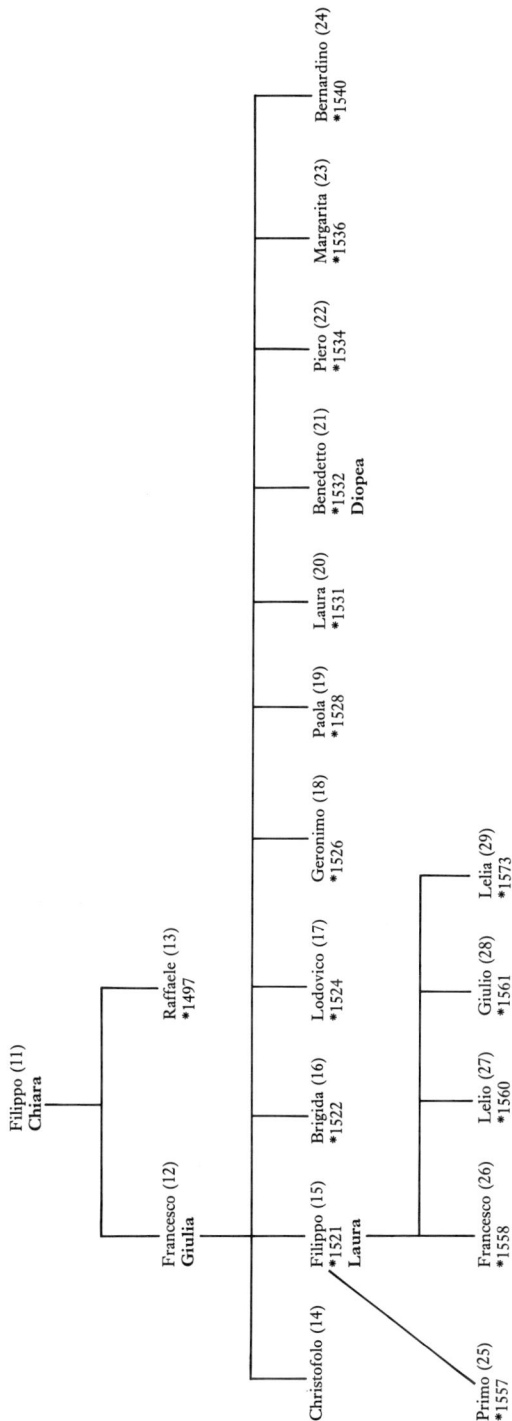

Filippo (11)
Chiara

Francesco (12)
Giulia

Raffaele (13)
*1497

Christofolo (14)

Filippo (15)
*1521
Laura

Brigida (16)
*1522

Lodovico (17)
*1524

Geronimo (18)
*1526

Paola (19)
*1528

Laura (20)
*1531

Benedetto (21)
*1532
Diopea

Piero (22)
*1534

Margarita (23)
*1536

Bernardino (24)
*1540

Primo (25)
*1557

Francesco (26)
*1558

Lelio (27)
*1560

Giulio (28)
*1561

Lelia (29)
*1573

Genealogy of the Vinaccesi Family

A.3

The Descendants of Primo Vinaccesi in Brescia: c.1560–c.1700

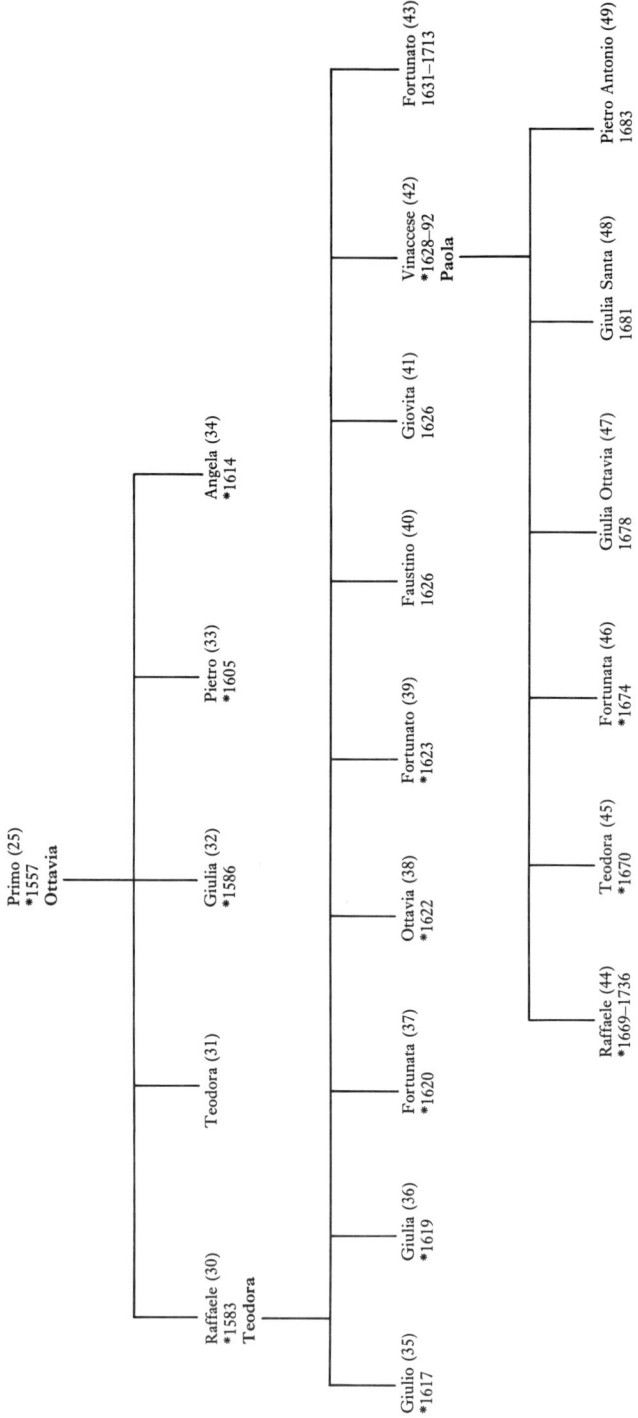

Primo (25)
*1557
Ottavia

Raffaele (30)
*1583
Teodora

Teodora (31)

Giulia (32)
*1586

Pietro (33)
*1605

Angela (34)
*1614

Giulio (35)
*1617

Giulia (36)
*1619

Fortunata (37)
*1620

Ottavia (38)
*1622

Fortunato (39)
*1623

Faustino (40)
1626

Giovita (41)
1626

Vinaccese (42)
*1628–92
Paola

Fortunato (43)
1631–1713

Raffaele (44)
*1669–1736

Teodora (45)
*1670

Fortunata (46)
*1674

Giulia Ottavia (47)
1678

Giulia Santa (48)
1681

Pietro Antonio (49)
1683

A.4

The Descendants of Bernardino Vinaccesi in Brescia: *c*.1540–*c*.1705

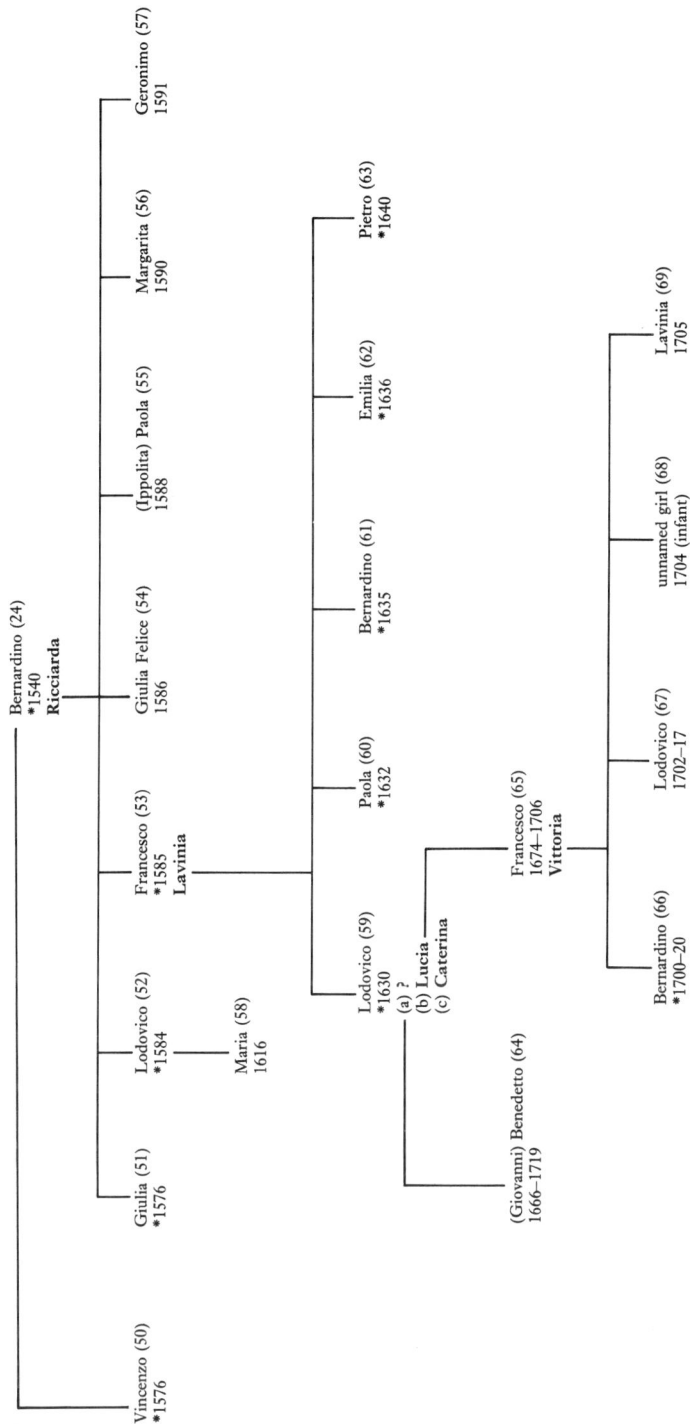

Bernardino (24)
*1540
Ricciarda

Vincenzo (50)
*1576

Giulia (51)
*1576

Lodovico (52)
*1584

Francesco (53)
*1585
Lavinia

Giulia Felice (54)
1586

(Ippolita) Paola (55)
1588

Margarita (56)
1590

Geronimo (57)
1591

Maria (58)
1616

Lodovico (59)
*1630
(a) ?
(b) **Lucia**
(c) **Caterina**

Paola (60)
*1632

Bernardino (61)
*1635

Emilia (62)
*1636

Pietro (63)
*1640

(Giovanni) Benedetto (64)
1666–1719

Francesco (65)
1674–1706
Vittoria

Bernardino (66)
*1700–20

Lodovico (67)
1702–17

unnamed girl (68)
1704 (infant)

Lavinia (69)
1705

A.5

The Descendants of Vincenzo Vinaccesi in Brescia: *c*.1575–*c*.1685

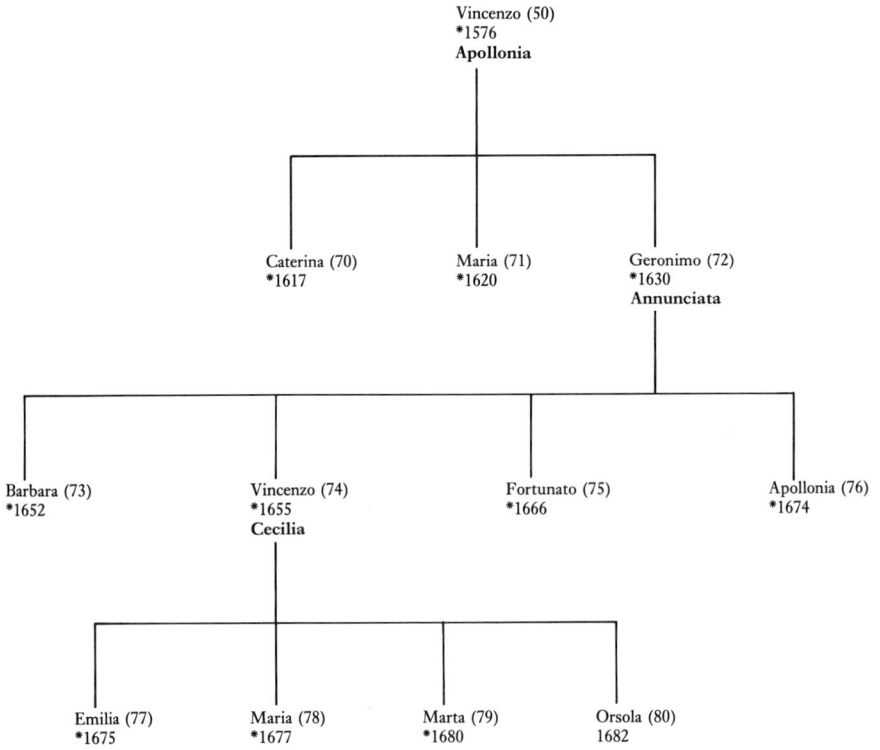

```
                          Vincenzo (50)
                          *1576
                          Apollonia
                               |
          ┌────────────────────┼────────────────────┐
          |                     |                     |
    Caterina (70)          Maria (71)          Geronimo (72)
    *1617                  *1620               *1630
                                               Annunciata
                                                    |
   ┌──────────────┬─────────────────────┬──────────────────────────┐
   |              |                      |                          |
Barbara (73)  Vincenzo (74)        Fortunato (75)            Apollonia (76)
*1652         *1655                *1666                     *1674
              Cecilia
                 |
      ┌──────────┼───────────┬──────────────┐
      |          |           |              |
 Emilia (77)  Maria (78)  Marta (79)   Orsola (80)
 *1675        *1677       *1680        1682
```

A.6

The Descendants of Benedetto Vinaccesi in Brescia and Venice: *c*.1665–1805

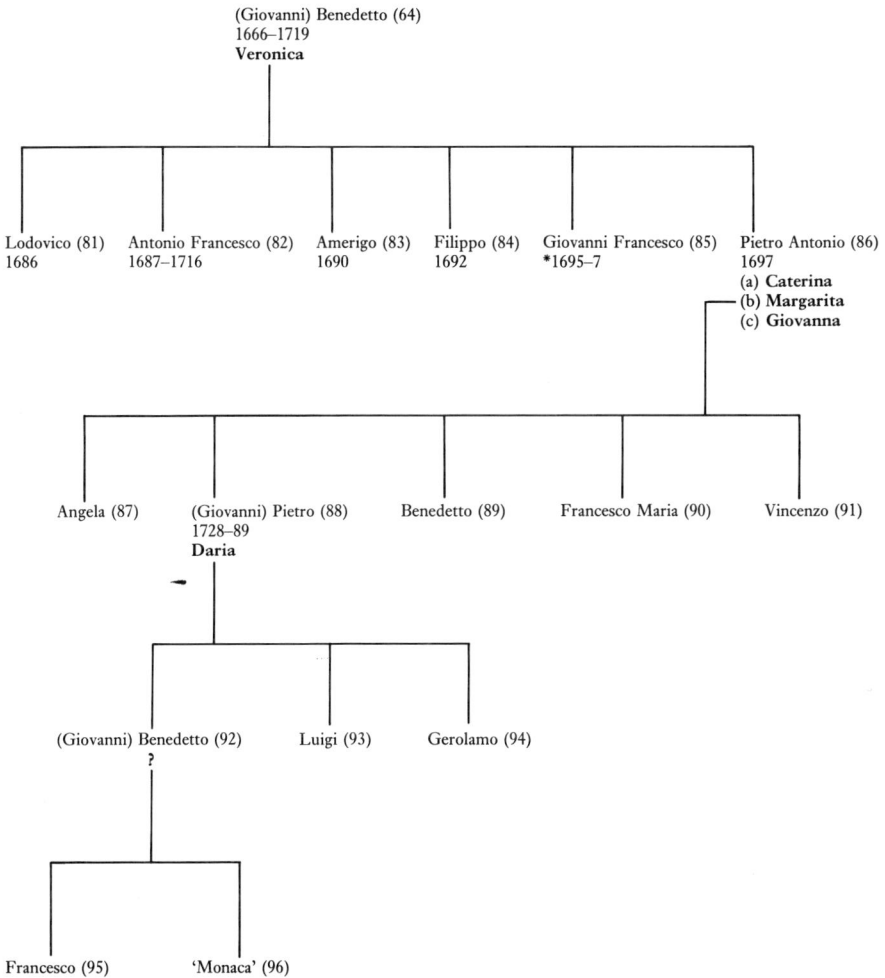

(Giovanni) Benedetto (64)
1666–1719
Veronica

Lodovico (81)
1686

Antonio Francesco (82)
1687–1716

Amerigo (83)
1690

Filippo (84)
1692

Giovanni Francesco (85)
*1695–7

Pietro Antonio (86)
1697
(a) **Caterina**
(b) **Margarita**
(c) **Giovanna**

Angela (87)

(Giovanni) Pietro (88)
1728–89
Daria

Benedetto (89)

Francesco Maria (90)

Vincenzo (91)

(Giovanni) Benedetto (92)
?

Luigi (93)

Gerolamo (94)

Francesco (95)

'Monaca' (96)

Genealogy of the Vinaccesi Family

A.7

The Vinaccesi Family in Brescia: *c*.1680–1805

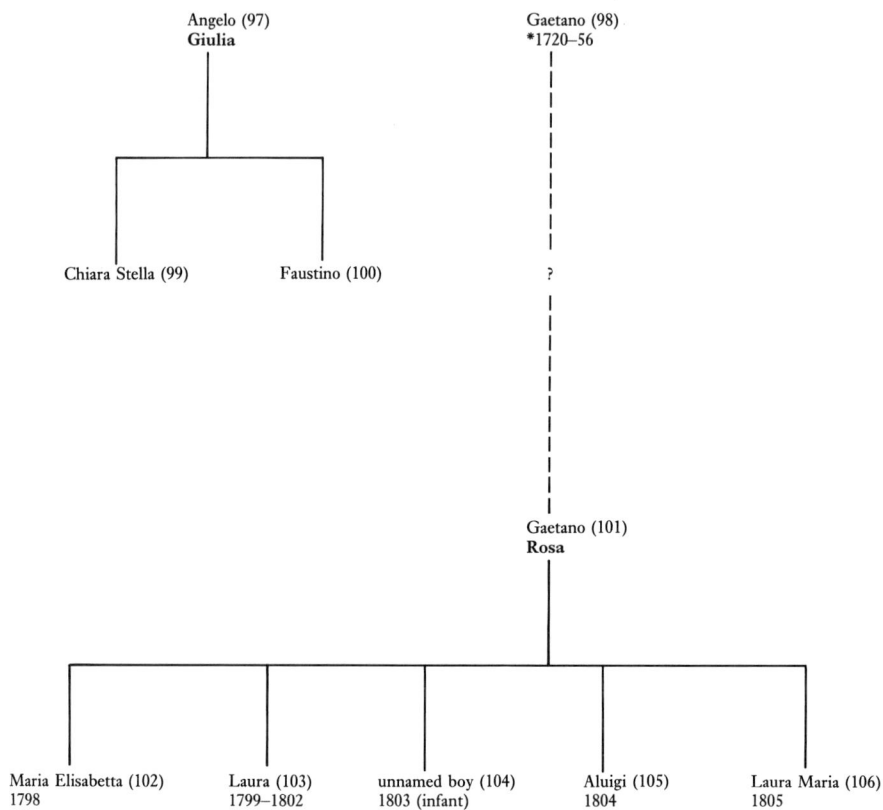

Angelo (97)
Giulia

Gaetano (98)
*1720–56

Chiara Stella (99)   Faustino (100)

?

Gaetano (101)
Rosa

Maria Elisabetta (102)
1798

Laura (103)
1799–1802

unnamed boy (104)
1803 (infant)

Aluigi (105)
1804

Laura Maria (106)
1805

Appendix B
Quotations and Transcriptions

This appendix presents in the original language, generally Italian, passages that have been given in English in the main text. In a few cases the English version is shortened from that given here.

The present transcriptions leave the original punctuation and capitalization intact (where needed, editorial interpolations in square brackets clarify the sense). Abbreviations (except for conventional ones, such as 'Sig.' for 'Signor') are resolved, all added letters appearing in square brackets. The letters U and V are distinguished according to the modern practice.

The order in which the quotations and transcriptions are presented in this appendix follows the order in which the English versions appear in the text. For ease of reference, the page numbers of the matching English versions are given in square brackets at the end of the title of each entry.

B.1. Giulio Antonio Averoldi, *Elogio di Fortunato Vinaccesi*, ed. Giovanni Averoldi (Brescia, 1889), 7–12 [see text, 2 and 24].

[In a footnote, Giovanni Averoldi makes the interesting comment that his ancestor's *Elogio* conforms to this writer's normal custom of avoiding scrupulously the use of the word 'che' (which, who, what, that, than, etc.), which our editor attributes to the 'whimsicality of a mind that seeks out difficulties in order to have the pleasure of overcoming them'.]

DOMINI FORTUNATI VINACCESI VITA ET INTERITUS

Transacto jam mense octobris, vale dixi uti proposui, pro nunc, notis super inscriptionibus. Adulto iam novembre, imò ad necem properante, certus factus sum de interitu Domini Fortunati Vinaccesij, cujus hic mentionem facere, ut ejus amicitiae morem geram, aequum et conveniens duco.

Tralasciamo di grazia il latino, e adoperiamo il nostro usuale idioma, e in tal maniera veramente questi miei insulsi fogli guadagneranno il titolo di *Miscellanea*.

È passato dunque a miglior vita il sig. Fortunato Vinaccesi oppresso da doppio colpo d'apoplessia in età d'anni ottantadue compiuti, età a cui pochi giungono.

Di sangue nobile, traeva la sua origine la famiglia Vinaccesi dalla città di Prato in Toscana (come chiaramente si legge in un libro a stampa varie volte mostratomi dal sig. Fortunato). A cagione di guerre civili Nicoluccio Vinaccesi lasciò Prato e andò a stabilirsi in Venezia l'anno 1374, e conosciuto subito il suo ingegno e giudizioso valore, fu ascritto alla cittadinanza veneta, e inviato Console a Rodi. Indi passarono i discendenti di lui a Brescia, ove, aggregati pure alla cittadinanza, con l'onorato impiego di negozio hanno sin'ora conservato decoroso il lustro ed il credito della famiglia, mentre l'arbore loro, non più fecondo di frutti, inaridisce.

Nacque il sig. Fortunato li 9 settembre 1631. Studiò in patria, e come d'ingegno spiritoso ed acuto risolse lasciare il nativo clima: desioso di erudire la mente con peregrine notizie, in età di anni ventisei, andò in Olanda, vide l'Inghilterra, parte della Francia e Spagna e quasi tutta l'Italia, mentre poi nel 1660 si tratteneva in Roma. Il diligente diario di questi suoi viaggi dà con esattezza le notizie.

La maggior sua dimora fu in Olanda, ove apprese le lingue greca, francese, spagnuola, olandese, inglese, e qualche poco di ebraica e tedesca. Colà s'impossessò appieno della geografia, in cui era versatissimo, e fece ampia provvigione di carte e libri (parte poi nel tempo susseguente distratti) a questa scienza spettanti, e seguitò anche in patria questo erudito diletto e genio. Coltivò in qualsivoglia loco le stanze de' più rinomati pittori, non per maneggiar pennelli, ma per conoscere le maniere e distinguere il bono, e di questa sua inclinazione alla pittura ne ha sempre dato il saggio con la scelta di rare tele. Con quei librai, come pure di Lione e Genevra, intavolò corrispondenza, sicchè in Patria chi bramava libri esotici, egli di bon core prendeva l'assunto di soddisfare le geniali premure. Acquistò pure varie altre cognizioni, delle quali si serviva nel discorso con applauso e santa invidia di chi l'ascoltava.

Avanti all'intrapresa de' suoi viaggi unì gran quantità di medaglie antiche di bronzo, (mentre allora la ingordigia e la lascivia in tale ricerca non era se non nell'alba) per indi poi al suo ritorno continuare questo delizioso e scientifico trattenimento, separando il fromento dal lollio e disporne la serie.

Restituitosi dopo sei anni, e due mesi a respirare l'aria paterna, e volendo por mano in queste commendabili reliquie della antichità, al primo incontro altamente si turbò, abbandonò l'impresa, nè mai più, mai più (tante e tante volte me lo ha attestato) ha posto l'occhio sopra le medaglie, nè mai le ha lasciate osservare ad alcuno. Il motivo del suo scontento fu la troppo facilità e connivenza de' signori suoi fratelli, in concedere contro il divieto la cassetta di esse medaglie nelle mani d'un prelato, il quale levò al sig. Fortunato l'incommodo d'applicarsi alla scelta, perchè quelle di maggior rimarco con gran disinvoltura se le appropriò.

Fra quatr'occhi, e niun altro lo sappia, svelo la persona del prelato; questi fu il sig. card. Pietro Ottoboni nostro vescovo, indi Pontefice

Massimo col nome d'Alessandro Ottavo. Egli adunque avendo penetrata l'unione di tali medaglie, vestitosi in abito nero e corto, e ben avanzate le tenebre, andò alla casa Vinaccesi, e chiese veder le medaglie. Attoniti i fratelli spiegarono il divieto dell'assente, ma ad un prelato di tal fatta non si potè negare il compiacimento, si fermò parecchie ore, le mirò, le maneggiò, e come pratico ed intendente quelle di suo gusto le ripose in un fazzoletto, e con un '*Goderò queste per amor loro*', partì, e unite le avrà all'altre da lui possedute.

Così deluso il sig. Fortunato mutò genio ed applicazione: sonava a meraviglia di flauto, di leuto alla francese e di chitarra, e a meglio fuggire l'ozio internossi al lavoro de' vetri per canocchiali, telescopi ed altri optici istrumenti. Travagliava egli in eccellenza, e li suoi vetri oggettivi erano molto ricercati ed apprezzati da Roma, da Olanda, come molte lettere allo stesso scritte e da me vedute, ne fanno piena testimonianza: e in certa occasione mi disse,, essergli stato pagato un suo vetro molte e molte doppie. A me donnone uno, intagliatovi attorno attorno il suo nome, e lo inserì nel mio canocchiale; di molti ne ha fatto regali ad amici e dilettanti esteri, e molti ha concambiati, e dopo sua morte ha lasciato bon numero di essi vetri, lenti ed altro con ordini all'erede, esteso nel suo codicillo, di regalarne i suoi amorevoli; e in quel paragrafo si esprime *averli lavorati, senza jattanza, in perfezione*.

L'arte però sua nell'ottica mai gli permise di lavorare due vetri atti e confacenti a' proprii suoi occhi, essendoglisi assai diminuita la vista.

Desideroso il sig. Fortunato d'aver sempre compagnia di genio, e conversazione erudita, essendo la sua abitazione lontana, aprì nel mezzo della città una stanza, soggiorno cotidiano di gente colta e letteraria; ivi teneva molti libri, pronto sempre a soddisfare le altrui ricerche e dimande in geografia, cosmografia, matematiche ed altre arti liberali, e lingue stranieri.

Erudito forestiere non giungeva, o pittore o dilettante di suono, o industre e rinomato artefice, il quale non avesse genio di seco lui abboccarsi, e passare ore e giorni in uniformi discorsi, e ogn'uno soddisfatto e contento partiva: io condussi da esso il rinomato Pre. Mabillon li 14 maggio 1685, quando per ordine del re di Francia viaggiava l'Italia; introdussi pure alla di lui conoscenza li 29 marzo 1686 Monsieur Vaillant di ritorno a Parigi; altresi giorni dopo il celebre Carlo Patino.

L'imprestar libri era di molto suo travaglio, dubitando, come infatti accade spesse fiate, o si perdono volontariamente, o per inavvertenza manchino carte, o anche si imbrattino. A me però, e forse a niun altro, offerì quanti libri avessi bramato; io però, conscio del suo genio, andavo assai riserbato in chiederne, e seppure alcuno ne addimandai, ero puntuale alla restituzione in brevissimo tempo. Molti bensì ne ho comprati da esso, ed esso alcuni di piccola mole m'ha donato.

S'impiegò nella stampa di libri, e componimenti altrui, ed oltre il genio ricavava vantaggio giusto, e conveniente alle sue fatiche. Propose egli la stampa del rarissimo e molto ricercato libro delle memorie bresciane d'Ottavio Rossi, e sortì col libraio Grumi l'intento. In ciò però non fu troppo felice come in vari lochi et occasioni in questi miei fogli miscellanei ho notato.

In tal metodo di lodevoli impieghi con tutta la candidezza di regolati costumi, con l'amore alle lettere e letterati, e con l'unione copiosa di volumi, ottimamente ha compiuti i suoi giorni il sig. Fortunato Vinaccesi, la cui perdita sarà un impegno di acerba ricordanza nell'animo degli amici.

Sorpreso da un colpo d'apoplessi conobbe vicino l'ultimo suo fato; e assalito dal secondo, con tutti i segni di vero e leale cristiano rendette lo spirito al Creatore alle ore sei e mezza della notte venendo li 25 novembre 1713. Fu sepolto nella disciplina di S. Alessandro avanti l'altare della Vergine.

B.2. *Stampa della Signora Marchesa Giovanni Miseroni ora consorte del Signor Conte Paola Sormani* [Venice, 1745], in *I-Vas*, Inquisitori di Stato, Processi civili 1743–1746, Busta 1030. n. 50, 6–7 [see text, 2–3]

Memoria

Tra le Famiglie più chiare che nell'Italia rendono l'Etruria al pari di qualunque Provincia Nobile, Glorioso per antichità di stirpe, per chiarezza de meriti, e per lustro di onori, fra le altre si ritrova essere stata quella de Vinacesi, la quale fino dall'Anno 1269. nella Città di Prato fioriva con splendore di dignità primarie, e parentadi con Famiglie le più Nobile della Città, come apparisce N. 2. 3., e quantunque si veda nel N. 4. che la Famiglia Vinacesi, assieme con altre principali di Prato s'impiegasse nella Mercatura, questo era all'uso di que' tempi, ne' quali appunto l'esercizio della Mercatura era proprio delle Famiglie Nobili.

Si legge che questa Famiglia Vinacesi fù insigne Benefatrice dell'Ordine de' Padri di S. Domenico N. 12, come pure di un'altro donato a primi il sito per fabricar il Convento, & a questo una pezza di Terra di valore considerabile nell'Anno 1306. N. 12. 13. 24.

Parlando delle Toghe, troviamo che Guidolotto de Vinacesi, e Guglielmo nel 1317. sono stati eletti per Procuratori, e Governatori della Città di Prato, e che Bellato Vinacesi era passato Governatore in Avignone.

Nell'Anno 1388. la Casa Vinacesi già nobile della Città di Prato fù anco aggregato alla Cittadinanza della Città di Firenze, e dichiarata Nobile Fiorentina, come consta nel N. 38. 39. 40. ne' quali sempre viene nominata la Famiglia Vinacesi come Nobile Patrizia Fiorentina, e come tale ne susseguenti Anni è sempre stata riconosciuta, ottenendo nella detta Città Cariche, e Posti cospicui proprie di Nobili di Firenze, come si vede Nicolussio Vinacese creato Priore del Supremo Magistrato nell'Anno 1470 N. 71.

La Famiglia Vinacesi ha indì contratti Parentadi con le principali Case di Firenze, e nell'Anno 1466. ha provato il Quarto nella Religione di Malta N. 72., e poi nell'Anno 1585 il Cavagliere Francesco doppo haver provato i Quarti delle Famiglie Medici, e Vinacesi vestì l'Abito di Cavagliere di Malta N. 81.

Appare similmente avere le Famiglie [*sic*] Vinacesi contratti Matrimonij con Casa Dini, con Casa Capponi principali di Firenze, e per sino nel 1509. aver maritata una sua Figlia con la sovrana Famiglia de Medici, stati per più Secoli Gran Duchi di Toscana N. 81. 82.

Trasferitasi poi da Firenze la Nobilissima Casa Vinacesi nella Dominante di Venezia quì ascritta alla Cittadinanza Veneta, mantenutasi sempre in rango Nobile, tuttavia si conserva nella Persona dell'Illustr. Sign. Pietro Vinacesi fatto, e dichiarato Conte dalla Ser. Casa Gonzaga ancor regnante in Guastala con suo Diploma amplissimo, in cui protestasi la detta Ser. Casa Gonzaga molto tenuta alla Casa Vinacesi, cioè all'Illustr. Signor Conte Pietro, e suoi Predecessori &c.

Resta ancora lo Stemma di Casa Vinacesi espresso in molti antichi, e moderni Monumenti nella forma espressa nel Libro, qual Stemma si supplica sia riveduto, & approvato come Gentilizio di Casa.

B.3.   Giuseppe Tassini, 'Notizie storiche e genealogiche sui cittadini veneziani', *I-Vmc*, Ms. P. D. 76/1–5, v. 90–1 [see text, 6]

Dalla Toscana. Fecero molte fabbriche massime in parrocchia dei SS. Apostoli e, secondo le cronache, facevano fazione in Venezia fino dal 1355.

1431   Cittadinanza di Francesco figlio di Raffaele Vinaccesi da Prato domiciliato a S. Canciano.

1449   Conferma della stessa cittadinanza ove il Vinaccesi è detto da S. Giovanni Grisostomo.

[Continues as family tree: see App. A.1. Then concludes as follows.]

1464   Griselda Vinaccesi, moglie di Giacomo Pierleoni, ha iscrizione mortuaria per cura a SS. Giovanni e Paolo.

B.4.   Pompeo Litta [and collaborators], *Famiglie celebri italiane*, xlviii/78, 'Giustiniani di Venezia' (Milan, 1840), table ix [see text, 13]

Ero unico maschio, siccome il padre e l'avo, per la consuetudine introdotta tra patrizj veneti di abbandonare il loro coniugale. appena si fosse conseguita successione maschile. Il bisogno di conservarsi ricchi erane il motivo, ma ciò non poco contribuì all'estinzione delle più antiche famiglie patrizie, e conseguentemente alla caduta della repubblica.

B.5.   Leonardo Cozzando, *Libraria bresciana* (Brescia, 1694), ii. 235–6 [see text, 22–3]

Benedetto Vinacese Cavaliere, sin da giovinetto fù assai vago, & amante del canto, e del sono, e perciò imprese a frequentare la scuola del Sign. D[on] Pietro Pelli Religioso secolare di molte virtù fregiato, ma nel canto, e sono di vari stromenti eccellente, e vi fece profitti notabili, come dall'opre poste in luce non oscuramente raccogliesi. *Sonate da Camera à 3 stromenti*. In Venetia 1687. Dedicate alla Principessa di Castiglione. *Il consiglio delli amanti, overo Cantate da Camera, à voce sola*. In Venetia 1688. Al Serenissimo gran Prencipe Ferdinando III di Toscana. *Sfere Armoniche, Sonate da Chiesa à 3 stromenti*. In Venetia 1692. Al Co: Alemano Gambara. *L'Oratorio di Gioseffe il casto*, recitato nella Serenissima Ducal Camera di Modena. *L'Oratorio di Susanna*. Ibidem.

B.6.   Brescia, Archivio parrocchiale di San Clemente, Matrimoni I (1566–1705), fo. 121^v [see text, 26]

Adi 27 Decembre 1685.

Il Sig[no]r Benedetto Venacese fig[li]o del Sig[no]r Ludovico, et D[on]na Veronica fig[li]a del q[uonda]m D[on] Francesco Illuminati, mia parocchiana dispensati dalle solite publicaz[io]ni, co[n] facultato contrahendi in qualibet hora, et loco; hanno contratto insieme matrimonio p[er] verba de presenti, con l'assistenza di me F[ra] Tomaso Fenarolo Curato di S. Clem[en]te di Brescia, in casa del M[olto] R[everendo] Sig[no]r D[on] Gio[vanni] Terrallio mio Parochiano; Presenti p[er] Testimonii, il pred[et]to R[everendo] D[on] Gio[vanni] [,] il Sig. Appolionio Tartaro, et D[on] Pietro Antonio Erazzio [Enazzio?] Pittore Cremonense habitante in Brescia.

B.7.   *I-BRq*, ASC, Registro 139, Fascicolo VIA 1687, Cittadella Vecchia, n. 254 [see text, 27]

Poliza di me Bened[et]to figl[i]o del Sig[no]r Lodovico Vinacese q[uondam] Sig[no]r Fra[nces]co Citt[adin]o di Brescia et habitante à Sa[n]to Cleme[n]te

Io Benedetto Vinacese sud[et]to d'anni no. 19
Veronica Luminati mia Moglie d'anni no. 18
Lod[ovi]co mio figl[i]o di mesi uno

Beni s[opr]a il Ter[ritori]o di Rocca Fra[n]ca

Possedo una pezza di terra, arad[rat]a, vid[a]ta, et adaquada nel Terr[itor]io sudetto in [contra]ta di S[an]to Rocco chiamata il Gerone descritta in l'est[im]o G[e]n[er]ale della M[agnifi]ca Città 1641. et cat[asta]ta in Cat[asti]co di Rocca Fra[n]ca al no. 3. posta prima alla partita del q[uondam] Gio[vanni] Bat[tis]ta Luminati q[uondam] Bart[olome]o; A qual pezza di terra sono coh[erenzi]e à mattina la strada Comune, à mezzo dì erano li S[igno]ri Alovisio, et fra[te]lli Rovati, et hora e [è] il S[ignor] Co[nte] Giac[om]o Sovardo [,] à Monte Stradella, et à sera il S[ignor] Co[nte] Cesare Martinengo, piò quattro P 4 t[avo]le— Qual pezza di terra mi è stata assignata in conto di dote della sud[et]ta mia moglie da D. Barbara r[elitta] [del] q[uondam] D[on] Fra[nces]co Luminati sua Madre

[*official note*] 1686: 31 Maij

B.8.   Mantua, Archivio di Stato, Archivio Gonzaga di Castiglione delle Stiviere, Busta 253/5, n. 101 [greeting and close omitted].
Giovita Vinaccesi, Brescia, to Guglielmo Corradini, Castiglione delle Stiviere, 10 Oct. 1672 [see text, 30]

Nell'amorevoliss[i]ma sua di 9 cor[rent]e recevo il pagam[ent]o delli due libri, che le mandò il S[igno]r Fort[unat]o mio fr[at]ello.

   Intendo quello m'accenna circa l'avanzo p[er] le robbe fatte fare p[er] cotesta Ecc[ellentissi]ma Sig[no]ra Prencipessa, che sijno in menà dell['] Ecc[ellentissi]mo Sig[nor]e Prencipe mio patrone p[er] renderci soddisfatti a primo comodo; con che faccendo fine le baccio di Core le mani.

B.9.   Mantua, Archivio di Stato, Archivio Gonzaga di Castiglione delle Stiviere, Busta 253/5, n. 102 [greeting and close omitted].
Fortunato Vinaccesi, Brescia, to Guglielmo Corradini, Castiglione delle Stiviere, 12 Feb. 1671 [see text, 31]

Ricevo dal Con[siglie]re d[i] S[ua] E[ccellenza] le £54: che V[ostra] S[ignoria] m'hà inviato p[er] il pagam[ent]o de gli avisi di 6. Mesi antecipati, che p[er] appunto già havevo rimessi all'amico di Venetia.

   Lo stesso mi ha recato p[er] cor[rier]e £7:10 p[er] li Barzino e Carnovale; resta solo a pagare li 2 Peregrini che costarono £3: di cui no[n] hebbi il rimborso forse scordato da V[ostra] S[ignoria].

   Per q[ue]llo de' Collari dell'Ecc[ellentissi]ma Sig[no]ra Principessa con suo comodo.

B.10.   B. Vinaccesi, Suonate da camera a tre, Op. 1: letter of dedication to Laura Pico della Mirandola [see text, 32–3]

ILL[USTRISSI]MA ET ECCEL[LENTISSI]MA SIG[NO]RA PRENCIPESSA.

Vostra Eccel[l]enza fregiata di rare, e cosi insigni prerogative, in nulla scemerà dell'invidiabil concetto, giustamente n'esigge, se dotata pur'anche d'intelligenza, non ineguale al nobilissimo genio, e buon gusto, che hà ne musicali componimenti non pertanto sdegnerà, d'accogliere con benigno compatimento un rozo parto, primizio però del mio, ben puoco di stubio [*sic*], e d'inclinazione alla virtù. Honore specioso, di cui m'eccita gagliardame[n]te à suplicar l'E[ccellenza] V[ostra] la brama, nodrisco d'accreditarmi se non conforme ambirei, almen come più posso: non disperando, anche un giorno farmi, di vantaggio conoscere.

Di Vostra Eccellenza

Humiiis[simo] [*sic*] Divot[issimo] ed Osseq[uiosissimo] Servo
BENEDETTO VINACESE

B.11.   B. Vinaccesi, *Sfere armoniche*, Op. 2: letter of dedication to Alemanno Gambara [see text, 35]

ILLUSTRISSIMO SIGNOr *Signor Patron Colendissimo*

AL Tempio veridico della Gloria, al Simolacro più venerabile dell'Honore; all'Idea massima della più adorata Gra[n]dezza, à V[ostra] S[ignoria] Illustrissima vengono ad humiliarsi Vittime del Genio, & Olocausti del debito le *Sfere Armoniche* delle mie Note. Compariscono con questo Titolo, non già suberbe [*sic*] d'arrogarsi il paragone con quelle Sovrane Melodie superiori all'humano Intendimento; mà perche concertate sotto il nostro Cielo, dove V[ostra] S[ignoria] Illustrissima risplende qual Astro di prima Luce & accordate al Tono più Sonoro della sua Fama, non ponno se non rapir come *Sfere* o Cuori più dedicati, e l'Anime più devote del suo gran merito. Io che pretendo frà questi di non haver chi m'avvanzi nella publicazione del mio ossequioso rispetto, presumo ancora di precedere nella speranza di veder graditi dall'Animo gentilissimo di V[ostra] S[ignoria] Illustrissima questi moti di Plettro, che goduta la sorte d'alzarsi con simili fantasie all'orecchio d'Italici dominanti, non devon formar disonanze al di lei Udito continuamente purgato da gli Encomi di chi al par d'ogni più Sovrana Potenza le sogetta volontario i sentimenti della propria humiliazione. Permetta V[ostra] S[ignoria] Illustrissima ch'io me ne vada altero di questo pregio; mentre alla varietà de Suoni, che le consacro, risponde la moltitudine de miei rassegnati doveri, e alle Cadenze d'una profonda Servitù termina il Carattere glorioso, che mi protesta

Di V[ostra] S[ignoria]

Umiliss[imo] Divotiss[imo] & Obligatiss[imo] Servi[tore]
Benedetto Vinaccesi

B.12.   B. Vinaccesi, *Sfere armoniche*, Op. 2: preface to the reader [see text, 36]

DILETTANTE AMOREVOLE

Venendo alla luce questa mia Terz'Opera sotto il Numero di Seconda, non vorrei, che ne restasse accusato l'Ordine, che venne prevertito da un supremo Comando; mà bensi condonati i trascorsi de miei Stromenti. Tanto più che facendosi essi sentir nella Chiesa, t'invitano in un Luogo dove più facilmente si perdonano gli errori, e dove l'Animo Virtuoso distende con più agevolezza il manto della sua Prottezione sù questi diffetti, che ponno venir scoperti da moderni Aristarchi di questo Genere, nel piccol Capo de quali vi sono Orecchie di Siracusa più grandi d'un Monte. Gli riccordo, che quelle s'addopravano da Tiranni per fare Ingiustizie, e queste non dovrian pronunciarsi contro le Sfere Senza il Titolo d'Empio; & io voglio in tè quello di Pio, & Amorevole, con che ti auguro felicità.

B.13.   *I-BRq*, ASC, Registro 854, Atti dei Deputati Pubblici 1688–95, opening 62 [see text, 38–9]

Adi 31 [dicem]bre 1689:
Furono esposte le cedole p[er] l'elett[ion]e d'un organista in luogo di Carlo Franc[esc]o Polarolo in termine di giorni cinq[ue]

Adi 2. Genaro 1690

Comparse il Sig[no]r Benedetto Venascesio p[er] l'elett[ion]e sud[ett]a
Comparse il Sig[no]r Giovan Alghisi p[er] nome del Sig[no]r Paris di lui fr[at]ello p[er] il concorso sud[ett]o

Adi 4 d[ett]o

Comparse il Sig[no]r D[on] Bernardo Borgognini p[er] il concorso sud[ett]o
Comparse il Sig[no]r Angelo Bofino à nome del Sig[no]r D[on] Oratio Pissamilio p[er] il concorso sud[ett]o

Adi 5 d[ett]o

Comparse il Sig[no]r Bartol[om]eo Antignati per il concorso sud[ett]o

[*lower down*] Gio[vanni] Quaglia

B.14.   *I-Vmc*, Ms. Cicogna 3079, fasciolo 5 [see text, 47–9]

Esposti li Proclami d'Invito à cadaun concorrente p[er] Maestro di questo Coro egualmente, che p[er] Maestri di Solfeggio, e Maniera, non che di Violino, e Violoncello con ordine registrato in d[ett]o Proclama che dovessero li concorrenti entro il termine di giorni 30. dare in nota li loro nomi, e quanto avessero voluto produrre p[er] il miglior riconoscim[en]to della loro Persone, la Deputaz[io]ne nostra onorata anche di pressiedere sop[r]a il coro hà preso in esame li nomi stessi dopo spirato il termine del Proclama p[er] informare sopra il particolar merito di cadaun concorrente.

Dovendosi pertanto da noi dare un esatto raguaglio à questa V[eneran]da Cong[regazion]e si dispensaremo da dir parola per ciò che riguarda la virtù della musica, poiche veramente questa scienza tanto vale quanto incontra, ed è conforme alla compiacenza di chi ascolta; che se si volessero da noi riferire private informazioni sarebbe lo stesso che non farlo, poiche cadauno viene sostenuto da illustri testimonianze, che parlano della Virtù del loro protetto con estimazione.

Noi pertanto p[er] obbedire al nostro dovere che si prescrive di dar un particolar raguaglio di ciascheduno si ridaremo unicamente à cose di fatto, cioè à refferire à questa cong[regazion]e gl'Impieghi, che averà cadaun sostenuto, e massimamente l'accoglimento, e l'aplauso con cui vengono ricevute le loro composizioni in questa città.

Diremo pertanto che tre sono li sogetti datisi in nota p[er] maestri di musica.

Il primo si è il Sig[no]r Tomaso Trajetta, il quale nel memoriale à noi presentato rissulta ch'egl'è Napolitano d'anni 40. in circa. Questi p[er] sett'anni esercitò l'Impiego di Maestro nel conservatorio di Napoli, indi partito fece molte composiz[io]ni in Roma, in Parma, in Vien[n]a, e scrisse p[er] la corte Eletorale Palatina dove p[er] le relazioni avute riuscì con aplauso. Fece anche nei Teatri di Venezia varie composizioni, le quali quando si voglia aver riguardo al giudizio della Città furono accolte, ed ammirate p[er] la pienezza, e vivacità delle immagini onde elle sono formate, come cadauno de' congregati avrà potuto rilevarlo dall'aplauso universale. Rapotto [Rispetto?] poi al suo contegno, e costumi non abbiamo cose in contrario, quanto si consta dalle informaz[io]ni praticate.

Il secondo è il Sig[no]r Salvador Perillo Napolitano d'anni 34. c[irc]a. Benchè questi non abbia prodotto alcun documento di sua Persona p[er] l'Impieghi in altri luochi sostenuti potrebbe credersi che riponesse egli tutta la sua confidenza nella estimazione che s'è formata con le due Opere Buffe fatte in Venezia. Di questo pure non abbiamo che aggiungere senon che aver rilevato di essere di buoni costumi.

Il terzo è il Sig[no]r Gregorio Sirolli Napolitano d'anni 50. c[irc]a. Nel memoriale da lui prodoto riferisce di esser stato Maestro di Capella nel conservatorio di Palermo parechi anni, di poi partito hà scritto più volte p[er] alcuni Teatri d'Italia più rinomati, come di Roma, Genova, Milano, ed altre città, ed in questi recenti anni anche in Venezia. Dalle molteplici chiamate di sua Persona può dedursi che il suo nome abbia riputazione, oltre di che in qualche privata adunanza di questa Città in cui s'adoprano delle sue Composiz[io]ni si parla delle med[esi]me con aplauso. Esso pure è di buoni costumi, ed in questa parte non abbiamo di nessuno che dire.

Passando poi al Maestro di Maniera un solo si diede in nota, e questi, e il S[igno]r Pietro Demezzo detto dalla Bragola di nascita Veneziano d'anni 40 c[irc]a, e di buoni costumi come si è rilevato. Non vi è dubbio che la persona non possi esser nota à cadauno di questa cong[regazion]e, il quale oltre aver sostenuto in varj Teatri la Parte di Tenore fù sentito con aplauso più volte anche in Venezia. Si può dedure dalla sua esperienza, e cognizioni un ottimo riuscimento anco nell'instruire, come hà riuscito in molte Chiese nel comporre.

Per Maestro di Solfeggio si diede in nota il solo il S[ignor] Matteo Boini di nascita Bolognese d'età 44. circa, ed esso pure di ottimi costumi. Egli hà composto di musica, ed hà molti scolari di solfeggio, da che si può giustamente confidare, che possi esser utile, ed abile p[er] il servizio di questo coro.

Per Maestro di Violino si diede in nota il S[igno]r Gio[vanni] M[ari]a Prandini d'anni 40. c[irc]a Veneziano d'ottimi costumi, dell'abilità del quale si dispensaremo far parola, giacche essendo sogetto di somma abilità, e fama, ed avendo dato saggi anche di sua moderazione nelli [*sic*] occasioni d'aver suplito in absenza del Martinelli in questo Coro abbiamo fiducia certa della di lui ottima riuscita à vantaggio del Coro.

Per quello riguarda al Maestro di Violoncello nessuno si diede in nota, perciò su tal punto dipendaremo dai comandi di questa Cong[regazion]e.

Darà questa Cong[regazion]e alle attestaz[io]ni presentate quella Considera[io]ne che crederà gli si convenga, poiche la Deputaz[io]ne nostra altro non ebbe in riguardo che di obbedire con sincerità, ed esatezza quanto si fù prescritto, desiderando che gli studj da noi praticati abbiano il compatim[en]to di questa Cong[regazio]ne. Grazie.

B.15.   *I-Vire*, Der. G. 1.48, Inserto 8 [see text, 71–2]

Ill[usstrissi]mi, et Ecc[ellentissi]mi Sig[no]ri. Pia, e Venerata Congregatione

Consumati, da me Benedetto Vinaccesi anni quindici in servitio di q[ues]ta Pia, e Venerata Congregat[io]ne, come Maestro di Musica delle sue figlie, devo finalmente applicar il pensiero alla quiete dell'animo, et ad un giusto desiderio che altri sott'entrino à questo peso, assai, e, per più riguardi, sopra ogni credenza gravoso. Hebbi sorte, l'anno 1698, d'esser prescielto in concorrenza di soggetti, accreditati per virtù, e per fama, con abondanza di voti, à questo impiego.

Hò procurato di rendermi non del tutto immeritevole d'un tanto honore, con assistere assiduam[en]te ad instruire le figlie stesse nel buon modo del dire, per quanto hà potuto portare il loro natural talento, che Dio non hà voluto permettermi di trovar eguale alle mie brame, et alla fortuna d'alcun'altro simile Pio luogo, dove apparisce più disposto à conciliarsi una qualsisia, più felice aura di aggradim[en]to. Mi sono adoperato appresso l'anima generosa del fù ecc[ellentissi]mo S[e]r Gio[vanni] Fran[ces]co Pisani per il rifacimento dell'Organo; degl'adornam[en]ti, e dorature del Coro; e l'Ecc[ellen]za sua, secondando le mie devotiss[i]me insinuationi, hà anco, del proprio denaro, à tutto adempito, con la nota magnificenza del suo genio, nella riguardevole forma, che tutt'hora si vede. Nè solam[en]te hò fatte seguir comprede d'instrum[en]ti con soldo de' benefattori, mà anco fatti condur più volte, à loro sole spese, Maestri di Violino, d'Oboè, e di Viola. Ritrovai, nel mio ingresso, il Coro numeroso non più che di venti figlie, comprese Maestre, Voci, ed Instrum[en]ti; Al presente lo lascio radoppiato al numero di quaranta, oltre alcune, che si vanno allevando, per renderlo maggiorm[en]te accresciuto. Quattrocento cinquanta, e più compositioni di vario genere, sono uscite in questo tempo, dalla mia penna à servitio del Coro stesso: numero, à cui non hanno arrivato più Maestri insieme, che in magg[io]r giro d'anni, mi hanno, con honor, preceduto. Queste, quali elle si siano, pur potranno servire à qualche occasione, et essiger forse da alcun'intendente di quest'arte, se mai fosse dalla sorte condotto ad udirle, qualche discreto compatimento. Nelle Domeniche, e feste di tutto l'anno, benche fuori d'obligo della mia Condotta, hò assistito al Coro, e suonato l'Organo sempre che nòn me l'habbia impedito il servitio da me dovuto al Ser[enissi]mo Principe, come organista della Ducal Capella di S. Marco, ò l'occasione di essere in solenni funtioni della Città, in qualità d'organista, ò in quella di Maestro. Per tutto ciò, mi rende consolato il riflesso di non haver in alcun conto mancato al debito, et all'ossequio, dovuto, e professato, e che sarò per sempre professare à così cospicua Congregat[io]ne, et alla dignità di chi vi pressiede; potendo io, ben sì, havermi desiderata magg[io]r fortuna, non già magg[io]r fervor di cuore nel ben servirla. Resta però ella hora da me humilm[en]te supplicata, in generoso gradim[en]to de' miei sparsi sudori, e delle vigili applicationi, sostenute in sì lungo corso di tempo, concedermi benigna permissione, che habbino quì il loro fine; onde con l'elettione di altro Maestro in mia vece, trovi in me sede la quiete, e sia reso degno d'incontrare, con raddoppiata mia indelebile obligazione, quella stessa magnanima bontà in sgravarmi da

questo carico, che mi fù, sopra ogni mio merito, dimostrata nel con-
ferirmelo.

1713. 29. Maggio

[*different hand*] Fù presentata nella V[eneran]da Congreg[atio]ne alli
N[obili] H[uomini] Pressidenti & letta da me Giacomo Aliprandi fattor
d[ett]o giorno

e con parte mandata da d[ett]i Ecc[ellentissi]mi S[ignor]i Pressid[ent]i fù
ballotata et Hebbe:

De Si	n[umer]o 6	
De No	n[umer]o 15	Non fù presa
N[on] S[inceri]	n[umer]o 2	

B.16.   *I-Vire*, Der. G. 1.48, Inserto 9 [see text, 72]

Dopo il lungo corso d'anni quindeci assiduam[en]te impiegati nel laborioso
esercitio di Maestro in q[ues]to nostro coro, avanzato nell'età con giusto
desiderio di quiete all'animo suo et di riposo, suplica il K[avalie]r
Benedetto Vinacesi la benignità di questa venerata Congregatione di
cortese licenza; Onde manda parte la carità de S[igno]ri Pressidenti che
resti la di lui suplicatione essaudita, acompagnandolo con pieno gradimento della sua benemerita virtù, savio et prudente morigeratissima con-
dota.

[in a different hand: voting figures as in Appendix B.15]

B.17.   *Raccolta di cose sacre che si soglion cantare dalle pie vergini dell'ospitale dei Poveri Derelitti* (Venice, 1777), 3–4 [extract] [see text, 77]

Ma forse non andrebbe lungi dal vero chi n'attribuisce la colpa in quella
tetra, debole, inconcludente maniera, punto esprimente la varietà dei
grandi concetti, che si contengono nella sacra salmodia, con cui fu trattata
la musica nei secoli a noi anteriori nelle chiese; d'onde annojati gli uomini
da quella uguaglianza di stil disadorno, cercaron di gustar il piacer di arte
cotanto divina ovunque la stolida scrupolosità lasciavala esprimersi nelle
forme più brillanti. L'error massiccio di un tal pratica fu vinto poc' a poco
dalla ragione che, avvalorata dalla divina autorità, fece conoscere che, non
si disdice alla maestà incomprehensibile del Signore, che noi adoriamo nei
templi, la musica più spiritosa, armonica e vivace. Professori eccellenti di
cotal arte, i quali nel giro di questo secolo ebbero a scriverne pel santu-
ario, tentarono gettarne i primi semi onde richiamarla quivi alla sua prim-
iera magnificenza: ma ben tosto si scontrarono in un torrente impetuoso di

opposizioni, che derivate da un zelo non illuminato di religione, stimavasi profanata la santità del luogo colla vivacità dell'espressioni.

B.18.   Vincenzo Coronelli, *Guida de' forestieri* (Venice, 1700), 27 [extract] [see text, 79]

Sono assai applaudite quelle [le voci ed istromenti] delle Figlie de' quattro Spedali, dove con molto grido cantano Cecilia, Appollonia, Coccina agl'Incurabili; Vienna, Cecilia, Antonina, e la Turchetta a' Mendicanti, dove in eccellenza suona l'Organo, et les Obois la Barbara; allo Spedaletto si distingue celebre Cantante la Vicentina; e per l'Arciliuto Barbara la Jamosa alla Pietà.

B.19.   Stefano Frilli, letter to Giacomo Antonio Perti dated 29 December 1699, *I-Bc*, P.145.19 [extract] [see text, 85]

e si farà la Giuditta recitata l'anno pass[at]o a S. Luca Mus[i]ca d[e]l K. Vinaccese, che se non l'abbatte la malinconia, spero, che non dispiacerà, e dimani a sera si deve far la Prova G[enera]le.

B.20.   Benedetto Vinaccesi, letter to Georg Friedrich, margrave of Ansbach, Staatsarchiv Nürnberg, Geheimregistratur Bamberger Zugang, Rep. 103a III Nr. 111 [see text, 85–6]

Ser[enissi]ma Altezza

Viddesi sempre l'Alma Augusta de' Prencipi proclive à le Virtù; reso audace da questo riflesso, ardisco humiliare all'A. V. Ser[enissi]ma questa debolissima fatica, parto de la mia penna, non ad altro oggetto composta, che à quello solo dovesse servire per divertimento suo, all'hor che le piaccia dar qualche posa alle Marziali applicazioni, con le quali empie di gloria il suo Eccelso Nome. Sò che ardito è il volo ch'io tento, ma sò pur anco, che al genio di V. A. non solo sono naturali i suoni degl'Oricalchi guerrieri, ma quegl'ancora degli stromenti d'Apollo, e che favorisce, e protegge con pari Magnanimità, e le spade, e le penne, vero Mecenate della Virtù. Divisai questo Drama pastorale tutto vaghezza, e con l'idea della minor soggezzione, sì nel numero de' Personaggi, sì per la qualità degl'apparati, acciò che ad un minimo cenno del volere, possa agevolmente comparire con diletto alla vista dell'A. V. Ser[enissi]ma. Il supplicarne l'aggradimento, fora troppo ingiurioso alla Clemenza graziosa di V. A., che Eroe della gloria, non rimira nella picciolezza dell'offerta, che la vastità del cuore dell'offerente, il quale, se non porge quanto deve, almeno dà quanto può. Io nel presentare all'A. V. S. questo imperfettissimo figlio del mio ingegno, presento con l'ossequio tutto me stesso in profondissima Venerazione, per esser in grazia dalla sua altissima generosità habilitato al decoroso ornamento di vivere

Dell'A. V. Ser[enissi]ma

Venezia li 6 Ottobre 1702

        Humilissimo, Divotissimo, Obligatissimo Servitore Ossequiosissimo

                                     Benedetto Vinaccesi

B.21. Preface by G. P. Candi to the libretto of *Gli amanti generosi* (Venice, 1703), 7–8 [extract] [see text, 88]

Rimane solo, che la tua bell'anima sempre inclinata à compatire gli errori, tolleri con generosità anco le mie imperfezioni, l'avvantaggio delle quali sarà il non comparire così difformi, perche mascherate, & abbellite dalle virtuose, e spiritose note del Sig. Maestro il Sig. Cavalier Vinacese, come pure dalla singolare abilità de Virtuosi soggetti, che lo rappresentano.

    Protestando il Sig. Maestro medesimo haver intrapresa la composizione musicale di questo Drama à solo mottivo d'obbedire ad'un commando de Cavalieri à quali non ha potuto negarlo, mentre era fuori d'ogni sua intenzione il far più Musiche per Drami, esprimendosi in oltre d'aver in molte Arie secondato più il gusto commune, che il proprio genio.

B.22. *I-Vas*, Procuratia de Supra, Busta 91, Processo 207, Organisti, fo. 45ʳ [see text, 100]

Il Ser[enissi]mo P[ri]n[ci]pe fà saper, et è d'ordine dell'Ill[ustrissi]mi, et Ecc[ellentissi]mi Sig[no]ri Procuratori de San Marco de Supra

Che tutti quelli pretendono concorrer organista della Chiesa de San Marco in loco de D[omi]no Francesco Caletti detto Cavalli elletto Maestro nella Capella della medesima debbano comparer nella Procuratia di loro Ecc[ellenz]e à darsi in notta, mentre intendono nella prima reddutione conforme il solito devenire all'elletione del Carico d'organista predetto etc.

Pietra del Bando San Marco

Pietra del Bando Rialto

[*Note in a different hand below*] 1668: a di 18 genaro fu publicato sopra le scale di San Marco e rialto per me Carlo Finesti C[omandado]r di deta Procuratia

B.23.   I-Vas, Procuratia de Supra, Busta 6, Decreti in originale, Fascicolo 13 (1701), 5 February 1701 (1702 m.v.) [see text, 101]

Illustrissimi, et Eccellentissimi Signori Procuratori de Supra, e Padroni Clementissimi

Sono ai piedi dell['] Eccellenze Vostre l'età, le fatiche, la Famiglia, e posso dir la riputatione di mè Carlo Francesco Polaroli servo, e suddito Riverendissimo, e fedelissimo. Doppo il corso di tredici anni serviti nella Reggia Capella di S. Marco, coll'abbandono della Patria, e dell'impiego, co' la Prole nata, et in certo modo nudrita nella riverente fiducia di vivere, e morire in questo ministero, m'inchino alla grandezza dell'Eccellenze Vostre e formo un voto, che non giunge nuovo suplicando à titolo di clementissima grazia il mio passaggio da Vice Maestro à Maestro. Questa gradatione, che condusse il Precessore sino [sic] già undeci anni (all'onor del grado nel ritiro rispettoso delle mie instanze) potrebbe valermi d'essempio, e conciliarmi luogo di compatimento se 'l rispetto dell'osse-quio, e della Fede viva non m'additasse la sola benignità dell'Eccellenze Vostre, da cui deve dipender unicamente il destino della mia Fortuna. Il ben essere di sette Figlioli trà Maschi, e Femine, e quel che più mi stringe, la Fama, e l'estimatione, più preziosa della vita. In procinto si grande m'inginocchio alla riverita, e venerata gratia dell'Eccellenze Vostre, e come Creatura della medesima imploro d'esser fatto degno, non col tes-timonio delle prove già rese, mà coll'alto benigno giudicio di questo istesso Sacrario, che mi creò tant'anni fà Vice Maestro, e peccarei d'ingratitudine, se non invocassi in si preciso bisogno quell'eccelso Genio, che mi chiamò al prossimo grado della sua adorata beneficenza. In questa umilmente confido, e da questa sospiro colla bocca à terra l'ultima perfet-tione della stessa beneficenza, perche al fine come presso Iddio una gratia è fondamento dell'altra, cosi a' piedi dell'Eccellenze Vostre che han le veci di Dio l'avermi decorato già due lustri del carattere di Vice Maesto, valerà à consolarmi colla pienezza della loro clemenza. Grazia

B.24.   *I-Vas*, Procuratia de Supra, Busta 6, Decreti in originale, Fascicolo 13 (1701), 5 February 1701 (1702 m.v.) [see text, 102–3]

Illustrissimi, & Eccellentissimi Signori Procuratori di Supra

Venero Io Antonino Biffi nato in questa Città servo, e suddito humilis-simo dell['] Eccellenze Vostre, come felice preludio della mia più grande fortuna l'inveterato costume di questo Gravissimo, e Sapientissimo Consesso, che fù di sciegliere al cospicuo honore di Maestro della Capella Ducal di San Marco, chi havesse ancora il grado di Sacerdote, per confor-mare al luoco, ch'è sacro, all'ufficio, ch'è pio un carattere ancora, che fosse religioso. La costanza di questa essemplarissima massima, accreditata dal corso de secoli, & inalterabilmente osservata nelle passate successive elettioni aggiunge coraggio all'humilissima mia confidenza nel presentarmi alla grandezza dell'Eccellenze Vostre supplichevole di tal posto, e perche Sacerdote, & perche hò sempre impiegato le deboli mie applicationi in soli sacre funtioni ne' Tempij, ò nell'amaestramento di Fanciulle ne' pij Hospitali. Non accettate da mè nessuna di quell'altre occasioni, che diverse da questo istituto potevano alterare questo mio sempre osservato proponimento. A tal fine non volsi assoggettarmi à Prencipi Esteri se ben invitato replicatamente con speciosi progetti, & alettato con lucrose esibitioni, reputando mercede maggior d'ogni prezzo l'honor di servire all'ossequiato mio Prencipe in questa Ducal Capella, e Maestro nel Choro riguardevole de Mendicanti. In questo mè lecito esponer il prestato servitio d'anni dieci in qualità di Contrapuntista, e nel suono dell'Organo senza rimorso d'alcuna mancanza, anzi con la consolatione d'haver senza repugnanza alcuna obbedito ai comandi de Signori Maestri, che supplivano in caso dell'altrui absenza àgl'Organi Superiori col mezzo della mia pronta rassegnatione. La puntualità dunque da mè sempre osservata in questo non breve servitio, le mie non discreditate compositioni nel pio Hospitale de Mendicanti, ch'hà servito di passaggio à trè miei precessori P. Nadal Monferrato, Legrenzi, e Partenio, da quello à questo riguardevole posto, mi fanno sperare il concorso generoso dei Voti dell'Eccellenze Vostre, che humilmente imploro, promettendo nell'essercitio della carica, succedendomi conseguirla non esser diverso da quello fui nell'occasion dell'attual servitio della Chiesa medesima. DIO, à cui hò sin'hora consacrate le mie deboli fatiche conduchi l'Anime dell'Eccellenze Vostre all'elettione di quello, che voglia con maggior pontualità, e possa con maggior applicatione, staccata d'altri impegni, & obligationi adempire al grande impiego della Publica Capella, & à mè se restassi eletto doni la gratia della sua invocata assistenza per ben essercitare à maggior sua gloria, & al miglior servitio dell'Eccellenze Vostre quell'ufficio, che humiliato, e prostrato supplico dalla gratia, e dalla grandezza del genio di cadauna di Vostre Eccellenze. Gratia, &c.

B.25. *I-Vas*, Procuratia de Supra, Busta 150, Decreti e terminazioni 1700–7, fo. 23(bis)^r [see text, 103–4]

Adi 5 Febraro 1701. M. V.

Ritrovandosi vacante il posto di maestro della Capella Ducal di S. Marco del S[ig]n[o]r R[everen]do Gio[vanni] Domenico Parthenio si rende necessario divenire all'alletione di altro soggetto, il quale per la propria virtù et habilità et prove datte di se med[esi]mo sij capace et addattato à sostener impiego così riguardevole et considerato con quel estimatione, che corrispondi al decoro et al servitio della stessa Ducal Capella. Però essendo statto scritto dall'Ill[ustrissi]mo et Ecc[ellentissi]mo S[igno]r P[rocurato]r Cassier alle corti senza l'effetto che si sperava, et fatti successivamente li soliti proclami ad intelligenza di chi volesse esibirsi come per relatione di Anzolo Carminati Coma[nda]dor si sono datti in nota li qui sottoscritti, cioè si devenira alla Ballotatione. All'elletto restera ingiunto l'obligo di adempire pontual et esatamente a tutte l'incombenze, che appartengono à tal ministero, e doverà conseguir la proviggione, et emolumenti appunto praticato con il defonto Maestro Parthenio. Dovendo all'eletto cessar ogn'altro emolumento, ma solo goder il solito salario spettante alla carica di Maestro su[dett]o

p[er] il Sign[no]r D[on] Antonio Biffi	Sì	9	Rimase elletto il S[igno]r
	Nò	5	D[on] Antonio Biffi
p[er] il Sign[no]r Benedetto Venacesi	Sì	3	
	Nò	11	
p[er] il Sign[no]r Carlo Polaroli	Sì	8	
	Nò	6	

B.26. *I-Vas*, Procuratia de Supra, Registro 211, Mandati e licenze 1694–1712, fo. 54ᵛ [see text, 104]

Ill[ustrissi]mo et Ecc[ellentissi]mo S[ignor]i Proc[urato]ri de Supra

Nota è sempre stata l'attentione et pontuale servitù di me D. Giacomo Spada p[rim]o Organista della Chiesa Ducal di S: Marco all'impiego riverito con cui sono statto decorata dall'Osequiata aut[ori]ta di V[ostre] E[ccelenze] [;] assiduo sempre è stato il mio esercitio con quel bono vivo desiderio dell'animo con il qualle ho sempre sospirato di sacrificare tutti li miei sudori, et la vita stessa in adorato olocausto di V[ostre] E[ccellenze] et nel Reggio servitio del Prencipe. Logorata hora la mia salute per le continue incessanti mie occupationi nel laboriosissimo impiego, et in bisogno con il parere de Medici, che mi assistono di qualche respiro, nell'Aria homogenea al mio temperamento del Paese nativo, supplico la carità di V[ostre] E[ccellenze] à permettermi benigna licenza per mesi quatro in circa, obligandomi a far servire in questo frà tempo nelle fontioni che caderanno alle mie parti da Alvise Tavelli mio Allievo, et della maggior à me ben nota habilità senza alcun aggravio alla cassa di V[ostre] E[ccellenze] con che io preso vigore con tale breve riposo possa con spirito sempre più vivo, et più fervido continuare il sacrifitio di me me[desi]mo in una perpetua rassegnatione a' comandi ossequiati di V[ostre] E[ccellenze] la gratia de qualli hu[milissimamen]te adoro et sospiro [*closing formula*]

B.27. *I-Vas*, Procuratia de Supra, Registro 150, Decreti e terminazioni 1700–7, fo. 62^v [see text, 106]

Adi 7 Settembre 1704

Publicati gl'ordinarij Proclami per Organista della Ducal di S. Marco in
loco di S[ig]n[o]r Antonio Lotti assunto all'essercitio del gia sostenuto da
D. Giacomo Filippo Spada, per qualli si diedero in nota li sottoscritti che
premesse le solite prove furono poi ballotati per gl'Infrascritti
Ill[ustrissi]mi et Ecc[ellentissi]mi S[igno]ri P[rocurato]ri a Rossoli coperti
cioè da . . . [names listed] et rimase elletto D[o]n Benedetto Vinacesi
come dalle sottoscritte ballotationi appar con gl'oblighi tutti salario et utilità godeva il prec[essor]e Ant[oni]o Lotti Organista

Andrea Paulati	Si	9
	Nò	7
Alvise Tavelli	Si	6
	Nò	10
Gio[vanni] Marco Martini	Si	9
	Nò	7
Benedetto Vinacesi	Si	10
	Nò	6

B.28. *I-Vas*, Procuratia de Supra, Registro 152, Decreti e terminazioni 1713–21, fo. 16^r [see text, 110]

Havendo n[ostr]o Benedetto Vinaccesi Organista da Anni dieci in quà
della Chiesa Ducale di S. Marco, dedicati a questa Procuratia una Muda
di Motteti à piu voci per servizio della medesima chiesa; hanno perciò
gl'Ill[ustrissi]mi, et Ecc[ellentissi]mi S[igno]ri Proc[urato]ri Inf[rascrit]ti,
cioe . . . [names listed] Terminato, Che in Testimonio di aggradimento
alle di lui lodevoli fatiche siano datti allo stesso per una volta tanto de
dinari della Cassa della Chiesa ducati Cento V[alut]a Cor[ren]te

Si 9   Nò 0   Non sincero 1   Presa

B.29. *I-Vas*, Sezione notarile, Testamenti, Busta 606, Andrea
Sandelli, no. 48 [see text, 111–12 and 113]

Volendo io, Benedetto Vinaccesi, q[uonda]m Lodovico disponere delle
cose, massime attrovandomi obligato al letto indisposto; Perciò hò fatto
scrivere dal Sig[no]r Andrea Sandei come mia confidente persona il
p[rese]nte mio Tes[tamen]to et ultimà volontà per poi p[rese]ntarlo al
Medemo come Nod[ar]o per la sua validità.

Prostrato però prima con la Mente, e con il cuore avanti il Crocifisso Giesù; lo prego per li meriti del suo pretiosissimo sangue sparso per me voler suffragare questa povera anima mia nel punto estremo con la sua santa Grazia, e per sua infinita misericordia condurla in Porto di salute. Nel che imploro l'intercessione della b[eata] V[ergine] M[aria] mia Avvocata, e di tutti i santi miei Protettori[.]

De miei Funerali, come io li desidero senza Pompa, cosi io mi rimetto in tutto e per tutto nella mia Amatissima Consorte, e Figlio, pregandoli più tosto abondare in suffraggi, che in Pompe.

Come sono tenuissime le mie fortune, e fù sempre ne tempi andati numerosa la mia Famiglia, havendo ciò non ostante collocati cinque Figli Religiosi a Gloria di Dio, cosi dichiaro, che hò convenuto valermi per supplire alla Fontioni necessarie d'alcuni Capitali di raggione Dimissoriale della Sig[no]ra Veronica mia Consorte, come spicca da Publici Instromenti, e scritture: Però intendo, ordino, commando, e voglio, che tutti li miei Mobili in qualunque luoco esistenti, [inserted above: organo, Habiti, e Biancherie per mio uso] siano, e s'intendino di raggione della stessa Sig[no]ra Veronica, in pagamento di quanto le devo per le cause soprariferite, potendo sopra li medemi pratticar, in ogni evento, qualunque atto di Pagamento, sapendo benissimo, che ne meno sarano sufficienti alla sodisfattione del suo Giustissimo Credito, pregandola aggradire quel che hò, in risarcimento di quel di più ch'ella merita.

Dichiaro in oltre, che li Quadri tutti, che si ritrovano nel primo piano della mia Casa nella Camera appresso la Scala, e qualch'altro anche disperso in qualche altra stanza, di mano di diversi Pittori moderni, questi sono di particolar raggione del Sig[no]r Giacomo Ganassoni, al quale doverano essere ad'ogni piacere restituiti[.]

Del Ressiduo di tutto quel, che hò, et aspettar mi potesse, instituisco herede universale Pietro mio Figlio: Pregandolo voler vivere con il Santo Timor di Dio, ben regere, e governarsi, impetrandogli dal Cielo unita con la mia Paterna, la Celeste Benedittione[.]

E questo voglio sia il mio Testamento, et ultima volontà a Gloria di Dio.

[*own hand*] Io Bened[et]to Vinaccesi affermo

Die Domenicę 31 Mensis D[ecem]bris 1719

Publicatum fuit ob Mortem mihi cognatam dicti Testatoris ad' instantiam D[omi]nę Veronicę Illuminati eius uxoris cui intimata fuit pars offitii Aquarum pro quinque pro centenario de' Legatis[.]

In Dei Eterni No[m]i[n]e Amen Anno ab I[ncarnatione] D[omini] N[ostri] I[esu] C[hristi] 1719 Ind[ic]e 12, Die vero Mercurii Vigesima Mensis Decembris Rivoalti. Il Sig[no]r K[avalie]r Benedetto Vinacesi q[uonda]m Lodovico sano per la Iddio Gratia di mente, sensi, et intelletto, seben aggravato da male nel letto, stando nella casa di sua habitatione posta in questa Città in Contrà di S. Severo, ha p[rese]ntato a me Andrea Sandei N[odaro] V[eneto] alla p[rese]nza delli qui sottoscritti Testi la p[rese]nte carta aperta quale disse essere il suo Tes[tamen]to et ultima volontà scritta da me Nod[ar]o come sua confidente persona. Quale fatti uscire li Testi le fù letto da solo a solo giusto l'obligo mio, e quelli [?] dove mi fece agiongere come in esso si vede, e lo sottoscrisse. Quelli poi richiamati tornò p[rese]ntarmelo confirmandolo in tutte le sue parti come stà, e giace. Pregandomi p[rese]ntarlo in Canc[elleri]a Inferior accio sia ivi custodito, et occorendo il caso di sua morte Io debbi pigliar aprir compir e roborar giusto le leggi. Interrogato da me Nod[ar]o della Consimile delli 4 Hospitali par[ticolarmen]te di quello della pietà, et altri luochi, et opere pie nominatamente Rispose. Se havessi lascierei con tutto il cuore [*closing formula*]

[*signed*] Io D[on] Pietro Barozzi q[uon]d[am] Gio[vanni] Bat[tis]ta fui testimonio alla sud[et]ta presentazione pregato e giurato

Io Giacomo Ganassoni q[uonda]m Andrea fui Testimonio come di contro pregato e giurato.

B.30. Venice, Archivio parrocchiale di San Severo, Registro dei morti 1715–1756, opening 16 [see text, 113]

Adì 25 [dicem]bre 1719

Sig. Cavalier Benedetto Vinaccesi q[uondam] Lodovico d'anni 53 in circa [;] mal di febre e streteza di peto di giorni 30. Medico Tosi[.] Lo fa sepelir sua moglie con capitolo.

B.31. Giovan Mario Crescimbeni, *Notizie istoriche degli Arcadi morti*, (Rome, 1720–1), iii. 52–3 [see text, 116–17]

BENEDETTO DI S. ANTONIO DI PADOVA

Benedetto di S. Antonio nato in Brescia da nobili genitori di Casa Vinacesi, visse nell'ordine delle Scuole Pie dieci solo anni; ma con tanta fama, e plauso sì nelle scienze, come nell'amena letteratura, quanto altri (voglia il vero) acquistato non ne avrebbe in lunghi anni di affannoso esercizio. Le fatiche Letterarie furono in lui talmente ostinate, che rubandoli tutte quasi le ore del sonno, lo impoverì talmente di spiriti, e di umori, che insortogli un'acutissimo, e fisso dolor di emicrania, lo portò nel termine di un mese all'altra vita à 4. d'Ottobre l'anno 1716. nella Città di Venezia, in casa paterna, ove erasi col consiglio de' Medici, per sentire il benefizio dell'aria, portato; e fu nella insigne Chiesa delle Monache di S. Lorenzo seppellito. Lasciò dopo di se in cordoglio, non che il Parentado, la nostra Colonia tutta, in cui appellossi Sindalio Fenicunteo, la quale aspettava di vederlo famoso dicitore su i Pergami; al qual fine aveva già composto un sodo, e bene scelto quaresimale, dopo aver dato saggio del suo cospicuo ingegno in varj Panegirici detti in Roma, particolarmente nella Patriarcale Basilica Vaticana, e in un' Avvento, che con molto suo onore spedì nell'insigne Collegiata Basilica di S. Maria in Trastevere.

> Euristene Aleate P[astore] A[rcade] della Col[onia] Mariana.
> [Il Padre Niccolò Maria di San Domenico, Genovese,
> Chierico Regolare delle Scuole Pie]

B.32. Venice, Archivio parrocchiale di San Severo, Morti 1715–1756, opening 6 [see text, 117]

Adì 5. ott. 1716

Il Molto Rev[erendo] Padre D[on] Benedetto di S. Antonio di Padova, figlio del Sig. Cavalier Benedetto Venacesi, d'anni 29 in c[irc]a, amalato già mesi uno, da febre e doglia di capo. Visitato dal Ecc[ellen]te Coen. La fa sepelir il sud[et]to signor suo padre con capitolo

B.33. I-Vas, Inquisitori di Stato, Processi civili 1743–1746, Busta 1030, no. 50. *Stampa della Signora Marchesa Giovanna Miseroni ora consorte del Signor Conte Paolo Sormani* [Venice, 1745], 86–8 [see text, 122–3]

'Inventario, e Stima de' Quadri di ragione del Sig. Pietro Vinacese'

Paesi Grune Istoriati	D.	18
Paeseti piccoli Storiati del Calzer	D.	6
Una Nonciada, e Giudicio di Salamon	D.	10
Un Quadro grande del Zanchi vecchio	D.	12
Un S. Pietro del detto	D.	4
Un Christo col Padre Eterno del Lettuini	D.	6
Un Quadro di Martin de Vos	D.	2
Una Copia di Tintoretto	D.	1
Una Copia di Tizian San Pietro Martire	D.	4
Una Giudita del Zanchi vecchio	D.	5
Ritratti		[—]
Una Testa di Vecchio del Cassani	D.	2
Un Paesetto	D.	2
Un Testa d'Omo, che pipa	D.	2

Un Porto de Mar del Brugel	D.	5
Il Ratto delle Sabine del Tiepolo	D.	8
Un Quadretto tondino Paese di Tizian	D.	8
Due Prospettive del Bolognese	D.	8
Un Quadretto piccolo con il Signor, S. Giuseppe, e Maria del Liberi	D.	4
Una Giudita del Tiepolo	D.	3
Un Baccanaletto di puttini in pietra		[—]
Una meza figura di Donna col Cimbano del Padoanin	D.	5
Una meza figura di Homo	D.	2
Un Paesetto	D.	2
Due Quadri compagni con Soaze dorate del Carboncin	D.	8
Quadro bislongo con molte figure dell'Ens	D.	6
Due Quadri meze figure coo [*sic*: con] soaza dorata	D.	6
Ritratto		[—]
In Camerin		
Quadretti prospetive, oselami, e figure	D.	[—]
Camera del Specchio		
Tre sotto balconi del Duramano fiori	D.	3
Una Madonina, e due altri Quadri di divozione	D.	3
Una Madonina copia di Sassoferrato	D.	2
Sala		
Un Sottobalcon	D.	1
In un'altra Camera		
Un Madonna con altri Santi in tavola	D.	6
Madonna del Zanchi vecchio	D.	6
Altra Madonna del Tiepolo	D.	6
Due Sopraporte fiori, & un altro Paese	D.	2
In Tinello		
Una Palude	D.	1
In Camera vicina alla Cusina		
Quadri, & una tela imprimada	D.	6
	D.	191

Hò stimato ad' instanza della Sign. March. Giovanni Miseroni Consorte in 2do Voto del Sig. Pietro Vinacese, per far sopra quelli la sua Assicurazione di Dote, & in fede

Domenico Clucerino Pittore [30 Agosto 1743]

B.34.   B. Vinaccesi, *Suonate da camera a tre*, Op. 1: note to the reader [see text, 142]

CORTESE LETTORE.

Non ti meravigliare se trovi Menuetti framischiati trà queste Sonate da Camera, essendo cio seguito solo per incontrar il genio, di chi godesse il Ballare. Se usi compatimento, mi animerai maggiormente à farti godere la Seconda Opera, che sarà da Chiesa, e di diferente studio [.] Amami, e vivi felice.

Appendix C

Tables

C.1. Census Returns of the Vinaccesi Family in Brescia

The table is organized in six columns. The first column gives the year or span of years by which the census is known (in the case of the Biblioteca Queriniana this date appears after the letters 'VIA' on the *fascicolo* containing the return). The second column gives the location. 'Q' stands for 'Biblioteca Queriniana, Archivio Storico Civico, Polizze d'estimo in ordine cronologico dall'anno 1517 all'anno 1734 e in ordine alfabetico', 'S' for 'Archivio di Stato di Brescia, Polizze e petizioni d'estimo, Estimo civico del 1641'. The letter is followed, after a slash, by the appropriate *registro* number (for 'Q') or *busta* number (for 'S'). Note that most returns in 'Q' survive in duplicate, one copy being found in each of the two *registri* (nos. 139 and 249) for the letters VIA–VIR. The third column identifies the *quadra* and the serial number under which the return was filed ('CN' stands for 'Cittadella Nuova', 'CV' for 'Cittadella Vecchia'). The fourth column names the one or more respondents in the order in which their names appear in the return (an identification number in parentheses following a name refers the reader to the family trees in Appendix A). The fifth column gives the date on which the return was presented and sworn. A sixth column is reserved for additional comments.

Year of census	Location	*Quadra* and serial nos.	Respondents	Date return presented	Comments
1534	Q/139 and 249	CN unnumbered	Francesco (12)	1533	
1548	Q/139 and 249	CN 24	Francesco (12)	undated	
1565	Q/139	CN 6677	Bernardino (24) and brothers	30.05.1565	
1568	Q/139 and 249	CN 25	Geronimo (18)	undated	
1568	Q/139 and 249	CN 39	Lodovico (17)	undated	
1568	Q/139 and 249	CN 45	Filippo (15)	undated	× 2 in Q/139
1568	Q/139 and 249	CN 47	Piero (22)	undated	× 2 in Q/139
1568	Q/139 and 249	CN 48	Bernardino (24)	undated	
1568	Q/139 and 249	CN 49	Benedetto (21)	undated	
1568	Q/139	CV unnumbered	Giulio (28)	undated	
1588–95	Q/139	CV 87	Francesco (26)	undated	
1588(–95)	Q/139 and 249	CV 203	Bernardino (24)	undated	
1588(–95)	Q/139 and 249	CV 276	Primo (25)	undated	
1588(–95)	Q/139 and 249	CV 576	Benedetto (21)	undated	

Year of census	Location	*Quadra* and serial nos.	Respondents	Date return presented	Comments
1614–19	Q/139	CN 22	Bernardino (24)	16.09.1614	
1627	Q/139	CN 173, 174	Primo (25)	29.03.1627	
1627	Q/249	CN 179	Primo (25)	undated	= Q/139, CN 173
1627	Q/139	CN 196	Bernardino (24)	undated	× 2
1627	Q/249	CN 197, 202	Bernardino (24)	undated	= Q/139
1627–37	Q/249	CN 193	Filippo (15) Lodovico (17) Geronimo (18) Benedetto (21) Piero (22) Bernardino (24)	03.02.1574	Note date
1630–4	Q/139 and 249	CV 42	Vincenzo (50)	12.06.1630	
1630–4	Q/249	CN 84	Primo (25)	12.06.1632	
1637	Q/139	CN 5	Primo (25)	27.06.1637	
1641	S/13	CV 27	Francesco (53)	20.07.1641	
1641	S/13	CN 152	Raffaele (30) Pietro (33)	27.07.1641	
1653	Q/139 and 249	CN 12	Giovita (41) Fortunato (43)	18.11.1657	
1653	Q/139 and 249	CV 140	Francesco (53)	20.03.1657	
1653	Q/139	CV 529	Lodovico (59) Bernardino (61)	15.03.1658	
1653	Q/139	8 Faustino 27	Geronimo (72)	27.09.1653	
1661(–7)	Q/139 and 249	CV 70	Francesco (53)	16.04.1661	
	Q/139 and 249	CV 71	Lodovico (59) Bernardino (61)	01.01.1661	
1661–7	Q/249	CN 70	Giovita (41) Vinaccese (42) Fortunato (43)	16.04.1661	
1661–7	Q/249	CN 189	Geronimo (72)	27.09.1653	Note date
1687	Q/139	CN 74	Geronimo (72)	24.12.1685	
1687	Q/139	CV 254	Benedetto (64)	31.05.1686	
1687	Q/139 and 249	1 Aless. 68	Paola Rebusca	30.05.1685	
1687	Q/139 and 249	1 Aless. 119	Giovita (41) Fortunato (43)	29.12.1685	
1687	Q/139 and 249	2 Aless. 163	Lodovico (59) Bernardino (61)	31.05.1686	

C.2. Baptisms, Deaths, and Marriages of Members of the Vinaccesi Family Recorded in the Parish Archives of Three Brescian Churches

The table summarizes information contained in the parish archives of Sant'Alessandro, San Clemente (kept at Sant'Alessandro), and Sant'Afra

(kept at Sant'Afra in Eufemia, formerly Sant'Eufemia). The first column
has the date of the entry, the second column the name of the church. The
third column identifies the type of register, the volume number, and the
span of years covered by the volume. The fourth column gives the name
of the person for whom the entry is made, followed by the appropriate
identification number taken from the family trees in Appendix A. Note
that the volumes described as 'Nascite' at Sant'Alessandro record baptisms, not births.

Date of entry	Church	Register type	Vol. no.	Span of years	
23.04.1585	S. Clemente	Battezzati	I	1541–1647	Francesco (53)
10.05.1586	S. Clemente	Battezzati	I	1541–1647	Giulia Felice (54)
12.04.1588	S. Clemente	Battezzati	I	1541–1647	Ippolita Paola (55)
09.01.1590	S. Clemente	Battezzati	I	1541–1647	Margarita Ippolita (56)
02.11.1591	S. Clemente	Battezzati	I	1541–1647	Geronimo (57)
24.06.1626	S. Clemente	Battezzati	I	1541–1647	Lelia: daughter of Piero
19.03.1636	S. Aless.	Nascite	III	1664–1702	Emilia (62)
17.06.1673	S. Afra	Matrimoni	IV	1653–1676	Lodovico (59)
02.08.1674	S. Afra	Battezzati	VIII	1689–1694	Francesco Giuseppe (65)
07.07.1678	S. Aless.	Nascite	IV	1664–1702	Giulia Ottavia (47)
09.08.1681	S. Aless.	Nascite	IV	1664–1702	Giulia Santa (48)
30.05.1683	S. Aless.	Nascite	IV	1664–1702	Pietro Antonio Gioseffo (49)
27.12.1685	S. Clemente	Matrimoni	I	1566–1705	Benedetto (64)
05.04.1686	S. Afra	Morti	III	1651–1707	Lucia: wife of Lodovico (59)
18.11.1687	S. Clemente	Battezzati	II	1647–1720	Antonio Francesco Diego (82)
30.06.1689	S. Clemente	Matrimoni	I	1566–1705	Lodovico (59)
21.01.1691	S. Clemente	Battezzati	II	1647–1720	Amerigo Emanuel Gaetano (83)
06.06.1692	S. Clemente	Battezzati	II	1647–1720	Filippo (84)
18.07.1692	S. Aless.	Defonti	II	1658–1702	Vinaccese (42)
10.02.1697	S. Clemente	Battezzati	II	1647–1720	Pietro Antonio (86)
31.07.1697	S. Clemente	Defonti	II	1696–1783	Giovanni Francesco (85)
04.01.1702	S. Clemente	Battezzati	II	1647–1720	Lodovico Tito (67)
10.02.1704	S. Clemente	Defonti	II	1696–1783	unnamed girl (68)
?.03.1705	S. Clemente	Battezzati	II	1647–1720	Lavinia Gioseffa Rosa (69)
04.12.1706	S. Clemente	Defonti	II	1696–1783	Francesco (65)
25.11.1713	S. Aless.	Defonti	III	1702–1756	Fortunato (43)
14.03.1717	S. Afra	Morti	IV	1708–1726	Lodovico (67)
10.05.1720	S. Afra	Morti	IV	1708–1726	Bernardino (66)
11.02.1736	S. Aless.	Defonti	III	1702–1756	Raffaele (44)
16.11.1737	S. Clemente	Battezzati	III	1720–1805	Chiara Stella (99)
14.01.1739	S. Clemente	Battezzati	III	1720–1805	Faustino Antonio (100)
15.06.1756	S. Aless.	Defonti	IV	1756–1773	Gaetano (98)
11.11.1798	S. Clemente	Battezzati	III	1720–1805	Maria Elisabetta (102)
27.06.1804	S. Clemente	Battezzati	III	1720–1805	Aluigi (105)
20.09.1805	S. Clemente	Battezzati	III	1720–1805	Laura Maria (106)

C.3. Music Masters at the Ospedaletto

The table lists the musicians and music teachers employed at the Ospedaletto in seven series:

(*a*) *Maestro di coro* (also called *maestro di musica*)
(*b*) *Maestro di solfeggio* (also called *maestro di canto*)
(*c*) *Maestro di maniera*
(*d*) *Maestro di violino* (also called *maestro d'istromenti*)
(*e*) *Maestro di violoncello* (also called *maestro di viola*)
(*f*) Organist
(*g*) Notes on other *maestri*.

The first and second columns give the year of appointment and, where known, the year in which the appointment was terminated (for whatever reason). The third column names the person. The fourth gives his salary, noting subsequent increases. The fifth column is for additional remarks. Years marked with an asterisk are to be interpreted *more veneto*. All salaries are expressed in ducats current (equivalent to 6 *lire* 4 *soldi*).

Year		Name	Salary	Comments
Appt. began	Appt. ended		(ducats current)	
(*a*) *Maestro di coro*				
1612*	?	Giovanni Bassano	?	
1624*	?	Unnamed Somaschian father	?	
1633*	?	Pietro Retti	24	
1634*	?	Francesco Vio	24	
1635*	1647*	Giovanni Rovetta	24	
1647*	1655*	*Musical activity suspended*		
1655*	1663	Massimiliano Neri	50	
			90	from 1662*
1670*	1676*	Giovanni Legrenzi	?	
1676*	1688	Carlo Grossi	100	
			160	from 1678*
			200	from 1688*
1688	1698	Paolo Biego	200	
1698	1715	Benedetto Vinaccesi	200	
1715	1716	Unnamed temporary *maestro*		
1716	1733	Antonio Pollarolo	150	
			200	from Aug. 1718

Year		Name	Salary (ducats current)	Comments
Appt. began	Appt. ended			
1733	1733	Bartolomeo Cordans		as provisional *maestro*
1734	1743	Antonio Pollarolo	200	
1744	1747	Nicola Porpora	250?	doubling as *maestro di solfeggio*
1747	1766	Gaetano Pampani	200	
			330	from Aug. 1747
			350	from Aug. 1748
			400	from Aug. 1749
(b) Maestro di solfeggio				
1715	1716	Antonio Pazzello	?	
1716	1722	Orazio Molinari	40	
1722	1727	*Post suspended*		
1727	1730	Pietro Scarpari	90	doubling as *maestro di maniera*
1730	1733	*Post suspended*		
1733	1740	Francesco Broccoli	50	
1740	1743	*Post vacant*		
1743		Girolamo Bassani	50	
1746	1758	Girolamo Brunelli	80	doubling as organist
			100	from Dec. 1749
			120	from Jan. 1753
(c) Maestro di maniera				
1716	1722	Pietro Scarpari	50	
1722	1727	*Post suspended*		
1727	1730	Pietro Scarpari	90	doubling as *maestro di solfeggio*
1730	1733	*Post suspended*		
1733	1743	Antonio Barbieri	100	replaced during absences by Girolamo Bassani or Pellegrin Tomii; suspended Feb.–May 1741
1743	1747	Nicola Porpora	250?	doubling as *maestro di coro*

Year		Name	Salary (ducats current)	Comments
Appt. began	Appt. ended			
?	1761	Pellegrin Tomii	?	date of first appt. unclear
(d) Maestro di violino				
1662*	?	Unnamed teacher	?	remunerated privately
1716	1722	Pietro Serta	50	
1723	?	Carlo Tessarini	42:14	paid 1 sequin per month
1727	1730	Carlo Tessarini	40	
1730	1733	*Post suspended*		
1733	1765	Antonio Martinelli	90	doubling as *maestro di violoncello*
			100	from May 1746
			120	from Sept. 1747
(e) Maestro di violoncello				
1699*	1703*	Giacomo Taneschi	?	remunerated privately
1708*	1710	Giacomo Taneschi	?	remunerated privately
1716	1719	Nadalin [Bonamici]	50	
1719	1722	Bernardo Aliprandi	40	
1722	1727	*Post suspended*		
1727	1730	Bernardo Aliprandi	40	
1730	1733	*Post suspended*		
1733	1765	Antonio Martinelli	90	doubling as *maestro di violino*
			100	from May 1746
			120	from Sept. 1747
(f) Organist				
1746†	1758	Girolamo Brunelli	80	doubling as *maestro di solfeggio*
			100	from Dec. 1749
			120	from Jan. 1753

* = m.v.

†Prior to 1746 this duty was carried out by various persons: the *maestro di coro* himself, one of the *figlie*, or someone employed casually.

(g) *Notes on other* maestri:

At some time during the period 1698–1713 the Ospedali employed an oboe teacher whose salary was paid by a benefactor, as emerges from Vinaccesi's letter to the governors of 29 May 1713.

Between 1716 and 1722 Camillo Personé was employed at an annual salary of 40 ducats to teach the *violone* (double-bass). In 1722 the governors decided to entrust the teaching of the instrument to the violin teacher they intended to appoint, and no separate teachers of the *violone* are subsequently recorded.

In December 1716 Lucia Catterina Vignola was admitted to the Ospedaletto as a *figlia di coro* on condition that her grandfather continued to teach her the trumpet free of charge.

C.4. Productions of Francesco Silvani's *L'innocenza giustificata*

The table is laid out in five columns. The first gives the year and, if known, the season of the production; the second gives the theatre (omitting the word 'teatro' for brevity); the third gives the title as shown in the libretto or otherwise; the fourth gives the composer when his identity is known beyond doubt; the fifth gives a location for one extant libretto, using standard RISM sigla.

Year	Season	Theatre	Title	Composer	Libretto location
1699	carnival	Venice, Sant'Angelo	L'innocenza giustificata	Vinaccesi	I-Vgc
1699	autumn	Genoa, Falcone	Carlo, re d'Allemagna		I-Bu
1700	carnival	Mantua, Ducale	L'innocenza giustificata	Vinaccesi	I-Bc
1700	carnival	Florence, Cocomero	Carlo, re d'Allemagna		I-Bu
1701	carnival	Crema	L'innocenza giustificata		I-Mc
1711		Milan, Ducale	L'innocenza giustificata	‡	I-Rsc
1712	spring	Ferrara, Bonacossi	L'innocenza difesa	Orlandini?	*
1713	carnival	Ancona, Fenice	La Giuditta di Baviera	Predieri	I-Fano
1713	autumn	Bologna, Formagliari	Carlo, re d'Allemagna	Orlandini	I-Bc
1713		Forlì, Comunale	La Giuditta di Baviera	Orlandini	I-MOe
1714		Palermo, S. Cecilia	L'innocenza giustificata	Fioré	I-Rsc
1714	summer	Parma, Ducale	Carlo, re d'Allemagna	Orlandini	I-Mb
1714	autumn	Verona, Palazzo	L'innocenza difesa		I-Vcg
1716	carnival	Naples, San Bartolomeo	Carlo, re d'Allemagna	Scarlatti	I-Bc
1720	carnival	Rome, Pace	L'innocenza difesa	Fioré	I-Vgc
1721	carnival	Florence, Pergola	L'innocenza difesa		I-Bc
1722		Turin, Carignano	L'innocenza giustificata	Fioré	I-Vgc
1722	carnival	Venice, Sant'Angelo	L'innocenza difesa	Chelleri	I-Vgc

1722	autumn	Wolfenbüttel, Ducal	L'innocenza difesa	Hurlebusch	D-W
1723	autumn	Bergamo	L'innocenza giustificata		I-Mb
1723	autumn	Crema	L'innocenza giustificata		I-Rsc
1725	carnival	Prague, Sporck	L'innocenza giustificata	pasticcio	D-W
1726		Kassel, court	L'innocenza difesa	Chelleri	†
1731	summer	Fano, Fortuna	L'innocenza giustificata	pasticcio	I-Vgc
1731	summer	Braunschweig, court	L'innocenza difesa	Chelleri	D-W
1731	autumn	Genoa, Falcone	L'innocenza giustificata		I-SA
1732	autumn	Hamburg, Gänsemarkt	Judith oder Die siegende Unschuld	pasticcio	D-B
1734	summer	Florence, Pergola	L'innocenza giustificata		I-Bc
1738	spring	Rome, Dame	Carlo il calvo	Porpora	I-Vgc
1739	carnival	Faenza, Accad. Remoti	L'innocenza giustificata	pasticcio	I-FZc
1739		Lisbon, Trindade	Carlo calvo		I-Rsc
1739	autumn	Venice, Sant'Angelo	Feraspe	Vivaldi	I-Vcg
1740		Vienna, Hofburg	L'innocenza difesa		I-Mb

* No libretto survives. The information comes from the work-list of the article on Orlandini in the *New Grove*. Either the date or the attribution must be incorrect, since in the libretto of the 1713 production in Bologna the music is described as 'nuovamente composta dal Sig. Giuseppe Orlandini'.

† No libretto survives. The information comes from the work-list of the article on Chelleri in *Die Musik in Geschichte und Gegenwart*.

‡ Some writers attribute this setting, on uncertain grounds, to Chelleri.

C.5. Employees of the Procuratia de Supra (Seventeenth and Eighteenth Centuries)

This table excludes posts held at San Marco. The first figure for each entry denotes the annual salary in ducats 'al valore di piazza', whose value exceeds that of ducats current by at least 20 per cent (asterisks indicate salaries subject to a *decima* of 30 per cent); the second figure records the Christmas bonus (*regalia*).

Name of post		Annual salary	Christmas bonus
Italian	English		
Gastaldi (2)	Chief Administrators	200*	5
Quadernier	Book-keeper	200*	5
Nodaro	Notary	180*	5
Proto	Architect	120	5
Ragionato	Accountant[†]	100	5
Fiscal	Legal Officer	80*	5
Acconcia reloggi	Clock-repairer	72*	
Custode del campaniel	Custodian of the bell	60*	
Fanti (2)	Orderlies	60*	2
Capitanio di piazza	Officer in charge of the Piazza	50*	2
Commesso	Clerk	48*	5
Deputato all'archivio	Archivist	?	5
Guardian impizzar	Lamplighter	44?	
Masser	Steward	20*	2
Scoa piazza	Sweeper of the Piazza	21:16?*	
Porta via scoazze	Refuse-Remover	12	
Custode della loggetta	Custodian of the Loggetta	?*	
Custode di palazzo	Custodian of the [Doge's] Palace	?*	
Cazza cani	Dog-shooer	?	

* Salaries subject to a *decima* of 30 per cent.
[†] Between 1618 and 1622, and again between 1661 and 1721, the office of *ragionato* was suppressed. During these periods the *quadernier* took over the responsibilities of the post.

Sources: *I-Vas*: Procuratia de Supra, Registro 42, Libro di scontro 1728–35, 3 July 1728; Busta 70, Cariche ed impieghi delle Procuratie, Processo 154, fascicolo 3, fos. 1–5, *passim*; Registro 153, Decreti e terminazioni 1721–35, 21 Dec. 1727. Venice, private collection of Dr Girolamo Marcello, Cod. 168, undated document.

C.6. Established Posts at the Ducal Church of San Marco in 1730

The first column gives the year in which each post was established; the second and third columns name the posts and append a translation or description of each; the fourth column gives the number of persons holding each post; the fifth column gives the annual salary in ducats 'al valore di piazza', whose value exceeds that of ducats current by at least 20 per cent (asterisks indicate salaries subject to a *decima* of 30 per cent). Other posts not listed but known to exist from Damiano Donati's register for the year 1714 (*I-Vmn*, Ms. Cicogna 801) are those of music librarian (*custode dei libri di musica*) and chaplain to the doge.

Yr. established	Italian name	English trans.	No of persons	Annual salary
829	Primicerio	Bishop of the Diocese of Venice	1	160
1266	Sagrestani	Sacristans	2	130
1527	Sottosagrestani	Sub-Sacristans	2	50
1328	Canonici di dentro	Internal Canons	10	130
	Canonici di fuori	External Canons	14	unpaid
1485	Sottocanonici	Sub-Canons	6	130
1514	Maestro di coro e cerimonie	Master of the Choristers	1	130
1440	Diaconi	Deacons	2	54
	Subdiaconi	Subdeacons	2	48
1489	Capi di coro	Head Choristers	2	30
1404	Giovani di coro	Senior Choristers	30	21
1479	Chierici (Zaghi)	Junior Choristers	24	12
1324	Appuntador di chiesa	Monitor	1	50*
1479	Maestro di grammatica	Tutor to the Choristers	1	80
1485	Maestro di canto di chierici	Singing Master to the Choristers	1	24
1597	Custode di zaghi	Custodian of the Choristers	1	24
1524	Custode della Soprasagrestia	Custodian of the Sacristy	1	50*
1491	Maestro di cappella	Master of the Music	1	400
1607	Vice-maestro di cappella	Deputy Master of the Music	1	120
1404	Musici sive cantori	Singers	36	†
	Concerti	Instrumentalists	34	‡
1316	Organisti	Organists	2	200
1518	Alzafogli	Bellows-operator	1	25*
1335	Guardiani di chiesa	Churchwardens	4	21
1545	Guardiani delle portelle	Doormen	?	24*

* Salary subject to a *decima* of 30 per cent.   † The salary-range for singers was 25–100 ducats.   ‡ The salary-range for instrumentalists was 15–60 ducats.

Source: I-Vas, Procuratia de Supra, Busta 89. Processo 202, 'Giovani di coro'.

C.7. Number and Composition of the Singers and Instrumentalists at San Marco, Venice

The dates 1685 (instrumentalists), 1687 (singers), 1714, and 1720 are years in which the membership of the *cappella* was reviewed and new appointments to vacancies were made in accordance with an agreed policy. Except in the 1685 list, which represents an 'ideal' plan that was never realized, the figures are those achieved in the first round of appointments following the respective review. The final column in the table of instrumentalists lists the composition of the orchestra described in a plan dating from the middle of the eighteenth century (*I-Vmc*, Ms. Gradenigo 173, Chiesa di S. Marco, fo. 295^r); it is not clear, however, whether this plan, which lists only 32 players, refers to an existing membership or a projected one; it presumably predates the comprehensive reform of the *cappella* carried out under Galuppi from 1765 onwards. Note that organists are excluded from the table of instrumentalists.

Instrumentalists	Year			
	1685	1714	1720	*c.*1760
Violins	8	13	12	12
Violas	11	7	10	8
Cellos*	2	3	3	3
Double-Basses	3	3	4	4
Theorboes	4	3	2	—
Oboes	—	1	1	2
Cornetts	2	1	—	—
Bassoons	1	—	—	1
Trombones	3	2	1	—
Trumpets	—	1	1	2
TOTAL	34	34	34	32

Singers	1687	1714	1720
Sopranos	6	12	9
Altos	7	6	9†
Tenors	13	10	9
Basses	10	8	9
TOTAL	36	36	36

* Including the larger form of bass violin usually called in Venice 'viola (da brazzo)'.
† Including one advertised vacancy left unfilled after the auditions on 15 December 1720.

C.8. Productions of Giovanni Battista Neri's *L'enigma disciolto*

The table is laid out in the same manner as Appendix C.4.

Year	Season	Theatre	Title	Composer	Libretto location
1698	spring	Reggio Emilia, Citadella	L'enigma disciolto	C. F. Pollarolo	I-Bc
1699		Ronciglione	L'enigma disciolto		I-Vgc
1700		Treviso, Onigo	L'enigma disciolto		I-Rsc
1703		Vicenza, Nuovo	L'enigma disciolto		I-Rsc
1705	carnival	Venice, San Fantino	L'enigma disciolto	C. F. Pollarolo	I-Bc
1708		Brescia, Erranti	L'enigma disciolto		US-Wc
1709		Udine, Mantica	L'enigma disciolto		*
1710	carnival	Bologna, Formagliari	L'enigma disciolto	Arresti?	I-Bc
1710	autumn	Verona	Gli amici rivali		I-Mb
1711		Lugo	L'enigma disciolto		I-Bc
1714		Pesaro, Pubblico	L'enigma disciolto	Arresti?	I-Rsc
1715	carnival	Venice, San Fantino	Gli amici rivali	C. F. Pollarolo	I-Vnm
1716	autumn	Modena, Molza	L'enigma disciolto	A. Bononcini?	I-Bc
1718	carnival	Parma, Ducale	L'enigma disciolto		I-PAc
1722		Vicenza	La fede nell'incostanza	Galuppi	YU-Lf
1722		Chioggia, Bogan	Gli amici rivali	Galuppi	*
1723	autumn	Reggio E., Citadella	L'enigma disciolto	Tonelli-Allegri	I-MOe
1726	autumn	Venice, San Moisè	Amor indovino	Cortona	I-Bc
1728	autumn	S. Gio. in Persiceto, Castello	Le vicende amorose		I-Bc
1728	December	Bologna, Marsigli-Rossi	Le vicende amorose		I-Bc
1729	May	Vicenza, Grazie	Le vicende amorose		I-Mb
1734	carnival	Rimini, Arcadico	Le vicende amorose		I-Bc
1736	carnival	Bologna, Angelelli	Le vicende amorose	Schiassi?	I-Bc

* No libretto survives. The information is taken from the *Drammaturgia di Lione Allacci* (Venice, 1755).

C.9. Contents of Vinaccesi's *Motetti a due e tre voci* (1714)

The present numbering follows the order in which the works appear in the index (*tavola*) at the end of the *Canto* partbook. The first column specifies the type of feast for which the motet is intended; the second column gives the title (i.e. the textual incipit); the third column identifies the scoring (organ is understood in all cases); the fourth column outlines the plan of movements ('A' = aria; 'R' = recitative; 'a' = 'Alleluja').

No.	Feast	Textual Incipit	Scoring	Mvt plan
1.	Per S. Marco	Inter cantica votiva	SAB	ARAa
2.	Per la B.V.M.	Adorata stella maris	SAB	ARAa
3.	Per un Santo	Floret iam in horto caeli	SAB	ARAa
4.	Per la Risurezzione	Alleluja | Gaudeat orbis et echo sonora	SAB	ARAa
5.	Per la Pentecoste e Per ogni Tempo	Aurae dulces, aurae amaenae	SAB	ARAa
6.		O quae cuncta fortissime	SAB	ARAa
7.		Cum luce tua benifica	SAB	ARAa
8.		Turtur amans lamentatur	SAB	ARARAa
9.		Cantate Domino	SS	ARAa
10.		Amor care, o Jesu dilecte	SS	ARARAR–a
11.		Conversae in pias lacrimas	SA	ARAa
12.	Per il Santissimo Sacramento	Densae nubes solem velant	SAB	ARAa
13.		Ad amantis Christi mensam	SAB	ARAa
14.		Si nescis, cor meum	SB	ARAa

C.10. Correspondence of the 'Motets' in Padua (Biblioteca Antoniana) and Assisi (Sacro Convento di San Francesco) with Movements from Vinaccesi's *Motetti a due e tre voci* of 1714

Individual movements are numbered in accordance with the plan of movements given in the last column of Appendix C.9. Thus in a work with 'ARAa' structure '1' represents the initial aria, '2' the following recitative, and so on. Where movements are in *da capo* form, the letter 'a' (following the appropriate number) denotes the 'A' section, 'b' the 'B' section.

1714 Collection		Assisi	Padua	Extracts
1.	Inter cantica votiva		B.II.608/2	3b
2.	Adorata stella maris		B.II.616	2 + 3a + 4
			B.II.621	3a + 3b
3.	Floret iam in horto caeli		B.II.617	1a + 1b

1714 Collection		Assisi	Padua	Extracts
3.	Floret iam in horto caeli		B.II.611	3a + 3b
4.	Alleluja | Gaudeat orbis		B.II.615	3a + 1
5.	Aurae dulces, aurae amaenae		B.II 610	1 + 3
6.	O quae cuncta fortissime	Mss. N. 320/5		1a + 1b
			B.II.606	2 + 4
			B.II.605	3a + 3b
7.	Cum luce tua benifica			not copied
8.	Turtur amans lamentatur		B.II.607	1a + 1b
			B.II.613	5a + 5b
9.	Cantate Domino	Mss. N. 320/1		1a + 1b
		Mss. N. 320/3		3a + 3b
10.	Amor care, o Jesu dilecte			not copied
11.	Conversae in pias lacrimas	Mss. N. 320/2		1a + 1b
12.	Densae nubes solem velant		B.II.608/1	1a
			B.II.612	2 + 4
13.	Ad amantis Christi mensam		B.II.614	1a + 1b
			B.II.609	3a + 3b
14.	Si nescis, cor meum	Mss. N. 320/4		1a + 1b

Appendix D
A Catalogue of Benedetto Vinaccesi's Works

The present catalogue is intended also to serve as an index to the works by Vinaccesi discussed in the present study, page references being given after each entry. It lists not only extant works, both complete and fragmentary, but also lost works and compositions known only from references in documents.

1. SACRED MUSIC
    General 71–2, 73, 243–75, 277

1.1. **Masses**

General 65–6

Messa concertata a 8 (SATB, SATB, 2 violins, 4 violas, 2 basses, organ, fragmentary). 243, 245, 246–51

Kyrie (a) 246, 247, 249, 250–1
Gloria (a) 246
Credo (a) 246, 247–9

1.2. **Vespers**

General 66–7

Vespers, performed Venice, 28 September 1704, lost. 73
Vespers, performed Venice, 27 December 1712, lost. 75
Magnificat (1696, lost). 42

1.3. **Compline**

General 67

Compieta a 8 (SATB, SATB, 2 violins, organ). 243, 245, 249–56

Cum invocarem (B flat) xii, 243
In te Domine speravi (A) 243, 252, 253, 254
Qui habitat in adjutorio (F) 243, 252, 254–5
Ecce nunc benedicite (a) 243
Nunc dimittis (e) 243

Compline, performed Venice, 5 March 1704, lost. 73

1.4. Motets

General vii, 110, 212, 220, 236, 237, 256–76, 280

Mottetti a due e tre voci (Venice, Sala, 1714). 108–10, 243, 261–4, 265, 267–76, 280

Ad amantis Christi mensam (SAB, organ) 263
Adorata stella maris (SAB, organ) 263, 270
Alleluja | Gaudeat orbis (SAB, organ) 268
Alme Jesu, sponse care (A, bass) xii, 244, 245–6, 259, 261
Amor care, o Jesu dilecte (SS, organ) 273
Astra campi, belli flores (A, 2 violins, viola, bass) 244, 245, 258–9, 260
Aurae dulces, aurae amaenae (SAB, organ)
Cantate Domino (SS, organ)
Conversae in pias lacrimas (SA, organ) 270, 272
Cum luce tua benefica (SAB, organ)
Densae nubes solem velant (SAB, organ) 273–6
Floret iam in horto caeli (SAB, organ) 268
Inter cantica votiva (SAB, organ) 267, 269, 270–1
O quae cuncta fortissime (SAB, organ)
Si nescis, cor meum (SB, organ) 268
Turtur amans lamentatur (SAB, organ) 268, 273

1.5. Motet fragments

Adeste canentes (SSB, organ) 244, 264–5, 266
Caelestis horti (ATB, organ) 244, 264
Mensa dulcis et iucunda (TTB, organ) 244, 265
O Maria, si me amas (SAB, organ) 244, 264
Stellarum fulgores (ATB, organ) 244, 264
Videte, filiae Sion ([S]AB, organ, incomplete) 244, 264

1.6. Doubtful works

Angelici chori (S or T, 2 violins, bass, also attr. Bassani) 244, 259
Beatus vir (SATB, orchestra, spurious) 244
De profundis (1696, lost and authorship uncertain) 42
Huc festini (Cantata de omni sancto, A + ?, lost) 244
Licet irae (Cantata, A + ?, lost) 244–5

2. ORATORIOS

General vii, 188–217, 277

Il cuor nello scrigno (text: F. Arisi), performed Cremona 1696, lost. 43, 188
Li diecimila martiri crocefissi (text: A. Paolini), performed Brescia 1698, lost. 43–4, 49, 188, 189, 201 n.

Quanto mi vien da ridere (B, continuo, titled *Il disinganno de gli amanti*) 159, 160, 166, 167, 168, 176, 179 n., 186–7
Su la sponda d'un rio (S, continuo) 159, 166, 167, 168, 178

6. SONATAS

General vii, 127–55, 186

Suonate da camera a tre, Op. 1 (Venice, Sala, 1687). 2 violins, cello, harpsichord. xii, 27–33, 36, 38, 129–55 *passim*, 186, 220, 277
Sonata I (C) xii, 129, 137, 138, 140, 143, 144, 145, 150, 153
Sonata II (d) 129, 138, 140, 141, 144, 145–6, 153
Sonata III (e) 129, 137, 138–9, 139, 140, 141, 144, 153
Sonata IV (F) 33, 130, 138, 139, 141, 144, 149, 150, 151, 153
Sonata V (g) 130, 138, 140, 141, 144, 144–5, 148, 153, 154
Sonata VI (A) 130, 137, 138, 139, 143, 150, 153

Sfere armoniche o vero Sonate da chiesa, Op. 2 (Venice, Sala, 1692). 2 violins, cello, organ; only organ part survives. Keys: d, C, b, g, e, B flat, A, c, G, F, a, D 32, 33, 34–7, 38, 155

Suonate da camera a tre, Op. 4, pt 1 (date and place of publication unknown). 2 violins, cello, harpsichord, lost. 38, 155

Bibliography

ALALEONA, DOMENICO, *Studi su la storia dell'oratorio musicale in Italia* (Turin, 1908, ²/1945).

ALGAROTTI, FRANCESCO, *Saggio sopra l'opera in musica* (Livorno, ²/1763).

ANON., *Capitoli et ordini per il buon governo del Pio Hospitale de Poveri Derelitti appresso SS. Giovanni e Paolo consacrati alla gloriosa Vergine protettrice di detto Hospitale* (Venice, 1668; revd. edn. 1704).

ANON., *Raccolta di cose sacre che si soglion cantare dalle pie vergini dell'ospitale dei Poveri Derelitti in Venezia* (Venice, 1772).

ANON., *Stampa della Signora Marchesa Giovanna Miseroni ora consorte del Signor Conte Paolo Sormani* [Venice, 1745].

APEL, WILLI, *Italian Violin Music of the Seventeenth Century* (Bloomington, Ind., 1990).

ARISI, FRANCESCO, *Cremona literata* (3 vols., Parma and Cremona, 1702–41).

ARNOLD, DENIS, 'Orphans and Ladies: The Venetian Conservatoires (1690–1797)', *Proceedings of the Royal Musical Association*, 89 (1962–3), 31–47.

—— and ARNOLD, ELSIE, *The Oratorio in Venice* (London, 1986).

ARRIGHI, BARTOLOMEO, *Storia di Castiglione delle Stiviere sotto il dominio dei Gonzaga* (2 vols., Mantua, 1853–4; repr. with an additional vol. by Emilio Ondei, Mantua, 1968).

AVEROLDI, GIULIO, *Le scelte pitture di Brescia additate al forestiere* (Brescia, 1700).

—— *Elogio di Fortunato Vinaccesi*, ed. Giovanni Averoldi (Brescia, [1889]).

BALDAUF-BERDES, JANE L., *Women Musicians of Venice: Musical Foundations, 1525–1855* (Oxford, 1993).

BARETTI, JOSEPH [GIUSEPPE], *An Account of the Manners and Customs of Italy, with Observations on the Mistakes of some Travellers, with Regard to that Country* (2 vols., London, ²/1769).

BAREZZANI, MARIA TERESA ROSA SALA, MARIELLA, ROSSATO, DANIELA, and PAGANI, GIUSEPPE, *La musica a Brescia nel Settecento* (Brescia, 1981).

BIANCONI, LORENZO, *Music in the Seventeenth Century* (Cambridge, 1987).

BOISGELOU, PAUL-LOUIS ROUALLE DE, 'Table biographique des auteurs et compositeurs de musique dont les ouvrages sont à la Bibliothèque Nationale' (MS, c.1800). Paris, Bibliothèque Nationale, Vm.⁸ 22.

BONTA, STEPHEN, 'From Violone to Violoncello: A Question of Strings?', *Journal of the American Instrument Society*, 3 (1977), 64–99.

—— 'The Uses of the *Sonata da chiesa*', *Journal of the American Musicological Society*, 22 (1969), 54–84.

BORGIR, THARALD, *The Performance of the Basso Continuo in Seventeenth-Century Italian Music* (Ann Arbor, Mich., 1987).

BROSSARD, SÉBASTIEN DE, 'Catalogue des livres de musique théorique et pratique . . .' (MS, c.1724). Paris, Bibliothèque Nationale, Vm.⁸ 20 (original) and 21 (copy).

BROSSARD, SÉBASTIEN DE, *Dictionnaire de musique* (Paris, 1703).

BRUNATI, GIUSEPPE, *Dizionario degli uomini illustri della Riviera di Salò* (Milan, 1837).

BRYANT, DAVID, 'The *cori spezzati* of St Mark's: Myth and Reality', in Iain Fenlon (ed.), *Early Music History*, i. *Studies in Medieval and Modern Music* (Cambridge, 1981), 165–86.

BURNEY, CHARLES, *The Present State of Music in France and Italy* (London, 1771).

BURROWS, DAVID, 'Style in Culture: Vivaldi, Zeno and Ricci', *The Journal of Interdisciplinary History*, 4 (1973–4), 1–23.

CAFFI, FRANCESCO, *Storia della musica sacra nella già cappella ducale di San Marco in Venezia dal 1317 al 1797* (2 vols., Venice, 1854–5).

—— 'Storia della musica teatrale in Venezia' (MS notes, *c.*1850). Venice, Biblioteca Nazionale Marciana, Cod. it. IV–747 (= 10462–5).

CAYLUS, COMTE DE, *Voyage d'Italie, 1714–1715*, ed. Amilda-A. Pons (Paris, 1914).

CHARLES, ROBERT HENRY, *The Apocrypha and Pseudepigrapha of the Old Testament in English with Introductions and Critical and Explanatory Notes to the Several Books* (Oxford, 1913).

CHIAPPELLI, ALBERTO, *Storia del teatro in Pistoia dalle origini alla fine del secolo XVIII* (Florence, 1913).

CISILINO, SIRO, *Stampi e manoscritti preziosi e rari della Biblioteca del Palazzo Giustinian Lolin a San Vidal* (Venice, 1966).

CORONELLI, VINCENZO, *Guida de' forestieri* . . . (Venice, 1698; and subsequent edns.).

COZZANDO, LEONARDO, *Libraria bresciana, prima e seconda parte nuovamente aperta dal M. R. P. Maestro Leonardo Cozzando, Servita Bresciano* (Brescia, 1694).

—— *Vago e curioso ristretto profano e sacro dell'historia bresciana* (Brescia, 1694).

CRESCIMBENI, GIOVAN MARIO (ed.), *Notizie istoriche degli Arcadi morti* (3 vols., Rome, 1720–1).

CROWTHER, VICTOR, 'Alessandro Stradella and the Oratorio Tradition in Modena', in Carolyn Gianturco (ed.), *Alessandro Stradella e Modena: Atti del Convegno internazionale di studi, Modena 15–17 dicembre 1983* (Modena, 1985), 51–64.

—— *The Oratorio in Modena* (Oxford, 1992).

DALLA LIBERA, SANDRO, *L'arte degli organi a Venezia* (Venice, 1962).

DAVERIO, JOHN, 'Formal Design and Terminology in the pre-Corellian "Sonata" and Related Instrumental Forms in the Printed Sources' Ph.D. diss. (Boston University, 1983).

—— 'In Search of the Sonata da Camera, before Corelli', *Acta musicologica*, 57 (1984), 195–214.

DE FELICE, EMIDIO, *Dizionario dei cognomi italiani* (Milan, 1978).

DOLCETTI, GIOVANNI, *Il 'Libro d'Argento' dei cittadini di Venezia e del Veneto* (5 vols., Venice, 1922–8).

DOTTI, BARTOLOMEO, *Satire del Cavalier Dotti* (Geneva, 1757).

—— 'Sonetti del K[avalie]r Bortalamio Dotti et enigmatici' (MS, *c.*1700). Venice, Museo Civico Correr, Ms. Cicogna 1283.

DREYFUS, LAURENCE, 'Early Music Defended against its Devotees: A Theory of Historical Performance in the Twentieth Century', *Musical Quarterly*, 69 (1983), 297–322.

DURANTE, SERGIO, 'Alcune considerazioni sui cantanti di teatro del primo Settecento e la loro formazione', in Lorenzo Bianconi and Francesco Degrada (eds.), *Antonio Vivaldi: Teatro musicale, cultura e società* (Florence, 1982), 427–81.

ELLERO, GIUSEPPE (ed.), *L'Archivio storico IRE: Inventari dei fondi antichi degli ospedali e luoghi pii di Venezia* (Venice, 1984).

FERRO, MARCO, *Dizionario del diritto comune e veneto* (10 vols., Venice, 1778–81).

FÉTIS, FRANÇOIS-JOSEPH, *Biographie universelle des musiciens et bibliographie générale de la musique* (8 vols., Paris, ²/1868–70).

FUKAČ, JIŘÍ, 'Křižovnický hudební inventář', diss. (2 vols., University of Brno, 1959).

FUX, JOHANN JOSEPH, *Gradus ad Parnassum* (Vienna, 1725).

GEORGETTI VICHI, ANNA MARIA (ed.), *Gli Arcadi dal 1690 al 1800: Onomasticon* (Rome, 1977).

GIAZOTTO, REMO, *Antonio Vivaldi* (Turin, 1973).

GROPPO, ANTONIO, 'Catalogo purgatissimo di tutti li drami per musica recitati ne' teatri di Venezia dall'anno mdcxxvii sin oggi' (MS, 1741, updated to 1767). Venice, Biblioteca Nazionale Marciana, Cod. it. VII–2326 (= 8263).

—— *Salmi che si cantano in tutti li vesperi dei giorni festivi di tutto l'anno dalle figliuole nelli quattro ospitali di questa città* (Venice, 1752).

[GROSLEY, PIERRE JEAN], *Nouveaux mémoires ou observations sur l'Italie et sur les Italiens par deux gentilshommes suédois*. (3 vols., Paris, 1764).

HABÖCK, FRANZ (completed Martina Haböck), *Die Kastraten und ihre Gesangskunst: Eine gesangsphysiologische, kultur- und musikhistorische Studie* (Stuttgart, 1927).

HANSELL, SVEN, 'Vinaccesi, Benedetto', in Stanley Sadie (ed.), *The New Grove Dictionary of Music and Musicians* (London, 1980), xix. 780–1.

HARRIS, ELLEN T., *Handel and the Pastoral Tradition* (London, 1980).

HAYBURN, ROBERT F. (ed.), *Papal Legislation on Sacred Music, 95 A.D. to 1977 A.D.* (Collegeville, Minn., 1979).

KALEY, DIANA E., *The Church of the Pietà* (Venice, [1980]).

KING, A. HYATT, *Catalogue of the Music Library, Instruments and Other Property of Nicolas Selhof. Sold in The Hague, 1759* (Amsterdam, 1973).

—— *Some British Collectors of Music* (Cambridge, 1963).

KLENZ, WILLIAM, *Giovanni Maria Bononcini of Modena* (Durham, NC, ²/1962).

KÜMMERLING, HARALD, *Katalog der Sammlung Bokemeyer* (Kassel, 1970).

LA BORDE, JEAN BENJAMIN DE, *Essai sur la musique ancienne et moderne* (4 vols., Paris, 1780).

LIMOJON DE SAINT-DIDIER, ALEXANDRE TOUSSAINT, *La Ville et la république de Venise* (Paris, 1680).

LITTA, POMPEO, and continuers, *Famiglie celebri italiane* (Numerous vols. and fascicles, Milan and Turin, 1819–99).

LUIN, ELISABETH J., 'Repertorio dei libri musicali di S. A. S. Francesco II d'Este nell'Archivio di Stato di Modena', *Bibliofilia*, 38 (1936), 418–45.

MABILLON, JEAN, *Museum italicum seu collectio veterum scriptorum ex bibliothecis*, (2 vols., Paris, 1687–9).

MARCELLO, BENEDETTO, *Il teatro alla moda*, ed. Andrea d'Angeli (Milan, 1956).

MARTYN, THOMAS, *A Tour through Italy: Containing Full Directions for Travelling in that Interesting Country* (London, 1791).

MARX, HANS-JOACHIM, 'Die Musik am Hofe Pietro Kardinal Ottobonis unter Arcangelo Corelli', *Analecta musicologica*, 5 (1968), 104–77.

MATTHESON, JOHANN, *Der vollkommene Capellmeister* (Hamburg, 1739).

—— *Grundlage einer Ehren-Pforte* (Hamburg, 1740).

MAYLENDER, MICHELE, *Storia delle accademie d'Italia* (5 vols., Bologna, 1926–30).

MAZZUCHELLI, GIOVANNI, *Gli scrittori d'Italia* (2 vols. published, Brescia, 1753–63).

MELCHIORI, GIOVAN-BATTISTA, *Vocabolario bresciano-italiano* (3 vols., Brescia, 1817).

[MESCHINELLO, GIOVANNI], *La chiesa ducale di S. Marco* (3 vols., Venice, 1753–4).

MISCHIATI, OSCAR. *Indici, cataloghi e avvisi degli editori e librai italiani dal 1591 al 1798* (Florence, 1984).

MISSON, FRANÇOIS MAXIMILIEN, *A New Voyage to Italy* (2 vols., London, 1695).

MOORE, JAMES H., *Vespers at St. Mark's: Music of Alessandro Grandi, Giovanni Rovetta and Francesco Cavalli* (Ann Arbor, Mich., 1981).

NEWMAN, WILLIAM S., *The Sonata in the Baroque Era* (Chapel Hill, NC, 1959).

NUGENT, THOMAS, *The Grand Tour* (4 vols., London, ^{2}/1778).

PASQUETTI, GUIDO, *L'oratorio musicale in Italia* (Florence, ^{2}/1914).

PILO, GIUSEPPE M., *La chiesa dello 'Spedaletto in Venezia* (Venice, 1988).

QUANTZ, JOHANN JOACHIM, *On Playing the Flute*, ed. and trans. Edward R. Reilly (London, 1976).

ROCHE, JEROME, 'Musica diversa di Compieta: Compline and its Music in Seventeenth-Century Italy', *Proceedings of the Royal Musical Association*, 109 (1982–3), 60–79.

—— 'Rovetta, Giovanni', in Stanley Sadie (ed.), *The New Grove Dictionary of Music and Musicians* (London, 1980), xvi. 279.

ROMAGNOLI, ANGELA, 'La componente strumentale ne "La Susanna" di Benedetto Vinaccesi', in Rosa Cafiero and Maria Teresa Rosa Barezzani (eds.), *Liuteria e musica strumentale a Brescia tra Cinque e Seicento* (Brescia, 1992), 333–53.

ROSAND, ELLEN, *Opera in Seventeenth-Century Venice: The Creation of a Genre* (Berkeley, 1991).

ROSSI, FRANCO, *La Fondazione Levi di Venezia: Catalogo del fondo musicale* (Venice, 1986).

SARTORI, CLAUDIO, *Assisi: La Cappella della Basilica di S. Francesco, i. Catalogo del fondo musicale nella Biblioteca Comunale di Assisi* (Milan, 1962).

—— *Bibliografia della musica strumentale italiana stampata in Italia fino al 1700* (2 vols., Florence, 1952 and 1968).

SAUNDERS, HARRIS S., 'The Repertoire of a Venetian Opera House (1678–1714): The Teatro Grimani di San Giovanni Grisostomo', Ph.D. diss., (Harvard University, 1989).

SCARPA, JOLANDO (ed.), *Arte e musica all'Ospedaletto* (Venice, 1978).

SCHLAGER, KARLHEINZ (ed.), *Einzeldrucke vor 1800* (17 vols. to date, Kassel, 1971–).

SCHMIDL, CARLO, *Dizionario universale dei musicisti*, (2 vols. and suppl., Milan, 1926–38).

SCHMIDT, GÜNTHER, *Die Musik am Hofe der Markgrafen von Brandenburg-Ansbach* (Kassel, 1956).

SCHMITZ, EUGEN, *Geschichte der weltlichen Solokantate* (Leipzig, 1914).

SELFRIDGE-FIELD, ELEANOR, *Pallade veneta: Writings on Music in Venetian Society, 1650–1750* (Venice, 1985).

—— *Venetian Instrumental Music from Gabrieli to Vivaldi* (Oxford, 1975).

—— 'The Viennese Court Orchestra in the Time of Caldara', in Brian Pritchard (ed.), *Antonio Caldara: Essays on his Life and Times* (Aldershot, 1987), 115–51.

SILVANI, FRANCESCO, *Opere drammatiche del Signor abate Francesco Silvani veneto* (4 vols., Venice, 1744).

SMITHER, HOWARD E., *A History of the Oratorio, i. The Oratorio in the Baroque Era: Italy, Vienna, Paris* (Chapel Hill, NC, 1977).

SNYDER, KERALA, 'Österreich, Georg', in Stanley Sadie (ed.), *The New Grove Dictionary of Music and Musicians* (London, 1980), xiv. 8–9.

SORAGNI, UGO, 'La Strada Nuova di Brescia', in Carlo Pirovani (ed.), *Lombardia: Il territorio, l'ambiente, il paesaggio* (5 vols., Milan, 1981–2), ii. 153–68.

SPAGNA, ARCHANGELO, *Oratorii overo melodrammi sacri* (2 vols., Rome, 1706).

STROHM, REINHARD, *Italienische Opernarien des frühen Settecento* (2 vols., Cologne, 1976).

TAGLIAVINI, LUIGI FERDINANDO, 'Vinaccesi, Benedetto', in Friedrich Blume (ed.), *Die Musik in Geschichte und Gegenwart*, 13 (1966), cols. 1651–2.

TALBOT, MICHAEL, 'The Function and Character of the Instrumental Ritornello in the Solo Cantatas of Tomaso Albinoni (1671–1751)', *Quaderni della Civica Scuola di Musica [di Milano]*, 19–20 (1990), 77–90.

—— 'The Marcian Motets of Benedetto Vinaccesi', in Franco Rossi and Francesco Passadore (eds.), *Giovanni Legrenzi e la Capella Ducale di San Marco* (Florence, forthcoming).

—— 'New Light on Vivaldi's *Stabat Mater*', *Informazioni e studi vivaldiani*, 13 (1992), 23–38.

—— 'The Taiheg, the Pira and Other Curiosities of Benedetto Vinaccesi's *Suonate da camera a tre*, Op. 1', *Music and Letters*, 75 (1994).

—— *Tomaso Albinoni: The Venetian Composer and his World* (Oxford, 1990).

—— 'Vivaldi in the Sale Catalogue of Nicolaas Selhof', *Informazioni e studi vivaldiani*, 6 (1985), 57–63.

—— and TIMMS, COLIN, 'Music and the Poetry of Antonio Ottoboni (1646–1721)', in Nino Pirrotta and Agostino Ziino (eds.), *Händel e gli Scarlatti a Roma: Atti del Convegno internazionale di studi (Roma 12–14 giugno 1985)* (Florence, 1987), 367–438.

TASSINI, GIUSEPPE, 'Notizie storiche e genealogiche sui cittadini veneziani' (MS, mid-19th cent.), 5 vols., Venice, Museo Civico Correr, Ms P.D. 33 D 76.

TEBALDINI, GIOVANNI, *L'archivio musicale della Cappella Antoniana in Padova* (Padua, 1895).

TEMPERLEY, NICHOLAS, Contribution to 'The Limits of Authenticity: A Discussion', *Early Music*, 12 (1984), 3–25.

TERMINI, OLGA, 'Organists and Chapel Masters at the Cathedral of Brescia (1608–1779)', *Note d'archivio per la storia musicale*, NS, 3 (1985), 73–90.

TERMINI, OLGA, 'Singers at San Marco in Venice: The Competition between Church and Theatre (*c*1675–*c*1725)', *[RMA] Research Chronicle*, 17 (1981), 65–96.

—— 'Vivaldi at Brescia: The Feast of the Purification at the Chiesa della Pace (1711)', *Informazioni e studi vivaldiani*, 9 (1988), 64–74.

TIMMS, COLIN, 'The Cavata at the Time of Vivaldi', in Antonio Fanna and Giovanni Morelli (eds.), *Nuovi studi vivaldiani: Edizione e cronologia critica dell'opera* (Florence, 1988), 451–77.

—— 'The Dramatic in Vivaldi's Cantatas', in Lorenzo Bianconi and Giovanni Morelli (eds.), *Antonio Vivaldi: Teatro musicale, cultura e società* (Florence, 1982), 97–129.

—— '*Prendea con man di latte*: A Vivaldi Spuriosity?', *Informazioni e studi vivaldiani*, 6 (1985), 64–73.

TUNLEY, DAVID, *The Eighteenth-Century French Cantata* (London, 1974).

VALENTINI, ANDREA, *I musicisti bresciani ed il Teatro Grande* (Brescia, 1894).

VINACCESI, FRANCESCO, *Panegirici recitati da tre celebri oratori [. . .] adonate del Beato Giovanni Marinoni . . . in occasione del triduo solenizzato nella chiesa de RR. PP. Teatini li 4, 5, 6 settembre 1763 . . .* (Venice, 1763).

VIO, GASTONE, 'I maestri di coro dei Mendicanti e la Cappella Marciana', in Maria Teresa Muraro and Franco Rossi (eds.), *Galuppiana 1985, studi e ricerche: Atti del Convegno internazionale (Venezia, 28–30 ottobre 1985)* (Florence, 1986), 95–111.

VOLLEN, GENE E., *The French Cantata: A Survey and Thematic Catalog* (Ann Arbor, Mich., 1982).

WEAVER, ROBERT L., and WEAVER, NORMA W., *A Chronology of Music in the Florentine Theater 1590–1750: Operas, Prologues, Finales, Intermezzos and Plays with Incidental Music* (Detroit, 1978).

WEILBACH, FREDERIK, *Frederik IV's italiensrejser* (Copenhagen, 1933).

ZACCARIA, VITTORE, 'Benedetto Vinaccesi (Brescia 1670c.–Venezia 1719): Profilo bio–bibliografico', *Musica sacra*,[2] 7 (1962), 12–15, 86–9, 119–25.

ZENO, APOSTOLO, *Poesie sacre drammatiche [. . .] cantate nella Imperial Capella di Vienna* (Venice, 1735).

ZOBELEY, FRITZ, *Die Musikalen der Grafen von Schönborn-Wiesentheid: Thematisch-bibliographischer Katalog. Teil I: Das Repertoire des Grafen Rudolf Franz Erwein von Schönborn (1677–1754), vol. i: 149 Drucke aus den Jahren 1676 bis 1738* (Tutzing, 1967).

Index

The present index includes names (of persons and places), titles (of poetic, dramatic, and musical works), and selected subjects. The names of publishers, cities, and countries are indexed only when they are part of the book's argument. Vinaccesi's compositions are indexed separately, with full page-references, in Appendix D.

The alphabetization follows the word-by-word system (treating words separated by an apostrophe or a hyphen as distinct). I have left initial definite articles in their normal position when alphabetizing titles, but not in other cases. Short particles (e.g. 'in', 'by') introducing subheadings are ignored for the purpose of alphabetization. The name '(Giovanni) Benedetto Vinaccesi' has been reduced for brevity to 'V' in qualifying expressions and subheadings. The numbers in brackets added to the given names of members of the Vinaccesi family are those used to identify individual family members in Appendix A and elsewhere. The appendices themselves have not been indexed.